# TOO PROUD TO BEND

## Journey of a Civil Rights Foot Soldier

*Sixty years in these folks' world*
*The child I works for calls me girl,*
*I say "Yes ma'am" for working's sake*
*Too proud to bend,*
*Too poor to break*

—Maya Angelou, "When I Think About Myself"

## NELL BRAXTON GIBSON

# Too Proud to Bend

Journey of a Civil Rights Foot Soldier

Nell Braxton Gibson

ISBN: 0692257438

ISBN 13: 9780692257432

Library of Congress Control Number: 2014921083

Nell B. Gibson, New York, NY

*Dedicated to Bert III, my literary muse, and*
*John, my musical muse,*
*and written for*

*Bert Jr., Anne, and Rosemary, who shared the journey,*
*but especially for Erika Anne, that she may*
*know her history as she conquers new frontiers.*

# TABLE OF CONTENTS

# ACKNOWLEDGMENTS

I OFFER MY THANKS TO Bert Gibson for his support through the years, to Erika Gibson for being my greatest cheerleader, staying up late at night and helping me arrange chapters and sort through photographs, teaching me how to submit material online, redesigning my website, and helping me overcome all the little things that baffled me electronically in sending my manuscript and photographs to the editors. I thank Bert Gibson III for his belief in me and his belief in this memoir.

There is no way I could have written this book if my mother, Anne Braxton, had not saved my diary notes from 1962 and sent them to me with encouragement to use them for recording my civil rights experience. She and my dad, John Braxton, and my sister, Rosemary Braxton, spent years recording their memories, e-mailing information from our past, and sitting with me and recalling incidents and historical data that made the book come alive. I could never have pulled all the facts and fun together without them, and so I give them my profound thanks.

I give special thanks to Russell Campbell Sr. for turning over the 1962–63 letters I wrote to him so that I could rediscover my nineteen-year-old self, and for sending student movement documents, newspaper clippings, letters to his parents, and photographs. Thanks also for numerous interviews, phone conversations, and e-mails that helped me recall our movement days. A deep thank you to Anna Jo Scruton, who was enormously helpful and supportive in sending old photographs, letters she wrote home to her parents from Spelman, and conversations and letters during the writing of this book that led to the recovery of many precious memories from our college days. A big thank you to Lonnie King for sitting with me in an Atlanta, Georgia, hotel in 2010 and going back over the founding of the Committee on Appeal for Human Rights so that the facts would be correct. I thank Frank Smith for the interviews he gave and the memories he recalled from our student movement days, and Katy Dawley for newspaper information on Dr. Borinski, memories of Camp Woodland and her trip to Tougaloo from Oberlin, photographs she sent over the years, and telephone conversations and e-mails that helped me put old memories into their proper context. And I thank Bea and Lew Wechsler for reading, rereading, and editing my first rough drafts, and to Lew Wechsler for giving me permission to use excerpts from his book, *The First Stone.* Both Bea and Lew played pivotal roles in the development of this book.

I am deeply grateful to Dr. Robert Kurtz for being so candid in interviews about our Camp Woodland days. I thank him for allowing me to use as much of those interviews as I deemed necessary in order to enhance the authenticity of this book. I thank Faye Wattleton for allowing me to use passages from her book, *Life on the Line,* and Gail Lutz and Jerel Morris, for reliving their deepest feelings and memories surrounding the death of their brother, Howard Skinner. And I would never have remembered many of the names from my elementary school days had it not been for Robert Calhoun. I especially thank him for steering me toward zip drives in the days before jump drives became available, and for hanging with me through the decades to help with information that was fresher in his mind than in mine because of his annual trips back to Mississippi. A big thank you to McGustavus Miller for helping me recall the names of people from camp that no one else remembered, and I thank Ann Redding for her help and support.

A very special thanks to Nancy Wilson and her writing classes at Lehman College for listening to years of readings as this book developed and for being willing to offer feedback and suggestions in order to improve it. And I cannot thank Sasha Wilson enough for his loving but critical eye to detail that led to many needed suggestions about what should remain and what should be omitted from the pages of this book. Every suggestion helped tighten up sections of the manuscript and kept me on point. Thank you, Wanda Jones, for reading numerous revisions of this book and offering your encouragement and insight over many years. Thank you, Jinx Roosevelt, for transcribing my talk with a group of seventh and eighth graders at Manhattan Country School, thereby allowing me to weave that talk into the fabric of this memoir.

Thank you, Robert Moss, James Gathers, Walter Hunter, and Eddie O'Neal, for sharing information on the days when you played college ball and ran track for my father, and for your continued encouragement as I worked to complete and publish this manuscript.

Last, this book would never have had the authenticity it has were it not for Mindy Lewis and her intermediate and advanced memoir-writing classes at the West Sixty-Third Street YMCA in New York City. Thank you, my fellow writers, for the suggestions, encouragement, and support you so lovingly offered. Thank you, Delo Washington, for information on Georgia culture, especially the Gullah/Geechee people of Savannah, Georgia. And profound thanks to Jeannine Otis, Irene

Jackson Brown, and David Link for the time they spent helping me with the songs I used as chapter headings and assisting me in finding and giving credit to the right composers and writers. Thank you, Anthony Turner, for your help; thank you, Neruda Williams, for building my first website; and thank you, Brenda Richardson, Joyce White, Martha and Randy Cameron, for your continuing encouragement.

# A Note to Readers

A LOT HAS BEEN MADE of the word *Negro* in recent years, but I use it throughout this memoir, and this is why. It was the acceptable name used in the fifties. Back then if the word *Black* had been used by a white person, it would have been a step above being called the N word. If it had been used by another African American, it would have provoked a fight. That's how negative the word was in those days. Sensitivity to this fact is apparent even in an excerpt of President Kennedy's Civil Rights Address of 1963. In it he uses the term people with "dark skin" rather than "Black people."

The word *colored* was the restrictive word for those of us living in the South—the one used on bathroom doors and water fountains (colored only vs. white only), so we seldom used it among ourselves. A few African Americans sometimes used it to include all people of color, as in the National Association for the Advancement of Colored People (NAACP), but the word did not have the universal acceptance it has today—as in "people of color."

In the fifties and early sixties, the word *Negro* carried the dignity and respect that the term *African American* carries today. It wasn't until the mid- to late sixties, when the Black Panther Party was founded, that Stokely Carmichael popularized the term *Black power*, and James

Brown recorded, "Say it loud, I'm Black and I'm proud," that the negative connotation of Black was reversed, and Black became beautiful. Therefore, in order to be true to the times I write about in this memoir, I use the word *Negro*.

The reader will also notice that my chapter titles are either the names of songs or lines from songs. This is because music has played such an important role in my life.

One of the reasons I wrote this book is because so much that is historical in nature has been written about the young people who made up the rank and file of the student movement. I have written a personal memoir about those days, understanding that sometimes historical documentation can cause readers from later decades to come away with the impression that earlier student activists were so single-minded in their work for justice that they thought of nothing else, leaving the more typical experiences of college life behind. My hope is that with the passage of fifty years, and with so much of our history already documented, readers are now ready to take the kind of long view of history that allows for the more multidimensional aspects of the lives of civil rights activists to emerge from typical college campuses. That is not to say that students who were willing to forego school dances, sporting events, and parties in order to pursue the greater cause did not exist. Only that there were also those of us who were serious about the liberation of our people but who struggled with decisions—about whether to cut classes in order to walk picket lines, whether to risk being arrested or show up for a test—and who also enjoyed more typical aspects of campus life, such as snowball fights, political debates, bid whist, and rock-and-roll music, in addition to walking picket lines and going to jail. We were as multidimensional back then as today's college students, attempting to fully experience our (often) first-time lives away from home while engaging in the struggle for equal rights. We were not perfect, and it was not easy to find a balance between the lives we lived and the Jim Crow world we were trying to change. Most of us came from ordinary families in which parents and grandparents had high hopes for us, in spite of the oppressive conditions under which we lived.

So this is one story among many that chronicles one life among thousands of young lives, told as honestly as I know how to tell it. It is the journey of a young girl trying to figure out who she was and trying to define who she was becoming during one of the twentieth century's epic movements—the battle for human rights.

# PROLOGUE

# ANOTHER MAN DONE GONE[i]

*Another man done gone, another man done gone*
*They hung him in a tree, they let his children see*
*When he was hangin' dead*

THE FIRST TIME I saw my father cry was June 13, 1963, the day after Medgar Evers was assassinated in the front yard of his home in Jackson, Mississippi. That was one year after our family moved from Mississippi to Sacramento, California. I was twenty-one years old. At the request of the Bishop of Northern California, Dad was scheduled to address the predominantly white parishioners at Trinity Cathedral,

---

i "Another Man Done Gone" is a traditional chain-gang song that comes out of gangs working in the southern United States beginning in the 1880s. Blues and folk singer Leadbelly, who once worked on a chain gang, was one of the earliest artists to record the song. Since that time, a number of artists have recorded it, including Odetta, Woody Guthrie, and Johnny Cash.

where our family was among the few Negro members. My father, my sister, Rosemary, and I were seated together on one side of the parish hall when the host for the evening introduced Dad to the assembled crowd. Applause resounded as he stood and approached the podium. Thanking the host, my father took the microphone and cleared his throat. He attempted to speak but only managed to whisper a few inaudible words. He cleared his throat for a second time and tried to speak again. This time his voice cracked, and tears filled his eyes. A long pause followed.

"I'm sorry," he finally managed to say, his usual commanding voice barely audible. "My dear friend Medgar Evers, was assassinated last night in Jackson, Mississippi. We were among the first people Medgar came to see when he began his work with the NAACP in Jackson." Dad's voice trailed off to a whisper. "Please excuse me." After returning the microphone to its stand, he walked to where Rosemary and I were sitting. "Let's go," he said.

Bewildered, my sister and I rose and followed him from the silent room where a stunned audience sat. The three of us walked outside to the church parking lot, got into our car, and drove onto the freeway without exchanging a word.

I had never known my father to walk away from anything, not white southern policemen who threatened him, or bigoted gas station attendants who refused to let us use their restrooms, nor the rednecks who shot up our neighborhood in Mississippi. Athletically built, my father was a six-foot-tall gregarious charmer who commanded attention just by entering a room. He was the person everyone gravitated to, the eloquent speaker who captivated audiences with poignant stories, delighted listeners with Shakespearean recitations, the one who had people roaring with laughter at the remembrance of an outlandish incident. But on June 13, 1963, my father was none of those things. On that day he was a man consumed with grief over the death of a beloved friend.

In the back of the Pontiac as the three of us silently moved along the freeway toward home, I thought of all the strife that had brought us to California, and I remembered all we had lived through in the one short year since our arrival. We had come to the politically conservative capital city of Sacramento after generations of forebears on both sides of my family had called the South home. My parents, sister, and I had lived in Georgia, Alabama, Florida, Texas, and Mississippi, the longest sojourn being eight years in racially torn Mississippi. Following nearly a decade of lynchings and intimidation of Negroes in the Magnolia State, Mother and Dad had decided to leave the South for good. We were part of the "great migration" of Negroes from that part of the country to the East, North, and West. My parents and I had spent most of the summer of 1962 working in New York State while my sister attended the World Youth Festival in Helsinki, Finland. Upon her return to the United States, the four of us drove across the country to California, where Mother and Dad hoped to find racial peace. They arrived without jobs, friends, or a place to live, only the telephone numbers of two acquaintances from Mother's distant past. One was a former schoolmate from Spelman, a college for Negro women in Atlanta, Georgia; the other was a man her father knew from Tuskegee Institute in Alabama, where my maternal grandparents had attended college. Both the Spelman and Tuskegee graduates had children who were the same ages as my sister and me, and I looked forward to meeting them. I had always enjoyed the children of my parents' acquaintances, and they would be my first friends in California.

Dad had done all the driving from New York to Sacramento without help. Mother hadn't done any highway driving since surviving a near-fatal automobile accident in South Carolina in 1954, and Rosemary and I were not allowed to do highway driving. We were exhausted when we pulled into a filling station in downtown Sacramento. It was barely dusk, but the station was already closed. Rosemary, Dad, and I remained in the car, while Mother got out and went to the public phone booth. She was in her early forties and still a classic beauty with no wrinkles on her face, and lipstick was the only makeup she ever needed. When I was younger and self-conscious about my five-foot-ten-inch frame, she would tell me that she was the tallest woman in her family. That was true, but having my five-foot-three-inch mother tell me how tall she was compared to her mother and aunts, as I stood towering over her—and most of my teachers—didn't help at the time. Mother dropped a coin into the pay phone and called her college friend. Masking a weariness we all felt, she responded cheerfully to a voice on the other end of the line.

"Hi there, this is Anne Thomas Braxton..." The easy laugh I'd so often heard when she greeted women from her past followed her initial greeting. Her relaxed response always put me at ease when she reconnected with old acquaintances for whom the passage of time made little difference.

"My family and I just arrived in town and..." Mother was explaining. "Yes, we have two daughters. Nell is twenty years of age and Rosemary...yes, time does move quickly," I heard her say in response to the person on the other end of the phone.

We'd spent our whole lives taking in stranded Negro friends and asking them to take us in when we traveled, because hotels in the

South refused to let Negroes register, and there was no place else to go. People always made room, often giving up the best beds to weary travelers, while they slept on cots or rollaway beds. There was never a need to explain why we needed to stay. All of us were in the same boat. Now, after days of sleeping in the backseat of the car next to my younger sister, I could hardly wait to stretch out my aching body.

"We wouldn't mind sleeping on the floor," Mother was saying.

*Well,* I thought, *sleeping bags are a lot better than the backseat of the car.*

Mother returned the phone to the cradle and dropped another dime in the slot.

"Hello, this is Anne Thomas Braxton..." she began. "I got your number from my father, Jesse O. Thomas."

There was a pause, followed by "Yes, that's right." And then the explanation. "My family and I have just driven in from..."

Maybe, I thought, the first person only has room for two of us, and the other person is being asked to take the other two.

Mother soon hung up the phone and returned to the car where we waited expectantly.

"What'd they say?" Dad asked.

"They said no."

"Both of them?"

"Yes."

The car was silent.

*So,* I thought, *this is what happens to Negroes when they move to California. They forget where they've come from, forget how we helped one another in the South. Instead they turn their backs on friends who need them*. All the way across the country we'd been singing, "California, Here I Come." Now I didn't know if I even wanted to stay here.

Daddy, who never swore in front of women, mumbled something under his breath and pulled the car into a corner of the filling station, where we would spend the night.

From New York City to Sacramento, we had stopped and stayed with friends. The last friends we'd stayed with lived in Denver, Colorado. Since we didn't know anyone between Denver and California, Dad had driven nonstop through the Rockies and the Sierra Mountains into California.

Our parents had decided to leave the South after Rosemary and I spent several summers in New York's Catskill Mountains. Having had that experience, they knew we would never return to Mississippi to live. All visible signs indicated that racial discrimination there would not end anytime soon, so at the end of the 1962 school year, our parents decided to move to California. They were so anxious to leave that they'd made the decision without securing jobs or a place to live in their newly chosen home. It was a courageous decision for them to make, but for me, barely out of my teens, it was an adventure.

The first morning after we arrived in Sacramento, I awoke to see the face of a Negro man peering into our car. It turned out that he lived next door to the filling station where we'd spent the night and had noticed our Mississippi license plate.

"Good morning," he said. "I see you've driven in from Mississippi."

"Yeah," my father answered, unwinding his body and getting out of the car. He walked a few steps away with the stranger and explained our situation.

"Would you like to come in and use my bathroom to freshen up?" we could hear the man say.

The four of us took sponge baths in his bathroom while our "angel" provided juice and the name of a Negro real estate broker. Dad asked where we could find the nearest Episcopal church and was told that Trinity Cathedral was a few blocks away. My father used the phone book to get the telephone number and then placed a call to the cathedral. He reached one of the canons there, who gave him the name and address of a nearby restaurant where he said he would meet us. Canon Howard Perry and Dean Malcolm McClenaghan both came to the restaurant and treated us to the first real breakfast we'd had in days. They listened as Dad related the journey that had brought us to California. Learning of our long-time membership in the Episcopal Church, the clergymen invited us to services at the cathedral and promised to tell Bishop Clarence Hayden about us.

When breakfast was over, Dad called Mr. J. R. Smith, the Negro real estate broker whose name he'd been given. Mr. Smith met us on a corner near the restaurant and took us to a house we could rent in the Oak Park section of the city.

Not long after our breakfast with Canon Perry and Dean McClenaghan, Bishop Hayden called Dad to his office and put him to work speaking in churches throughout Northern California in order to sensitize his predominantly white congregations to the atrocities taking place in Mississippi.

A year had passed since that first night and day in Sacramento, and Dad was still on his speaking tour. On June 13, he was scheduled to speak at Trinity Cathedral, the church to which we now belonged. I loved hearing my father speak and looked forward to hearing what he had to say one year after we'd left Mississippi. The speech had been planned long before Medgar Evers's assassination and was coming on the heels of several racially tense months in the Deep South. I was relieved to be far away from the hostilities that had bubbled up in Alabama and Mississippi that summer, yet I missed being at the heart of the struggle for integration with my friends. In Birmingham, Martin Luther King Jr. and Ralph Abernathy had led fifty people on a demonstration to desegregate the downtown stores. All fifty-two persons (including King and Abernathy) had been arrested. Following their release from jail, schoolchildren had become demonstrators for the first time and found themselves face-to-face with attack dogs. They were sprayed so hard with fire hoses carrying a hundred pounds of water that they were plastered against storefronts or propelled through the streets like rag dolls

In Jackson, Medgar Evers had informed the governor of Mississippi and the mayor that the National Association for the Advancement of Colored People (NAACP) was planning to end racial discrimination there, and he had gone on television[ii] to appeal to Negroes for support. At his invitation, Lena Horne had gone to Jackson to give a concert and speak at an NAACP rally. Afterward, Mr. Evers delivered his now famous "Freedom has never been free" speech.

On June 12, having watched televised accounts of the activities taking place in Mississippi and Alabama, my mother, father, sister, and I joined millions of Americans who gathered in front of their television sets that night to see President John F. Kennedy address the nation. Part of what he planned to say was meant to quiet an anxious country

---

ii Evers was only able to gain access to television time with the help of the Federal Communications Commission, because the state and city would not otherwise have allowed such a thing to happen in 1963.

following Governor George Wallace's attempt to block the admission of the first two Negro students admitted to the University of Alabama. The governor had stood in the university entranceway in order to keep Vivian Malone and James Hood from entering. And so President Kennedy spoke that night about the moral crisis we faced as a nation, and he urged people at every level of government to work to curb the unrest. His speech touched me most deeply when he addressed white Americans, saying, "If an American, because his skin is dark...cannot enjoy the full and free life which all of us want, then who among us would be content to have the color of his skin changed and stand in his place?"[iii] It was the first time I'd heard a US president speak so compassionately about the plight of Negroes.

These words coming from the president of the United States gave me a renewed sense of hope for my country, a belief that the awful life of Negroes in the Deep South might change during my lifetime. But it didn't take long for my newfound hope to be shattered. Shortly after midnight in Mississippi (a little after nine o'clock in California), television programming was interrupted with the announcement that Medgar Evers had been killed on the front lawn of his home.

Numbness overtook me, and everything else—including my family—disappeared. I felt as if I were all alone in the world. In my mind, I could see the Evers family's front lawn, which we had passed many times when we lived in Mississippi. I was immediately gripped with fear, wondering if his family was safe, wondering if the killer shot Mr. Evers and drove away or hid to see if other family members would appear, so he could shoot them, too. I snapped back to the present moment when

---

iii YouTube, MCamericanpresident, June 11, 1963, John F. Kennedy, Civil Rights Address, American President: An Online Reference Resource, www.MillerCenter. org/americanpresident.

Dad turned off the television. I hadn't even been aware that he'd gotten up; we all rose and headed to our bedrooms without speaking a word.

---

ON OUR RETURN HOME from the cathedral the night Dad was to give his address on conditions in Mississippi, he pulled the car into our garage on Hogan Drive, and the three of us got out. Inside the house, Rosemary and I washed up for dinner, while Dad and Mother retreated to their bedroom, where he no doubt finally released his emotions and told her why we were home early. Later they emerged, and the four of us sat down to eat dinner. Afterward, we cleared the dishes and stacked them in the sink before turning on the television news. To our amazement, there stood a poised Myrlie Evers, Medgar Evers's lovely young widow, speaking through her pain to a crowd assembled in Jackson.

"Nothing can bring Medgar back, but the cause can live on. It was his wish that this movement be one of the most successful that this nation has ever known. We cannot let his death be in vain."[iv]

It was one of the worst days in American history to date—far worse for her than for the rest of us—yet there she stood, eloquent in her grief, pulling the movement back together again. If anything could give us courage, it was her simple words that night. And indeed her words did give my father the courage he needed to keep his commitment to a Trinity Cathedral audience on a succeeding night.

My tears flowed freely as Mrs. Evers spoke, and I allowed my thoughts to wander back to my first encounter with her husband, in September 1955, when I was thirteen years old. It was one year after we

---

iv  Juan Williams, *Eyes on the Prize: America's Civil Rights Years, 1954–1965, A Robert Lavelle Book* (New York: Viking, 1987), 221–25.

moved to Mississippi from Florida. In late August, one month before my encounter with Mr. Evers, fourteen-year-old Emmett Till had been murdered, and every Negro in the area was on edge. Medgar Evers was Mississippi's newly appointed NAACP field director. He had driven ten miles north from his home in Jackson to Tougaloo College, where we lived, in order to meet with my parents.

In the twilight after dinner, Rosemary and I were playing hopscotch on the sidewalk in front of our home. His car pulled up on the far side of the five-foot-high hedge that surrounded our front yard just as Rosemary threw a small stone into the fourth square and jumped forward into the first two squares. The car engine shut off, the car door was slammed shut, and a handsome fair-skinned Negro man emerged from between the opening in the hedges. He walked along the sidewalk to where we were playing. "Hello, my name is Medgar Evers. I'm with the NAACP, and I'm here to see your parents."

Mr. Evers and his family had not been in Jackson long, and he was not yet the well-known civil rights leader he would become, so I was surprised to hear him announce his membership in the NAACP. I could not believe he would trust children he had just encountered with that information, because there was deep fear among many Mississippi Negroes about their association with the organization. Local whites swore the NAACP bred communists, and they intimidated NAACP members by getting them fired from jobs, fire-bombing their homes, and sometimes even murdering people they thought were members. In the weeks following the lynching of young Emmett Till, fear in the Negro community was palpable, yet here was this man Rosemary and I had never seen before, standing on our sidewalk announcing his membership in the NAACP and asking to see our parents, who were themselves unapologetic lifelong members of the organization. His gentle manner and his acknowledged membership led me to trust him immediately, so I invited him into our home to meet with Mother and Dad. I didn't discover until years later that my parents had asked him to come to Tougaloo that night so they could offer their support and assistance in recruiting new members for the organization.

Mr. Evers stopped by our home often to work with Dad and was among the progressive speakers who addressed integrated audiences at Tougaloo in defiance of Mississippi's laws against race mixing. Although they looked nothing alike and carried themselves very differently, Mr. Evers reminded me of my father, because I knew courage was a quality that could get a Negro man killed. Even though I was only thirteen years old, I often joined the college students and faculty members who gathered to hear Medgar Evers whenever he came to Tougaloo to speak. He was mesmerizing, speaking of equality of the races with a passion rarely heard from a Negro man.

I was twenty-one years old when he was assassinated eight years later, and I knew he was the reason that one of the first things I did after my birthday was register to vote.[v] I knew how hard he had worked for that right in Mississippi, knew how many millions of Negroes throughout the generations had died for that right, how many of them still living in Mississippi were being denied the right. I had registered first-time Negro voters in Georgia as a nineteen-year-old, and now I counted myself lucky to be in the position of reelecting a president who had hastened my entry into the civil rights movement by telling young people,

---

v  In 1963, the voting age was twenty-one. It was not until 1972 that it was lowered to eighteen.

"Ask not what your country can do for you—ask what you can do for your country...what together we can do for the freedom of man."[vi]

I had not had the privilege of voting for John F. Kennedy in his first presidential election, and that made me all the more anxious to participate in his reelection. But that was not to be. Five months after Medgar Evers's assassination, President John F. Kennedy was felled by an assassin's bullet in Dallas, Texas, shaking my world to its foundation. With the assassinations of two men I deeply respected and admired, I began to reexamine my own life. I felt an urgency to acquire all the knowledge I could fill my head with, a need to grasp everything, to reach out and get all the learning I could hold, in order to survive in the world. I felt I had an obligation to society and the world, because I wasn't put here simply to enjoy life. I had a purpose—a duty to myself and to others. I saw that I was put here to give, to understand, and to help and love all mankind, and I didn't want to stop with one small gesture. I wanted to enlarge the scope of my work until I had helped all humankind in some unique way. I felt my duty was to help humanity, and I hungered for a chance to explore and experience a new awareness, a new reason for being. I was just beginning to live, and life was so precious that I didn't want to deny myself any experience, for fear that it might never come my way again.

---

vi  From President John F. Kennedy's 1960 inaugural address.

# CHAPTER 1

# HEAVEN HELP US ALL[1]

VEILED IN A MIST of fog and confusion, I hold tightly to my mother's hand as we make our way along the crowded street. My father walks ahead of us in the dark, carrying suitcases. We move past Negro homes where people are throwing buckets of water on flames leaping from the roofs of houses. People are screaming, crying, and using garden hoses on patches of burning grass. Despite my mother's calm, I sense fear. Babies are crying, and women are sobbing softly, so I can tell this night is unusual. Families beside us have loaded what they could salvage onto flatbed trucks and the tops of cars: sofas, chairs, radios, mattresses, suitcases, lamps, and fans are all tied down with rope and cord. Older people and women with babies ride inside the truck cabs as the exodus of Negroes surges forward. Streetlights cast shadows on the road. When we approach the outskirts of town, my father spots a large black sedan idling in the distance, and the three of us go to it. He climbs into the front seat. Mother and I step onto the

---

1 Composed by Ronald N. Miller, 1970 EMI Music Publishing. Recorded by Stevie Wonder.

running board and settle down in the back. The windows are rolled up, making the air inside steamy and difficult to breathe.

I wake and sit upright in bed, drenched in perspiration, close to tears. The motion startles my husband, Bert, who wakes up to see what the matter is.

"It's my nightmare," I tell him.

"What nightmare?"

"The nightmare I've had ever since I was a little girl, the one where Mother, Daddy, and I are escaping the city in a mass exodus of Black people. It's like a premonition of something bad that's going to happen."

"Something that's going to happen, or something that's already happened?" he asks.

"I don't know. I used to think it happened, but when I asked Rosemary if she remembered it, she said no."

"Come here," Bert says, taking me in his arms and holding me until I fall asleep again. It is the spring of 1978. I am a wife and mother in my midthirties, and I've been troubled by this dream for as long as I can remember, a dream that always leaves me anxious.

During the summer of that same year, my parents come to New York from California for a visit. Prodded by Bert's suggestion, I wonder if the dream I've had all my life is really a memory of some event from long ago. So when Mother and I are alone in the kitchen preparing dinner, I describe the dream to her and ask her if anything like that ever happened to us. Self-consciously and a bit sheepishly I add, "Rosemary says she doesn't remember it."

Mother is so astonished by my question that she stops helping with dinner and stares at me with her mouth open. "Of course she doesn't remember," Mom finally says. "She wasn't born yet. *You* were only fourteen months old! What you are describing is the Beaumont race riot."

I turn off the stove, get out my tape recorder, go into the living room where Dad and Bert are reading newspapers and discussing sports, and ask my father and mother to tell me everything they remember about that long-ago night. Dad puts down his paper, gets up from the chair he is sitting in, and joins Mother and me at the dining-room table. Bert puts his paper down too and comes to sit and listen.

———————◆———————

IT WAS SUMMER. THE month was June, and my mother, father, and I were boarding with Mr. and Mrs. Matthews, because Mother and Dad had not found a home of their own yet. Mother read me a bedtime story, while flashes of flames from nearby oil rigs created reflections against the windowpanes. When my bedtime story was over, Mother turned off the lights so she could open the doors and windows and let air blow through the screens to keep the house cool. No one had air-conditioning back then. After putting me to bed, she sat alone, waiting for Daddy to come home from his office at the Negro branch of the YMCA on Neches Street in Beaumont where he was the boys' work secretary.

Meanwhile Daddy sat alone in his office, waiting until it was time to lock up and go home. It was strange, he thought, the building being so unusually quiet. It had been quiet like that on the previous night, too, and that was odd because the Y was the place where men went to talk, shoot pool, and play cards and table tennis. There wasn't much else for Negroes to do in segregated Beaumont, Texas. Following a long wait, Dad decided the evening would probably end as it had the night before, without a single person stopping by. So he locked the windows and doors, left a few lights burning for safety, and headed out toward the nearest bus stop. He was almost there when he saw a bus coming, so he started running toward it, waving his arms for the driver to stop, but the driver never even slowed down. Agitated, my father headed to another bus stop and boarded it when that bus came to a halt. Settling into a seat, he noticed that there was only one other passenger. That too was odd, because city buses were usually full of people riding home from work or places like the YMCA at that time of night.

When the bus reached our neighborhood, my father got off to walk the last blocks to our house. That's when an elderly Negro woman called out from a rocking chair on her front porch, "Hey, mister, what's all the screaming and yelling about?"

For the first time, Dad became aware of noise in the distance. "I don't know," he said. "Maybe it's a fire."

Without giving it much more thought, he continued walking home. Mother greeted him at the front door. The two of them laughed when Dad told her about the old woman on her porch who inquired about the noise.

"Some people are so nosy," he said. "They want to know what's going on blocks away from where they live."

Not long after that they retired for the night.

The following morning, when Daddy started out to work, a Texas Ranger stopped him.

"Where you goin'?" the ranger demanded.

"I'm going to work," Dad told him.

"You ain't goin' nowhere. Beaumont's under martial law. You go on back home. Ain't nobody goin' to work today."

By the time Dad returned home, Mother was on the telephone with Wendell Douglas, the executive secretary of the YMCA where my father worked. Mr. Douglas had called to say that an hour after Daddy left the Y, a gang of whites marched up Neches Street yelling racial obscenities and firing bullets into the YMCA building. They had shot out all the lights and left bullet holes in the wall behind the desk where my father had been seated. The first bus that passed by Dad the night before had been commandeered by angry whites, who pulled every Negro off and beat them. Every Negro, that is, except for Dr. Charlton, a physician who was so fair-skinned, the thugs mistook him for white. Mr. Douglas told Mother he and his family were leaving town, and they weren't planning to return until the rioting blew over. He had called because he knew Mother and Dad had one young baby and another on the way and he wanted to offer them safe passage out of the city.

Listening to my parents relive the events of that 1943 June night, I suddenly become aware of the fact that the "mist" in my dream was smoke rising from the homes of Negro families—homes that had been torched by rioters. And hearing of the bullet holes behind my father's desk, I shudder to think of how close I came to losing him that night. Had he not left the office early, bullets that ended up in the wall behind his desk might well have killed him.

Bringing myself back to the story unfolding in my dining room, I learn that after we entered the Douglases' car, it joined a long procession of vehicles leaving the city. Mother and I sat on the backseat with Mr. Douglas's wife, Bill, and their toddler, Wendell Joseph. Dad and Mr. Douglas rode up front as the adults tried to piece together what had happened.

"His wife, Bill?" I interrupt.

"Yes, her name was Bill," my parents confirm. As they do, I realize I have southern girlfriends named Charles, Harold, Sammy Lee, and Spencer. In that light, the name Bill seems less strange. Bill, they continue, was the most frightened of anyone in the car. As a child, she had survived the notorious June 1, 1921, race riot in Tulsa, Oklahoma, and the experience had left her desperate to get out of Beaumont with their young son, lest *that* riot have a similar effect on him.

The Greenwood section of Tulsa, known in 1921 as the Negro Wall Street, was completely leveled in less than twelve hours, leaving some three thousand Negroes dead, and over six hundred homes and successful businesses lost. Greenwood was one of the most affluent all-Negro communities in the United States. It had twenty-one churches, twenty-one restaurants, thirty grocery stores, a hospital, a bank, a post office, libraries, schools, law offices, and two movie theaters. The entire state of Oklahoma had only two airports, but a reported six Greenwood Negroes owned their own planes. Twenty-two years after the destruction of that city, the memory of the race riot that took place there still haunted Bill Douglas as our two families escaped Beaumont.

Beaumont, Texas, was the city to which my parents had moved two years after they were married, so my father could accept a better-paying job than the one he'd left behind in Georgia. But the city in which they had placed their hopes exploded the night a white woman claimed she was raped by a Negro shipyard worker. Based on her accusation, the police rounded up Negro men at random and threw them into jail. Later, under FBI interrogation, the woman admitted to having lied, but her initial claim had caused a Negro worker at an all-night ice stand to be shot and killed by whites in a passing car and had led to mass disorder throughout the city.

Under further investigation the underlying cause of the violence was revealed to have stemmed from the hiring of Negro shipyard workers who performed technical skills that commanded good pay, while white workers, lacking those skills, were relegated to lower-paying jobs. Their anger over the hiring of Negroes for the better jobs boiled over when rumor of the "rape" of a white woman spread through the city.

I learn later that Beaumont wasn't the only city that experienced a race riot during the summer of 1943. Negro-white relations were shaky all across the country where tension and fear gave way to distrust between the races. The new status among Negroes, based on their having been trained in government service jobs, had grown from sixty thousand to three hundred thousand hires between 1940 and 1944, and that had caused deep resentment among whites in the South as well as the North. Among the riots that took place that summer were an outbreak in Harlem and two in Detroit, the worst of which occurred in June.[2]

LEAVING BEAUMONT THAT HOT June night, we headed for Houston, eighty-four miles to the west. The Douglases planned to stay with relatives there. Mother attempted to locate the mother of a Spelman College classmate of hers who she hoped would take us in, since Negroes were not allowed entrance into hotels except as maids or cooks. Jim Crow laws forced us to rely on relatives and friends when we traveled and sometimes to even impose on Negro strangers. It would remain that way for the next twenty-one years.

---

2 Benjamin Quarles, *The Negro in the Making of America* (New York: Collier Books, Macmillan Publishing Company, 1964), 226–28.

After our arrival in Houston and welcome into her home by my mother's classmate's mother, Dad kept in touch with friends in Beaumont who let him know when it was safe to return. Weeks later we went back and moved into a new place on Threadneedle Street in the Pear Orchard section of Beaumont, one of the few Negro neighborhoods that had escaped the riot. For many Negroes who returned, the city would never again be the same. It had once held a promise of dreams fulfilled for those who flocked to her gates during World War II, but after the riot a large number of Negroes from Texas in general, and Beaumont in particular, moved to the West Coast seeking employment in the shipyards there, where they again hoped for lives better than the ones they had left behind.

My recurring dream of our escape from Beaumont ceased as soon as I learned the origin of it, but I believe that that early memory was the launching pad from which my lifelong commitment to justice began.

# Chapter 2

# Don't Fence Me In[3]

Four months after the Beaumont riot my sister, Rosemary, was born at home on Threadneedle Street. Before she arrived, my maternal grandmother, Nell, for whom I am named and on whose fiftieth birthday I was born, came from Atlanta, Georgia, to be with us. My grandmother was a small-boned, fair-skinned woman, the eldest of ten—eight girls and two boys—all offspring of an interracial marriage between a Cherokee Indian woman born Ida Anne Scott and a Negro man named Nelson Turner Mitchell. My grandmother's straight black hair had a gray streak in the center, and she wore it pulled back into a bun, revealing a face that reflected more of her Cherokee ancestry than her African American genes. As the firstborn, she was often called "Sis" by her siblings, who sometimes also used her given name until I was born. Then she became "Big Nell" and I was called "Little Nell." She stood barely five feet tall and weighed little more than a hundred pounds. Her father, Nelson T. Mitchell, was a linguistics professor who had taught at Wiley College in Marshall, Texas, and who spoke several

---

3 Music by Cole Porter, lyrics by Robert Fletcher and Cole Porter, 1934.

languages. His oldest child, who was my grandmother, spoke Spanish as fluently as she did English. I called her "Madre."

———————

PRIOR TO MADRE'S ARRIVAL, Mother prepares a special room for my sister's birth by sterilizing sheets baked in the oven along with an Irish potato. When the potato is done, Mother knows the sheets are sterile, and she takes care in moving them from the oven to the birthing room, along with sterilized blankets, baby clothes, and the linen that will go in the baby's bassinet. After the room is readied, it will not be entered until the day of my sister's birth. When that day arrives, Madre, a proper southern lady by anyone's standards, sits me down beside her as my mother goes into labor. Madre, who did not believe in discussing the origins of birth with a toddler, takes out a book and begins reading me a story. But in spite of her attempts to distract me, I can hear my mother's moans filtering through the wall of the room next door, rising above my grandmother's voice. And those moans concern me. I am anxious to know if she's all right.

"Why is Mommy crying?" I ask my grandmother. "Does it hurt to have a baby?"

"Be still, baby," Madre admonishes as she continues to read.

"Is Mommy all right?" I want to know, growing more impatient, but my grandmother reads on.

"Sit down, baby, and listen to the story."

I try hard to obey Madre and listen, but I can't be still. A baby is being born in the room next door, and I want to know what's happening. Mother has prepared me for the birth by letting me touch my sister inside her swollen belly and by telling me the big event will happen at home, but she didn't tell me there would be pain. So I'm curious about what is happening and have a very difficult time sitting still and listening to a story.

After what seems like an eternity, I hear the unmistakable cry of a newborn baby and scamper from the footstool in front of Madre's chair. Racing ahead of her, I run into the birthing room, barely containing myself. "I want to see the baby!" I squeal, grabbing hold of the bassinet and tipping it forward while I stand on tiptoes. "Be careful," Madre gently warns.

"Her name is Rosemary," whispers Mother in a tired voice from her bed across the room. "Mosemary!" I exclaim, christening her with the family nickname that is frequently used for years thereafter.

Rosemary is pampered and cooed over for months before Madre returns home, and by the time my sister is seven months old, she is placed in a playpen on the front porch. She can see me while I play with neighborhood children, and Mother can take care of household duties. I have great fun with most of my playmates, but there is one little boy who terrorizes all the rest of us. Neighborhood mothers complain to the bully's mother, but she seems unconcerned. Rosemary sits and watches everything that goes on between those of us who are playmates. And even as a baby, she senses that the rest of the neighborhood children are afraid of that one little boy.

One day, the little bully notices my sister in her playpen and climbs our steps. "Look at the baby," he coos, reaching into the playpen to touch her. Suddenly she grabs his hand and sinks her four teeth into his arm. His bloodcurdling scream brings Mother racing to the front porch and brings his mother running from her house. Mother pries Rosemary loose from him, and the bully flies down the steps into his mother's arms. After that day, the neighborhood kids play together without being bullied by him. The bite that the little boy received from Rosemary is the beginning of her fierce loyalty to me—a loyalty that has lasted a lifetime.

Mother holding Rosemary, who is being kissed by Nell

We are not in Beaumont much longer after Rosie's birth. The riots have taken their toll on countless Negroes, and by the time my sister takes her first steps, we have moved to San Antonio, Texas. In our new home the neighbors are Negro, Caucasian, and Mexican, and we children are in and out of one another's homes with great regularity, absorbing one another's cultures through music, language, games, and food without realizing how much we are learning about our different cultures. Rosemary and I eat spicy beans and rice and hot tamales, repeating the Spanish words we hear, and our friends speak English as they wolf down collard greens, corn bread, and black-eyed peas in our home. Mariachi music and country-and-western songs echo through their houses, while songs by the Inkspots and the Mills Brothers play in ours.

During our early San Antonio days, Mother stays home to take care of us, and Daddy starts his new job. He works hard to get a program going for the children of servicemen at a USO site. Going door to door, he recruits children for an after-school program, in spite of the fact that he does not have a car, an office, money to run the new program, or a place for the children he is recruiting to play.

Seeing how hard he is working to get the program off the ground, Mother laments, "You don't even have a place for the children to gather for your new program."

With characteristic optimism, Dad replies, "But I've got the most important thing. I've got the kids."

The Negro owner of a local filling station, who has observed Dad signing youngsters up for his new program, offers my father a spare room at his filling station. He says it can be used as an office, and since the station is across the street from a park, my father designates the playground there as his athletic field. Over time, the work he does with children leads him to found the Alamo East Side YMCA, San Antonio's first Y for Negroes.

Eager to do her share to contribute to the household, Mother decides to try her hand as a door-to-door sales representative for "Real Silk" stockings. She is excited about the opportunity to test her skills as a salesperson, because when she was a little girl, her parents wouldn't even let her sell Girl Scout cookies. As well-to-do Atlanta socialites, they shuddered at the thought of their only child going door to door, so they bought up her quota of cookies and sent her back to her troop with the money.

I grow up thinking of my mother as the most beautiful woman in the world. Her youthful skin is smooth and flawless, a rich blend of cinnamon and ginger, and there is a hint of freckles on her cheeks. Her long black hair is swept up in a profusion of curls the way Daddy likes it, and her lips are perfectly shaped. She has doe-like eyes that are as fresh and sparkling as a child's. She wears no makeup except for bright red lipstick. She stands five feet three inches tall next to our father's muscular, six-foot frame.

When Mother begins her new job, our paternal grandmother, Mary, comes from Jacksonville, Florida, to care for us. This grandmother we call "Dear." She, like Madre, is biracial, but her conception and birth are the result of a violent rape against her mother, Ellen Bass, by a southern white man. Dear is a large warm-hearted woman who stands five feet eight inches tall and weighs nearly two hundred pounds. Her arms swallow Rosemary and me up in her ample bosom. She is a thoughtful and loving grandmother and mother-in-law who spoils Mother with the little things her own parents didn't think to do. On this trip, Dear has traveled on a Jim Crow train all the way from Jacksonville, Florida, to San Antonio, Texas, with a homemade cake to celebrate Mother's birthday. Rosemary and I are her first grandchildren, and being the mother of two sons, she takes delight in her granddaughters.

Our family falls into a comfortable rhythm following Dear's arrival, but that comfort is interrupted when Mother's door-to-door selling proves too strenuous for her. In the midst of her third pregnancy, our mother suffers a miscarriage and ends up spending time in bed recovering. Dear takes care of her during her convalescence, nursing Mother back to health before returning to Jacksonville. By the time Mother is on her feet again, news of Dad's outstanding work in San Antonio has reached Austin, Texas. Administrators at Tillotson College send a telegram inviting him to come and create the school's first football program. If he accepts, they say, he can also coach the track team. In the midst of their negotiations, administrators in Austin discover that Mother has a bachelor's degree in English and a master's in guidance counseling, so they sweeten the pot with an offer to her to be dean of women and a professor of English.

It is 1947 when we move into the old army barracks Tillotson College uses for faculty housing. The units are leftover accommodations that the segregated troops lived in during World War II. We live at the end of one row of barracks across a dirt path from another set. In the beginning, what most worries Mother about our move is whether or not her three- and five-year-old girls will be able to negotiate the small shower stall. All we have known up to that point is bathtubs, and our young mother isn't sure how to help us to use the tiny stall. But we master it and allay her fears.

By fall, I am enrolled in the first grade at the Blackshear Elementary School, which is across the street from Tillotson College. Like all southern institutions at the time, it is segregated. I am excited to be entering the first grade.

Rosemary is enrolled in a Catholic preschool a few blocks past the Blackshear Elementary School that I attend. Because Daddy leaves home before breakfast for track practice, and Mother's English class begins at the same time we have to be in school, the task of getting Rosemary to school falls to me. At five years old, I take my responsibility very seriously, following my parents' instructions to the letter. I hold my sister's hand, look both ways before crossing the busy street separating the college from my school, and then cross. I walk past Blackshear Elementary to get to Rosemary's school, where we greet nuns who float past us in long black habits and black headpieces billowing out from white headbands. I make sure my sister is safely in her seat and then leave to return to Blackshear and my own classroom.

It isn't until the end of the school day that I discover Rosemary has sat at her desk just long enough for me to get to my own school. Then she leaped up, darted through her classroom door and past the nuns, ran past my school, and crossed the street full of traffic alone. She arrived home just in time to meet Mother leaving for work. Standing in our front door, she wailed, "I'm not going back to that school!"

After several days of my sister running away from school, Mother and Dad take time off from their jobs to find out what is making Rosemary so unhappy at school. There they discover that she is not the only dissatisfied child in the school. Other parents report that other children are unhappy, too, so my parents decide the best thing for them to do is find a new preschool for Rosemary. My sister's new school is much farther away from Blackshear than her old one, so Daddy makes room in his schedule to take her each morning. I'm given the responsibility of picking her up in the afternoon after I have come home, had a snack, and changed out of my school clothes and into play things.

One day on my way home to change into play clothes before picking Rosie up from school, I run into a man on campus who is going around taking photographs of children on his Shetland pony. He asks me if I want to take a picture and says he will bring it back in a few weeks to see if Mother wants to buy it. I say yes and climb up on the pony, remembering stories Madre has told me of wanting a Shetland pony of her own when she was little girl. After the man leaves to photograph other children, I change into my play clothes and race to get Rosemary from school without having my snack. I believe that if I can pick her up early enough, maybe we can get home before the man leaves the campus, and she can have her picture taken on the pony, too. But her teacher holds us up, and by the time we get home, the man with the pony is gone. Weeks later he returns with a beautiful sepia photograph of me in front of our home on the pony. Mother buys it, and for years it graces a table in our living room.

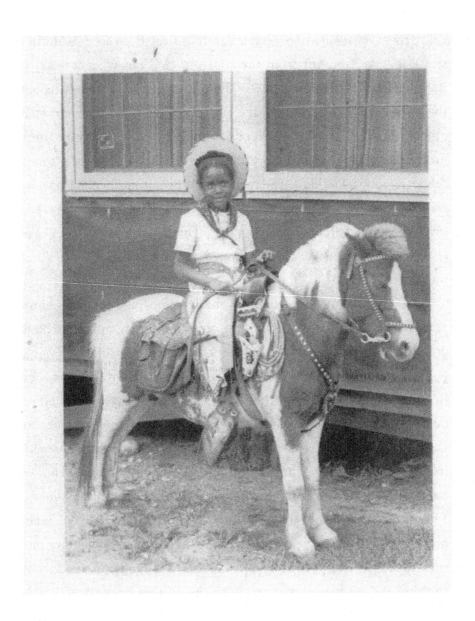

Nell on Shetland pony

Our friends in Austin are the children of other faculty members. Some live on campus, others down the street from the college. Most are members of the Jack and Jill Club[4] we belong to, and nearly all of them attend St. James Episcopal Church, where Father Murray is the priest, and Daddy is a licensed lay reader. Mrs. Murray and their daughter, Malvina, play the organ and piano for Sunday services, and their son, Jimmy, is one of our closest friends. Rosemary and I, and Jimmy, Ora Ann, Joan, Janet, and Louisa Bell all attend Sunday school together and sit together in the front pew during the adult service. Sunday school plus the adult service makes for a long day. We children struggle to keep quiet and pay attention in church, but by midmorning, we are easily distracted and begin to whisper and giggle during the service. In the middle of our fun, Father Murray interrupts his sermon, calls the name of the child he catches talking, and demands that the foolishness cease. The church becomes so quiet we can hear ourselves breathe. Having gotten our full attention, Father Murray resumes preaching as we sit absolutely still. There will be time for fun again after the service has ended, but for now we are determined not to be embarrassed again.

When Jimmy comes to play at our house, we swing on our jungle gym, build cities in our sandbox, and eat make-believe dinners of onion-grass salad, potatoes made from stones, and sunbaked, mud-dried meatloaf inside our log cabin playhouse. While our make-believe pies bake, we head for the grass, where we search for four-leaf clovers. Whoever finds the first one will be declared lucky. I always want to find one first, but Rosemary or Jimmy usually beat me to it, leaving all

---

4 Jack and Jill is a children's social organization which our parents used to bring us together for recreation in a city where Jim Crow facilities were off-limits. The organization is still used today by middle-class African Americans who want their children to meet other young people with similar backgrounds and values.

the three-leaf clovers for me. As the two of them head for the grass, our dog, Mike, runs toward me jumping up and down on his leash. Since I know I won't find the four-leaf clover, I greet him. "Come here, Mike. Come here, boy." Mike is a beautiful dog with the coloring and long hair of a collie and the body of a chow.

When Daddy brought him home to us in San Antonio, he was so tiny, he fit in the pocket of our father's coat. Rosemary and I loved Mike from that first night. We fed him from the table, snuck him into bed with us, and wiped him every time he urinated, considering him more of a brother than a pet.

He becomes our greatest protector, even biting Daddy once for spanking us, and although Dad was upset by the attack, he didn't scold Mike because, he said, he bought him to protect us. When our parents go to PTA or faculty meetings, they lock Mike inside the house with us, knowing he will viciously attack anyone who tries to get in. In fact, our playmates are the only people he doesn't lunge at.

Mike jumps up on me, and I pet him, while Rosemary and Jimmy impatiently call to me to join them in search of a four-leaf clover. Finally, I leave Mike to search for clovers as the three of us start to sing, "I'm looking over a four-leaf clover that I overlooked before. First is the sunshine, the second is rain, third is the roses that bloom in the lane..." I don't know why we sing this song when we look for clovers, but we always do. I start to pull up clovers, and my allergic reaction to grass causes me to sneeze. Jimmy and Rosemary are asthmatic, but the grass doesn't bother them. Soon Rosemary is squealing, "I found one! I found one!" She has found the first four-leaf clover of the day and is declared lucky.

Our neighbors, Junior and Melvin, often come over to join us, and we go to the three-story sliding fire escape we discovered one day located outside the administration building. The five of us climb up the front of the fire escape to the second story and slide down. The momentum carries us down so fast, we can't stop ourselves from landing on our rear ends in the dirt.

Rosemary, who is small-boned and built more like our mother's side of the family, is the first to climb to the third floor. She slides down so fast that she bounces several feet into the air before landing in the middle of the slide on the ground-floor level and sailing into the dirt. Seeing her fly up like that scares the living daylights out of the rest of us, so we refuse to go up three stories. But she repeats the stunt so often that she shames us into trying it, too.

I feel too scared to climb to the top, but everyone else does it and starts calling to me, "C'mon, Nell!" I refuse, but they keep after me, each in turn climbing to the top and sliding down. Jimmy, who is three years older than I am and the only boy I know who is taller than I am, climbs all the way up and careens down. Now I really feel foolish about refusing to climb to the top, but I'm afraid. "C'mon, Nell!" they all yell. "C'mon!"

When they are all at the bottom again, I climb to the first level, turn around, and look down. "Go on," they urge. "You scared?" Yes, I am scared, but I'm not about to admit it. My heart is pounding so hard I can hear it. I start the climb to the top and am surprised at how short it is. Then I turn around and discover why. It is steeper than the bottom part. I stand at the top of the fire escape above the trees. The clouds float over my head, and I hear birds singing. I can see the whole campus from here and wish I could stay and enjoy this quiet beauty. "C'mon, Nell. Hurry up!" I look down and gasp at how small everyone seems. I look at the top part of the fire escape and wonder if I will stay connected to the metal slab as I slide. I sit and feel only slightly better to see that the distance between the second and third floor landings is a little closer.

"C'mon!" Everybody is yelling at me at once.

"I am!" I yell back. "One, two, three," I say to myself.

"Come on! Let go!" they all scream. I push forward onto the metal, take a deep breath, and let go. Down I fly, hitting the familiar second landing and then careening to the bottom.

"Wasn't that fun?" Rosemary screams.

"No," I want to say, "that was the scariest thing I've ever done." But I nod my head, hoping no one notices how much I'm rubbing my rear end. I don't think I will ever climb that high again, but I do every time our friends scream, "C'mon! You scared?" One day while we are playing on the slide, a security guard appears and tells us we can't play on the fire escape anymore. "It's too dangerous," he says, but Rosemary and I yell back, "Our Mother doesn't care what we do." That evening when we get home Mother is waiting at the door with her hairbrush. She uses it to give us both a tanning.

My sister and I are enrolled in ballet and tap classes, where we wear pretty, sleeveless white dotted-Swiss dresses trimmed at the hem in two rows of black rickrack. The dresses are tied in back with wide white sashes. When guests come to our home, Mother and Daddy have us dance, sing, and recite the poems by Negro authors that we have memorized. We also learn Negro spirituals and master all three verses of the Negro national anthem, "Lift Every Voice and Sing." We are taught that the last verse is to be sung reverently, like a prayer.

*God of our weary years, God of our silent tears*
*Thou who has brought us thus far on the way;*

*Thou who has by thy might*
*Led us into the light,*
*Keep us forever in the path, we pray...*[5]

At Christmas I amaze everyone by memorizing and reciting Clement Clarke Moore's "A Visit from St. Nick" also known as "The Night Before Christmas."

Many Saturday mornings, Rosemary and I linger in bed to listen to our favorite children's program, *Big John and Sparky*, on the radio. Afterward, we follow the job chart Mother has printed up with hand-drawn pictures: clean your room, hang your pillows on the clothesline in the sun, rearrange your socks and underwear drawers, air your mattresses, and sweep your room. After we are done with chores, we play band.

"Mommy, may we have a pot to make instruments?" we ask. She searches for the dented pots she keeps for this time of the day and gives us a couple of wooden spoons as we head out to join other faculty brats carrying similar makeshift instruments. We line up behind our pint-size four-year-old bandleader, Petey Williams, the eldest son of the college's director of music. Whistle dangling from a shoestring around his neck, stick in hand, Petey lifts his makeshift baton and blows his whistle, and we begin. Beating pots and humming a tune, we parade around the campus, a ragtag band of three-, four-, and five-year-olds moving past couples on benches, students crossing the grass, and teachers walking the grounds. We march back and forth over the campus until we exhaust our repertoire of songs.

On the way back, we usually pass the home of the only child on campus who is not allowed to come out and play. Locked behind a screen

---

5 "Lift Every Voice and Sing," words by James Weldon Johnson, music by Rosamond Johnson, copyright 1921.

door, he watches as we parade in front of his house. We don't know why his mother locks him in, but we feel sorry for him. Even on the rare occasions when she leaves him inside so she can hang her wash on the line in back, she locks him in with an outdoor hook she has placed at the top of their screen door. He lives at the opposite end of the barracks from our unit, and as soon as his mother disappears behind the barracks (which had no back doors), he pleads with us to let him out. On this day one child peeps around the corner where his mother is hanging the wash while I, the only child tall enough to reach the hook, tiptoe up the front porch steps to unhook the latch. The hook is barely out when he flings the door open, dashes past me, and runs away. We all scatter like frightened birds. When his mother returns and discovers he's been let out, she begins calling for my father, the only adult who can run fast enough to catch her son. "Coach! Coach! Catch him, catch him!" Dad starts out, running, searching as he runs, unaware that I am the culprit who has let the little boy out. When my father finds him he picks him up and brings him home kicking and screaming. His mother whips him and locks him inside again, where he stays until the next time one of the kids stands watch, and I can tiptoe up to free him. I think we all hated to see him caged in like that.

On weekends when Dad's teams do not have games to play, he and Mother play contract bridge. They carry Rosemary and me with them to the homes of friends where we play with the children, while they deal cards and bid. They play late into the evening, and we children climb onto one big bed, slowly drifting off to sleep to the sounds of shuffling and dealing cards and our parents' laughter in the background. At the end of the night, Rose and I are carried out to the car of a friend who drives us and our parents home.

When Dad is on the road with the team and rain keeps us from playing band outside, Rosemary and I play "Sunshine School" inside with Mother, who is inventive in taking on the characters in our storybooks. We listen to the tales of Uncle Remus, rejoicing when Brer Fox is outsmarted the by animals who are deemed duller than he. Animals who, like our slave ancestors, outsmarted their owners while feigning ignorance. *Tales of the Arabian Nights* enthralls us, because we know people in Arabia are brown like us, and there are few storybook heroes in whom we can see ourselves. Heidi and Hansel and Gretel are favorites, too, but I like Hans Christian Andersen best, because as a gangly youngster, I often feel like an ugly duckling. Tall, unsure of myself, and somewhat shy, I listen to the story over and over, hoping to someday become a beautiful swan the way the ugly duckling does.

In Sunshine School with Mother, Rosemary and I study geography, arithmetic, and history. "Today we are going to study the map of Europe," Mother says, pulling out an atlas and running her finger around the outline of a country. When the lesson is over, we make decorations that Mother tapes to the windows or saves for the Christmas tree. "Let's make a new kind of star for the Christmas tree this year," she says, laying out precut squares of special paper that is shiny and colorful on one side and white on the other. Using a pattern she has cut from one of her women's magazines, she swirls a compass around and around, tracing intricate patterns of elongated ovals.

"What are we going to do with those?" Rose and I want to know.

"You children can cut them along the solid lines, and I'll show you how to fold them on the dotted ones."

We follow her instructions, singing as we work. Cutting shiny reds, greens, blues, golds, and silvers, we set aside the pieces until we are shown how to fold and paste them. Before our beautiful multipointed stars are completely sealed, Mother strings a piece of shiny thread through them and shows us how they will be hung over a branch of the Christmas tree.

Sometimes we play dress-up in our mother's clothes, putting on "Little Lady" perfume and lipstick, which is really lightly colored ChapStick. As a special treat, she paints our fingernails with clear polish. "May we wear red like Madre?" we plead.

"No," she tells us, "little ladies don't wear red." But when she lets us go down to a neighbor's house to have our nails done, we return with scarlet-red nails like our grandmother's.

At Christmastime, Daddy makes extra money barnstorming through the South playing against teams at other historically Negro colleges. The more experienced coaches counsel the younger ones like our dad about the roads they should stay clear of to avoid night riders and Klansmen. The team fills two station wagons and one sedan with twenty-five boys and coaches who make their way from Tillotson to sister Negro schools, where they stop to use the only toilets available to Negroes. There, they relax before being sent off with twenty-five sandwiches that they can't buy from whites along the roads without humiliating themselves by going to the back doors. They also take twenty-five cartons of milk and twenty-five slices of cake to get the energy and nourishment they will need before playing basketball.[6] With all the segregation in the South at this time, few of the people we associate with ever go to the back door of an establishment for food. I think it is the pride passed down from one generation to the next that keeps us from those back doors.

---

6 Interview with coaches Stan Wright and John Braxton, the Rusty Duck Restaurant, Sacramento, CA, August 27, 1995.

If on Christmas Eve Dad is late getting home from a trip, Mother sends us to bed. I lie wide-awake in my bed across the room from Rosemary, praying for my father's safe return. Even as a child, I sense the roads are dangerous for Negroes traveling along dark two-lane highways, and my daddy's safe return is more important than any gift Santa can bring. Since my prayers are always answered, I think God and Santa Claus must be the same.

Should he return from a trip early, Daddy goes out to find a Christmas tree to chop down, or at least I think he goes to chop down a tree, because on Christmas morning, Rosie and I wake to find one standing in the living room decorated with colored lights, aluminum-foil chains, and the stars, bells, and angels we have made with Mother in Sunshine School.

One year Rose and I get an electric popcorn machine. A Rudolph the Red-Nosed Reindeer radio is left another year. Life-size Negro dolls with real hair come from our great-aunt Maude and Uncle Brit another Christmas. Aunt Maude is one of Madre's seven younger sisters, and the dolls she and her husband send are as soft and cuddly as real babies. They even have brown eyes that open and shut. We think they are the most beautiful dolls we've ever seen—one is dressed in a pink nylon dress with a matching bonnet, the other in blue. Both wear white baby shoes and are named Maude Dale and Carmen.

We welcome each New Year with black-eyed peas, rice, pig ears, chitlins, greens, cornbread, and buttermilk. When the yuletide season is over, we burn the fir tree in the front of the barracks and let its pungent aroma prolong our holiday memories.

Austin summers, like those in San Antonio, are hot and humid. So, just as we've done in other cities, we turn off the electric lights at night and open the front door to let the air blow through the house and cool it down. In the darkness Rosemary and I strip down to our underpants and box by the beams from a streetlight that streak across the living-room floor. Our parents act as "trainers," coaxing us from opposite corners, "Bob and weave, bob and weave." When Rose and I have worn ourselves out, the four of us celebrate with bowls of ice cream and watch Daddy form shadow animals on the wall with his hands.

Texas—with its open spaces, rolling tumbleweeds, and untamed horses galloping across the prairies, their manes flying in the breeze—gives us a unique sense of freedom. In the daylight hours, we play cowboys and Indians, shooting cap pistols and feigning death. We run barefoot across the campus (which is our playground boundary), chasing the bad guys and sometimes capturing them. All the while, Rosemary and I keep an ear cocked for the special tune Dad has written for Mother. If one of our parents whistles it, and the other answers, we know they are sending messages to each other. But if there is no response from the other parent, then Rosie and I know we are being called home to dinner. Saying good-bye to playmates, we make our way back across the campus, sometimes finding that while we played on one side of the main road running through the campus, fresh tar has been poured over it. Rosie bets me she can run across the newly tarred road without burning her feet. I bet her she can't. She races across, swearing she didn't feel a thing. Being a full head taller than she is, I follow, only to get stuck in the middle with soft tar clinging to the soles of my feet. Somehow it never occurs to me that, being taller and heavier, I will sink deeper into the tar. At home, Mother soaks my feet in a tub of cool water and coats them with medicated ointment, admonishing us both to take our shoes the next time we go across campus to play. We promise we will but hardly ever do.

September arrives, and the air gets cool as the changing colors of the leaves announce the start of fall. In October, Mother and Dad host a cowgirl/cowboy party at a dude ranch in celebration of Rosemary's fourth birthday. Everybody comes dressed in cowboy clothes. Rosie and I wear checkered shirts, boots and spurs, suede cowgirl skirts with white fringe around the hem, cowgirl hats, and holsters with cap pistols tucked inside. We children take pony rides and play cowboys and Indians—sometimes letting the Indians win and sometimes the cowboys. We roast hot dogs and toast marshmallows over a campfire while we sing country songs. Even though it is Rosemary's birthday, the day is magical for me, too, because until this day I did not know Negroes could hold celebrations in such a lovely spot. At the same time, I find myself wondering if white people can use places like this all the time, and Negroes are only allowed to use them on special days. I wonder, but I don't ask. Southern children of my generation don't question their parents about such things. I know a world different from the one I live in exists somewhere "out there," a world where white children go to different schools, see different movies, and worship in different churches, but it isn't until the day of Rosemary's birthday party that I think of their world as having more in it than ours.

That winter it snows for the first time in anyone's memory, and Mother surprises us by making snow ice cream. Rosie and I scarf it down and then race outside to build a snowman, but there isn't enough snow to make one like those we've seen on Christmas cards, and our measly job disappoints us. A month later we find ourselves aboard a train headed for Los Angeles. There the Tillotson football team will play a semipro team called the San Pedro All Stars in the Angel Bowl Classic.

Jim Crow laws prohibit Negroes and whites from riding in the same coach, so a special car is hooked onto the back of the train for us to ride in.[7] It is the custom of white conductors to reserve the two front seats of the Negro coach for themselves, placing baskets of fruit, candy bars, magazines, and newspapers on them. After collecting tickets from the other passengers, they return to our segregated car and sell the items they've placed in the front seats, because we are not allowed to eat in the dining car. When the porter enters our car, Rosemary sparks laughter from everyone by answering his question, "What'll you have?" with, "Pabst Blue Ribbon!" which is the response to a famous beer jingle. The football players say they know this is going to be a "good-time" trip if the baby daughter of the coach and the dean of women is ordering beer.

The train clickety-clacks along the track as Rosie and I stretch out across its seats. Bedding down with blankets and pillows, we listen to football players with nicknames like Ironhead and Zigaboo sing us to sleep with a song about a woman who wears red silk stockings and green perfume.

---

7 In 1865, the provisional legislatures established by President Andrew Johnson adopted the notorious Black Codes. "Some of them were intended to establish systems of peonage or apprenticeship resembling slavery. Three states at (the) time adopted laws that made racial discrimination of various kinds on railroads. Mississippi gave the force of law to practices already adopted by railroads by forbidding 'any freedman, negro (sic) or mulatto to ride in any first class passenger cars, set apart, or used by and for white persons....' The Florida legislature went a step further the same year by forbidding whites to use the cars set apart for use (by) Negroes, as well as excluding Negroes from cars reserved for whites, but it did not require the railroads to provide separate cars for either race, nor did it prohibit mixing of the races in smoking cars. Texas carried the development further in 1866 with a law that required all railroad companies to 'attach to passenger trains one car for the special accommodation of freedmen.'" C. Vann Woodward, *The Strange Career of Jim Crow*, second revised edition (Oxford University Press, 1966), 23–24.

# CHAPTER 3

# WE ARE FAMILY[8]

I T IS THE EARLY summer of 1948, and the four of us—Mother, Daddy, Rosemary, and I—are in Atlanta with a large contingent of Madre's siblings and their families to celebrate Cousin Yvonne's graduation from Fisk University. Yvonne's commencement makes her the first descendant of (her grandfather and) my maternal great-grandfather, Nelson T. Mitchell, to graduate from his alma mater, and her accomplishment creates an expectation of a possible family tradition at Fisk. Great-aunts and great-uncles have arrived from across the country. Aunt Ruby and Uncle Kelley have driven from Marshall, Texas; Yvonne's parents, Aunt Gertrude and Uncle Sam, have flown in from Los Angeles along with Uncle Dynamite; Aunt Louise and Uncle Dyche have come from Newark, New Jersey; Aunt Mabel and Uncle Ezra have come in from New York; and Aunt Maude and Uncle Brit have traveled by train from Chicago. With so many family members descending on Madre and Papa's home, my grandmother finds her budget stretched to the limit, and every available room of her two-story house filled, including

---

8 Music composed by Bernard Edwards and Nile Rodgers, recorded by Sister Sledge, 1979.

the screened-in back porch where army cots have been opened for Dad and Uncle Dynamite,[9] and down in the basement, where pallets have been laid out on the floor for Rosemary and me. Uncle Dynamite's and Dad's cots are set up amid crates of 7-Up and Coca-Colas and wooden baskets of fresh Georgia peaches. There are also bedrooms in the finished attic, which is used as a third floor. Madre's married sisters and brothers-in-law—the ones who have come from New York, New Jersey, and Chicago—sleep there.

At age six, I am delighted to be in the basement, where Rosie and I can be audience to the best show in town: our grandmother and her siblings reminiscing about times past. Lying on our pallets, we enjoy the conversations coming from the sewing room where they sit making clothes, one memory triggering another without rhyme or reason.

"Remember the time Louise and Maude went shopping at Rich's and tried to go down the up escalator?" Gertrude asks, referring to the day her sisters went down to Atlanta's leading department store and decided to try the new moving staircase instead of the elevator. Arriving at the up escalator instead of the one headed down, they found the steps disappearing faster than they could put a foot down.

Aunt Gertrude stands to mimic her sisters standing at the top of the up escalator. Pulling her foot up, she demonstrates how each sister put a foot on the top step over and over again, only to jerk it back as one step after another disappeared. Peals of laughter echo through the basement as everyone recalls the moment. When the laughing subsides, someone else begins a new tale; like the time each one disguised herself and pretended to be Gertrude in order to sneak into the sanatorium and visit Lucille,

---

9 Our great-uncle, Nelson T. Mitchell Jr., is called N. T. by his blood relatives, but during his days as a student at Morehouse College, one of his friends added a "T" in front of his initials, changing them from N. T. to T. N. T. From that day forward he was known by his friends, including Dad, as Dynamite. Upon hearing Daddy call him Dynamite, Rosemary and I begin calling him Uncle Dynamite.

who was suffering from tuberculosis. Finding humor even in the difficult times, they recall the furtive looks of hospital staff as each disguised sister smuggled in the special foods Lucille loved. Gales of laughter ring out as they congratulate themselves on having foiled the administration.

Then Aunt Mabel begins her story of a cross-country trip she took alone by bus from Asheville, North Carolina, where she was teaching school, to Los Angeles to visit two of her sisters. Halfway through Utah, the bus she was on broke down. As the only Negro aboard, she knew she didn't stand a chance of being allowed to stay in a hotel. But of all the members in our family (because of her Cherokee-Negro heritage), Aunt Mabel is the most Asian-looking. Mustering up her courage in Utah that fateful night, Aunt Mabel walked into the hotel and said, "I am Haru Hisami, and I need a room for the night," and that is how she was able to get a bed in Utah.

NELL'S GREAT-AUNT MABEL

When they are having fun, our great-aunts are among the happiest people we know, but when they are sad, their sobbing can cast a cloud over everything. Concerned at seeing grown-ups cry, Rosemary and I once asked our mother why they were weeping.

"The Mitchells are high-strung," she told us.

On the first floor of the house, the well-appointed living room leads straight into a formal dining room. A beautiful crystal chandelier hangs over the table, which is encircled by chairs covered in a silk and satin material. Covering the table is a white damask tablecloth, with the signatures of each family member embroidered by Madre in white silk thread. The outline of my hand has been traced and embroidered next to my grandmother's name at one end. When I am old enough to write in script, I will sign my name beside the handprint, which I measure against my growing hand each year. After Rosemary is born, her handprint is added to the tablecloth between Mother's and Daddy's names, to be followed by her signature when she is older. Papa sits at the opposite end of the table from Madre, and when the whole family is together, each member sits where his or her signature appears. (Rosemary sits between our parents near Papa's end of the table, and I sit at the opposite end of the table, closest to the breakfast room and kitchen, next to Madre.) Our grandmother's sisters and brothers, and their spouses and children, fill in the other places.

At the start of each morning when Papa goes out, everyone's breakfast waits until he returns from his walk. Rosie and I, awakened by the smell of bacon, grits, scrambled eggs, and beef brains, bound out of bed, wash up, and get dressed as fast as we can. Then we hurry up to the kitchen for freshly squeezed orange juice. The aroma of coffee wafts through the house as Madre gives us the "everyday" silverware and china with which to set the table. Eager and hungry, we go about our assigned tasks.

"Where's Papa?" we ask.

"He's taking his morning constitutional," Madre tells us, meaning he is walking in the neighborhood, and depending on whom he runs into or stops to talk with, he could be gone from half an hour to more than an hour.

The smell of his Cuban cigar alerts us to our grandfather's return and means we can finally be seated for breakfast. As soon as he washes his hands and takes his place at the head of the table, piping-hot food appears and is set in silver chafing dishes or on sterling silver trivets. Unless Rosemary and I have been asked in advance to say grace, Papa does the honors. The two of us stifle giggles whenever Papa says the blessing, because he is known as a brilliant orator, and our family places great importance on the enunciation of words. But when Madre calls on him to say the grace, Papa mumbles, "Gra—Ga-a-a—. Amen." The first two words are likely "Gracious God," but he races through the blessing so fast we wonder if even God understands him. After he blesses the food, Madre asks that all the serving dishes be passed around the table in the same direction so food won't be coming at people from both directions. We eat while Papa shares news of the city that he has picked up during his morning walk. "Mr. So-and-so says the city legislators are planning..." or "a new house is going up over on Such-and-such Street."

In the evenings, Madre rings a small silver bell to gather us for dinner. At dinnertime Papa asks Rosemary and me what we've learned during the day. Even though I'm only six years old, Papa can ask the question in such a way as to make me feel there is little point in being alive if I've been up and about all day and haven't learned anything new. Sometimes I forget to find out something new until just before dinner and go scrambling for a newspaper, so I will have something to contribute. I have to read more than a few paragraphs, because I know Papa will ask questions about the article that he expects me to answer. It is through our daily sharing of newly learned information that Rosie and I begin to take part in dinner conversations. Once in a while, our contribution is interesting enough for other members of the family to enter into the discussion, which means we are rescued and can finish dinner in peace.

On one side of the dining room there are windows along the entire wall, and a long window seat overlooks the front yard and a portion of the tennis court in back. Just off the other side of the dining room is one of my favorite places in the whole house—Madre's bedroom. It has a four-poster mahogany bed covered with professionally laundered eyelet-edged linen and a fireplace where Rosemary and I sit with Madre on cool evenings eating homemade yogurt and just-baked devil's food cake. Our small rockers sit beside her large one in front of the fireplace facing an assortment of short, colorful Mexican brooms with curved handles, part of the collection of treasures she brings back from her annual trips to Mexico. A large black telephone stands on her bedside table beside a radio that is tuned to classical music in the mornings, soap operas in the afternoon, and when I was younger, President Roosevelt's fireside chats in the evenings. A mahogany dresser and large framed mirror are off to the left across from the foot of her bed. To the right of the dresser is the door to the black-and-white tiled bathroom that joins Madre's bedroom to Papa's.

Madre's side of the bathroom has crochet-laced towels with the letter T embroidered on the front. Cotton, tweezers, night cream, and bubble bath sit on a glass shelf over the sink, and a trash basket covered in mirrored squares is on the floor beside the basin. Papa's side is dominated by a long leather razor strop and an assortment of natural-bristle shaving brushes.

Papa's bedroom is where Mother slept when she was a child, but it has been transformed for him over the years, as travel consumes more and more of his time. His bed is also a four-poster mahogany one, with green-and-white-striped linen. A night table stands next to it with a gooseneck reading lamp, writing pads, and a Philco radio alternately tuned to the news, the Voice of America, and Walter Winchell. When the room is empty, Rosemary and I slip behind the night table and switch the radio on. We watch the orange filament in the tubes at the back glow off and on. We can stand mesmerized for what seems like hours, watching the filament grow bright orange when we turn the radio on and dim again when we turn it off.

When Papa is home, Rosie and I linger in the doorway of the bathroom to watch him shave. He wears brown leather slippers, laundered khakis, handsome leather bracers,[10] and a white undervest. After popping a straightedge along the leather strop, he dips one of his brushes into a porcelain cup with soap shavings, lathers his face, and glides the razor down one side of his cheek, clearing mounds of white foam from his smooth chocolate skin. Sometimes he hums as he shaves or carries on small talk with us. When he's finished, he rinses his face with water and splashes on Bay Rum aftershave, filling the bathroom with its intoxicating smell. It's a smell I love, because to a little girl with limited travel experience, it causes me to imagine the places my grandfather has seen: England, Italy, France, and Cuba.

---

10 suspenders

There is a second door in Papa's bedroom near his chest of drawers that leads to the screened-in back porch, where the smell of recently picked peaches rises from wooden baskets at the end of the porch closest to the kitchen. A large wooden drying rack with the day's newly washed "undies" sends the smell of fresh laundry from the other end of the porch. Two cases of bottled sodas are next to the drying rack alongside a wooden ice cream barrel that awaits the newest batch of Madre's homemade peach ice cream.

In the afternoons, Rosie and I watch *Howdy Doody* and *The Pinky Lee Show* on Madre and Papa's television, or we cheer on contestants on *Queen for a Day* or *Strike It Rich*, "the show with a heart." Sometimes we go outside to the pond to see the koi fish and then head down the slope to the tennis court in back to play a set. If our aunts are on the court, we pick blackberries from the bushes along the path and take them in to Madre, hoping she will make fresh blackberry pie to go with freshly whipped cream or with wedges of cheddar cheese on the side.

Some days we renew summer friendships playing at the homes of Carol Ann and Connie Jackson (whose brother, Maynard, will become Atlanta's first Negro mayor), or with Hope and Melle Dowdy, who live across the street from Madre and Papa, or we visit with Ernestine and Aurelia Brazeal, daughters of the dean at Morehouse College.

In the evenings, my sister and I wander down to the basement sewing room where Mother, Madre, and our great-aunts sit, sewing and sharing memories. There we sometimes hear the women, all of whom love sports, describe the fights of the "Brown Bomber," who seems more like a family member than a national hero. They speak of Joe Louis in a way that makes us feel as if his victories are lifting the whole race. Their conversations prime us for future evenings when we will gather around the black-and-white console television in the living room to watch Jersey Joe Walcott, Sugar Ray Robinson, and later, Hurricane Jackson.

One night as we prepare for bed, Rosemary doesn't join me in the fun we usually have eavesdropping. She seems listless and out of sorts. She has been this way for two or three days now, and when I kneel down to say the prayer we repeat every night, "Now I lay me down to sleep, I pray the Lord my soul to keep. Bless Mommy, Daddy, sister, all our loved ones. Amen," she doesn't join me.

"Mommy," I say when I am finished, "Rosemary didn't say her prayers."

Mother has noticed Rosemary's listlessness, too.

"She doesn't feel well," Mother says and then asks my sister to give her a kiss. Mother can tell by the warmth of Rosie's lips that she has a raging fever. She gives Rosie half an aspirin but knows it is too late to call the pediatrician we see when we're in Atlanta, so she lays Rosie on the pallet next to me for the night and calls him first thing in the morning. That day Dr. Hackney's office is so full that his assistant says she cannot fit us in, so Mother and Daddy seek an appointment with another baby doctor, Dr. McClendon. But he is unfamiliar with Rosemary's health history and misdiagnoses her condition.

Unaware of the misdiagnosis, our parents return to Madre's and follow the doctor's instructions, but Mother can see that the medicine isn't helping Rosemary, so she calls Dr. Hackney's office again. She is told for the second time that the office is filled with regular patients, and she can't be squeezed in. Mother keeps calling back until she convinces the assistant to let her speak with the doctor. After listening to Mother describe Rosemary's symptoms, Dr. Hackney realizes her condition is serious enough for him to make a house call, which he does. Upon his arrival at Madre's, the doctor takes one look at Rosie and shakes his head.

"She already has a foot drop," he says. "There's nothing I can do."

My little sister has contracted infantile paralysis in her right leg, which, by the time Dr. Hackney arrives, is paralyzed from her knee to her toes. He refers her to a specialist, who concurs with his diagnosis and wraps her leg in a cast.

No one knows how Rosemary contracted polio. All we know is that there is no known cure. In 1948, when she is stricken, there are twenty-seven thousand new cases, with a disproportionate number affecting Negro children.[11] Our family wonders whether the segregated public swimming pool is to blame. In other parts of the United States, people wonder about the water in swimming pools transmitting polio, too, and across the country, recreational pools dry up as the disease reaches epidemic proportions. The Infantile Paralysis Center is founded for Negroes at Tuskegee Institute in response to the Jim Crow laws that bar access to resources available to whites. Madre drives the four members of our family from Atlanta to Tuskegee, Alabama, where progress with the disease is being reported and because Tuskegee is a major provider of health care for Negroes in the region. People have claimed that Madre and Papa's friend, Dr. George Washington Carver, has "miracle" peanut oil that might be a cure for polio,[12] but later research shows it is

---

11 Information obtained from the Tuskegee University Historical Center for Science during a 1997 visit.

12 Information obtained at the Infantile Paralysis Center, The Carver Museum, on January 23, 1998. Carver had been dead since 1943 but people were still extolling the virtues of his peanut oil.

the massage, not the peanut oil, that has helped prompt partial recovery of muscle usage for some people who visit Tuskegee. During our time in Alabama, we meet with Tuskegee Institute's leading polio specialist, Dr. John W. Chenault, who takes on Rosemary as a patient. But our hopes are dashed when he says there is little anyone can do. "The worst has passed," he tells us.

Now Rosemary—the first child to climb the three-story fire escape at Tillotson, the one who crossed the busy thoroughfare and ran home from nursery school in defiance of Catholic nuns, the baby who bit a neighborhood bully—is reduced to crawling in order to accommodate the weight of the heavy cast on her leg. Later she will use crutches and be fitted for a brace that children at school will tease her about. Proper exercise, we are told, can help, with corrective surgery after she reaches puberty. In anticipation of that surgery, members of our family take turns each night performing exercises that strengthen her foot and leg muscles.

We lay Rosemary on a flat surface with one of us seated beside her. Cupping the heel of her right foot in the palm of our hand and resting her toes against the forearm, we bend her foot forward, pushing her toes toward her knee, and then we relax her toes. We do this over and over again, hoping the exercise will strengthen the muscles that have been paralyzed and make them strong enough for her eventual surgery. The activity becomes a family ritual performed each night before we go to bed.

A pall falls over Madre and Papa's house at 212 Griffin Street, as Yvonne's graduation festivities become a footnote to the hit taken by the youngest member of our family. The steady thud of her cast against the floor is a constant reminder of the disease that has claimed the lives and limbs of far too many children and adults, as well as the legs of President Franklin D. Roosevelt, who was stricken with the disease in 1921.

Our grandparents' home soon empties of relatives headed back home following Yvonne's graduation in Tennessee. With the house empty of relatives, insult is added to injury when the parents of the friends we've had all our lives refuse to let their children come play with us. Their absence brings an abrupt end to our games of dodge-ball, hide-and-seek, and "Mother, may I?" And it ends our afternoons of running through the water sprinkler in Melle and Hope's backyard. Children come to our front hedges now to see what Rosemary looks like with her cast, or to invite me to come to their homes to play, but Mother says I can't play anywhere where Rosie isn't welcomed, too. This is my earliest lesson in understanding the price one pays for Justice. I sleep next to Rosie every night and never come down with the disease, but that doesn't convince the parents of our playmates that their children will be safe around her.

Madre is so devastated that Rosemary was stricken in her home that she goes from doctor to doctor asking if they can graft the skin from her leg to Rosemary's so that the area that has been paralyzed can be filled out. Each doctor tells her that the type of grafting she seeks cannot be done. With our grandparents' home under virtual quarantine, my sister and I are forced to spend every waking hour with each other. The imposed isolation eventually becomes a bone of contention that makes me feel as if the family takes Rosie's side whenever she and I get angry with each other, and I resent it. One day in the middle of an argument, Rosie kicks me in the shin with her cast. Smarting from the pain, I reach out to slap her face, but she draws back, and my fingernails rake across her cheek. Blood sprays over the front of her clothes as she screams and crawls into the arms of our great-aunt Maude, who is still in Atlanta. She picks up Rosie and chastises me, reminding me that Rosemary is all I have, and I am all she has. Aunt Maude says we need to be kind to each other. Then she demands and gets my embarrassed apology.

I retreat to the outdoor oasis that is always there for me when I'm sad—the shade of the corner mimosa tree—where I withdraw into daydreams. Ashamed and frustrated, I stretch out on a blanket under the tree and withdraw into happier times when Rosemary and I lay there with friends, stringing Madre's blankets across the tree limbs for shelter. Sometimes we'd fall asleep and remain until Madre rang the dinner bell.

In the evenings after dinner we'd go back and lie face up in the grass, counting stars to make wishes on. *"Star light, star bright, first star I see tonight. I wish I may, I wish I might, have the wish I wish tonight."* But on this afternoon, I lie alone beneath the tree staring up at clouds that I turn into genies in my mind, genies who lift me onto magic carpets and fly me around the world. Stopping in Africa, I become the daughter of a noble chief, in love with the bravest village warrior. In Japan, I walk through narrow streets in a beautiful kimono, my long black hair piled high and filled with pearls. Back in the United States, I pirouette across a stage as snowflakes fall on Swan Lake.

⎯⎯⎯◆⎯⎯⎯

AT THE END OF the summer our family returns to Austin, where Rosemary learns to walk with crutches and is fitted with a brace. She goes through each stage of her recuperation without complaint and without asking why it happened to her. She tells me she knows Daddy understands how she feels, because he has told her how he wished a thousand times that the disease had struck him instead of her. "I'm a man," he said to her, "and I can cover my leg with pants."

Meanwhile, my sister continues to do all the things she has always done—go to tap and ballet classes, run track, and march in our ragtag band, and she is the first child back on the giant fire escape at Tillotson, brace and all. In fact, she compensates so well that I sometimes forget the toll polio has taken on her. As time passes, she tells me of the mean things other children say or do to her because of her brace, but mostly she pushes ahead without complaint. The Murrays, the Means, and our other Austin playmates help us return to normal life. Polio changes us, though. We take less for granted, and we grow closer to each other. For years the two of us go door to door with dime cards, raising money for the March of Dimes in the hope that a cure for the disease can be found. And my secret wish is that Rosemary will be chosen as a March of Dimes poster child, but she never is.

# CHAPTER 4

# TUMBLING TUMBLEWEED[13]

O N CHRISTMAS DAY 1948, two shiny new bicycles from Papa sit under the tree, and before the day is over, they have provided good exercise for both of us. We can see that by riding the bike, Rosemary's leg is being excrcised and maybe even strengthened, so we are encouraged to ride often. Dad lectures us on bicycle safety and warns us not let anyone ride double on the back of our bikes or sit on the handlebars. We promise to heed his warnings. By spring we are riding well enough to go to the top of a paved hill, near the big fire escape we use as a slide, and coast down. At the bottom of the hill, we get off our bikes and push them back to the top, so we can coast down again.

Our friends Junior and Melvin come to the hill to play, and they ask if they can borrow our bikes and ride. We tell them we aren't allowed to lend them to anyone, but they continue to beg and plead. Finally, ignoring Rosemary's warning to keep the promise we've made to Dad, I let Junior get on the back of my bike so he and I can coast down the

---

13 Original version recorded under the title "Tumbling Tumbleweeds," composed by Bob Noland, Sunset Music, 1934.

hill together. Midway down Junior starts to lose his balance, and as he struggles to regain it, I lose control of the bike. I flip headfirst over the handlebars, hit the gravel road full force on the right side of my face, and slide to the bottom, emitting a bloodcurdling scream as I slide. Junior tumbles over me on the gravel, skinning his knees and elbows. At the bottom of the hill, I struggle to my feet and pick up my dented bike. I begin pushing it toward home with Rosemary leading the way. Mother hears my cries before we reach home and is standing in the front door when we arrive. Seeing the loose gravel embedded in my right eye and blood streaming down my face, all she can think is, *My God, she's a girl, and her face will be scarred for the rest of her life.* She leads me into the house and begins to gently remove bits and pieces of gravel from my face as Rosemary explains what happened. No scolding or punishment is issued when Daddy gets home; my parents agree that I've already learned my lesson.

I stretch out across the bed that night with a sick feeling in the pit of my stomach and tightness on the right side of my face. When I awake in the morning, my right eye is swollen shut in a grotesque mass. I look and feel like a freak. Seeing myself in the mirror, I wonder if I'll ever be able ever see out of that eye again. At school, classmates shrink back at the sight of me, and over the ensuing weeks, scabs on my face become hard and ugly. By Easter Sunday I would give almost anything to stay home from church, but I know my parents won't let me do that, so I don't even ask. I get up and get dressed for church with the rest of the family. Rosemary and I go straight to Sunday school. When we enter, our longtime friend, Jimmy Murray, comes over and greets us as if nothing has happened. I am so relieved by his kindness that I'm put immediately at ease. This is an Easter I will never forget, because Jimmy (the son of our priest) helps me understand the lessons we've been learning in Sunday school, the ones that say people are more important than what they look like, and the hideous scar on my face doesn't change our friendship.

⸻

DADDY'S YOUNGER BROTHER, EDWARD, has entered Tillotson as a new student. Dear has sent him there so that Dad can keep an eye on him and be a positive influence in his life. Like many younger brothers, Edward looks up to Daddy and wants to be like him. As a little boy, he was so proud of his older brother that he asked Dear to change his last name from Shipp to Braxton, but she said, "No. You were born a Shipp, and Shipp is the name you'll keep." Nathaniel Edward Shipp was born fifteen years after our father, who was away at boarding school. Nathaniel was the name Dear had chosen for him, but when a woman down the street named her son Nathaniel, my grandmother called her new baby Edward, and it is the name he has used ever since.

At Tillotson, Edward dates some of the most beautiful women on campus, but Rosemary and I tease him about them, because they are all named Gloria, except for one, whose name is LaGloria. Our favorite among his girlfriends is a beautiful East Indian woman named Gloria Sealey. Rose and I trail Edward and Gloria all over the campus, hiding in bushes and jumping out to surprise them, much to the annoyance of our uncle.

Edward would like nothing more than to follow in his brother's footsteps and be a football star, but he is not the athlete our father was, and when he realizes this, he takes another path. He joins the air force and by June 1950 is sent, with so many others, to fight in the Korean War.

While he is overseas, we check the mail every day, hoping for a letter from him. He is conscientious about writing home, but there is one letter I remember more than all the others. It is written from the back of a moving truck in the glare of exploding bombs. In it he describes the chaos taking place around him. He describes his truck flipping over and the driver being wounded. His machine gunner is killed, and Edward is thrown into the gutter. When he comes to he is in a hospital bed, from which he finishes his letter. He tells us it is the faith he learned at his mother's knee that saved him.

Everyone is greatly relieved when his tour of duty ends, and he returns safely to Tillotson and reunites with Gloria Sealey, whom he will one day marry.

———— ◆ ————

IN THE SPRING OF 1951, Mother resigns her position as dean of women at Tillotson due to what she calls "a matter of principle." To this day she will not say what the principle was, but Dad supports her decision. That same spring, Tillotson cuts football from its athletic program, leaving the boys Daddy has recruited from all over the country without the scholarships he has used to bring them there and ensure their college educations. Knowing how hard-pressed the boys are for funds to finish their schooling, Dad goes to the president of the college and pleads with him to continue the financial aid, so the boys can stay in school. The president refuses, making Daddy so angry that he resigns his position, too.

My father has always had a special relationship with the athletes we call "Daddy's boys." There was a combination of respect, camaraderie, discipline, and friendship so close that it was not uncommon for us to answer the front door and come face-to-face with an athlete panting breathlessly, "Coach said I could borrow his tux." Nor was it unusual for my father to give the allowance I had been counting on all week to one of his boys whom he knew was strapped for funds. The connection between him and them was partially a reflection of the closeness he had with his maternal grandfather, Lewis Bass, and his relationship with Dr. A. S. Clark, the mentor he acquired at boarding school when he was a young teenager.

Daddy was reared by his widowed mother, Mary Hattie Bass Braxton, the grandmother Rosemary and I call Dear. Her parents, Ellen and Lewis Bass, helped her rear our father after Dear's husband, Zachial, was accidentally killed in his churchyard while trying to break up a fight between two men. Zachial Braxton was the minister of the church where he was shot, and his death led to my father's premature birth. When she went into labor, Dear went back to her parents' farm in Brown's Hill, Georgia, to her mother, Ellen, who was a midwife. And it was in the tiny town of Brown's Hill, a small spot between Unadilla and Cordele (pronounced Cordeal), that my father spent his first six years. Lewis was not Dad's grandfather by blood. In fact, my father never knew his biological grandfather, and he never wanted to know him, because his grandfather was the white man who had raped Dear's mother, Ellen. Dear was the third child of Ellen Bass, and after her birth, Lewis accepted her as one of his own. Lewis loved her son, my father, as if Dad were his own flesh and blood. In fact, he spent so much time with Dad when he was a young boy that Ellen accused him of enjoying Daddy more than he enjoyed his own sons. Her claim may have had some validity since, by the time Dad was born, Lewis had fewer farming responsibilities in his old age and more free time to spend with his grandson. He taught my father (whose family name was J. T.) to churn butter, cure meat, and bury potatoes in the ground covered with pine needles. They did that so the potatoes would last through the winter. Lewis taught Dad everything he knew, except his secret for making a form of ice that lasted and kept perishable food from spoiling before the days of refrigeration.

Then, when Dad was six years old, the years of hard work in the fields took their toll on Lewis, and he dropped dead without warning. My father was devastated, as was his mother, Dear. With the death of the only father she had known (since she never knew the white man who raped her mother) and the only grandfather her son had known, Dear was forced to consider new options. Those options included staying on the farm with her newly widowed mother or beginning a new life as a young widow somewhere else. After prayerful consideration and long discussions with her mother, my grandmother, Mary Bass Braxton, decided she would move to the coastal city of Savannah, Georgia, with her son, J. T., and carve out a new kind of life for the two of them.

Mother and son began life in Savannah, where living was easy along the river in a city with old-world charm and southern grace. In those days Savannah was one of the most liberal cities of any in the state of Georgia, one in which a sense of liberalism had emerged after Sherman marched from Atlanta to the sea at the end of the Civil War.[14] The year Mary and J. T. moved to Savannah, the city offered Negroes better work than they could find in nearby towns. That gave them a

---

14 Interview with Dr. Delo Washington, professor of African American Studies, California State University at Stanislaus, September 1, 1995, Stockton, CA.

sense of power and independence that didn't exist for members of their race in most other southern communities.

Mary found day's work with the Solomons, an affluent Jewish family who owned a chain of drugstores. To bring in the extra money she needed to supplement her income from the Solomons, she made hot fish sandwiches that J. T. sold after school to the Geechees who worked along the waterfront. When the sandwiches were sold, J. T. delivered his mother's freshly baked breads to restaurants near Savannah's Yamacraw River. In the fall, he enrolled in the Maple Street Elementary School, where his best friends were Charlie Livingston and "Boy Blue." The adventuresome three were inseparable, running errands together after school, playing along the riverbank, even getting into trouble together. In those days, Negro children who played in one another's homes did not find it unusual for their mothers to discipline all the children who were disobedient while in their care, and my grandmother was no exception. She was known to whip every child in her yard if one of them disobeyed, so J. T., Charlie Livingston, and Boy Blue always chose carefully whose house they would play at, steering clear of the Braxton yard unless there was no other choice. But my grandmother was also a loving woman who worked hard to provide as happy a childhood as she was able to for her son. When J. T. was seven, she scrimped and saved enough money to buy a bicycle for his birthday, making him so happy that he rode it up and down the street every evening. Annoyed by his pedaling back and forth, a neighbor man chastised Mary Braxton for spending her money "so foolishly."

"You shoulda bought that boy a pair of long pants 'stead of a bicycle," he told her.

"When he gets to be a man," my father's twenty-five-year-old mother shouted back, "he can buy himself all the long pants he wants, but he's only gonna be a boy once, and this is his time to have a bicycle."

Life along the Yamacraw River was good for Mary and her son, J. T., but the Solomons' pharmaceutical stores did not fare as well in Georgia as they did in North Carolina and Florida, so they decided to move to Jacksonville, where business was thriving. They wanted to take Mary with them the way they took her on their trips to New England, the Caribbean, Canada, and England so she could clean, cook, and take care of their children, who had grown to love her.

As a widow with only a sixth-grade education, Mary knew a traveling life would not allow her son to get the kind of education she'd dreamed of for him, but she wasn't likely to get a job as good as the one she had with the Solomons anywhere else. So considering the major move they were planning, she weighed her options carefully. She was determined to see her son finish high school, and she knew if she moved to Florida with the Solomons he could lose the opportunity to fulfill that dream. Schools in Georgia only required Negroes to finish sixth grade, and Mary doubted Florida schools would be any better. After much prayer, she decided to send J. T. back to Brown's Hill to live with her mother, Ellen, who was taking care of six other grandchildren. Ellen's daughter Cora had returned home following her divorce and died a short time after her return, leaving her children for Ellen to rear. Within months of Cora's death, her sister Julanne died, and Julanne's children came to the farm to live with their grandmother, too. Concerned over her mother's ability to care for so many grandchildren, Mary decided to leave the Solomons' employ and move back to Brown's Hill to help out.

Before she left, she went to Jacksonville with the Solomons to help them set up their new home. Never shy about her son, she told anyone who would listen about how smart her (then) twelve-year-old was. A Negro mortician named John Rucker was one of the people my grandmother bragged to, and he was impressed with her stories about her son. So Rucker told her about a boarding school for Negro children in Cordele, Georgia, where students could work for a portion of their tuition and receive a good preparatory school education. When Mr. Rucker learned that my grandmother was preparing to leave her precocious son with her mother in Brown's Hill, Georgia, he offered to drive her and her son to Cordele to see the Gillespie Normal School (for underprivileged Negro boys and girls) and meet its founder, Dr. A. S. Clark.

Rucker, Mary, and J. T. met with Dr. Clark and took a tour of the school grounds. Then Dr. Clark and Mary sat down and worked out the financial arrangements that would allow my father to enroll in the seventh grade as a work-study student. With my father firmly settled in school, my grandmother returned to her employers, where she would earn money to help with Dad's education. The remainder J. T. would earn working at the school.

John Thomas Braxton thrived at the Gillespie Normal School. His mother's pride in him gave him the confidence he needed to try out for every activity the school offered. If he heard about an opening in the glee club, he auditioned for it. When football and basketball tryouts were held, he competed for and won places on both teams. He tried out for, and won, a spot in the band and on the track team, and he earned coveted roles in plays. If there was a poem to be learned, he checked the book out of the library and memorized it. He joined the debate club and became such a good orator that he is still remembered for a recitation from Elijah Kellogg's work "Spartacus to the Gladiators" and for his role as Marc Antony in *Julius Caesar*. He mastered the piano, the ukulele, and the trumpet, playing the trumpet in the marching band during halftime of the same football games in which he was quarterback. Dressed in his football uniform, he took to the field with the band in order to hold on to his music scholarship. Then he raced back to the locker room to receive the plays he had to call during the second half of the game and executed them.

Dad understood hard work, because he worked hard for everything he got. It therefore came as no surprise that he understood better than most how much the boys he recruited after he became a coach needed the scholarships he'd gotten for them at Tillotson College. He had been hired to start the school's first football team and had done so, in spite of the fact that Tillotson didn't have a football field. And the fact that the school was also without a track did not stop him from winning track meets or recruiting boys for both teams the same way he recruited youngsters for the Y in San Antonio when his office was a borrowed room at a filling station and his recreation area an empty lot in the city park.

In bringing boys to Tillotson, he had convinced parents in Texas who had never seen the inside of a college that their sons' ability to play ball could bring home the family's first bachelor's degrees. He had gone to New York City and convinced parents there that their sons would be safe in the Jim Crow South, where the lynching of Negro men was more common than anyone wanted to admit. He had lined up young track prospects from Boys High School in Brooklyn who'd earned their reputations in New York City's Police Athletic League, and he'd gotten their parents to agree to send them to the South, in spite of the fact that the boys themselves were nervous about the trip. Some of them even met to talk about the realities of southern racism and overt hostility but in the end decided to take their chances together with Dad.[15]

When they arrived, they found themselves helping Dad clear away grass and tree roots to prepare a makeshift football field and practice lanes for a track, instead of warming up for practice. Then, after the track was ready, they arose each morning at six o'clock to run laps around the field and up and down steep hills before they'd even had breakfast. And at the end of the day, they returned to the practice area for evening workouts. When it rained they practiced at Anderson High School or the Dorie Miller Community Center. Their conditioning was tough, but they all stuck it out.

To inspire them, Dad took them to track meets at the University of Texas, where they gathered together using stopwatches to compare their times with the times of white runners on the track below. They huddled together a stone's throw away from a sign that read, NO NEGROES ALLOWED.[16] During my dad's first year at Tillotson, the track team won four of five trophies at the first Texas State University relays.[17] And within three years of his arrival, newspapers as far away as Pittsburgh were proclaiming, "Coach John Braxton's high-flying Eagles came home first in the 440 and one-mile relays and James Gathers, Tillotson freshman...put on a dazzling finish to win the 100-yard dash in 0:9.7."[18]

From that initial track team, my father produced one of the first Olympians ever groomed by a Negro coach at an all-Negro college.

15 Interviews with Walter Hunter, Robert Moss, and James Gathers, October 2001.

16 Ibid.

17 "H-TC Inducts Gathers into Athletic Hall of Fame," *The Villager: A Community Weekly* 19, no. 49 (1992), 1.

18 Joel Smith, "Crack Tillotson Track Team Wins Tuskegee Relays," *The Pittsburgh Courier*, May 13, 1950.

James Gathers represented the United States at the 1952 summer Olympics in Helsinki, Finland, finishing the 200-meter dash in a photo finish dead heat with Thane Baker. The race was a sweep for the US with Andrew Stanfield winning the gold medal and Gathers and Baker both clocked at 20.8 seconds.[19]

Gathers was an unassuming young man with a love for my father so great that some twenty-five years later, at a reunion party in New York City, he stood and made a short speech and insisted that Dad accept his Olympic medal.

"No," my father protested. "It's *your* medal, you *earned* it."

"Please, Coach," Gathers insisted, shoving his medal into Dad's hands, "I want you to have it."

It was on behalf of boys like Gathers that my father approached the president of the college to ask Tillotson to keep its promise and honor the athletic scholarships it had awarded them. He was devastated when the president refused.

---

19 Although it was inconclusive as to which athlete crossed the finish line first, Thane Baker was awarded the silver medal and James Gathers the bronze. Corrected text supplied by Robert Moss (Gathers' teammate), May 5, 2015.

# Chapter 5

# Grandma's Hands[20]

M Y PARENTS' DECISION TO leave Austin comes as a shock to me. I love the third grade and my sweet teacher, Mrs. Cook, who makes school a happy place. And I have found a close friend in Mary Ann McAllister, for whom I wait each day, along with other children whose parents work past elementary school hours. We sit next to each other sharing after-school snacks of saltine crackers, cheddar cheese, and apple juice and often wear our matching red-and-green-checked dresses with the white Peter Pan collars to school on the same days. When it's time to go home, we collect our little sisters and walk to our houses.

In class, Mrs. Cook teaches us to write script by making swirling curls and loops on the backboard, which we work hard to copy. Madre comes to Austin for a visit and stops by the school, where she and Mrs. Cook spend an entire recess period talking about my progress. Happy as I am, the last thing I want to do is leave Austin. But even worse than

---

20 Composed and recorded by Bill Withers.

leaving an adored teacher and dear friends, Mother and Daddy say we must also leave our beloved dog, Mike.

Mike has been with us since the night Daddy brought the little brown-and-white bundle of fur home in his overcoat pocket. My parents never explain to my satisfaction the reason that we can't take Mike with us, but the parents of a six-year-old boy we know agree to take him, and Dad delivers him to them.

In less than a week, Mike turns up in our front yard again with sad eyes that seem to ask what he's done to be sent away. Rosemary and I welcome him back with open arms, even though we're upset to see his new owners have shaved his beautiful coat—the gorgeous hair that flowed when he strutted around the backyard, tossing his head from side to side. We plead with Mother and Dad to let us to keep him, but they say we can't, that he belongs to someone else now. Dad gets a rope, ties it to Mike's collar, and leads him back to his new owners. It's the last time we see him, and the last time I love any dog as much as I loved Mike.

---

MY PARENTS HAVE ACCEPTED jobs at Bethune-Cookman College in Daytona Beach, Florida, where Dad will become the new assistant coach of football and basketball and head coach of tennis and track. Mother will be dean of women. We plan to travel through Atlanta and Jacksonville and visit both sets of grandparents on the way to our new home.

Rosie and I, who've never known life outside of Texas's big skies, fields of bluebonnets, free-running stallions, and exciting rodeos, are sad to be leaving. We wonder where we will find hot tamales at football games, and if we'll play horseshoes with new friends in another city;

whether there'll be windmills, tumbleweeds, and oil wells, and if the friends we make will wear cowgirl skirts, Western hats, and boots with spurs, and carry cap pistols strapped to their hips.

Madre arrives in her shiny black Buick to drive us from Austin to Atlanta. From there we will board a train to Jacksonville, then move on to Daytona Beach. We pack the car with summer clothes, fresh fruit, fudge, and fried chicken. The food we pack is the sort that will not spoil easily as we make our way across the segregated southern states. We pack ice in the thermos, knowing it will melt into water for us to drink and keep us cool as we travel without air-conditioning. Rosemary and I are too young to know that the reason our parents and grandmother have taken such care to pack this kind of food and water is because Negroes can't stop and eat in restaurants or stay in the hotels we'll pass. All we know is that when we do stop, it will be with family members in eastern Texas and friends in Alabama.

Riding along in Madre's car, Rosemary and I entertain ourselves reading Burma Shave signs.

*Watch your speed.*

*Take it slow.*

*Let our little shavers grow.*

*BURMA SHAVE*

We cheer when Madre passes cars that are moving slowly and beg her to go faster, so others will not catch us. "Don't let 'em pass you, Madre!" we shout, and she laughs and speeds up.

Our first stop is in Marshall, Texas, where Aunt Ruby and Uncle Kelley live. Aunt Ruby is one of Madre's youngest sisters. She is the only one who has remained in the town where she and her siblings grew up. Ruby and Kelley teach at Wiley College, where Madre and Ruby's father taught foreign languages many years ago.

After taking care of our bathroom needs, we sit down to eat dinner. Then Rosemary and I fall asleep. As we drift off, we can hear Madre and Aunt Ruby on the front porch catching up on the latest news with local families.

Following a good night's sleep, we are off again, stopping in Tuskegee, Alabama, where our friend "Baby" McMullen Reid lives. Aunt Baby and her husband operate one of the few filling stations owned by Negroes in the South. This is where Madre fills her car up and where we put up for the night. Following another good night's sleep, we are on our way to Atlanta. When we get there we have a light meal, take hot baths, and climb between freshly laundered sheets.

In the morning, Rosemary and I awake to the sounds of Daddy at the piano, playing and singing, "When It's Darkness on the Delta." Lying in the back bedroom that now belongs to Papa, I can picture my father having already spun the piano stool down to the height he needs before sitting down to sing. Rosemary and I get up, wash our faces, brush our teeth, get dressed, and enter the living room where Dad has just begun another song, called "The Rosary."[21]

Rosemary stretches out on the gold brocade couch behind Dad, and I walk across green oriental rugs past a small mahogany end table, momentarily catching sight of myself in the full-length gold-leaf mirror behind the table. Entering the solarium, I slide onto Papa's brown leather easy chair and watch fish swimming in the bowl on a wrought-iron stand on the other side of the solarium. I close my eyes and listen

---

21 "The Rosary," words and music by Robert Cameron Rogers and Ethelbert Nevin. Music and words copyrighted August 29, 1898, Boston Music Co.

to the music coming from my father's fingers. *One day I'll play the piano, too,* I think, *so he and I can sit and play duets together.*

After several days of rest in Atlanta, Mother and Dad begin preparing for the next leg of our journey. We will go see our paternal grandparents in Jacksonville before Rosemary, Mother, and I go to Daytona Beach, and Dad leaves for New York on a trip he has taken every summer since we lived in San Antonio. Boarding the only transportation he can afford—a Jim Crow bus—Dad will travel to New York City to work toward earning a master's degree in health and physical education.

Standing next to Mother, where I am helping to repack clothes for the next leg of our trip, I suddenly become sad. *I don't want to leave Madre,* I think. *She has driven all the way to Texas to pick us up, and now we're all leaving her.* "I want to stay in Atlanta," I tell Mother. "I don't want to leave Madre." Mother is startled by my sudden announcement but says she will discuss it with Daddy. After they talk, and after she talks with Madre, she tells me I may stay. I am overjoyed, but in my haste to be company to Madre, it hasn't occurred to me that Rosemary may want to go with Mother and Daddy. My sister and I have never been separated, but she has no intention of staying in Atlanta. She wants to go with Mother and Dad. Now the reality of being in Atlanta without her makes me sad.

I stand teary-eyed at the train station beside Madre as Rosemary, Mother, and Dad board the train for Jacksonville. After the train pulls away, my grandmother and I return home and wait for their call to let us know they've arrived safely in Florida. When Rosemary and I talk, she tells me she is going to stay in Jacksonville with Dear and Grandpa Singleton (the man my paternal grandmother has married), and Mother is going to go ahead to Daytona Beach and search for a house for us to live in while Dad is in New York.

One day blends into another as Madre and I fall into an easy routine, sleeping together in her four-poster bed, getting dressed in our Sunday best to shop at Rich's department store downtown, and visiting with her friends. In the evening, we make ice cream from the fresh peaches we take out of the wooden baskets on the back porch. I help separate the soft ones from the firm while Madre peels, pits, and slices them. Then she pulls the ice-cream maker to the kitchen door, and I pour rock salt down the sides of the wooden barrel. Madre churns cream, sugar, vanilla extract, and other ingredients, and I add peaches to the mix and watch the cream thicken. When the mixture is thick enough, my grandmother places it in the freezer compartment of her refrigerator. I retrieve the dasher and lick what is left of the ice cream from it.

With the ice cream chilling in the freezer, Madre sets about baking a devil's food cake, which we will eat hot from the oven with our peach ice cream. Later in the week we make fudge and divinity candy to eat during the day.

My grandmother is a Tuskegee alumna who also holds a certificate from the John Robert Powers School of Charm in New York City. She is the quintessential southern lady, one who would never be described as a "woman." In our fifties world, a woman is someone who has "been around," seen the underside of life, whereas a lady is genteel, refined; my grandmother is a lady from head to toe. She stands barely five feet tall and weighs a little over one hundred pounds. Her fair skin is set off by long, straight black hair with its one-inch band of gray that starts at the roots in the middle of her forehead and runs to the hair ends. She still wears it in a bun at the crown of her head. Over the next few years, the one band of white hair will span across her forehead, making the entire front white. The back of her hair will stay black in spite of the passage of time, thanks to her frequent trips to the hairdresser.

Her fingernails are immaculately manicured, and her dresses so freshly starched and ironed that she appears to be eternally on the verge of entertaining or leaving to shop downtown. She wears face powder, red lipstick, stockings, and high heels every day even if she has no intention of leaving the house, and she never ventures outside without a hat and gloves—black leather gloves and a black hat for driving, gray cotton gloves and a straw hat for gardening, and white gloves and a dress hat for everything else. In the fall when she needs a coat, she will fold it over her arm with the smooth flat side turned out. "A lady never allows the collar and sleeves of her coat to flop over her arm," she tells me.

When standing and waiting for a bus or trolley, she stands in one of the five ballet positions, and admonishes Rosemary and me to do the same. She never refers to children as "kids" and insists that one *rears* children and *raises* crops.

Each night, after taking me through my multiplication tables and helping me get ready for bed, she removes her stockings and shoes, dress, lace slip, and teddy, and gets into a Barbizon nightgown. In front of the bedroom mirror, she takes down her hair and brushes it a hundred times before wrapping it in a silk scarf for the night. Then she takes a Kleenex tissue and removes her makeup with cold cream. She moisturizes her face and then places an adhesive "frownie" triangle between her eyebrows to get rid of the wrinkles. When she has finished her nighttime ritual, she brushes out my Shirley Temple curls and rolls them on brown leather kit curlers and ties a silk scarf around my head. Then the two of us climb into her bed and talk until we fall asleep.

Some nights when we talk, she reminisces about a young Spaniard whom she loved deeply before she met Papa. She says they spoke to each other in Spanish, using special names for each other. When she describes him to me, I think of George Raft, who is Madre's favorite movie actor. Her Spanish suitor gave her a diamond ring from Tiffany's in New York to seal their engagement and insisted she keep it when her parents refused to let her marry him.

"My mama and papa disapproved of him," she tells me, "and I always did as they said." Her parents' objections seem to have been based on his being Spanish, which confuses me greatly because my great-grandmother was Cherokee, and my great-grandfather was a free Negro. Of all people, they should have understood an interracial love.

"Are you sorry you didn't marry him instead of Papa?" I ask.

"Oh no, baby. Then I wouldn't have you and Rosie."

Lying there talking, I tell her I love her so much, I don't want to live without her. "If anything has to happen to either one of us, I hope God takes me instead of you," I say.

"No, baby, I've already lived my life, but your whole life is ahead of you. I pray God will take me instead."

During the day, Madre keeps me enthralled with stories about the bullfights she's attended during her annual trips to Mexico, describing the grace of matadors and the way they use their capes. She has rarely seen a matador lose a contest, she says, but she has seen one get gored.

Because Papa spends so much time in Washington with government work, Madre sleeps with a loaded revolver under her pillow. Even with wrought-iron bars on the windows and the protection of her purebred chow, Ouija, she tells me that one night when she was alone, she lowered her guard and let a stranger into her home. "He tried to rob me," she tells me, "but I convinced him that he didn't want to ruin his life that way. After that I bought a gun that I keep right here," she says, patting her pillow. She shows it to me and explains how the safety works. She tells me I must never touch it. I never do.

Each morning I awake to the sweet smell of my grandmother's Jean Nate perfume. By the time I arise, wash up, brush my teeth, and enter the living room, she has already finished breakfast and is peeling fruit in the kitchen for me to eat. I am just in time to see the mailman jerk his hand back through the brass mail slot next to the front door. Ouija has been standing there waiting for him, and as soon as the mail comes through the slot, she growls and snaps at his hand. She has bitten so many mailmen that many of them have taken to leaving the letters on the front porch or calling from the far side of the hedge for someone to come out and get the mail.

A few weeks go by before Madre enrolls me in the Oglethorpe Elementary School for its half-day summer school program. Oglethorpe is the school Mother attended when she was a little girl, and her former teachers still work there. Many of my Atlanta playmates are at the Oglethorpe summer school, too, placed there by their parents or by grandmothers like mine who need a rest during the day from their energetic charges.

During many days Madre sews pretty sundresses for me on the sewing machine in the basement, and she buys matching ribbons that she ties around my curls. Her housekeeper starches and irons all my clothes, even my lace-trimmed socks and underwear, making me feel like a princess as I head off to school.

Marie Thomas's family lives down the street from Madre. Our families are not related, but our parents have been friends for as long as either of us can remember. Marie comes up to play in the afternoons after I return from school, and the two of us go down to the basement to make patterns for doll dresses out of old newspapers. Using scraps of material Madre has given us, we take the newspaper patterns, place them against the material, and cut out clothes for our dolls that we sew on the Singer machine. In the late afternoon, we wash down sandwiches with 7-Up or Coca-Cola from one of the crates on Madre's back porch and then polish off homemade fudge or devil's food cake.

On the Fourth of July, my grandmother and I travel across town to the house of her brother Cyrus, where we celebrate with family and friends who have come from all over the city to enjoy his famous barbecued spare ribs. Uncle Cyrus (whom Rosemary and I call "Uncle Pappy" for reasons we cannot remember) and Aunt Julia's annual backyard barbecue gives me a chance to visit my four-year-old cousin Pat, whom I adore. She's a pretty little girl with long black hair and, until the arrival of her little sister, Deirdre, is the only cousin Rosemary and I have of our generation. Aunt Julia is Uncle Pappy's second wife. His first wife, Janey, died when their daughter, Marilouise (who is of Mother's generation), was a little girl. Many years passed before he married again and began this new family. I spend time with Pat while the grown-ups talk and then enjoy barbecue before returning home with Madre.

Back at her home, I help Madre with Japanese flower arrangements. There is a lot about the Japanese culture that my grandmother embraces—the oriental rugs in her living room, her koi pond, Japanese flower arranging, and a song she teaches us about "dainty little Japanese playing 'neath the cherry trees. Cherry blossoms fluttering down, seem to kiss their faces brown." Her first baby even had a Japanese name. "Haru," she tells me, "means springtime and flowers in Japanese." Little Haru's neck was broken by a doctor during her delivery, which is the reason Madre went home to Marshall, Texas, to give birth to our mother, her second baby. She wanted to be with the familiar doctors she had known while growing up in Texas. In homage to Haru, Mother and Daddy gave my sister Rosemary Haru as a middle name. Her first name is the name of Mother's closest friend when she was growing up, the friend we call Aunt Rosemary.

After gathering fresh flowers from her garden, Madre and I fill two crystal vases with water and begin placing them in each one. "When we make three levels of flowers like we are doing here, they represent heaven, man, and earth," Madre says. When we have completed our task, the first vase of flowers goes in the living room. The second is placed on the circular mirror in the center of the dining-room table. In the afternoon my grandmother instructs me to practice walking with books on my head to keep my posture straight, and in the early evening I do my ballet exercises.

My days in Atlanta are filled with so many fascinating activities that were not available in Austin that I don't realize how fast the summer is passing. Before I know it, my grandmother and I are on our way to the train station to meet Rosemary, who is returning to Atlanta for a few days while Dear takes our twelve-year-old cousin Arno back to Detroit after he has spent the summer in Jacksonville with Dear and Rosemary. She alights from the train, waves good-bye to Dear and Arno, and gives Madre and me each a long hug and a kiss. As soon as we are in Madre's car, I launch into a monologue of all the things I've been into during the summer. When I finally stop talking, it's Rosie's turn to tell me all about Jacksonville. I am reduced to uncontrollable laughter with her stories about our cousin Arno, especially when she relates the story of the day he ignored Dear's warnings about her old-fashioned washing machine—the one with double cylinder wringers that squeeze water from the clothes. Throwing caution to the wind, Arno gets his fingers caught in the double wringers along with the clothes, and Dear has to rush to the back porch, where her washing machine sits, in order to free him. His hands are a bit swollen when he finally gets them out, but his pride is more hurt than he is.

When night falls, Rosemary and I get into our pajamas and watch old World War II and Esther Williams movies on the *Late Late Show*. After all programming goes off the air, we stand and sing the national anthem and then watch the screen until the test pattern appears. Only then do we drag ourselves off to the back bedroom, get into bed, and fall asleep.

During the day, we watch children's TV shows and sing the commercial jingles that come on between the shows.

*"Brusha, brusha, brusha, new Ipana toothpaste*
*Brusha, brusha, brusha, Ipana for your teeth."*

When the Hazel Bishop lipstick commercial comes on, we tell Madre she should "wear Hazel Bishop no-smear lipstick, because it won't rub off when you kiss us." That's all the incentive she needs to leave a red lip imprint on each of our cheeks and proclaim, "Now I've branded you, so everyone will know you're mine." But to please us, she does go out and buy a tube of Hazel Bishop lipstick "to make my little darlings happy."

In the afternoon after her favorite soap operas are over, Madre sits Rosemary and me down beside her and tells us the story of our maternal ancestors.

MISSOURI ANNE (NELL'S GREAT-GREAT-GRANDMOTHER [FAR RIGHT], WITH
DAUGHTERS, ALICE (FAR LEFT), PRUDENCE, AND A GRANDDAUGHTER (REAR)

"My mama came from proud people," she says, beginning with
the story of her grandmother, Missouri Anne, who was a full-blooded
Cherokee. "Anne is a name that has been passed down through every
generation of women in our family since Missouri Anne. My mama was
Ida Anne, Aunt Gertrude is Gertrude Anne, your sweet little mummy
is Anne Amanda, and you're Nell Anne.[22] My grandmother was part of
the great Cherokee Nation whose tribe numbered in the thousands."

The Cherokee survived more than a hundred years of the white
man's disease and whiskey, until they were moved west. The move

---

22 At this writing Aunt Gertrude's granddaughter is Kimberly Anne, and her great-
granddaughter is Heather Anne. In my family line, in addition to my mother Anne
and me (Nell Anne), our daughter is Erika Anne.

was supposed to take place in gradual stages, but when Appalachian gold was discovered in their territory, there was an outcry for an immediate wholesale exodus, and in the autumn of 1838, soldiers from General Winfield Scott's troops rounded up members of the tribe and concentrated them into camps before sending them west to "Indian Territory." On the long trek, one of every four Cherokees died from cold, hunger, or disease. They called the march the Trail of Tears.[23]

"Missouri Anne's family made the journey as far as Edwardsville, Illinois, where she met her future husband, who had arrived in Illinois from South Carolina. We think he was indigenous, too, because he left home after an altercation with a white boy 'over a racial thing,'" Madre says. "His surname was Scott. I don't remember his first name."

"What tribe was he from, Madre?"

She says she isn't sure. "He was a teen when he whipped the white boy in a fight, but afterward he feared so much for his life that he fled South Carolina. The day he left, his mother walked him to the town bridge where they said good-bye. With tears in her eyes, she reached into her pocket to get the only money she had. It was a fifty-cent piece, and she placed it in his hands and then said good-bye.

"After he married my grandmamma, Missouri Anne, and started a family, each one of their children used that fifty-cent piece as a teething ring. Their daughter, Ida Anne, was my mama. She was the only one of their children to defy them and marry a man they didn't approve of. But my papa was the most educated of all my mama's sisters' husbands and the one who advanced the farthest professionally."

---

23 Dee Brown, *Bury My Heart at Wounded Knee: An Indian History of the American West* (New York: Holt, Rinehart & Winston, February 1971), 7.

IDA ANNE SCOTT MITCHELL (NELL'S MATERNAL GREAT-GRANDMOTHER)

Nelson Turner Mitchell Sr. (Nell's maternal great-grandfather)

Madre's father was Nelson Turner Mitchell, a free Negro who graduated from Fisk University and became a linguistics professor at both Wiley and Bishop Colleges in Marshall, Texas. He moved his family from Edwardsville, Illinois, to Marshall when Madre, the first of their ten children, was a little girl. She tells us she is proud to be named Nellie Ida, for both her parents, but after she reached adulthood, she changed her first name from Nellie to Nell.

Rosemary and I listen to the story of our ancestors, absorbing Madre's pride in our family history. *One day,* I think, *I will tell this story to my children, and they will be proud, too.*

Too soon, the time comes for Rosemary and me to say good-bye to Madre and leave for Jacksonville, where we'll meet Daddy, who is on his way back from New York, and Dear, who has returned from Detroit. Daddy will take us to Daytona Beach, where Mother (who has found a new house) is waiting.

In Atlanta, we board the train for our trip to Jacksonville, where Dear's brother Dempsey, the owner of a cab company, will pick us up in one of his taxis. After loading our luggage into the trunk of the taxi, he drives to Dear and Grandpa Singleton's home at 1542 Evergreen Avenue. As Uncle Dempsey approaches the house, Rosemary and I spy Dear standing on the top step of the front porch. As soon as the taxi stops, Rosemary and I throw open the back door and race to throw our arms around Dear. She plants kisses on each of us as she swallows us up in her ample bosom. What a comfort to be in the arms of our grandmother, inhaling the aroma of her Blue Grass perfume. Dear is one of the sweetest people I've ever known, so sweet that some folks say, "Even bees won't sting her." They're right about that. During our time in Jacksonville, Rosemary and I follow her out to the honey farm in her backyard and wait near the honeycombs until she emerges with honey from the hives without any protection but her housedress. She repeats this trip often during our stay and is never stung. Dear and Grandpa's home is the antithesis of Madre and Papa's stately residence. The front porch has a swing and rocking chairs, and the front yard is filled with a profusion of flowers. In addition to the bee farm, the backyard is full of ducks and chickens and guarded by their black-and-white dog, Bobby.

The friends who know her now would never guess how hard this grandmother's life has been, because her strong faith has taught her to look for the growth that comes from hardships rather than wallow in the negatives. Dear was eighteen years old and seven months pregnant when she witnessed the murder of her thirty-two-year-old husband, Zachial Braxton. He was a Baptist minister who was accidentally shot in his churchyard while attempting to break up a fight between two men. His murder sent my grandmother into premature labor with my father, who was born on May 10, 1914. As my grandfather, Zachial, lay dying, he extracted a promise from his brother, Dave, to give his wife, Mary, half the hog farm the brothers jointly owned, but Dave never honored the agreement. So with only a sixth-grade education and no source of income, Dear was forced to return to her family's farm in Brown's Hill. She was there when she gave birth to my father.

Dear's parents, Ellen and Lewis Bass, lived on the Peavy plantation, where they worked as share tenants/croppers. Following emancipation, the family picked enough cotton and corn to acquire their own land. They raised the cotton and peanuts they sold at local roadside stands when their harvest was plentiful. Dear's mother, Ellen, was one of the most revered midwives in the Unadilla, Georgia, area, where she is still remembered today. She delivered our father just as she delivered most of the children in the area—Negro and white. Her greatest source of income came from white women, who were her largest clientele, but if two white clients went into labor at the same time, a dispute often occurred, because Ellen honored the practice in those days of staying with the baby and new mother for two weeks following the birth to make sure both mother and child were healthy before she left. The majority of Negro women couldn't afford to pay for such a long stay, since they had to get back to the fields and kitchens of their employers the day after giving birth, so Ellen delivered their children and moved on.

Dear, whose given name was Mary Hattie, was the third of Ellen and Lewis Bass's fourteen children, and one of ten who lived past the age of four. Ellen was the eldest, followed by Gila, who left the most lasting family impression and the most notorious family story by surviving an encounter few southern Negro men lived to tell. Family legend has it that a white man once made the mistake of slapping Gila's wife, so enraging Gila that without thinking, my great-uncle jumped down from the seat of his buggy and shouted, "*Nobody* slaps my wife! *I* don't even slap my wife!" And in a fit of rage he pulled a pistol and fired a single shot, killing the offender. With the homicide of a white man hanging over his head, and the prospect of a lynching in his future, Gila and his family fled Georgia and sought refuge in White Plains, New York. There he is said to have settled into ordinary life, steering clear of family members with whom contact may have revealed his whereabouts.

Dear was born after Gila, followed by John (for whom my father was named). Dear's brother John was called Juggy and was reported to be a crack shot who could bring down birds on the wing and kill wild turkeys with a double- or single-barrel shotgun. After Juggy came Cora, Julanne, Dura (pronounced Dury), Lewis Jr., Dempsey (the brother who owned the cab company in Jacksonville), and Betty Mae. The Basses were a religious family who attended Mt. Moriah Baptist Church in nearby Perry, Georgia. Their strong faith was undoubtedly how they came to accept the circumstances of my grandmother's birth and the grace with which they lived with it.

Dear was conceived during one of her mother's responses to a pregnant white woman in the last stages of labor. Following the baby's delivery, Ellen, the midwife, began her customary two-week stay. One night after the new mother was asleep, her husband crept into my great-grandmother's sleeping quarters and raped her. It wasn't until she had gone six weeks without a menstrual period that Ellen realized she was pregnant. Understanding the perils associated with his wife's midwifery and the dangers to his own life were he to avenge her condition, Lewis accepted my grandmother as a full-blooded Bass, never making any distinction between her and the rest of the Bass children, despite her fair complexion and long, wavy brown hair. And he came to love my father as if Dad were his own flesh and blood. My father adored Lewis, too, who was the only male figure in the young boy's life. In addition to being a sought-after midwife, Ellen was also a gifted self-taught herbalist. In fact, people in the area relied so much on her herbal formulas, they preferred them to the prescriptions they received from local physicians. Their decision to use her remedies created such strong opposition by white doctors in the area that Ellen was forced to earn a special certificate in order to continue her herbal practice.

My grandmother's life on the farm with a young baby presented many challenges for the eighteen-year-old widow. The most frightening came on the night Dear awoke to discover my prematurely born father wasn't breathing. Terrified, she began screaming hysterically. The thought of losing her new baby after having just lost her husband was more than she could bear. Her mother, Ellen, rushed to her side, took one look at the baby, grabbed him up in her arms, and got him breathing again. Then she placed him in a basket lined with herbs, balanced the basket on her head, and walked miles through the night to a freshwater stream. There she bathed him and wrapped him in blankets and then walked back home and returned him to his mother's arms. For the next two years, Ellen bathed him in pot liquor (the essence of juices left in the pot after vegetables are cooked) and only allowed him to drink water from the freshwater stream she had bathed him in that fateful night. Some people say his grandmother's pot-liquor baths and fresh stream water are what kept my father injury-free throughout his days of competitive sports. All we know is that he was one of the few athletes of his day who did not suffer injuries.

ON OUR SECOND MORNING in Jacksonville, Rosemary and I are awakened by a crowing rooster. We drag ourselves out of bed, wash up, and go out to collect eggs from the chicken coop. We take them to Dear so she can prepare them for breakfast. We eat and help clean up before following her onto the front porch, where she begins each morning's conversation the same way. She stands on her front porch and proclaims to every neighbor within earshot, "I've got the finest two sons anywhere."

And every morning the refrain comes back from across the street and down the block, "That's right, Miz Singleton, you sho' do."

"I *know* I do," she insists, and then she shares with everyone along Evergreen Avenue the latest news about her sons and their families.

How Daddy is coming back from New York City where he's been working on his master's degree, and Uncle Edward is finishing his bachelor's degree at Tillotson College after serving in the Korean War.

In the afternoon, Dear goes out to the backyard and catches the fattest chicken she can find. Taking its head in her hand, she climbs the steps to the back porch and swings the bird around in quick little circles until its neck snaps. Its headless body hops wildly around the yard with feathers flying and blood spattering. Other chickens go squawking and fleeing in every direction until the quivering, headless bird jerks slower and slower, eventually toppling over. At that point our grandmother goes down the steps and into the yard, grabs the chicken by a foot, and returns to the back porch, where she plucks and cleans it before washing and singeing it over a burner on the kitchen stove. Afterward she sections and flours it for frying.

While she finishes cooking dinner, Rosemary and I sit on the front porch visiting with neighbors and snapping fresh string beans from the garden. As usual we have little to share with Dear's friends, because she has already told them everything about us. They know why we have come, how long we are staying, and where we are going. In fact, they know so much about us, they can tell us our own business.

"Hey, Nell! Hey, Rosemary!" they yell from their rocking chairs. "Ya'll movin' to Daytona Beach?"

"Yes."

"Goin' be leavin' Texas, huh?"

"Yes."

"Reckon ya'll will ever go back?"

"We don't know."

Before long, Grandpa Singleton rides up on his bicycle. He says hello to us, gives each of us a hug, and enters the house to wash his hands and face. Henry Singleton and Dear were married before we moved to Daytona Beach, and he is the only paternal grandfather Rosemary and I ever know. Our grandpa works for the railroad and moonlights as an electrician and carpenter. He can neither read nor write but is a good man and a wonderful grandfather who loves us unconditionally. His beautifully chiseled body has been honed to perfection by the biking he does all over the city and in the afternoons and evenings he spends playing softball. On several evenings during our stay in Jacksonville, we pack a picnic basket and go to the colored park to cheer him on in one of the local ball games.

Our grandmothers have lived very different lives, but both played important roles in forming our understanding of respect for all people, including ourselves, during some of the worst days of segregation. Madre warns us about people whose lack of values can "pull us down." Dear tells us that ditch diggers and street sweepers are just as good as we are. Madre says no one in the world is better than the two of us. Dear says we are no better than anyone else in the world. We believe them both.

Both grandmothers are also expert seamstresses. Each summer the clothes Madre and her sister Mabel make supply Aunt Mabel's wardrobe as a schoolteacher for an entire year in Asheville, North Carolina. Dear makes our Easter dresses and Grandpa Singleton's suits. A three-piece navy-blue pinstripe suit she makes for him looks like it has come right off the rack of a department store.

In the early evenings when the heat drives everyone outside, we sit on the front porch where Dad, who has finally arrived from New York, settles onto the large white swing at a right angle to the three wooden rockers facing the street. All the rockers are glossy and bumpy from years of paint buildup. Dear sits in one rocking chair, and Rosemary and I sit on the floor at the edge of the porch, dangling our legs over the flower beds. There we listen to new stories and relive old memories while washing down fresh hot pound cake with jelly between the layers with glasses of cold milk.

Dear rocks back and forth, and Daddy swings, regaling us with stories about how good an athlete our grandmother once was. She's the one who taught him to play ball and to revere the New York Yankees because "they were the greatest baseball team in history." Dad says that when he was a boy, Dear could run so fast that she was able to outrun him, and it was years before he could beat her in a race.

Dear sits listening and smiling until he is finished and then declares self-assuredly, "I can still outrun you, you know, J. T." Having made the improbable declaration, she projects a wad of the snuff that has been lodged in her cheek. It sails over a corner of the porch and into one of the flower beds. Afterward, she dabs at the corners of her mouth with the hankie she's slipped from a pocket of her housedress. When the storytelling is over, we turn on the radio to hear the latest prizefight or listen to a baseball game. By that time, every radio along Evergreen Avenue is tuned to the same station; neighbors up and down the block are sitting on their front porches taking in the night air. Calling to one another back and forth up and down the block, they celebrate a great baseball catch or a stunning uppercut and recap what has happened between innings or between rounds of the fight.

Grandpa Singleton joins us on the porch, easing onto the floor with Rosemary and me. Whispering gently, he attempts to calm the dog whose barking has suddenly been triggered by the excitement on the porches up and down the block.

"Hush now, Bobby. Hush your barkin'," Grandpa says, waving to Bobby, who can't stop jumping up and down behind the side-yard fence. We can see him behind the hand-painted sign, Bad Dog, but he's never bad with Rosie and me. Still attempting to soothe Bobby, Grandpa reaches into his shirt pocket and removes a pouch of loose tobacco. From a pants pocket he extracts a box of thin square papers, opens a square, and taps tobacco gently onto it. Then he rolls himself a cigarette and pulls out a small pack of matches. Lighting his freshly made cigarette, he leans back against a column of the porch and inhales deeply, sending circles of smoke into the night air. Meanwhile, the game rolls on to an exciting finish and whoops and hollers in the neighborhood.

Satisfied with the game's outcome, Dear rocks back and offers everyone on the porch ice cream, warning Rosemary and me, "It's store-bought now, not homemade like your grandmother's in Atlanta." After the ice cream has been consumed, Rosemary and I take baths and lie down on the pullout sofa bed in the living room, which has a window that opens out onto the front porch. From there we look away from the porch to the other side of the room to watch Dear in an adjoining bathroom. She takes down her long brown wavy hair and (like Madre did every night) brushes it one hundred times before parting it down the middle and making two long braids. Dear has only one strand of gray hair and is so proud of it that she tries to make a part in her hair that reveals that one strand of gray. To her disappointment, no one ever notices it unless she points it out.

After the lights are turned out, I lie in bed next to Rosie, who has already drifted off to sleep, and listen to the clickety-clack of a distant train, its whistle beckoning as I become drowsy. *One day*, I tell myself, *I'll be on one of those trains, riding to places I can only dream of now.*

The rooster's crow awakens me and is soon followed by the clinking of empty milk bottles that were left last night at the front door for the milkman to collect. He leaves full bottles in their place before making his way down the steps and on to the next house. The aroma of ham and eggs wafts through the house from the kitchen as Rosemary and I wash up and get dressed. When we enter the kitchen, ham is sizzling in the frying pan, and Dear is scooping cream off the top of a bottle of fresh milk.[24] The cream will go into Grandpa's coffee, and whatever he doesn't use will be put back in the bottle and shaken until it is mixed with the rest of the milk, so Rosemary and I can have it with our breakfast. It is Sunday, and Dear is preparing a huge country breakfast of ham, fried chicken, bacon, grits, biscuits, homemade preserves, and apple butter. If we ask for coffee, our grandmother will give us a concoction of warm water, milk, and molasses, and we are convinced we are having a children's version of real coffee. After we have eaten everything on our plates, we will be given pound cake. Dear has used her bare hands (instead of an eggbeater or whisk) to beat it, producing some of the finest-grain cake I've ever had.

---

24 These were the days before pasteurized milk was common, and rich cream formed in the neck of a glass bottle of milk.

DEAR (NELL'S PATERNAL GRANDMOTHER)

On Sunday mornings like this one, when we don't go to the local Baptist church with Dear, everyone seated around the dining room table has to say a Bible verse after the blessing has been said, and no one can repeat a verse that has already been spoken. I sit on pins and needles until my turn comes, because my favorite verse is, "Suffer the little children to come unto me and forbid them not, for such is the kingdom of heaven." I like that verse, because it makes me feel as if I am as much a part of God's kingdom as everyone else. I'm always afraid someone else will say it before my turn comes, and then I'll have to think of another one to recite.

Before long it is time to leave Jacksonville and head to our new home. We say good-bye to Dear and Grandpa, their dog, Bobby, the duck farm, the chickens, and all the neighbors. Daddy, Rosemary, and I get into Uncle Dempsey's taxi and head toward the train station.

"Bye now, ya'll be careful," Dear says as we pull away from the house. The cab moves down the block, and I look back over my shoulder through the rear window to see Grandpa standing next to his bike, waving. We wave back as he swings a leg over the bicycle seat, settles himself, and pedals off to work. Dear waves good-bye to him and begins talking to neighbors across the street, no doubt about the finest two sons anywhere.

# CHAPTER 6

# FLORIDA BY THE SEA[25]

D AYTONA BEACH'S PINE AND cypress trees, kudzu-laden swamps, and Spanish moss are a lush contrast to the rugged beauty of Texas tumbleweed and wild stallions. Rosemary and I revel in the freedom we have to crack open coconuts and eat them as the juice runs down our chins and arms, and to pull sugarcane from the open field across the street from our house and suck on it while we help Mother and Dad unpack from our trip.

Our new pink stucco house at the dead end of Jefferson Street still smells of fresh paint and recently sealed hardwood floors, and a bathtub replaces our tiny barrack shower stall. But this city has barracks, too. They are on the campus of Bethune-Cookman College behind our house, and that's where many of the other faculty members and their children live. A shallow ditch and a thicket of trees run along the side of our house at the end of the street where, during hurricane season, the ditch fills with water and sends snakes onto our partially paved road.

---

25 Words and music by Irving Berlin, copyright 1925.

At the other end of Jefferson, the street intersects with Second Avenue (the main thoroughfare in the Negro section).

What sidewalks there are on Jefferson Street become visible near Second Avenue, but taper off and disappear into the dirt the closer one gets to our house. This is the end of the street, where tufts of grass strain to push themselves up between cracks of the disappearing sidewalk, cracks we hop over on our way to and from school playing "step on a crack, break your mother's back."

Soon after we arrive in Daytona Beach, Rosemary, Dad, and I begin working in the front yard, getting rid of the rocks so new grass will grow. Spying beautiful bands of color in the grass, Rosemary reaches for them saying, "Look at the pretty snake."

"Get back!" Dad yells, using his sickle to chop off the snake's head. "That's a coral snake. One of the deadliest snakes there is." He tells us that the beautiful bands of color are what distinguish it from other snakes and that we must never pick up any snake with colors like that.

Across the street from our house is a field partially planted with sugarcane. On the other side of the field is a street called College Row where other Negro professionals live, including Joyce and George Engram, whose children, Carol and George Jr., will be new schoolmates of ours. Over the years our two families become close enough for us to spend weekends with the Engrams at their summer home in Volusia Beach, which in the early fifties is a sparsely inhabited stretch of waterfront where middle-income Negro families are building weekend homes. There Rosemary, Carol, George Jr., and I dart in and out of the surf chasing their pet boxer, Princess Anne. When we tire from that, we fall onto the sand and build castles or search for shells until it's time to gather around the fire and roast hot dogs and marshmallows.

Weekends at the beach are a godsend on days when the temperature reaches ninety degrees before nine in the morning, and the humidity is so heavy our sunglasses fog up.

When not at the Engrams' beach home, our only other respite from the heat is to walk to a crowded segregated public pool or go fishing at Vero Beach with our parents and their friends, the Matthewses. On fishing days, Rosemary and I are awakened in the early dawn, dressed in jeans and T-shirts, and hustled, halfway between sleep and wakefulness, into the Matthewses' waiting car. There we settle into the backseat, where the two of us tug the lap robe back and forth until we're comfortable enough to doze off again. We don't wake up until the car stops, and the doors swing open to the salty ocean air. Then we climb into a chartered motorboat and bounce across the ocean at top speed until we come to a spot where the rainbow trout, perch, and bass are running. We settle ourselves in the rocking boat, and Dad and Coach Matthews cast their reels out over the water. Resting his rod on a notch on the side of the boat, Dad helps Rose and me put night crawlers on our hooks, and he shows us how to cast our bamboo pole lines over the side of the boat.

"You've got a bite," he gently coaxes me, seeing my line bob up and down. "Pull him in slowly now, so you won't lose him. Easy—easy. Don't jerk the line." Mother squeals like a child when I eventually pull a fish in and toss it in the ice chest. My sister and I learn a lot about patience sitting in the intense heat waiting for fish to bite. This is the only part of fishing that I hate; sweat running down my body in the sizzling sun and having to talk in whispers so as not to frighten the fish as the boat rocks back and forth. At day's end, Rosemary's and my reward for our patient endurance is the feel of cool ocean spray across our faces as the boat speeds back across the water toward the shore.

Sometimes we go fishing at night, and my sister and I sit at the edge of the dock and drop our lines through the cracks of wood where a large flashlight helps us spot schools of trout and bass. Those are the trips where Dad and Coach Matthews haul in so many crabs that the nets often split under the weight. After they've filled the large galvanized washtubs we've brought with us, we head for home. There, we throw the ice we've saved from our fishing trip into the metal tubs and place them in the garage to keep the fish we've caught fresh until morning. Then Rose and I sit with Dad on the back-porch steps, scaling the fish. Afterward, Dad guts and fillets them, while Mother makes room in the deep freeze to store the bulk of our catch.

The next day she cooks everything we are unable to fit into the deep freeze. The back door of our house is in the kitchen, and it opens to our backyard, where Dad stands boiling the crabs and corn on the cob in two cauldrons that sit over an open fire. Rosemary and I help Mother make coleslaw and lemonade in the kitchen and wait to welcome the friends and neighbors we've invited over for a big fish fry. The men fill their plates and tell fish stories, and the women sit and talk about children and recipes.

"Leroilyn is learning a new cantata for a piano recital next week," Mrs. Hacker will say.

"Ever Carol is rehearsing a new dance for the next children's recital," Mrs. DuBose tells everyone.

Only half listening to our parents' admonishments: "Slow down. Take your time. Eat like little ladies and little gentlemen," we children sit near our log cabin playhouse wolfing down fried fish, crab, hush puppies, corn on the cob, and lemonade as fast as we can. Afterward, we hop on the jungle gym to see who can swing the highest before we launch into a game of hide-and-seek. Late in the afternoon, Mother goes into the kitchen and returns with a plate of freshly baked pecan brownies. Guests who know of her legendary treats plead, "Please, Anne, I can't eat another morsel," as they reach for a square or two. Wrapping up the leftover fish, Dad begs departing guests to take the packages with them, urging, "I've still got a freezerful to cook."

In August, when football practice begins, our father writes the football players he left back at Tillotson College with revoked athletic scholarships and tells them that if they can make their way from Texas to Florida, he has scholarships waiting for them at Bethune-Cookman. His relationship with his boys is so strong that those who can manage to hitchhike or scrounge up enough bus fare to get to Florida make the trip. Our friend Nina French leaves Tillotson to come to Florida, too. Miss French is a friend of my parents from Brooklyn. She attended graduate school with Dad in New York City, and he encouraged her to come to Texas to work. Mother and Daddy call her Frenchie, but Rosemary and I (for reasons we no longer remember) nickname her Miss Ridiculous. Frenchie is a beloved professor and a superb athlete who is so gifted that Dad chooses her to play on his faculty teams whenever the faculty men play the male students, and he picks her to play against male faculty members from rival schools when the faculty men at Bethune-Cookman play against them.

Professors from the other schools often tease Dad when Frenchie takes to the basketball court or baseball mound. "Brax, you must be outta your mind, puttin' a girl on your team."

But Frenchie silences them all, striking them out from the mound or dribbling rings around them on the basketball court. Her athletic skills make Rosemary and me feel that girls can do anything boys can do, and we are proud to be on the sidelines cheering her on.

Our parents enroll my sister and me in the Keyser Laboratory School with other faculty children, where there are fewer than twenty students per class. Keyser is called a laboratory or practice school, because it is the place where college students who want to become teachers receive their training. They come to our classrooms and assist our teachers. I am nine years old and in Mr. Thomas's fourth-grade class. Mr. Thomas is the first male teacher my classmates and I have ever had, and he is a strict disciplinarian who dispenses punishment by hitting our open palms with a thick ruler or paddling our behinds with a fraternity paddle.[26]

The first evangelist I ever have the opportunity to meet is Rosemary's teacher, Mrs. Rose Marie Bryon a guardian of our Christian faith and cultural heritage. This amply built honey-colored woman is the mother of two young sons and a pretty teenage daughter named Joy Sandra. We adore and look up to Joy Sandra, a sweet youngster on the verge of womanhood. Her open smile, spirited personality, and kindness draw the younger ones of us admiringly close to her. She is a blossoming fair-skinned girl with naturally pink lips, medium-brown hair, and sparkling brown eyes. She's a pleasure to be near because, without seeming to try, she manages to put the younger ones of us at ease.

At school, Mrs. Bryon breathes life into familiar Bible stories and into the writings by Negro poets, thereby instilling in us a sense of racial pride along with our spiritual development. Her biblical stories paint such vivid pictures that we can imagine the events happening to us. In her version of Christ's temptation in the wilderness, she tells of

---

26 Corporal punishment was allowed in all the elementary schools I attended.

two little boys playing on a mountaintop. Mrs. Bryon takes on the role of Satan (the bad little boy), and in a devilish little boy's voice, she says to the young Jesus, "Throw yourself down off this mountain. If your father is really God, He won't let you get hurt."

Then she switches to a sweet little boy's voice and answers, "No, I won't. You leave me alone, Satan."

Switching back to Satan again, she says, "If you fall down and worship me, I'll give you all the toys we see down there on the road."

But the young Jesus is not fooled by that either and sends Satan away. When she finishes her story, Mrs. Bryon asks how many of us would be strong enough to turn away from temptations like the ones Satan offered Jesus and do what we know is right. Every child's hand shoots into the air, because we all want to be like Jesus.

Because she introduces Jesus to us as a little boy, Mrs. Bryon helps us see ourselves in him and lets us know he wasn't always perfect. Like the time the twelve-year-old Jesus wandered away from his parents to talk with the elders during a visit to Jerusalem. She tells us about the anxiety his decision caused his parents and impresses upon us the anxiety we can cause our parents by not staying close to them on trips. Through her stories we learn that God understands and loves us children, even though we are not perfect.

During one chapel period, as Mrs. Bryon moves around the room telling one of her Bible stories, a younger member of the assembly faints. Great commotion breaks out as the child is lifted into the arms of teachers and carried out, pale and weak. She is a very thin fair-skinned little girl who seldom plays with the rest of us, choosing instead to sit in the shade of a tree and watch us at recess time. On the morning that she is rushed out of the assembly, I wonder if she has been overcome by the story Mrs. Bryon is telling about King Solomon suggesting a baby be divided between two women who both claim to be the child's mother, but before chapel is over our principal, Mrs. Davis, returns to share some information with those of us who are in assembly. She says that the little girl is a "blue baby," who was born with a heart defect, and that her condition causes blood that flows from her veins and arteries to mix together and make her light-headed. "Sometimes when this happens, her skin turns a bluish color, and her lips become purple. At times like these she might faint. We are all members of the Keyser family," Mrs. Davis explains, "and we all need to know what to do if she has another seizure and no adults are around." Should that happen, Mrs. Davis tells us, we must immediately find a teacher, who will know how to handle the situation. With an explanation of her condition, we children begin to feel more protective of the little girl. It is within this same context that I come to understand what it means to be part of the Negro family, and why it is important for us to stand together whenever one of us is in trouble. We are to take care of one another.

There are other teachers who help strengthen my faith, my cultural identity, and my belief that Negroes need to stand together, too. They provide lessons through spirituals and poems by James Weldon Johnson, Langston Hughes, and Paul Lawrence Dunbar, through which our rich heritage shines. During dance recitals and musical performances in the college auditorium, where our parents and other faculty members sit in attendance, we recite the poems we have learned, often providing explanations for the reason they've been written. Sometimes during our presentations, a child emerges who is so talented that she is asked to perform on special occasions, such as when Mrs. Bethune entertains visitors and donors to the school. On one of those occasions, I hear Frances sing for the first time.

In an effort to raise money for her school, Mrs. Bethune often invites wealthy donors to tour the college during the day and stay for a presentation in the evening. Sometimes the performance might be a professional group of artists. At other times she might entertain her guests with local talent. Frances, the niece of our next-door neighbors, the Bergmans, often plays on our jungle gym when she visits her aunt and uncle, but until the night of her performance, Rosemary and I have no idea how musically gifted she is. When our eight-year-old friend rises to sing "Ave Maria," we hear one of the purest soprano voices we've ever heard. A hush falls over the audience as her angelic tones float above the crowd. I sit in rapt attention, thinking of Paul Lawrence Dunbar's poem "When Malindy Sings."

> Aint you nevah hyeahd Malindy?
> Blessed soul, tek up de cross!
> Look hyeah, ain't you jokin', honey?
> Well, you don't know whut you los'.
> Y'ought to hyeah dat gal a-wa'blin',
> Robins, la'ks, an' all dem things
> Heish dey moufs an' hides dey face,
> When Malindy sings.[27]

At the end of her performance, Rosemary and I go up to tell her how much we have enjoyed her singing. She shyly thanks us and then turns to go home with her parents. Had she grown up a decade later, Frances might have gone on to become an operatic sensation, but we

27 "When Malindy Sings," Paul Laurence Dunbar.

live in a time and place where such opportunities rarely present themselves, and so she becomes a nurse and moves to New York to pursue her medical career.

Immersed in the richness of Negro culture, I begin to appreciate, on a profound level, the hardships my people have endured. The litany of how millions of Africans died in the belly of slave ships or at the bottom of the Atlantic Ocean during the infamous Middle Passage is repeated again and again by teachers and mentors. How those who survived arrived on these shores to be stripped naked and sold on auction blocks like animals; robbed of their languages, customs, music, instruments, and the beauty of their clothing. But they survived. They survived the beatings, the rapes, the brandings, and the grueling work in the fields from sunup to sundown. They survived having their children being sold away. They learned to read and write in spite of laws against such learning, and they defied the odds—becoming educators and midwives, doctors and lawyers, scientists, writers, musicians, artists, law-abiding citizens. The rich history of my people gives me strength and an appreciation for all those who made my life possible.

Adults in our community take responsibility for passing along the bits and pieces of our history to every Negro child they encounter as a kind of communal education. They seem to sense that without their constant attention to the pride they are instilling in us, we might come to accept the oppression under which we live as our fate, our destiny. We absorb the positive aspects of our legacy, but we also know there is an unspoken ugliness to the lives we are living, one that threatens not only our culture but our very existence. For although my sister and I do not witness it firsthand, we have overheard talk of the Ku Klux Klan riding through the Bethune-Cookman College more than once. On one occasion they roared through on the eve of an election. Their demonstration was to be a warning to the students and faculty not to vote the following day. Having received word that they might come, Mrs. Bethune turned on lights in all the buildings on campus and kept them burning until dawn. Then she led Negro voters to the polls unharmed.[28] On another occasion, Mrs. Bethune sat in front of one of the dormitories with students and faculty members singing hymns when the Klan appeared. Upon seeing her, they rode off into the night.

Eventually the day comes when the effects of racism hit me personally. It is on a day when Rosemary and I are playing in our front yard. Mother and Dad are still at work, and our neighbors, the Bergmans, are keeping an eye on us from their house next door. Our parents have always been able to trust us to follow their rules when they are not at home, and they feel they can leave us alone for short periods of time, as long as the neighbors are at home next door. And our new dog, a mutt named Thunder Mike, is there to protect us, too.

On this particular day we have drawn hopscotch lines in the dirt on the street in front of our house. Rosemary throws a rock into the first square and is jumping toward the "free circle" at the top when two little white boys appear seemingly out of nowhere. They approach us and say, "You wanna play?"

"Yes," we say. We ask them if they want to swing on our jungle gym in the backyard. They say they do, so we go into the backyard and get on the swings and the teeter-totter. After a while, the boys become curious and ask if they can see the inside of our house. We know we're not

---

28 From a reprint of the tract by Genevieve Forbes Herrick, "Loved, Feared and Followed," *Bethune-Cookman ADVOCATE* (Daytona Beach, FL: Bethune-Cookman College, 1950), 4. The original text appeared in *Collier's Weekly*, September 23, 1950.

allowed to let anyone in the house when Mother and Dad are not at home, but we decide it will be okay this one time. We take them through the kitchen door and into the dining room and living room. Just as we lead them toward our bedroom, we hear Dad at the back door. We are so mortified by his coming home early and by that fact that we have let strangers in the house that we rush the boys into our bedroom closet. We hope Dad will collect whatever he has come home for and go back to football practice without detecting them, so we tell them to be quiet until he leaves and we can get them out of the house.

Calling out as he enters, Dad yells, "Nell, Rosemary, are y'all all right?"

"Yes," we answer.

He collects what he came home for, says good-bye, and starts out the kitchen door again. Thankful to have escaped being discovered, Rosie and I tell the boys they should leave through our bedroom window, which is next to the dead-end wooded area beside our home. That way our neighbors won't see them and call out to our father. We raise our bedroom window and coax the older boy into jumping out into the grass below. As he does, he calls for his younger brother. That's when our father bursts through the kitchen door again. Crossing the dining and living rooms in what seems like two strides, he stands beside us at the bedroom window.

"You know better than to have people in the house when Mommy and I are out!" he yells, searching the room for the younger brother whom he heard the older one call out to. The little boy is so frightened by Dad's return that he has run back into the closet. Flinging open the closet door, Dad grabs the boy by one arm and carries him out the front door.

"Don't you ever come back here again. Do you understand me?" Dad yells to the trembling child, lowering him onto the sidewalk. Then he returns to the house and gives Rosemary and me a whipping before he returns to football practice. I lie on my bed sobbing, and Rosemary cries on hers. I can't help wondering if we've been whipped because we've let strangers into the house, because we've let white people in the house, because we've let boys in, or because of all those things. To this day, I still don't know the answer.

———————

A FEW MONTHS AFTER that incident, Rosemary and I are walking along the ditch beside our house on our way to see Carol and George Engram on College Row. The same two white boys suddenly appear and beckon to us to come see where they live. We follow them through the trees on the other side of the ditch where, to my surprise, just yards away from the Negro section of town is an entire community of working-class white people. In all the time my sister and I have walked back and forth beside the ditch and thicket of trees to the Engrams' house, I never imagined we were so close to white people. Standing there looking at the boys' house, I wonder if they've been watching us come and go all that time without our knowing it. The four of us crouch down at the edge of the trees, and they point to a tract house very much like ours where their mother is in the backyard hanging clothes on the line. As we move closer to the edge of the trees, she turns in our direction and begins screaming. Her husband bolts from the back door to see her pointing at their sons beside Rose and me. "Get away from here and don't ever come back, or I'll make sure you're sorry!" he screams. We tear out for the Engrams' as fast as we can run and never attempt to see the boys again. They never seek us out again, either.

That day I consciously begin to accept the prescribed standards of southern laws, and I become more aware of the rules that I've accepted throughout my life without question, like the rule Mother and Dad have about our going to the bathroom before we leave home and waiting until we return home to go again, unless we are attending a function at Bethune-Cookman, where the restrooms are open to everyone. When we are away from the college campus, we do not drink anything, and we learn to swallow vitamins and other pills without water. We avoid public restrooms because Mother says they are filthy, but we never leave home without Kleenex, in case we get stranded and are forced to go into one. I am nine years old before I see the first restrooms marked COLORED, WHITE WOMEN, and WHITE MEN. It doesn't take much imagination for me to understand that the room marked colored is to be used by both men and women; nor does it take long to discover that the colored restroom is seldom cleaned, since the smell spills outside into the surrounding area. Besides, it is a generally known fact that Negro maids are paid to clean the "white" restrooms but not the colored ones. Years pass before I ask Mother why she and Dad didn't tell us the truth about the conditions under which we lived, why they never told us public facilities were segregated but instead said we had to go to the bathroom before we left home because public toilets were filthy.

"I didn't see any reason to fill your minds with a hatred of all white people just because some of them were bigots," she said, "and I *did* tell you the truth. The public toilets *were* filthy."

After we've been out all day without the use of a toilet, the minute we return, we all make a mad dash for the bathroom, everyone yelling,

"First!" The fastest one inside gets to use the toilet first, while everyone else stands wiggling impatiently outside the door. With three females in the family, Dad sometimes gets an empty jar he keeps for emergencies and heads for the garage to relieve himself there.

Like many southern parents, ours try to shield us from overt racism by telling us only what they feel is essential, so my understanding of the intensity of the intolerant times in which we live is a slow and gradual awakening, understood through an accumulation of experiences and incidents that occur over a period of time.[29]

Growing up in a Negro community means the images we see are of Negro people. Negro art is prominently displayed, and we learn to appreciate Negro artists of all genres. Negro images of God teach me to think of God as dark-skinned.

Mrs. Bethune (who later becomes Dr. Bethune) still lives on the campus of Bethune-Cookman College as president emeritus during our tenure in Daytona Beach. Both she and Mrs. Bryon are such good friends and such strong influences in the community that I begin to see the possibility of God being a woman, too. That image is reinforced when Rosemary and I learn and recite James Weldon Johnson's poem "The Creation" at one of the performances we children put on for the college community. In his poem, Johnson describes God as "a mammy bending over her baby." After learning the poem, whenever I look into the eyes of Mary McLeod Bethune, I feel like I'm looking into the face of God, and I say to myself, "If God is a woman, then God must look like Mary McLeod Bethune."

---

29 It wasn't until I became a mother myself that I began to understand why our parents didn't want to do anything in an oppressive, segregated society that would cause Rosemary and me to question our worth as human beings, especially while our self-images were still being formed.

Rosemary actually gets to meet the great lady before I do on the day Mrs. Bryon sends my sister to Mrs. Bethune's home to deliver a letter. Placing the letter in Rosie's hand, Mrs. Bryon tells her she is to deliver it to Mrs. Bethune. My seven-year-old sister takes her teacher's instruction to mean she is to deliver the letter personally, so when she arrives at Mrs. Bethune's front door, she tells the woman who answers that she has a letter for Mrs. Bethune. The young woman tells Rosemary she is Mrs. Bethune's secretary and will take the letter. But Rosemary refuses to hand it over, saying her teacher told her to deliver it. The woman explains again who she is and says she will take the letter, but Rosemary, who has never heard of a secretary working in anyone's home, will not release the letter. Overhearing the exchange from inside the house, Mrs. Bethune calls to her secretary saying, "Let the child come in." Rosemary enters and hands the letter over.

An amused Mrs. Bethune thanks her and asks, "What's your name?"

"Rosemary Braxton," my sister pipes up.

Mrs. Bethune begins to chuckle, saying, "Why, I know your parents and your grandparents, too. Come here and give me a hug."

Not only is Mrs. Bethune a good friend of Madre and Papa, but having only one son, she often refers to our mother as her daughter. After Rosemary's initial meeting with her, the two of us become regular visitors to the Bethune home, enjoying the invitations without question and without fully realizing how privileged we are. Small chairs await each arrival. We take seats and then listen to her reminisce about days gone by.

She tells us she started Bethune-Cookman College on October 3, 1904, in "a shack," with a dollar and a half and some soapboxes for furniture. She called her new school the Daytona Educational and Industrial Training School. It had five little girls whose parents agreed to pay fifty cents a week for tuition.[30] Her son, Albert McLeod Bethune, was the school's only boy.[31] She says that money for the school came in slowly, but then she heard that a man named James A. Gamble (son of the founder of Proctor and Gamble) had a winter home in Daytona Beach. Mrs. Bethune invited him to visit, not realizing that Gamble was already attracted to her school because he felt it was "a Christian effort on behalf of Negro children."[32] When he entered her office, which was furnished with a wooden crate and a wobbly chair, he demanded, "Where is this school of which you wish me to be a trustee?"[33]

"In my mind, Mr. Gamble," she shot back, "and in my soul."[34]

James Gamble was so taken aback by her commitment that he not only gave her financial assistance, but he also gave her advice. And he eventually became chairman of the board, remaining in the position until his death twenty years later.

Rosemary and I admire Mrs. Bethune, but as children with easy access to her, we don't fully understand the respect with which the rest of the world holds her. We go to her home when invited for afternoon visits, knowing full well that she could have chosen to spend time with any of her great-grandchildren or any number of adults. That she chooses to spend that time serving the two of us lemonade and cookies in her sunroom and sharing stories of her childhood and early days is a privilege we relish but will not fully appreciate until we are a lot older.

---

30 Catherine Owens Peare, *Mary McLeod Bethune*, (New York: Vanguard Press, 1951), 88.

31 In 1923, the former grade school for girls merged with Cookman Institute and became Bethune-Cookman College. It was accredited by the Southern Association of Colleges and Secondary Schools as an "A-grade" college and to this day is dominated by Faith Hall.

32 Herrick, "Loved, Feared and Followed," 4.

33 Peare, *Mary McLeod Bethune*, 96.

34 Ibid.

Listening to memories of her childhood makes me feel as if we are living in a golden age by comparison. Of all the things she tells us, the one that stands out most vividly in my mind is the day she and her mother went to deliver clothes to the white folk who had owned the McLeods during slavery. During that trip, young Mary McLeod stopped at the playhouse of the child her mother ironed clothes for in order to play with the two little white girls inside. Rocking one of the dolls she had been handed, young Mary picked up a book to look at.

As soon as she touched it one of the girls yelled, "Put down that book! You can't read!"

The white child was confident in her assertion, Mrs. Bethune told us, because slavery, which outlawed teaching Negroes to read and write, had not been over for long. Embarrassed by the sudden outburst, Mary McLeod put the book down. She said she had only picked it up out of curiosity, but as she returned it to the table, she promised herself that one day she would learn to read, and she would teach other members of her race to read, too, so no one else would ever again tell a Negro child to put down a book.

As she came of age, Mary McLeod Bethune became especially concerned about young girls like herself who were denied an education. That concern pushed her to build a school in the South where she said "the need was greatest."[35] She wanted the school to be in an inexpensive neighborhood, because she had no money. The rest, she says, she left to God. During her early teaching days in Florida, some people directed her to a piece of land and a dilapidated house that she could rent for $200—five dollars down and the balance within two years. The owner

---

35 Herrick, "Loved, Feared and Followed," 3.

of the land said the place was a "public dump heap,"[36] but he agreed to sell it to her.

"He never knew it, but I didn't have five dollars," she confided to one of her biographers. "I promised to be back in a few days with the initial payment, which I raised selling ice cream and sweet potato pies to workmen on construction jobs. I took the owner his money in small change wrapped in my handkerchief."[37] She says the most intangible asset in starting her school was her partnership with God. "I believe in God, and so I believe in Mary Bethune."[38] It seems fitting that the other strong female influence in our lives at the time is Rose Marie Bryon (my sister's teacher), because she and Mrs. Bethune are close personal friends, and both have a fervent belief in God.

To make sure the children she cares about have a healthy relationship with God, Mrs. Bryon establishes the Children's Crusade for Christ, which Rosemary and I join. Under her direction, we take part in producing a weekly fifteen-minute radio program featuring hymns, Bible verses, and life lessons. We and our fellow crusaders record the show each Saturday morning for its airing on Sunday morning for children who are not in church like we are. To prepare for the taping, we gather several times a week after school in Mrs. Bryon's classroom for rehearsals; there, our only interruptions are Mrs. Bryon's splitting headaches. Her pain is often so severe that she's forced to stop playing the piano in the middle of a hymn and send a child across the room for her black leather handbag. Taking hold of the straps, she opens it and digs around inside until she locates a blue-and-white package of BC (bicarbonate of soda). Ripping it open, she pours the white powder into

36 Peare, *Mary McLeod Bethune*, 94.
37 Ibid. 95.
38 Herrick, "Loved, Feared and Followed," 4.

the glass of water another child has been sent to get and gulps the fizz-ing liquid down. Then, with a wave of her plump honey-colored hand, she begins playing again, and we return to singing, "My faith looks up to thee, thou Lamb of Calvary..." The songs we learn at Mrs. Bryon's piano come straight out of her Baptist hymnals and enrich the stock of traditional Episcopal hymns. As members of the Children's Crusade for Christ, we march in Bethune-Cookman's homecoming parades dressed in blue-and-white satin uniforms with red crosses emblazoned on a satin shield that spreads across our chests.

Months go by before Mrs. Bryon discovers Rosemary has had polio. One day she detects a slight limp in Rosie's gait and asks, "Why are you limping?" When Rosemary tells her she had polio three years earlier, a special bond develops between my sister and her teacher.

At the Keyser Laboratory School, my sister and I become cham-pion marble shooters, undoing Mother's nightly ritual of scrubbing our knees and elbows with a pumice stone and applying lemon juice to keep them "soft and ladylike." As two of the only girls who join the boys dur-ing recess, we hike up our dresses, get down on all fours in the dirt, and enter into major marble shootouts. During one game I lose every marble I have and then borrow Rosemary's prized "big bummy" to win mine back. But I end up losing hers, too. She is initially angry with me but lets go of her anger when we find other games to enter into, like the day we follow the boys around to the back of the schoolhouse to play mumblety-peg with pocketknives the fellows have smuggled into school. At other times we join in a game of coed kickball or play Little Sally Walker, jacks, and hopscotch with the girls.

My best friend in the fourth grade is Sonya Ferrell, who is also the teacher's pet. As long as I stay close to Sonya, Mr. Thomas treats me well, too, except for the day Sonya and I make a drawing that lands us in trouble. It is a sketch of a man and woman lying in bed together, holding hands, facing forward. Neither figure has genitals, because Sonya and I don't know what adult genitalia look like, so we draw figures like our dolls—one with long hair for the woman, the other with short hair for the man. We have drawn the picture because the older girls in our class have just returned from viewing a special filmstrip on reproduction, and they are teasing us for not being old enough to see it.

We retort, "We don't need to see it, because we already know where babies come from." To prove it, we make a drawing that Mr. Thomas promptly confiscates.

With the evidence in his hand, he calls us to the front of the class and hits each of our open palms so hard with his thick ruler that when I return to my desk, I can't even hold my pencil. The embarrassment alone mortifies us to the point of never attempting anything like that again and relegates the rest of my artwork to fruit, flowers, and houses, or youngsters sitting in a movie watching the picture show.

Daytona Beach, like other places we've lived, is conservative when it comes to morals and politics. With little exposure to any political understanding of things, Rosemary and I are dismayed in 1951 when the majority of our classmates begin wearing their I LIKE IKE buttons to school. They ask where our buttons are, and we rush home to find out why we don't have them. Mother and Dad say it is because they plan to vote for Adlai Stevenson. This places Rosemary and me in the minority of children whose parents identify with the national Democratic Party but shun southern Democrats who are the staunch segregationists known as Dixiecrats. Dixiecrats are the reason so many of the southern Negroes we know support the Republican

Party. Not that southern Republicans are that much better about race. Our schoolmates tease us for not supporting Eisenhower, saying, "Everybody knows he's going to win." Eisenhower's reputation as a war hero leads us children into discussions about our fathers—whose father fought in World War II, and whose father did not. Because our father is color-blind, the army refused to take him, and that also puts us at odds with the children whose fathers served the country during the war. Realizing the taunting we are putting up with, Mother tells us that the work Daddy did with youngsters at the Y in San Antonio when their fathers were away fighting was just as important as the work of the men who fought abroad. But when we tell this to our schoolmates, they are unimpressed.

Our first year in Florida moves rapidly to a close, and just as we have done since our days in Texas, Rosemary and I attend college graduation exercises with our parents. Going to the main lawn on Bethune-Cookman's campus, we take seats among parents, grandparents, and siblings of the graduates, and beside the other faculty brats whose parents will be in procession along with ours; seated together, we children await the beginning of the commencement exercises. We strain our necks to see Mrs. Bethune in her place of honor at the head of the line as the opening chords to "Pomp and Circumstance" are struck. Then we look for Mother and Dad in the long procession of hooded faculty members and nervous graduates. Settling into my seat, I shake off the goose bumps I always get when I hear "Pomp and Circumstance" and dream of the day when I will march in a similar line dressed in my cap and gown to receive my college diploma.

Every year I'm inspired by the number of athletes who receive special awards and honors—boys we've seen on the basketball court and the football field, or running around the track, without ever realizing what outstanding scholars they are, too. The ceremonies are brought to a close with the singing of the school's alma mater, a Negro spiritual, and the Negro national anthem, "Lift Every Voice and Sing."

On July 10, the college family gathers to celebrate Mrs. Bethune's birthday. Forming a huge circle, the college family stands around a large carefully constructed three-tiered cement cake near the entrance to the campus. The cake is a permanent fixture that reaches several feet high, and on this special day members of the community have come together to honor the president emeritus. Seventy-six children, dressed in our Sunday best, are given lighted candles, each representing a year of Mrs. Bethune's life. Each of us marches toward the cement cake and ascends the tiers holding a candle and standing at our assigned places. President Moore greets the crowd and calls on several dignitaries to speak. Afterward, the honoree rises to address the crowd, speaking of the founding of her school and the challenges that lie ahead. She encourages us all to continue to reach for higher goals. Then in the midst of her inspiring speech, she begins to refer to her homeliness, speaking of her wide nose, full lips, kinky hair, and dark skin. This part of her annual talk always confuses me, because when I look into her ebony face encircled by a halo of snow-white hair, I see the same beauty of Africa that is reflected in *Ebony* magazine's African kings and queens, and I can't understand why she thinks she's ugly. As soon as her speech ends, we sing, "Happy Birthday," and a real cake, prepared by the kitchen staff, is rolled onto the great lawn, sliced, distributed, and consumed by all present. Then all the lights on campus are extinguished, and the entire assembly sings her favorite song, "Let Me Call You

Sweetheart," as she sits beaming, with several great-grandchildren on her lap and at her feet.

———◆———

MOTHER, DADDY, ROSEMARY, AND I spend at least one evening a week at the movies for the remainder of the summer. We walk across our backyard, cut through the football field, and turn right up Second Avenue. Speaking to Mr. Rodriguez as we pass his newsstand on Fairview Street, we head into the Negro theater[39] to see memorable movies—*The Robe, Johnny Belinda, The Pearl, Singin' in the Rain, Cochise,* a number of Esther Williams movies, and *King Solomon's Mines. King Solomon's Mines,* a movie based on the book of the same title by H. Rider Haggard, tells the story of a search for diamonds in South Africa. It is one of the few fifties films about Africa that impresses and inspires me. I am overwhelmed by the beautiful landscape and dazzled by the size of the diamonds, but the thing that leaves the most lasting impression is an attraction between a white diamond miner and a Black South African woman. It is my earliest awareness of the possibility of interracial love between a Black woman and a white man, and I ponder the attraction between the two for a long time, because it goes against everything I have overheard adults say about southern laws prohibiting miscegenation—a word I come understand by the way it is used in hushed tones as adults speak of people loving one another across racial lines. But *King Solomon's Mines* opens the possibility of such a love, and I begin to think of the prospect of a Black woman

---

39 When Rosemary and I were growing up, Mother and Dad took us to (or allowed us to go to) the all-Negro movie houses in the cities where we lived. But if we lived where the movie houses were segregated (that is, if they seated whites downstairs and Negroes in the balcony), members of our family didn't go to the movies at all.

being attractive to a white man. It is something I will ponder again as a teenager.

During the day, when Dad is taking the track team through its paces, Rosemary and I go downtown to shop with Mother, where department stores stretch along the city's main thoroughfare, and the beach comes up to the sidewalk. A bridge crosses the water on Front Street leading to a sandy shore on the other side, where white children run in and out of the water, squealing at the chill of pounding waves. I know without being told that the color of my skin prohibits me from entering that world.

Shopping in Daytona is different from shopping in Atlanta where we get dressed in gloves and hats to take the trolley into the heart of the city. In Daytona Beach, the sand swirls up from the beach onto the sidewalks, and barefooted whites troll in and out of department stores in various stages of attire—sundresses and high-heeled shoes, dress pants, Panama hats, and shirts and ties, as well as beach shoes, bare feet, and bathing suits. But Negroes, not wanting to give salespeople any reason for refusing us service, dress in our best clothes to shop. Because of the intense heat, Mother lets Rosemary and me wear sandals downtown and allows us to leave our gloves at home. We carry parasols to protect our skin from the sun.

The end of summer brings on hurricane season, with high winds and blinding rains that bend palm trees like accordion drinking straws and upend everything that isn't anchored. Daddy, who harbors a fear of lightning from his days as a boy on the farm, gathers us in the garage each time a storms blows up and keeps us there until it has passed. One summer during hurricane season, members of the Bethune-Cookman faculty travel to Antioch College to participate in workshops sponsored by New York University. Both Mother and Dad attend the workshops, so our paternal grandmother, Dear, comes from Jacksonville to take care of Rosie and me. She helps us catch lightning bugs. We punch holes in jar tops so we can lie in bed and watch the lights in their tails glow off and on after she has turned out the bedroom light. She bakes pies and cakes and makes us candy, and in the early evenings, she sits with us on the front steps teaching us the constellations and telling us Bible stories.

Toward the end of the summer and her stay with us, a vicious hurricane blows up. Rosemary and I are playing on our jungle gym when it begins, and we are in one of our sassy moods. We ignore Dear's call for us to come inside and continue to play even after her admonitions. The Bergmans, our next-door neighbors, call to us from their kitchen window. "Mind your grandmother and go inside." But we ignore them, too, swinging higher and higher on our metal jungle gym as if we are possessed by demons. When the pounding rain finally soaks us to the bone, and lightning threatens to strike the jungle gym, we realize we should have gone inside when we were called. We hop off the swings and attempt to open the back door, but Dear has locked it. Then we try the front door, but that one is locked, too. That's when Rosemary and I make a pact with each other to find a way into the house where we will be undetected by Dear. We know our home better than she does, and we are already anticipating the whipping that awaits us once we are inside. We agree that whoever finds an opening first will let the other one in. Almost immediately, my sister discovers the unlocked garage door and runs into the house. As soon as she enters, I hear Dear secure that door and give Rosemary the whipping of her life. Afterward, Rosie tries to open the front door for me, but

Dear is hot on her heels. When my sister heads for a bedroom window, Dear foils her again.

Finally, cold and shivering, I decide to accept what I know is coming. So I walk up the front steps and knock at the door. Dear opens it and snatches me inside with such force that it takes my breath away. Then she gives me the whipping I knew was coming. I am so angry at her that when she stops hitting me, I scream out in a blind rage, "I don't love you anymore, and I'm not coming to your funeral when you die!" Without skipping a beat and with the mother wit that has sustained Negro grandmas for generations, she answers, "At the rate you're going, I may be coming to yours." Her response is fired back so fast that Rosemary falls on the floor laughing. Years later, Dear and I laugh about that day, too, but I am an adult before I learn that she never mentioned any part of what happened to Mother and Dad.

In Daytona Beach, I finally begin to think of myself as an individual. Before the move to this city, I always thought of myself as a member of a family and gave little thought to who I was apart from my parents and my sister. In Florida, I begin to develop my own identity, one that is separate from the other members of my family. I discover that I am an entity apart, unique, more conscious of the things I am learning outside my home—at Mrs. Bethune's, with Mrs. Bryon, and from Dr. Tucker, an elderly white woman who spent many years living in China.

Dr. Tucker is a tiny soul (to say she is five feet tall would be stretching the truth) with white hair. She is part of Bethune-Cookman's interracial faculty and frequently invites Rosemary and me over for tea in Chinese rice cups. She tells stories of her days in the Orient. "In China," she says, "the elderly are revered. They held me in high esteem there because of my age. They thought I was wise, because I have white hair."

We enjoy visiting with her, as we enjoy being in the company of most old people. They seem to always have time to teach us things, and they know so much that we find fascinating—foreign travel, history, species of trees and flowers.

In September, when the new school year begins, Eleanor Roosevelt comes to visit Daytona Beach. Actually, she comes to speak to a group of whites who have arranged her trip, but when Mrs. Bethune learns that the group plans to have Mrs. Roosevelt, who is a close personal friend of hers, speak before a segregated audience, she organizes a welcoming party to go to the airport and meet the former first lady. There, she informs her friend that no Negroes have been invited to attend the function where Mrs. Roosevelt is to speak. Typical of Eleanor Roosevelt, she not only decides against delivering her address to the segregated crowd, she agrees to ride through the Negro part of town in an open convertible with Mrs. Bethune. Rosemary and I are among the excited children and adults who line Second Avenue to watch Bethune-Cookman's "first lady" and America's former first lady holding their hands triumphantly in the air as they lead the impromptu motorcade through the Negro section of town. I stand at the side of Second Avenue, thrilled by the sight of these two strong women whose appearance together helps me understand that there are white people who will stand up for Negroes in spite of the laws governing southern society. That day is such a high point for us children that when two schoolmates get into a fight vying for the best spot from which to see the parade, they hide in the bushes to do battle so as not to embarrass Mrs. Bethune.

Fall gives way to winter, and Thanksgiving to Christmas. A new year approaches in which Dwight D. Eisenhower is set to be inaugurated thirty-fourth president of the United States. A decorated army general, Ike led the troops to victory in Europe during the Second World War and returned home triumphant. The country has rewarded him by electing him president, and he has requested that school-children lead his inaugural parade. Our school safety patrol is called together and told that we've been given the honor of leading the new president's parade in Washington, DC. Everyone, including those parents and teachers who did not support his election, help raise money for our trip. At the news of my impending participation, Aunt Mabel sends a pair of navy-blue-and-beige shoes from New York, and I am ecstatic! All our lives, Rosemary and I have worn ugly brown oxfords, while our friends have sported fashionable penny loafers and brown-and-white saddle oxfords. So when the shoes arrive from New York, and I try them on, I'm not about to admit they are too tight. "They fit fine," I say, because I have no intention of marching through the nation's capital in ugly brown oxfords when I can finally be dressed as smartly as my schoolmates.

We travel by train with our Negro safety patrol leaders to Washington in a Jim Crow car and check into a Negro hotel. Going to our room, my roommates and I unpack our clothes before I locate a pay phone down the hall and call my maternal grandfather, Papa, who is working in Washington as information specialist in the Office of Price Stabilization. After we have talked, he asks to speak with our safety patrol leader, so he can arrange a special tour for us. I call her to the phone and return to my room, the first hotel room I've ever stayed in.

Excitement mounts on the morning of the inauguration. We are proud of the fact that, of all the children from across the country, we have been chosen to lead the parade on the day Dwight Eisenhower is sworn in as president of the United States. It is the first time Mother has let me wear my hair in curls instead of braids, and like the other girls in our group, I have sat in our kitchen for hours as the hot iron comb, heated on the kitchen burner, was pulled through my hair to straighten it. Afterward, hot iron curlers were twisted and clicked to make my full curls. The process was arduous, but it was worth it to have the straight hair that beauty standards of the fifties dictated. I spend time admiring myself in the mirror on Inauguration Day. It is one of the rare occasions when I look in the mirror and love everything about me.

We arrive early to line up, passing other marchers and going to the front where we wait for the flags we are to carry to be distributed. As we stand talking excitedly about keeping our marching lines straight, a large contingent of white schoolchildren comes around the corner and walks past us. Eying us with disdain, they form several new rows in front of ours, making it clear that they are actually going to lead the parade, and we Negro children are going to march behind them. Realizing we have been forced to the back of the formation, I fight back the tears welling up in my eyes, and I promise myself that I will not let them see me cry. I'll be as strong as nine-year-old Mary McLeod was when the white girl told her to "put down that book."

I stand there humiliated with my fellow patrol mates, waiting for the parade to begin, chiding myself for believing that the president of the United States would choose Negro children to lead his inaugural parade. I'm especially embarrassed when I think of marching past Papa in Jim Crow formation. He was the first southern field director for the National Urban League, and by marching past him in segregated formation, I'll be betraying everything he has spent his life working to overcome.

# CHAPTER 7

# OVER THE RAINBOW[40]

NELL'S MATERNAL GRANDFATHER, PAPA, AS A RED CROSS PROFESSIONAL

M Y GRANDFATHER GREW UP on a rented plantation in
McComb, Mississippi, the second of six children (four boys and
two girls) born to Jeff and Amanda Thomas. His parents were children
when the Civil War ended, but the pain and embarrassment of slavery

40 From "Over the Rainbow," music by Harold Arlen, lyrics by E. Y. Harburg.

caused them never to speak of it to their children. When Papa was growing up, Negroes and whites lived and sharecropped side by side without regard to race, and their children played together and let their hogs eat and wallow in the same swamp. Young white children even called my great-grandfather "sir,"[41] Papa once told us.

Papa's father, Jeff, had three weeks of night-school training, amounting to the equivalent of a fourth-grade education. My great-grandmother, Amanda (from whom my mother Anne Amanda got her middle name), never attended school. Because he had a deep hunger for knowledge, Jeff Thomas taught himself and all his children to read music and to sing by note.[42] Papa had a wonderful baritone voice that I enjoyed each time I sat between Madre and him at First Congregational Church in Atlanta.

Our grandfather grew up thinking the land his family lived on belonged to them, because the crops they harvested did not go to feed white people but came to their own table. He was fourteen years old before he learned better. That was the year his mother, who had been ailing for most of his young life with an unexplained malady, died. It was also the year the land he had grown up on and come to love was sold away from his father. Papa was devastated when he learned that a neighbor and trusted friend had gone to the landowner and privately negotiated to rent the land his family had lived on for a larger sum than they could afford to pay.

When Jeff Thomas sat his children down to tell them what had happened, Papa asked his father, "How can a neighbor cause us to move off our land and out of our own home?"

"We do not own this land," his father told him. "We are sharecroppers."[43]

---

41 Jesse O. Thomas, *My Story in Black and White: The Autobiography of Jesse O. Thomas* (New York: Exposition Press, 1967), 11.

42 Ibid. 14.

43 Ibid. 12.

The sale of land forced the Thomases off the property they had lived on for more than twenty years, rendering them homeless. The event led my grandfather to decide then and there that he would never again live on property he did not own or could not afford to buy.

With his mother's death, and the land he'd grown to love gone, Papa saw no future in sharecropping. Considering a way to make money for himself, my grandfather recalled seeing people coming to McComb from New Orleans to attend the "big meeting," an annual outdoor revival service that took place on the fourth Monday in August. His uncle, a Baptist minister, was a preacher at the revival, and his father, a deacon known as Uncle Peace, took charge of the finances. The Negroes who came to attend the big meeting from twenty or thirty miles away showed off the finery that spoke of money to be made in the places where they lived. So on the day he returned home from his mother's funeral service, my fourteen-year-old grandfather decided to pack a small bag of clothes, board a milk train, and head for New Orleans.[44] He took the train as far as Natalbany, Louisiana, where he found work in the sawmills and dreamed of becoming an architect or a carpenter. But guilt caught up with him. He felt badly about the way he'd snuck off from home and realized his father had no idea where he was or whether he was dead or alive, so he sent home a peace offering of fertilizer, meat, and flour, hoping the gift would help prevent Jeff Thomas from having to mortgage crops to pay for rent. Instead of a reprimand, his father sent him a note thanking him for his thoughtfulness and supporting his independence. That note opened the door to my grandfather's infrequent visits back home.[45]

---

44 Ibid. 18.
45 Ibid. 20.

During one such visit, the brother of a young woman my grandfather was courting mentioned a school called Tuskegee Institute in Alabama. Papa had never heard of the school, but at the urging of his girlfriend's brother, he wrote down the name of the registrar and sent a letter requesting a catalogue. Within a few months he had applied and was accepted as a student. Once enrolled, he quickly won the respect of Booker T. Washington, Tuskegee's founder and president, and of Mrs. Washington and members of the student body. At the dedication of the school's newly constructed dining room, he was the student chosen by his peers to speak before the trustees, who included Theodore Roosevelt, William Wilcox, George Peabody, and Julius Rosenwald. Mr. Wilcox was so impressed by the speech that when he returned to New York, he sent my grandfather a fifty-dollar check—a lot of money to a poor Negro boy in the days when tuition and board totaled eighteen dollars a month.[46]

Upon graduation from Tuskegee, Papa became the New York and Pennsylvania field secretary for the school, raising money for the institution and abandoning any future he had envisioned in carpentry and architecture.[47] He went on to establish Tuskegee's alumni association and to serve as principal of Voorhees Industrial Institute (later Voorhees College) in Denmark, South Carolina. He met my grandmother on a return trip to Tuskegee from one of his many fund-raising ventures, and after a courtship, they were married just prior to his acceptance of the position of principal of Voorhees Institute. After Voorhees he became Negro economics examiner-in-charge of the US Employment Service for the Department of Labor, and following that job, he established the southern office of the National Urban League in Atlanta, Georgia, where he served as the first southern field director.

---

46 Ibid. 37.
47 Ibid. 60.

In 1920, while still employed by the Urban League, Papa founded the Atlanta University School of Social Work before taking a leave of absence from the Urban League to work as senior promotional specialist for the US Treasury Department where, in 1941, he established an organized approach to selling war bonds to Negroes. He left the Treasury Department to join the American Red Cross as the first Negro hired at an administrative level by its national body. While there he opened doors for a number of Negroes who might never have been considered for work with the organization and was instrumental in changing the Red Cross's policy regarding the segregation of Negro blood. In spite of the heroic work of Dr. Charles Drew regarding the equality of blood plasma, the Red Cross had continued to keep blood donated by Negroes separate from the other blood it collected. This practice left a bitter taste in the mouths of Negroes, who were reluctant to donate blood even in the midst of a war where Negroes were being wounded. Their reaction led the organization to take a timid step away from its policy, but not so much that it stopped giving people receiving blood the right to ask the race of the donor. Memoranda from my grandfather soon forced them to see that this was an unacceptable solution, and in 1948, in the interest of the war effort, the Red Cross altered its policy regarding the segregation of blood.[48] The real vindication for Papa came in 1951, when he departed from the American Red Cross to join the Office of Price Stabilization. At that time, he was heralded in an article published in the *Washington Post*. "Jesse O. Thomas Puts Negro in Bloodstream of Red Cross..."[49] The year I went to Washington to participate in Dwight Eisenhower's inaugural parade, Papa was still working in the Office of Price Stabilization.

---

48  Ibid. 174–75.
49  Ibid. 219.

As Eisenhower's inaugural parade begins, I look straight ahead and concentrate on putting one foot in front of the other, praying all the while for the ordeal to end. Almost immediately my feet start to ache. I don't know if they are aching because of the tight shoes I have on, or because I am part of a segregated group marching in a national parade, but the pain digs deep inside me. When we arrive at the place where Papa is standing, I glance sideways and attempt a smile. He stands on the sidewalk in his Red Cross uniform adorned with medals and ribbons, looking straight ahead, saluting as we pass. I don't know if he is saluting us or the flag. I hope it is both.

After I see him, the parade can't move fast enough, and when it does end, no one mentions what has happened. We talk about dinner and tours of Washington and then head back to the hotel. In my room, I sit at the edge of the bed and take off my shoes to discover I have walked calluses onto the little toes of both feet. Dinner that evening is quiet, but afterward I lie awake for hours trying to forget what I've been through that day.

Papa appears at our hotel at midmorning the following day to take me to see his living quarters. We ride in a taxi to his hotel and go up to his room. The floor is covered with a Persian rug, and the room is furnished with an antique floor lamp, a four-poster bed, a shiny black telephone, an end table, and two upholstered armchairs. We sit and talk about the family and then call Daytona Beach to speak with Mother, Dad, and Rosemary. Then we call Madre in Atlanta. That evening he takes me to dinner at a restaurant with linen tablecloths and linen napkins. It is my first meal in a formal restaurant, and I am awed by the Negro waiters in suits and bow ties, the chandeliers, and all the Negro people who have come here dressed in their finery. After dinner, Papa takes me to a Negro movie house, where the rest of my safety patrol group is waiting. He has arranged for all of us to see a film there.

On our third day in Washington, Papa greets Negro and white safety patrol members at the Treasury Department, where he once worked. There, he introduces the guides who will take us through the building on a tour he has set up. Before he departs, he makes it clear that we are to take the tour as an integrated group, not in segregated lines.

As we begin moving across the floor, the white kids strong-arm their way to the front of the line. The Negro children surge ahead of them. Then slowly, as we look down at the endless flow of new money, the groups begin to intermingle. We are seeing more money than any of us has ever seen before and more than most of us will ever see in one place again. Mesmerized by the new bills shooting out from machines on the floor below us and by the workers in surgical gloves who quickly collect and fan them apart before sending them to the next station, we ooh and ahh.

Papa meets us at the end of the tour and hands out souvenirs. He and I say good-bye, and the group moves on to other city tours. I am so proud of what my grandfather has done that day—the tour he has arranged and the way he has insisted we move as an integrated group through the Treasury building—that I could burst.

We leave the Treasury Department for a tour of the White House, where we view the Blue Room, the Gold Room, and the Red Room. Then we go to the Capitol, where the group divides along racial lines again to pose for photographs. Afterward we head for the Lincoln and Jefferson Memorials. Standing at the foot of the giant statue of Abraham Lincoln, I feel a sense of awe as I remember parts of the speech we have all learned in school, "...that this nation under God shall have a new birth of freedom, and that the government of the people, by the people, for the people, shall not perish from the earth." I am so rooted to the spot that I don't move when the rest of the group goes to buy souvenirs. When chaperones finally coax me away, I purchase mementos for Mother, Daddy, and Rosemary and then descend the stairs with the rest of my group and head toward the Washington Monument where we climb to the top to look out over the city of Washington.

NELL (THIRD PERSON SEATED FROM RIGHT) WITH SAFETY
PATROL ON CAPITOL STEPS WASHINGTON, DC)

The last stop of the day is the city zoo, where we sit on benches to eat bag lunches. An hour later, after having enjoyed seeing the animals in their cages, I have to use the toilet, but I haven't seen one in all the time we've been out in the city. I think of asking our patrol leader to stop so I can relieve myself, but I'm afraid I'll be scolded for not knowing there are no facilities for colored. I have already been wrong about leading the parade, and I don't want to show my ignorance by asking for a toilet in Jim Crow Washington. As the urge gets stronger, I know that as long as we keep moving, I will be all right. *When this part of the day is over,* I tell myself, *I'll go to the hotel and rush down the hall yelling, "First," the way we do at home.* We stop in front of the primates' cage to look at the apes, and a little white girl comes up beside us to get a drink from the nearby water fountain. As soon as the water spouts up, I feel a trickle down my legs, and before I know it, my ankles and socks are drenched. I slump to my knees, weeping. A schoolmate goes to the middle of the line to get our patrol leader. She brings her back to where I am. "Why didn't you tell me you had to use the toilet?" she asks.

I don't answer her. I can't. All I want at this moment is for the earth to open up and swallow me whole. *I'm a disgrace,* I think, *to myself, to my family, to my race; an embarrassment to my friends*—who have by this time formed a circle around me.

A young white boy passes by with his mother and points at me. His mother looks over, sucks her teeth, and says, "That's just some nigger peeing." I can finish her sentence: "That's the way they *all* are."

"I guess we'd better get all of them to a restroom," our patrol leader says, and they finally do. Negro kids to the toilets marked colored, white kids to the ones marked white.

We leave Washington the next day, and in the weeks and months that follow, I try to sort out the feelings I have about the trip. I share with my family the excitement of touring the White House and the sense of wonder I felt standing at the foot of the Lincoln Memorial. I describe Papa's living quarters, and I talk about the fun he and I had at dinner and about touring the Treasury Department with the group, but my humiliation of marching in Jim Crow formation in the parade and my accident at the zoo are shameful experiences I keep to myself.

The following fall Sonya and I enter Mrs. Holbert's fifth-grade class, feeling older and more grown-up than we did in the fourth grade. We love our new teacher so much that the two of us often take turns visiting her home after school. Mrs. Holbert has an enlarged thyroid that sends her into coughing spasms during many of our classes. The spasms are so violent that she often has to leave the classroom before they are under control again. By the time she decides to have the goiter removed, it is so enlarged that she dies from complications connected with the surgery. The day we are told of her death by our principal and released from school is one of the saddest days of our lives. It is the first time most of us have experienced the death of someone close to us. A pall falls over our class that no one can lift until the day that Bethune-Cookman College hosts a professional performance of the opera *Carmen*. It is the first event I have mustered enthusiasm for since my teacher's death.

Before we attend the performance, Mother reads the story of *Carmen* to Rosemary and me, so we will understand what is happening when we attend the opera. The four of us arrive at the auditorium just before the curtain goes up. The place is so full that the only available seats are at the back. Thoughtful ushers allow Rosemary and me to stand in the aisle once the performance begins, so we can see. Everything we witness is exciting, and the costumes are beautiful, especially Carmen's black-and-red ruffled skirt and off-the-shoulder peasant blouse.

At intermission we spot Mrs. Bethune in the front row and ask Mother and Dad if we may go say hello. We make our way to where she is seated with some white benefactors of the college. She introduces them as Mr. and Mrs. Rice, and they, in turn, introduce their little girl to us. Their daughter is a few years younger than we are, but the three of us strike up a conversation about the opera. When Rosemary and I realize she doesn't understand what is taking place, we begin to explain the story to her. Overhearing our explanation, the Rices are so impressed that they invite us to sit with them for the remainder of the performance to help their daughter understand what is taking place on stage. We view the rest of the performance from the front-row seats, continuing to whisper to our new little friend about what is taking place.

In the ensuing weeks, Rosemary and I attend a campus concert with Mother and Daddy, where the famed Fisk Jubilee Singers' a cappella interpretation of spirituals make me feel as if I am in a place of ancestral pain I can almost feel. The struggles they sing about in "Nobody Knows the Trouble I've Seen," "Steal Away," and "I've Been 'Buked, and I've Been Scorned," are so palpable, I feel as if they are leaving the imprint of slavery on my soul. Sung against the backdrop of the racial strife we are living in, the spirituals are a testament to the fact that we can make it through the hard times of our day, because our ancestors made it through the horrors of theirs.

At the end of the school year, students are told that the Keyser Laboratory School has run out of funds and must close its doors. Our principal says we will all have to attend new schools in the fall. The close of the lab school means that Sonya will be attending a new school on the other side of town where she lives, while Rosemary, Carol and George Engram, and I will attend Bonner Elementary, a public school in our neighborhood.

That same spring, Daddy takes his track team on the road to compete, while Mother teaches school. On the weekends, she fends off loneliness by spending time with her friend, Clarice Biggins, the wife of a co-owner of Biggins and Meeks, the Negro pharmacy on Second Avenue. Mrs. Biggins and her boys, Franklin (who is Rosemary's age) and Warner, who at four is three and a half years younger than Rosemary and Franklin, drive their car to our house and pick us up to take us to the airport so we children can watch the commercial planes, which are still a novelty, take off and land. We stand behind the cyclone fence with wind from the roaring propellers whipping our clothing into a flapping frenzy, and we watch the planes. I love seeing the crewmen struggle against the wind as they roll the stairs up to the airplane door. Uniformed stewardesses in hats and gloves emerge from inside and help passengers descend the steps. Mother and Mrs. Biggins stand near the fence in deep conversation while we children watch people greet loved ones who have awaited their arrival. I try to imagine where all those passengers have come from.

Another plane taxies down the tarmac and lifts into the air, disappearing into the clouds. Between takeoffs and landings Rose and I play tag with the Biggins boys, yelling, "Gotcha! Gotcha back!" When our mothers decide we've been entertained enough, we all pile into the Bigginses' car and head for their home, making a highly anticipated stop at the Dairy Queen for ice cream cones.

The Bigginses breed Airedales, so after the ice cream is gone, we children are allowed to play with the newest litter of puppies. We roll in the grass, letting the pups lick our faces, unaware until it's too late that we're also being eaten alive by the red bugs hiding in the grass. When Mr. Biggins arrives home, Mother, Rose, and I say good-bye and begin walking the long blocks from the Bigginses' home to ours, where we take baths before dinner.

That summer Mrs. Rice (the white woman who attended the opera *Carmen* with her husband and daughter) also drops by our home to invite Rosemary and me to join her and her daughter at the beach. She says her little girl has been asking for us to play with her ever since the opera. Mother is taken aback by the invitation, because the beach is segregated. When she reminds Mrs. Rice of this, our hostess admits she's forgotten she'll be breaking the law by taking us, but her daughter really wants us to be her guests so her mother tells ours, "They're just children. If it's all right with you, it doesn't matter to me." When Mother says we may go, we excitedly get into our bathing suits and terry-cloth cover-ups, grab swimming caps, shower shoes, towels, sunhats, and sunglasses, and we are off.

Inside the Rices' car, I have a sense of foreboding that accompanies my sense of excitement. On the one hand, I fear we will be turned away from the beach and not allowed to go in the water when we arrive; on the other, I am excited about finally having a chance to run in and out of the surf I've seen white children playing in from the other side of Front Street when we go downtown on shopping trips with Mother. Mrs. Rice drives the car over the bridge I have dreamed of crossing so many times and parks near the sand. She takes out blankets, towels, and a basket of food, then sits reading her magazine, while Rosemary and I run in and out of the surf with her daughter. When we tire of the water, the three of us eat lunch and then go back into the ocean to play some more. Our hostess speaks with acquaintances who occasionally wander by until the sun begins to melt across the sky. If any of them ask questions, she is so discreet in her responses that I am totally unaware of any discomfort some of them may feel. Slowly she gathers the leftover food, puts it in her basket, folds her towels and blankets, and beckons to us to climb into her car for the ride home. When we return to the Negro side of town and pull up in front of our home, we say good-bye and thank her for a wonderful afternoon. Mrs. Rice and her daughter pull away from our front yard, having single-handedly integrated Daytona's lily-white beach.

A few weeks into the summer, Mother and Dad buy a new 1953 Sahara-beige and desert-tan Chevrolet. The most important conversation we have about our first family car is whether or not to get a radio or a clock for the new car. Rosemary and I beg for a radio, so we can listen to music while we ride along, but Mother and Dad decide a clock is more practical. Little do I realize how important that decision will be for years to come, because it means that we will be forced to make our own music as we travel from town to town, and singing brings us closer together. The new car opens up a new world of activities for us—fishing trips on our own, more trips to the airport to watch the planes, frequent visits to Sonya's house across town, excursions with Mother and Dad to their bridge games, and evenings at the drive-in movies, where Rose and I go dressed in pajamas, because by the time the double feature ends, it is well past our bedtime.

Later that same summer, we take our first family trip to New York City, where Dad continues to work toward a master's degree in health and physical education. This trip will end years of our father's summer-school travel to New York aboard Jim Crow buses. My excitement about this trip mounts as Rosemary and I decide which clothes to pack for the summer and try to imagine the sights we'll see.

Madre's sister Mabel and her husband, Ezra Parrott, live in New York, and Mabel and Madre's youngest sister, Louise, lives in Newark, New Jersey. Of all our great-aunts, Mabel and Maude (who lives in Chicago) are the ones with whom we have the most fun. Aunt Mabel's propensity for fun began early, when as a child she goaded her younger siblings into climbing trees and throwing eggs and fruit down onto well-dressed passersby. She tells us she once placed a monkey in the family flour bin, frightening her mother and older sisters (Madre and Aunt Lucille) half out of their wits when they opened the bin and the animal, covered in flour, jumped out. Aunt Mabel got into so much mischief at school that Lucille and Madre pleaded with their father to transfer her to another school to keep her from embarrassing them. Their father complied. I adore my Aunt Mabel, because she is the aunt who sent me the stylish navy-and-beige shoes I wore in President Eisenhower's inaugural parade, and because she has always been fun to be around.

We drive from Daytona Beach to our first stop, Jacksonville, where we visit Dear and Grandpa Singleton. We sit and talk on the front porch with neighbors who already know everything about our trip; early the following morning we leave for Atlanta to see Madre. In Atlanta I learn of the fate of Ethel and Julius Rosenberg when I walk into the living room and find Madre in front of the television set, crying.

"What's the matter, Madre?" I ask.

"Oh, baby," she says, "I can't believe we live in a country that would take the lives of a mother and father and leave their innocent children orphans."

"Why would the country do that?"

"Because," she tells me, "the Rosenbergs have been accused of giving secrets of the atomic bomb to the Soviet Union."

She tells me that Ethel's brother, David Greenglass, who served as an army sergeant at Los Alamos, New Mexico, was accused of having turned over detailed diagrams of America's first atomic bomb to his sister and brother-in-law. He then supposedly charged them with giving the diagrams to the Soviet consul in New York City.[50] Despite the Rosenbergs' declarations of innocence, following a sensational trial, both are sentenced to die.[51]

At the age of eleven, this is all I know of the Rosenberg case, but it frightens me to think we live in a country where the lives of one's parents can "legally" be taken. I feel strong empathy for Michael and Robbie Rosenberg, and I find myself wondering—if the lives of their parents can be taken by the government, then whose parents are safe?

Before leaving Atlanta the following day to begin the next leg of our trip, we drive to St. Paul's Episcopal Church on Ashby Street to pray for a safe journey and to pray for the people in our country hounded by an

---

50 In its race to get a satellite launched before the Soviets, the US government has been participating in a "red scare" that is running through the country. In 1951, based on accusations that they are Communists, twenty-five hundred people alleged to be security risks are dismissed from federal employment without due process. Among the group are suspected alcoholics and homosexuals. Meanwhile, the British accuse a nuclear scientist named Klaus Fuchs of spying for the Russians at the US Los Alamos atomic bomb project. The accusation leads to Fuchs's arrest by British agents and to a trial, in which he implicates several Americans, including Ethel and Julius Rosenberg. Charles Sellers, Henry May, Neil R. McMillen, *A Synopsis of American History Since the Civil War*, Sixth Edition, Volume H (Boston: Houghton Mifflin Company, 1985), 386–87.

51 David Burner, Elizabeth Fox-Genovese, Eugene D. Genovese, Forrest McDonald, *An American Portrait: A History of the United States*, Second Edition, Volume 2 (New York: Charles Scribner's Sons, 1985), 709.

overzealous government on a rampage to destroy communism. In spite of my prayers, I am upset by our country's atmosphere of suspicion and intolerance of people whose beliefs are different from ours.

We have packed fried chicken, fresh oranges, peaches, grapefruit, Madre's fudge, and the remainder of a cake from Dear. This is the food that will sustain us while we are on the road, because we won't be able to stop and eat in any restaurants between Atlanta and Washington, DC, and we don't have friends to stay with in any of the states between Atlanta and Washington. We have filled our thermos with ice that will melt into cool water, and we have brought along our childhood training potty, even though we have long since outgrown it. We take it with us because it is the only toilet we will have on the road when we can't find a wooded area in which to relieve ourselves. In fact, driving along one stretch of road, I am forced to use the potty inside the car as Daddy drives along a two-lane highway. Rosemary holds a towel up to the window so passing truck drivers can't look in and see me relieving myself. We will empty it when we come to a wooded area or find a service station that allows Negroes to use the toilets and empty and clean it there. If the station attendant refuses to let us go to his lavatory, we'll drive off without buying any gas, regardless of how low our tank is. Once, an attendant started pumping gas into our car before Dad asked where the restroom was. When the man said he didn't have one (meaning he didn't have one for Negroes), my father said, "Hold it right there. I don't want any gas." The pump showed two cents' worth of gas had already gone in to the tank. Daddy threw two pennies on the ground and drove to the station across the street. "Do you have a restroom?" he asked the attendant.

Having witnessed what happened to his competitor, the man told Dad, "Sho', right there."

"Okay, fill up the tank," my father told him, and we used the toilet and emptied and cleaned the potty.

We drive through Georgia, South and North Carolina, and into Virginia, where we board a ferry at Kiptopeke, near Cape Charles. The ferry ride, Rose's and my first, gives Dad a chance to sleep in the car and Mother an opportunity to take the two of us upstairs to stretch our legs. While Daddy naps, we stand outside on the upper level of the ferry, the wind blowing through our hair, talking with fellow travelers about where we are going and where they have been. A feeling of exhilaration rushes over me as I meet and rub shoulders with people of all races riding across the water on the ferry.

As soon as we spot land, Mother says it's time to go back to the car. Awake and rested, Dad steers our car into a long line of autos exiting the ferry, and we begin a medley of traveling songs: "Swinging on a Star," "Sentimental Journey," and "I've Got Sixpence." We travel through towns that look more like the hamlets of my textbooks than the southern cities I've grown up in, and Daddy begins to sing a favorite song of ours, "Daddy's Little Girl."

We drive through Maryland and Pennsylvania and then enter New Jersey and a stretch of highway so rank with the scent of oil refineries that we'd roll up the windows if it weren't so hot. Finally we see the sign for Newark, where Aunt Louise lives, and follow the arrows that lead to an exit ramp. We enter heavily populated streets where adults stand outside talking, young boys play stickball in the middle of the street, and girls jump rope in a style we've never seen before; they call it "double Dutch." After going several blocks, we pull up in front of the two-story brick building where Aunt Louise lives. This is where we will spend most of the summer.

Aunt Louise, the youngest of Madre's seven sisters, is a divorcée who lives alone. The location of her apartment gives Mother and Daddy better access to NYU's Physical Education Camp at Bear Mountain than Aunt Mabel's Manhattan apartment does. Daddy parks the car in front of Aunt Louise's two-story building and then gets out and rings the doorbell.

Aunt Louise's head pops out of a window on the second floor. "Hi! I'll be right down!"

Seconds later, she is at the front door of the building, laughing and hugging Dad, then leaving him on the sidewalk and coming to the car to embrace us one at a time. She leads us up a dimly lit staircase to her apartment, where we use the toilet. Rosemary and I help our parents unload our suitcases and the packages Madre has sent to Aunt Louise and Aunt Mabel. Aunt Louise says we have to empty the car completely in order to park it on the street. "Otherwise," she says, "people will break in and steal whatever they see" because of our out-of-state license plate. Since we don't have money to put the car in a garage for the summer, we must park on the street. In the mornings Mother and Daddy will drive the car to the NYU camp where they will take classes.

Tired from the long drive and hungry for the first hot food we have had since leaving Atlanta, we wash our hands and take seats at the kitchen table. After saying grace and giving thanks for a safe trip, we dig into Aunt Louise's rice with gravy, turnip greens, tossed salad, hot cornbread, and roast beef. Then Rosemary and I take baths and slip between freshly ironed sheets in a bedroom that is next to the kitchen. Mother and Dad have the bedroom farther back from the kitchen, next to the living room, and Aunt Louise has made a place to sleep in the large pantry adjoining her kitchen. Rose and I fall asleep listening to our aunt and parents talking and laughing, catching up on the time they have been apart.

Aunt Louise arises early the next morning to make breakfast for us before she leaves for Newark's Lincoln Hospital, where she is a dietician. Mother and Dad eat their breakfast and leave for the drive to Bear Mountain. Mom will register for two courses, and Dad will continue to work on his master's. Rosemary and I are left alone in Aunt Louise's apartment with strict instructions not to open the door for *anyone*. By ourselves in a big city for the first time, we promise to obey. At first we have a great time eating cold cereal all day, watching soap operas on the first television we've had access to since leaving Madre's, and looking at the action on the street below. But it doesn't take long for the sameness of each day to become monotonous for two youngsters accustomed to running barefoot through the grass, playing on our jungle gym and in our log cabin playhouse, and visiting friends on the other side of the vacant lot in Daytona Beach. Being locked inside a hot city apartment is suffocating, compared to what we are used to.

One day Uncle Dyche (Aunt Louise's ex-husband) comes to a spot beneath the living room window and calls to us from the street below. We look out the window and talk to him for a while. Then he asks us to buzz him in downstairs. He has always been one of our favorite uncles, and we love him in spite of the fact that he and Aunt Louise are divorced, so we let him into the apartment. We tell him about members of the family he hasn't seen in a long time and bring him up to date on what we have been doing. We have a great time sharing family news, and he seems to understand how hard it is for us to spend days on end alone in the apartment. We are sad to discover that he has become an alcoholic since the days when we were little girls, but our love for him lets us overlook this weakness. Before he leaves he gives each of us money to spend on "something for yourselves." We watch from the upstairs window as he exits the building and talks with people on the street before continuing down the block. After he has gone a couple of blocks, he turns and heads back to the bar across the street from Aunt Louise's, unaware that Rose and I are still watching from behind the curtains. Late in the day we see him stumble out of the same bar on the arm of another patron and wander off into the evening.

The following day, in spite of the fact that we've been warned not to leave the apartment, the money Uncle Dyche has given us is burning such a hole in our pockets that we decide to go spend it. Rose stands in the upstairs window while I go to the corner candy store for goodies. She buzzes me in downstairs, and I run up with the contraband that the two of us devour: potato chips, candy, ice cream bars, cookies, and sodas—Orange Crush for her, grape soda for me. We hide the wrappers before the adults get back and make sure we eat dinner as if we've been waiting for it all day.

On the days that Uncle Dyche doesn't come by the apartment, we find other things to do to keep from getting bored. One afternoon Rosemary climbs outside the kitchen window and onto the roof of an attached house to bring in oranges that have fallen off a tree. The next day I go out to get more, but because I am heavier than Rosie, I make so much noise that a lady appears downstairs on the sidewalk and yells at me to stop stealing her oranges. I apologize, promise not to take any more, and crawl back to the safety of Aunt Louise's kitchen, shocked by the accusation. Back home in Florida, fruit that falls from the trees is free for anyone to take. We think the same thing is true up here, but when Mother and Dad come home, Aunt Louise tells them her neighbor reported Rosemary and me for stealing her fruit. Dad gives us a tongue lashing—first for going outside the apartment and second for taking fruit that isn't ours, but he doesn't whip us. He hasn't given me a whipping in over a year, when he whipped me for something he thought I did, despite my protestations. Afterward, when he discovered he was wrong, he apologized and promised never to hit me again. It was a promise he never broke.

That day he warns that we could have fallen off the roof and broken bones or killed ourselves, and he makes us promise we will not to go out on the roof again. The next morning when we get up, we find that a bowl filled with grapefruit, oranges, mangoes, and tangerines has been left on the kitchen table.

Getting together to pool resources and help one another out is a Mitchell family commitment that spills over into our generation. So it is no surprise when Aunt Mabel and Uncle Ezra take a bus from New York to Newark bringing food and clothing for us. Aunt Mabel has made the clothes from material left over at the French mending and weaving shop where she works at Grand Central Station. The dresses she's made have delicate lace and beautiful tucks stitched into the fabric. We share an evening full of memories and laughter before she and Uncle Ezra head back to Manhattan.

A few weeks after Aunt Mabel and Uncle Ezra's visit, Mother and Dad's schoolwork eases up enough for them to plan a trip to Palisades Amusement Park, a new adventure for Rosie and me. As youngsters we have gone to carnivals and circuses put on by the touring companies that traveled from town to town, but we've never been inside an amusement park before. At Palisades Amusement Park we ride the Ferris wheel, drive bumper cars, get on the Virginia Reel, and ride the roller coaster. When Mother was a girl, there were two places she dreamed of taking her children one day—Palisades Amusement Park and Coney Island in New York.

After the treat of going to the amusement park, weeks go by with the same dullness of soap operas, game shows, and people-watching from Aunt Louise's window. Then for the last weeks of August, we pack up all our things and move from Aunt Louise's apartment to Aunt Mabel and Uncle Ezra's apartment in New York. I am filled with excitement as we enter the Lincoln Tunnel; then I panic and begin hyperventilating when my claustrophobia kicks in. Mother unknowingly adds to my anxiety by explaining why uniformed men are stationed in the booths along the wall.[52] "To make sure the cars stay in their lanes and that drivers don't blow their car horns," she tells us. After what seems like an eternity, the mouth of the tunnel comes mercifully into view, and we emerge.

Aunt Mabel and Uncle Ezra live at 1947 Seventh Avenue in apartment number six on the third floor. After parking the car in front of their building, we take turns carrying luggage upstairs to their third-floor apartment. Ascending the second and third floor sets of stairs, I look out over the marble windowsills at the beauty of the avenue below. Stately trees in the center island give serenity to the busyness of the six-lane boulevard where cars whiz up and down, and people dodge between them, crossing against traffic lights.

Inside the apartment, we follow a long, dimly lit hall past a bathroom to the right near the front door and two bedrooms on the right midway down the hall. The dining room is straight ahead at the end of

---

52 The small stations with glass fronts where men were stationed no longer exist.

the hall, followed by an eat-in kitchen and a pantry, where Aunt Mabel has set up a cot for herself. She has given Rosemary and me a room at the front of the apartment just off the living room. Our bedroom is connected to the living room by a set of French doors. A lovely gray-and-white marble mantel graces the living-room fireplace, and a gold-leaf mirror hangs above it. A brocade couch similar to Madre's faces the fireplace, and there is a coffee table in front of it. The living-room windows look out onto Seventh Avenue and have two wingback chairs in front of each of them. A television is between the windows.

At night, Rosemary and I close the French doors and open the couch in our room and sleep on the bed that unfolds. After we are in our pajamas, we turn off the lights, open the French doors again, and watch television from the bed in the adjoining room. Uncle Ezra retires to the first bedroom down the hall, and Mother and Dad to the second. They share a small anteroom with a marble sink, a mirror, and a window across from the sink that overlooks an alleyway between their apartment building and the one next door at 1945 Seventh Avenue.

In the wee hours of the morning, after the *Late Late Show* has ended, and Rosemary has fallen asleep, I slip out of bed to sit in one of the chairs in front of the living-room window and watch the gleaming yellow taxis that speed up and down the avenue and the people calling to one another like it is midday. This is worlds away from our little southern city of lightning bugs, streetlights that go off at ten o'clock, and crickets that chirp through the night. Our town, with its one Negro-owned cab company and two taxis to take care of everyone, is no match for this city. In Daytona Beach, if both cabs are busy, the caller is told how long the wait will be before one of them is sent to pick him or her up. One driver has gone to get Miz So-and-so, and after he leaves her off, he has to pick up a prescription from the drugstore for Mr. Whoever before he can head to your house. We are told, "It'll be 'round about thirty-five minutes till he gets to that part o' town." Daytona Beach, with its blacktopped streets and disappearing sidewalks, is no match for New York's City's wide boulevards, high curbs, and fast-paced, all-night action, and I decide immediately that this is the way a city should be—full, rich, pulsating with life. On those summer nights sitting in Aunt Mabel's window watching the street below, I fall in love with New York City.

In the morning, Aunt Mabel rises early to shop for fresh vegetables so Uncle Ezra can make his daily juice. While she is gone, our uncle ties up the only bathroom in the house. He stays in it so long that Aunt Mabel has to coax him out when she returns from shopping so that the rest of us can use the toilet. After that first morning, Rosemary and I get up early to take care of our toilet needs before he wakes up. His extended morning ritual leads us to christen the bathroom, "Uncle Ezra's office." Each day when he emerges, he looks and smells as if he has been dressed by a valet. Clean-shaven, in a white dress shirt and dark tie, a pair of pants that match his dark suit, and shoes that look as if they've been professionally shined, he heads to the kitchen. Every strand of his wavy salt-and-pepper hair is pomaded into place, and his manicured fingernails are buffed to a shine. Donning a chef's apron, he washes the vegetables Aunt Mabel has brought home—carrots, spinach, celery, cucumbers, apples, beets, and fresh horseradish—and then peels and cuts them into bite-size pieces before feeding them to his electric juicer, all the while extolling the virtues of fresh vegetable juice to Rosemary and me. As soon as the juice is ready, he insists we drink the thick murky liquid that plops into the two glasses he has set aside for us. Today my sister and I go through the same juicing ritual, but back then it was all we could do to keep from gagging as we forced the concoction down.

After we've had our juice, everyone assembles around the dining-room table for a breakfast of grits, ham, eggs, and fresh muffins. When we are finished, Uncle Ezra and Aunt Mabel leave for work—she to the French mending shop in Grand Central Station and he to his job as a redcap at Grand Central. Before Mother and Dad leave for a new set of classes at NYU's Greenwich Village campus, they warn Rosemary and me not to open Aunt Mabel's front door for anyone. We follow their instructions to the letter, and because we do, Uncle Ezra cannot get back into his own apartment the day he leaves home without his front door keys and returns to get them. When we hear banging at the door, we turn up the volume on the television set to drown it out. That night when he comes home and asks why we didn't open the door for him, we remind him that we were told not to open it for anyone. Aunt Mabel falls out laughing when she learns he was locked out, but he doesn't see the humor in it at all.

During the days when the adults are out, we watch soap operas, stare out the window at sleight-of-hand games and checkers and dominoes matches on old card tables, and delight in the squeals of children running in and out of the fire hydrants on the street as they keep cool in the sizzling heat. We are intrigued by disputes on front stoops and amazed that taxis screech to a halt when people step off the curb and hold up a hand.

In the evening when the adults are back at home, we get permission to go to the candy store on the corner and buy sherbet for dessert after dinner. One day Rosemary races ahead of me to Aunt Mabel's, and I dawdle along, enjoying the sights on the block. Suddenly I find myself face-to-face with my boxing idol, Sugar Ray Robinson, who has just parked his pink Cadillac in front of Aunt Mabel's apartment building and is headed to the corner of 118th Street—the same corner I am walking away from. As we pass, our eyes meet, and I swear he smiles at me. Completely overcome, I can't even manage a hello. But by the time I reach the top step of the third-floor landing and Aunt Mabel's front door, I am talking a mile a minute in one long run-on sentence.

"I just saw Sugar Ray Robinson—he has the smoothest skin—he passed right by me—he smiled at me—he has the most gorgeous smile—he was wearing a tailored suit, and his hair was slicked back."

When I finally take a breath, Aunt Mabel says, "He comes here almost every week to visit friends around the corner."

"What! Sugar Ray Robinson visits people around the corner and no one told me!?"

As soon as dinner is over I sit in the living-room window and wait for him to come back to his car. I daydream about going back downstairs and collapsing as soon as he rounds the corner, so he can sweep me up and carry me off in his pink Cadillac. For years, I have sat with Madre, Mother, Dad, and numerous aunts and uncles watching Madre's television, screaming for him to win the fight and then comb his conked hair back for the cameras after he's won. "That's right, Sugar," I'd yell at the television. "Don't let 'em think he hurt you." Now I'm sitting in the window around the corner from where he is, waiting for him to return to his car. When he appears and gets into his car with friends and drives away, I have a memory that will carry me on a cloud for months to come, and a story I will share with friends as soon as we are back at home.

A week after my Sugar Ray Robinson sighting, Mother and Dad take us to see the Statue of Liberty. We climb all the way up into the crown to look out over the harbor. Then we head for the Empire State Building to view the city through high-powered binoculars. We leave there and go to Grand Central Station, where we visit Aunt Mabel at the French mending shop and then join Uncle Ezra for lunch at the Automat, which the adults are all excited about. The Automat is a place where customers get trays, line up, and choose their food from an array of plates revolving behind little glass doors. Customers move on in a line toward a cashier. For the life of me, I cannot understand what all the excitement is about. The Automat feels just like an upscale school cafeteria to me but with better food, especially the banana cream pie, but New Yorkers are excited to have a place they can go to and get a tasty, quick lunch without having to sit and wait for an order to be filled. After lunch Daddy heads back to school, while Mother, Rose, and I head uptown to St. Patrick's Cathedral for a tour before returning to Aunt Mabel and Uncle Ezra's apartment.

On Saturday, Aunt Louise arrives at Aunt Mabel's with a friend to take us to Jones Beach for a day of picnicking and swimming. She comes back on Sunday evening to take us to Coney Island, where Mother fulfills her dream of taking Rosemary and me on a ride called the Cyclone—a roller coaster whose eighty-five-foot drop is the steepest in the country. Dad, who has never experienced the ride, says he'll go in the car with Rosemary and me to keep us from being afraid. Mother volunteers to ride with the daughters of Aunt Louise's gentleman friend. Aunt Mabel and Uncle Ezra have stayed at home.

As the safety bar locks across the three of us, Dad, who is in the middle, puts an arm around Rosemary and me and says, "Don't be afraid, now. Daddy's here." The ride begins with cars slowly climbing a wooden frame that creaks and moans every inch of the way up. I look straight ahead, becoming extremely nervous when I am unable to see anything but a starry band of cobalt-blue sky. Suddenly we are plunged into a drop so steep that sheer centrifugal force lifts us off the seat and sends us into a terrifying free fall. Dad's arms fly from around the two of us, and he grabs the safety bar and holds on for dear life. The sisters in the car behind us with Mother let out a bloodcurdling scream, and before I can catch my breath, we've begun another ascent. At the top of the second plateau, we find ourselves staring out into space at a thousand twinkling stars. With our stomachs still back at the top of the first drop, our car abruptly whips around at a right angle and plunges downward into a death-defying spiral. People all around us are screaming and praying out loud. My hands and Dad's are in a viselike grip around the safety bar, but my daredevil sister claps and yells, "Wheee!" Frozen to the seat, too frightened to turn my head, I shift my eyes sideways to my father and see him staring straight ahead, zombielike.

We go through numerous dips, twists, and turns before coming to an abrupt stop that throws our bodies forward before slamming them back against the seat. I attempt to stand with rubbery knees. I step off the wooden platform, hoping my feet will find solid ground. Dad tests his sea legs. Mother stumbles out of the car behind us, laughing as her two companions hold on to each other feeling their way off the platform, neither of them trusting to stand alone. The ride has only lasted a few minutes, but it feels as if a whole lifetime has gone by. When Dad finds his voice, he asks if we want to go again. Unable to say a word, I shake my head no, but Rosemary jumps up and down and squeals, "Yes!" Dad slowly moves away from the ride toward a Nathan's hot dog stand, where he plops down on a bench. "Ya'll enjoy the rest of the rides," he says. "I'll be right here when you're through."

When we have had our fill of bumper cars, the Ferris wheel, the Tilt-a-Whirl, and other wild rides, we return to Nathan's and pick our dad up for the return trip to Harlem and the safety of Aunt Mabel's apartment. Back at Aunt Mabel's, we burst through the door with stories about the fun we've had. Aunt Mabel and Uncle Ezra listen enthusiastically until Dad begins to describe the terrifying ride on the Cyclone. As he tells of his fear, Aunt Mabel laughs so hard she falls backward in a chair.

"A big old grown man like you ought to be ashamed of yourself, being scared of a roller-coaster ride," she says. "No ride in the world would scare me!"

"Have you ever been on the Cyclone, Mabel?" Daddy asks.

"No, but I'm not afraid of *any* ride."

Our ninety-eight-pound, five-foot-tall aunt is the same person who, as a girl, frightened her mother and older sisters by putting a monkey in the flour bin, the one who coaxed her younger siblings into throwing fruit and raw eggs down from a tree onto well-dressed passersby. She is the sister who so embarrassed her two older sisters (Madre and Aunt Lucille) that they petitioned their father to put her in a different school. She's the one everyone in her Harlem neighborhood knows by name, so we don't doubt her fearlessness—but Daddy does.

"The Cyclone's no ordinary roller-coaster ride, Mabel, I'm tellin' you."

"*No* ride can frighten me."

"Okay," Dad challenges, "come back with us next weekend." She accepts.

When the weekend arrives, we jam ourselves into Aunt Louise's friend's car for a return trip to Coney Island with Uncle Ezra, Aunt Mabel, and Aunt Louise. As soon as we get to the Cyclone, Rosemary and Mother jump into the first available car. Determined not to be outdone by my younger sister, I enter the car behind theirs with Aunt Louise. Aunt Mabel gets into a car with the person behind us because both Dad and Uncle Ezra refuse to ride.

The moment we plunge down the first heart-stopping drop, Aunt Louise flings herself against me and begins to scream so hysterically that I don't think she'll ever stop. Pinned against the seat, the air knocked out of me, I struggle to get the full force of my aunt's dead weight off my thin frame. Our car climbs the second plateau and shoots around the bend like a rocket. Shrieks and prayers of riders accompany this ride as they did the first one until we come to a halt. Rosemary and Mother hop out of the car in front of ours with broad smiles. An attendant has to pull Aunt Louise from the car she and I are in, because she is laughing and crying so hard she can hardly move. Aunt Mabel wobbles out of the car behind ours completely disheveled. When she finds her voice she declares, "There ought to be a law against a ride like that!"

She is just about to look for the Cyclone operator and give him a piece of her mind when a heavyset woman and her husband stumble out of their car. The woman's wig is hanging from one side of her head, and her pocketbook dangles from the bend in her elbow. Her slightly built husband wobbles off looking as if he's been pummeled mercilessly. The brim of his straw hat hangs around his neck like an African necklace; the edges of the crown are smashed down over his eyebrows. The crown is stuck to the top of his head. He feels his way along the walls of the ride like a blind man and then gingerly steps down while his wife storms off to find "the man in charge." Dad leans toward Aunt Mabel and whispers smugly, "I told you, Mabel."

"They ought to be locked up for scaring people to death like that!" she yells.

———◆———

BEFORE WE KNOW IT summer is over, and we are packing our car with everything Aunt Mabel and Aunt Louise can think of to send back to Madre. Early in the morning, Aunt Mabel stands alone on the sidewalk next to our car, confessing, "I surely hate to see you go." We pull away from the curb waving good-bye to the small frame of our aunt, lost against the vastness of the New York City skyline.

# CHAPTER 8

# THE RAINBOW CONNECTION[53]

FOR THREE MONTHS WE have been free to mingle with all kinds of people: white people who waited on us with a smile, Puerto Ricans who spoke Spanish to us in the street, Haitians who addressed us in patois at the corner candy store, and all hues and stripes of people in between. We have gone into public restrooms anytime we needed to use the toilet and taken trips to Palisades Park, Jones Beach, and Coney Island without thinking twice. Now we are headed back to Florida where the legal division between the races is strictly enforced, back to a place that stands as a constant reminder of everything we have left behind in New York. I savor the last memories of summer as we begin our drive home.

Motoring through New Jersey, Delaware, Maryland, Virginia, and the Carolinas, we consume the food our aunts have packed for us. In Atlanta, we deliver packages to Madre that her sisters have sent and spend a night before starting out for Jacksonville. We spend another

53 Written by Paul Williams and Kenneth Ascher, 1979.

night with Dear and Grandpa, sharing adventures of the summer, before continuing on to Daytona Beach.

Back in Daytona Beach, I regale my friends with a blow-by-blow account of the day I saw Sugar Ray Robinson. I describe St. Patrick's Cathedral and our climb to the top of the Statue of Liberty. I describe the view of New York City from the Empire State Building, and I talk about the way taxis race up and down the boulevards, screeching to a halt when someone raises a hand in the air. They listen in awe as I describe New York's night life from my perch at Aunt Mabel's window, and they are envious when I tell them I was up until midnight watching television. In our front yard, the signal of the end of summer can be heard in the distant boom-ditty-boom of a big bass drum far away on the Bethune-Cookman campus. The rhythms of the snare drums send Rosemary and me into the house for our batons and back out to the street to practice twirling and tossing them into the air and catching them behind our backs as we prepare for another season as majorettes. We mimic the steps of bands we have seen through the years at half-time shows during football games. FAMU's (Florida A&M University) strutters dipping and spinning behind their prancing drum major, and Southern's band members with their famous 320 steps a minute.

A few weeks later we are set for the tilt of the maroon and gold, Bethune-Cookman's annual homecoming, which the entire Negro community turns out to see. The pregame parade wends its way up Second Avenue as I, the head majorette, lead my troop of girls through the Negro section of town adorned in a gold-and-white satin uniform, high white majorette hat with gold braid, and white boots with gold tassels. Two rows of younger girls follow me dressed in green-and-white satin dresses. I can hear little girls on the sidelines say to their mothers, "I'm gonna be a majorette like her when I get big!" I prance and spin, twirl, and throw my baton in the air as we make our way up the crowded streets. At the end of the parade, we fall out and join people on the sidelines to witness what's left of the show. Afterward, Rosemary and I go home to change clothes for the football game.

Back in the days when we lived in Texas, the two of us sat on the bench with Dad and the players, huddled under a big wool blanket and waterproof poncho. We were just feet away from players running up and down the field in the bitter cold or chilling rain, eating hot tamales and drinking cocoa to keep warm, cheering as the wind got knocked out of opposing players tackled right in front of us. Seeing helmets clash and mud squish between their cleats, yelling for our boys as they tight-roped their way along the sidelines, a football cradled in their arms as they moved toward the goal, was heavenly for us.

In those days, we worried when assistant coaches had to hold Daddy back to keep him from grabbing an official who'd made a bad call. And we got a ringside view the night he tore a plank from a wooden bench and fitted it to the leg of a visiting player who'd been hurt during the game. Taking adhesive tape from a trainer's box, he made a splint with the wood and wrapped the boy's leg so well that a doctor in the city's emergency room refused to undo it. He said the leg had been set so well, it didn't need a cast. At the end of that game my chest nearly burst with pride when players lifted my father to their shoulders and carried him out of the stadium to the cheers of the crowd. But those days are gone now. At Bethune-Cookman we have to sit in the stands with Mother, a long way from the excitement of the game.

Arriving at the stadium, we sit as close to the band as we can get and cheer the Wildcats on. At halftime, we watch the battle of the bands and then fill up on hot dogs and sodas. Then, because the stench from the restroom is so rank, we crawl under the bleachers to urinate, shielding each other while we take turns relieving ourselves.

During the week Rosie and I attend skull practice[54] with Daddy while Mother goes to a faculty meeting. Rosemary and I enter a classroom with Daddy and begin our homework, while he draws Xs and Os in solid and broken lines across the blackboard. Soon players saunter into the classroom from the dining hall and take their seats to listen to Dad explain the plays that now fill the chalkboard. Rosie and I learn them, too, and look for them at the next football game.

---

THE START OF SCHOOL in a new building is uneventful, but Bonner Elementary (a public school) is nothing like Keyser. It exudes new smells—wet milk cartons, fresh paint, and newly waxed floors, as opposed to the old wood-framed building on the college campus. An American flag hangs at the front of my new classroom, and we begin each morning standing in front of it with our right hands over our hearts reciting the Pledge of Allegiance. The words "under God" have just been added, and our teacher wants to make sure we don't forget them.

After the pledge we sing songs from World Wars I and II—"Over There" and "From the Halls of Montezuma"—embracing a kind of patriotism that was absent at Keyser Lab. We sing, "This Is My Country," "The House I Live In," and "Bless This House," in the hope, it seems, that we will feel a deeper appreciation for our country. It is here at Bonner Elementary that I become aware of the panic sweeping the nation regarding communism and fear of the Russians winning the

---

54 A meeting the coach holds to teach his team new plays and special strategies.

Cold War, taking control of our country, and making "Reds" out of all of us. We are told that the only way to protect ourselves in this Cold War is to make better bombs than Russia makes. If we don't stay ahead of them, our teacher says, we could end up like the people in Europe who fell victim to Hitler and Mussolini, or those in China and Japan who are under the thumbs of Mao Tse-tung and Hirohito. We learn about the concentration camps here at home where Japanese Americans were interred because, our teacher tells us, of the color of their skin. But there is no mention of the Holocaust or concentration camps in Europe, so our knowledge of the war in that part of the world does not have the human face it has here at home with regard to the Japanese. The teacher ends our history lesson by assuring us that American troops have fought overseas to make the world safe for democracy.

Fear of a Russian invasion sends us crouching beneath school desks at the sound of air-raid sirens and propels us toward the nearest bomb shelter or outside into the schoolyard. It doesn't seem to matter that we don't understand who the Russians are or why they want to change us; we are terrified of being captured by them.

In October, Bonner Elementary announces plans to start a school band. Mother and Daddy say Rose and I may choose the instruments we want and become members. What I really want is a set of drums, but I know my parents will never agree to let me have them, so I ask for a trumpet. But Dad, who plays the trumpet, says it will ruin my lips and suggests I try the flute, so that is what I settle for. Rosemary chooses the clarinet. We work diligently to master our new instruments and become good enough to play in the school's concert and marching bands. The school orchestra performs in concerts in the school auditorium for teachers, parents, siblings, and friends. Our friend Frenchie comes with

Mother and Dad to hear us play and spends many evenings in our home sitting through our performances of the Fat Lady (bound with pillows held by belts and straps under oversize clothes) and the Thin Lady (who has been twisted into a sheet so tight it is hard to breathe). She and our parents roar with laughter at the characters we create, especially the adventures of "Mrs. En and Mrs. Dale" who perform slapstick routines using bits and pieces of conversations we've picked up from the adults.

Soon basketball season is underway with a crop of exceptional athletes Dad has recruited, including a standout from Philadelphia named John Chaney. He has been turned down by Temple University (the school he really wanted to play for) because of his skin color.[55] Chaney becomes a hero in Florida, where people come from all over the state to see him play. Nobody handles a ball like he does, dribbling rings around opponents. Sometimes when the team is on the road, Dad will wait to start Chaney just to build the crowd's anticipation. If Carl Richardson makes a great play or Mitch Payne dribbles through someone's legs, people in the stands can be heard whispering, "Is *that* Chaney? Is that Chaney?" When he finally enters the game, there is no doubt as to who he is. He's a magician with the ball.

At home games, Rose and I sit next to Mother in the stands behind Daddy and the team, cheering them to victory, while a pep squad whips the crowd into a frenzy. Girls in knee-length purple-and-gold pleated skirts and crewneck sweaters with megaphones and boys in dark pants and sweaters that match the girls' prance back and forth, leading us in syncopated cheers and rhythmic stomping and clapping that rock the stands.

---

55  He will return to Philadelphia years later to coach championship teams at Temple.

One boy breaks into an imitation of the St. Vitus dance, grabbing his chest, his back, then his legs, yelling, "I got it!"

The answer roars back from the crowd, "What?"

"I got it!"

"What?"

"It's in my head!"

"What?"

"It's in my chest!"

"What?"

"It's in my back!"

"What?"

"It's in my legs!"

"What?"

"I got the spirit!"

"What?"

"I got the spirit!"

Soon everybody breaks into "Give me that old BC spirit," to the tune of "That Old-Time Religion," clapping out a pulsating beat so hypnotic that even Mrs. Bethune looks as if she wants to join in.

At halftime, students from the physical education department take to the floor to build human pyramids and perform tumbling stunts. When they are finished, Rosemary and I grab a basketball and dribble up and down the court, shooting baskets over one another to the applause of halftime onlookers. At the end of the game everyone stands to sing the alma mater before filing out of the gym. Mother, Rose, and I sit in the empty stands, waiting for Dad to emerge from the locker room, while sweepers push big brooms across the floor and clean up the empty gym. By the time the cleanup crew has begun turning out the lights, Dad emerges from the locker room.

On Sundays, Rosemary and I set out for church, clutching collection plate coins that have been tied in the corners of our handkerchiefs and speaking to neighbors and friends along the way. "Good morning, Mrs. Dubose. Hello, President Moore." In Sunday school, we sing hymns, memorize psalms, and learn lines for seasonal pageants. One year I play the Christmas angel; another year, Queen Esther. This Easter I will be a mother rabbit, but the role that really made me famous took place in Austin, Texas, before we arrived in Daytona Beach. That Easter morning, I greeted the congregation with the words, "Jesus arose from the desk!" For the life of me I could not understand why members of the congregation struggled so hard to keep from laughing. I knew no one could come back from the dead, and I thought they knew it, too. The line I'd been given to learn, "Jesus arose from the dead," was obviously a mistake, so I corrected it with the only thing that made sense to me.

In these uncertain times of the "Red fear," the one thing that gives me solace is my membership in St. Timothy's Episcopal Church where, in addition to Sunday school, I begin Saturday catechism class. There Father Peaks prepares ten of us for confirmation by having us memorize rosary prayers and centuries-old creeds and complete workbook assignments.

At the end of Lent, Rosemary and I join the parade of children who walk up the center aisle toward the altar to leave the mite boxes we have filled with nickels and pennies during the Lenten season. Just before Easter, the members of my catechism class approach the altar rail—the girls in white dresses, white lace doilies on our heads, white gloves, and white socks, the boys in navy suits. Kneeling before the bishop, we are, one by one, confirmed in the faith. I arise with a sense of wonder at having become an adult in the eyes of the Church. On Easter I am proud to kneel at the Communion rail, extend my hands to receive my first Communion wafer, and take my first sip of wine—symbols of the body and blood of Christ.

The academic and liturgical years move forward, the spring bringing with it the conflict I usually feel on Mother's Day and Father's Day. I get a warm feeling singing, "M is for the million things she gave me," but I feel sad for children I pass on the way to church. I wear a red flower that tells everyone my mother is alive, but some children wear white ones to signify that their mothers are dead. I often wonder why there is a tradition that makes them expose their pain every year. On Father's Day, I hate seeing Daddy in his white flower, and I can't imagine how hard it must have been for him when he was a little boy to be one of the few children whose father was dead.

Rosemary and I enjoy attending our new school until the day we start home after band practice and are followed by a group of children yelling, "Hey, crip!" to Rosemary. Without thinking, I spin around and hit one of them as hard as I can with the carrying case of my flute. Stunned, they scatter as Rosemary and I run for home as fast as our legs can carry us. When we arrive, Mother and Daddy demand to know what happened, and we tell them. They don't want us fighting, they say, but hasten to add I was right to defend my sister.

The next day as we walk to school, we approach each tree and every corner with fear, expecting to be jumped by the kids who teased Rosie the day before, but no one bothers us that day or any day after that. In fact, the kids who did the teasing eventually become our friends.

Meanwhile at Bethune-Cookman, Mrs. Bethune is holding her annual fund-raiser, inviting famous people to observe students in their classrooms. Many of her guests are artists who tour the classrooms by day and perform for paying audiences at night. The special friendship Rosemary and I have with her leads her to seek us out and make sure we meet her guests. Dr. Ralph Bunche,[56] the first Negro Nobel Peace Prize recipient, is asked to be the main speaker at the school's fiftieth anniversary celebration. Marian Anderson, the first Negro singer to perform at the Metropolitan Opera, comes and gives a performance that year, too. But the artist Rosie and I are really enchanted with is a young classical pianist and composer in her twenties named Philippa Schuyler who is world famous. We find her concert mesmerizing.

———

A FEW WEEKS INTO the spring, my menstrual period begins, but not having been prepared for it, I am terrified to see blood on the toilet seat. Thinking I have injured myself, I search for the injury but can't find it. I don't know that Rosemary has seen the blood, too, and has told Mother, who calls me into her bedroom for a talk. She begins by telling me our female dog, Thunder Mike, is in heat. I listen without the faintest idea of why she is talking to me about the dog. At the end of the talk, she gives me a book that I take to my room. Flipping the pages, I see drawings like the ones in my Dick and Jane primer. I begin to read, trying to figure out what this book has to do with Thunder Mike.

---

56 On whom the Nobel Peace Prize was bestowed because, as United Nations secretary of the Palestine Commission, Dr. Bunche was instrumental in settling the 1948 Arab-Israeli dispute.

While I'm reading, Daddy returns from track practice and goes to his and Mother's bedroom. Then he enters our room and sits beside me on my bed. Because he teaches health education, he feels comfortable talking to me about the way my body is changing. He says this is a wonderful time in my life, says I am being prepared for womanhood. He goes through portions of the book with me, explaining how important personal hygiene is on the days that I have my period. Then he leaves. Continuing to read the book, I begin to understand what is happening to me. Daddy returns and gives me a box of sanitary napkins. He says I'll find instructions and illustrations inside that explain how I am supposed to use them. My father has ushered me into womanhood so lovingly that I promise myself that when I have a little girl, I will remember this day and prepare her with the same gentleness and concern.

The remainder of the year slips quickly by, and in the late spring we take a trip to Tougaloo College in Mississippi for what I assume is a trip where Dad will scout a team. While we are there, Dean Branch takes us on a tour of the campus. Our last stop is to a run-down house at the back of the campus with torn screens on all three porches, holes and splinters in the hardwood floors, and an exterior that hasn't been painted in years. No one has lived here for years, we are told as we enter. In the same breath, the dean turns to Rosemary and me and says, "Since this is a three-bedroom house, you girls can each have your own bedroom."

*What in the world is he talking about?* I wonder. *Mother and Daddy can't be thinking about leaving our beautiful new home in Florida for this abandoned shack in Mississippi.* But that is exactly what they are doing, and at the end of the academic year, they both resign their positions at Bethune-Cookman College. Dad accepts a job as athletic director and head coach of four different sports at Tougaloo College in Mississippi.

We say our good-byes to the Ferrells, the Bigginses, the Engrams, and Mrs. Bryon, who invites the four of us for dinner and singing around her piano. The thought of never being gathered round this piano again is a painful thing to imagine.

A few days later Rosemary and I visit Mrs. Bethune to thank her for the time she has spent with us and for the book she gave us at the beginning of the previous year called *Mary McLeod Bethune*.[57] In it there is "A Foreword to My Young Readers" that says:

*All my life I have worked with youth. I have begged for them and fought for them and lived for them and in them. My story is their story. Because I see young Mary McLeod in all struggling boys and girls, I can never rest while there is still something that I can do to make the ground firmer under their feet, to make their efforts more productive, to bring their goals nearer, to make their faith in God and their fellow men a little stronger. May those who read this volume...gather from it a new confidence in themselves, a new faith in God, and a willingness to work hard to reach the goals of a good life. Mine has not been an easy road. Very few of my generation found life easy or wanted it that way. Your road may be somewhat less rugged because of the struggles we have made. The doors of progress and advancement will open to the steady, persistent pressure of your skilled hands and your trained minds, your*

---

57 Catherine Owens Peare, *Mary McLeod Bethune* (New York: Vanguard Press, 1951).

*stout hearts and your prayers, more readily than they opened to me. I rejoice now, as I look back down my seventy-five years that I have been able to help in the movement for the extension of brotherhood through greater interracial understanding. I rejoice that in my own way I have been able to demonstrate that there is a place in God's sun for the youth "farthest down" who has the vision, the determination, and the courage to reach it.*

In a somewhat unsteady script, the book is signed, "To Nell and Rosemary with Love, Mary McLeod Bethune."

On the day she gives this book to us, she challenges us to find the courage to follow her example, and she extracts a promise from each of us to make the world a better place for the children who come after us, the way past generations of our people have made it better for us. We leave her feeling sad in the fact that with this move, we will be taken to a place where her personal memories and sage guidance are no longer right across the campus from where we live.

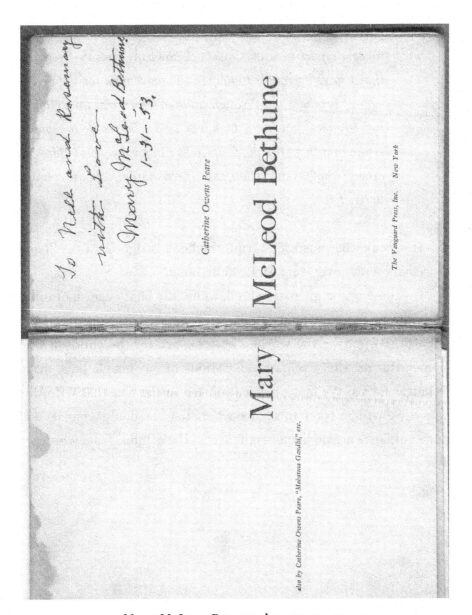

**MARY MCLEOD BETHUNE'S AUTOGRAPH**

# CHAPTER 9

# I'M ON MY WAY AND
# I WON'T TURN BACK[58]

THE MOVERS ARRIVE EARLIER than they are scheduled to come, sending Mother into a panic. Suddenly she must determine what will go ahead to Mississippi and what will be packed for our trip to New York, where Dad will finally submit his master's thesis. Rosemary and I help with the packing, while Daddy mops the floors and cleans the bathroom. Mother rushes out to the clothesline to get the sheets she has washed, sheets we slept on last night. Meanwhile, movers begin loading furniture into their truck. When Mother returns from the backyard with clean sheets to pack, she is horrified to discover the movers have packed almost all the furniture, including a dresser where her checkbook with all the money we will need for our summer in New York is stored. She races out to the van, describes the dresser, and asks if they will look for it. The movers, who have no idea why she wants to find the dresser, go inside and take a look, but the van is packed so tightly that they can't find it. Frantic,

58 Based on a Negro spiritual, "I'm on My Way to Canaan Land."

Mother insists that they let her look inside, which they do, but as soon as she enters the truck, she realizes the piece is so far inside that she won't be able to find it, either, and it is too late for movers to unpack all the furniture that is in front of it.

The van pulls away as Mother tries to determine the next best step for getting money for our trip. She goes to the Daytona Beach Savings and Loan, where she has done business for the three years that we've lived in the city. Explaining her dilemma, she requests a loan to carry us through the summer, promising to pay the money back as soon as she unpacks her bankbook in Mississippi. Like many southern businesses of the day, the Daytona Beach S&L makes it difficult for Negroes to do business, and in spite of the fact that she has been with them for years, authorities tell her they will provide the loan only if she produces her bankbook, which they know is in the van headed for Mississippi. Since these are the days before credit cards exist, Mother doesn't know what to do.

Meanwhile, we continue making farewell rounds to friends. We visit Sonya and her family and say good-bye to Frenchie, who Rosemary and I can't believe is not making this trip with us, too. With our home empty of everything, we spend the last night with the Biggins family. After a romp with the Airedale puppies and a wonderful dinner, Rosemary and Warner go to sleep. Franklin and I watch the grown-ups play bridge and then go off alone to talk about all the things we will miss doing together—trips to the airport and the Dairy Queen, rolling in the grass, and watching puppies being born. Then we finally fall asleep, too.

The following morning we say good-bye and begin the drive to Jacksonville, where we spend a few days with Dear and Grandpa

Singleton before heading to Atlanta. It is really painful to realize that our annual summer visits to Jacksonville will end with our move to Mississippi.

In Atlanta, I am riveted to the televised public investigation into the activities of Senator Joseph McCarthy. These hearings help me make the connection between the communism we have been discussing in school and the accusations against people accused of being communists here in the United States. Like a madman, the senator bangs his shoe on the table where television microphones are set up and yells at his questioners.

While I am fixated on the television, Mother works up the nerve to ask Madre and Papa to lend her the money we need to make it through the summer. Explaining the dilemma of her checkbook, she promises to repay them as soon as we get to Mississippi. Instead of opening their checkbooks, my grandparents send her to the Atlanta Savings and Loan, where they have an account, and tell her to secure a loan there, but they refuse to serve as the collateral she needs to secure the loan, and she is turned down.

My grandparents, who never approved of my parents' marriage, kept a respectable distance between themselves and my father since the day he and my mother were wed. And since they thought Daddy married Mother to gain access to their money, they are not inclined to help out in this dilemma. It is not until Rosemary and I are well into our teens that we learn of their feelings, so while we are growing up, we mistake their aloofness toward our Dad as formality, since they are rather formal people.

When the Atlanta S&L turns Mother down, Papa reluctantly lends her the money we need, but not without embarrassing her at the breakfast table on the morning of our departure by reminding her to pay him back as soon as we get to Mississippi. No one knows why he chooses to do this in the presence of Madre's sister Ruby and her husband, Kelley, who are visiting from Marshall, Texas, but that is what he does.

# CHAPTER 10

# CAROLINA IN MY MIND[59]

D AD IS OUTSIDE, LOADING our car with the last-minute packages Madre always brings out for her sisters in New York. Tension simmers just beneath the surface. Daddy is furious about having to create additional space in the trunk after he thought he had packed the car for the last time. Now, "just one more thing for Louise and one more box for Mabel" are being brought down the front steps. In my head I can hear him muttering beneath his breath about the latest parcels as he struggles to make room for them. Meanwhile, seeing his agitation, Mother attempts to act as a buffer between him and her family, because now Aunt Ruby and Uncle Kelley descend the steps with Madre, adding to the ill will in the air by admonishing Dad to be careful while driving.

The morning is relatively cool by southern standards, and we are hoping to get an early start in order to stay cool as long as possible. Rosemary and Mother descend the front steps and walk toward the car holding hands; Dad and I finish packing the last of Madre's packages.

---

59 "Carolina in My Mind," written and recorded by James Taylor, 1968.

My sister is speaking softly to Mother about a dream she had last night, a dream in which we had a terrible accident, and everyone was hurt but her. Mother tries to calm her fears by reassuring her that we will make our usual stop at St. Paul's Episcopal Church on Ashby Street to pray before we leave.

Finally the car is packed, and the four of us take up our usual seats inside, Rosemary behind Daddy on the passenger side, and me behind the driver's seat. After waving good-bye, we head for St. Paul's Church to pray, but when we arrive we find the church doors locked, so we pray in the car and settle in for the long drive. I thank God that Mother is at the wheel. I always feel safer when she is driving, because she learned to drive when she was a girl and has only taught Dad how to drive in the last year that we have had the car. I lay my head back against the seat, close my eyes, and recall the magic New York held for me a year ago—the taxis speeding up and down the avenues; sitting in Aunt Mabel's living room window while the rest of the house slept; watching cars move along Seventh Avenue until the wee hours of the morning; going to Coney Island and riding the Cyclone; our trip to Jones Beach. Soon I join in the usual medley of road songs we sing on trips, starting with "Me and Brother Bill," a song recorded by Bing Crosby and Louis Armstrong that is about two hunters running to escape the clutches of a grizzly bear. As we sing about the hunters running past their houses and a gin mill, I picture the two of them hopping over fences, ducking under freshly washed sheets, and flying past a dilapidated old shack with a hand-painted sign reading, "Bucket O' Blood."

While singing we find ourselves driving behind a grapefruit truck that spills bag loads of fruit every time it rounds a curve. Each time the fruit spills, we pull onto the shoulder of the road and gather the fallen fruit, so we can eat fresh grapefruit along with the food we have already packed. The added fruit will provide enough food to last us through the southern states, where we cannot eat without entering the back door of road stands, and my parents refuse to do that.

Finally, the motion of the car combined with our early morning start lulls me into a deep sleep and a wonderful dream about New York City. In the middle of my dream, I hear a car horn and screeching tires. I shift around on the backseat and try to curl into another comfortable position, reminding myself that Mother, an expert driver, is at the wheel. Suddenly the car jerks forward, and I feel a jostling sensation. I am still in a semiconscious state but groggily begin to be awakened by my sister's screams. Then her kicking, flailing, and hitting everything around her, including me, force me to open my eyes. When I do everything inside the car is topsy-turvy. The floor is where the roof should be, and the front seat has completely disappeared. I tell myself I am still dreaming.

"Daddy! Daddy!" Rosemary screams.

Fully awake now, I am aware of my sister beside me as I stare through an open window at our father standing next to the car in a bloody shirt. Only one of his eyes is visible. The other is covered in blood. Stunned, he stumbles forward in a daze, but he responds to Rosemary's screams and pulls the two of us through an open window of the car.

"Are y'all all right?" he asks.

We both nod. Standing beside him next to the car, the reality of what has happened begins to sink in. The car lies on its top and is almost completely flat. One tire still spins crazily. The windshield is cracked, and red dust is still flying everywhere. Papers and luggage are strewn over the ground. The three of us stand at the bottom of a twenty-foot embankment, helplessly surveying a horror that appears to be some-where between fiction and reality, while cars and trucks whiz by on the highway above.

"Where's Mother?" Rosemary shouts.

"I don't know," Dad answers, still not seeming to be fully conscious. Then he calls out, "Anne?"

"I'm here," she answers weakly. Slowly a blood-soaked hand emerges from the front window on the passenger side. Dad's eyes tear up as he takes hold of it and tries to pull her through the window. With each tug, she moans and at times cries out in pain. Watching him extract her from the car is agonizing and such a slow process that I want to tell him to stop, that he is hurting her too much, to leave her alone. Instead I stand silently watching, unable to utter a word. Slowly our beautiful mother emerges from the crushed vehicle. Her once lustrous black hair is matted with sand and blood, and her doe-like eyes are red, as if the blood vessels have popped. The fingers of her slender, cinnamon-colored hand are cut and bleeding, and she is clearly in a great deal of pain. When she is completely out and lying on the ground, she looks as if a bucket of blood has been dumped across her from her waist to her knees. Dad keeps pulling her across the ground despite her cries. "Please leave me alone."

"I can't," he tells her. "I gotta get you away from the car. It could blow at any minute."

Only then do I understand why he has refused to leave her alone. He pulls her another fifteen or twenty feet from the wreckage, then gets the lap robe to cover her—laying her head on some of the clothes that have been scattered about the wreckage. Mother looks up at Rosemary and me and whispers, "You girls help your father find his thesis. He's worked so hard. Don't let it fly away."

Rosemary and I move around the base of the ravine, disoriented, looking for papers, while cars and trucks barrel by above. Our beautiful mother lies nearby, broken and helpless. A slow chill comes over me as we pick up documents. It is the knowledge that we are Negroes in trouble in the Deep South, and everyone speeding by above is white. In my heart, I fear no southern white person will stop for us. As the thought crosses my mind, my fears are confirmed when a truckload of rednecks whizzes by, and the people sitting in the back point at us and jeer and laugh.

From the amount of blood our mother has lost, I know she will die if help doesn't come soon. The nauseating smell of blood and gasoline permeate the air as the sun beats down on us. Not knowing what else to do, I pray, "Oh God, forgive me for every wrong thing I've ever done. I'm sorry. I'll never swear again, never tell another lie. I'll never do anything wrong again if you will let my mother live. Please don't take her from me. Please, God, don't let her die."

While I am praying, a truck slows down and stops. A very tan old white man with skin like leather gets out and yells, "Y'all need any he'p?"

"Yeah!" Dad yells back as a young white boy about ten years old gets out of the truck and runs halfway down the embankment to survey the wreckage. The man drawls that he'll send an ambulance. Before he drives away, we ask him where we are.

"South Cah'lina, near Gaffney," he yells, then drives off.

Mother asks Rosemary and me again to help Dad find his thesis. This time, feeling that help is on the way, we begin to look for it in earnest. I say a prayer of thanks as the three of us gather the papers and place them in a stack.[60]

---

60 In 1954, there were no such things as jump drives or copy machines, only manual typewriters with carbon ribbons. The one backup my father had to his thesis was a blurred carbon copy of it on onion skin paper. The hard copy we began collecting at the foot of the ravine was the only one he had to turn in, in order to earn his master's degree.

Only now, moving and collecting papers, do I notice the heat and humidity, the perspiration running down my body, under my arms, down my sides, across my face, and down my legs. It finds its way to my ankles, and the left one begins to sting. I look down and see a bloody cut, but I don't have nerve enough to mention it. *What's a cut on the ankle,* I think, *when Dad may have lost an eye, and Mother is lying a few feet away dying?* Rosemary is the only one who escapes injury. It has happened just as she dreamed it would the night before.

Nearly forty-five minutes have passed since the man and his son left with the promise of help. Now another feeling starts to churn in the pit of my stomach. Suppose he hasn't gone for help at all? Suppose he has just promised to get help and instead has left us on the side of the road with a false sense of hope? Southern living has conditioned me for this possibility, made me suspicious, kept me from trusting any white person I don't know. I don't like this feeling, but I want to prepare myself for whatever lies ahead. In all the time we've been stranded, not one Negro family has driven by, but this is not unusual. Few of us drive along southern highways, so it is unlikely that one of our own will come to our rescue. My panic rises as we continue moving about in a stupor at the bottom of the embankment, searching for the scattered pages of Daddy's thesis. I fight the possibility that we could be in this ditch all night if someone doesn't come soon. Then it happens. A Negro family slows down and asks if we need help. Dad tells them someone has already gone for help, but I wonder if Mother can hold out until that help arrives—if it ever does. The family drives on, and another half hour passes as my sense of urgency escalates. Dad shows little emotion, and I don't expect him to. He and Mother have spent years perfecting the art of being (or at least appearing) calm, seldom showing what they truly feel in times of danger. Through the years their example teaches us how to confront adversity bravely.

Ten more minutes pass, then half an hour. Finally an ambulance appears. Two white attendants descend the hill. One quickly takes Mother's blood pressure and listens to her heart. The other hollers up to the driver for a stretcher. When the attendant closest to Mother has finished checking her, he turns to examine Dad's eye. As he cleans away the blood, I see a large cut above his eye and realize with gratitude that the eye itself is not damaged. I sigh with relief as a butterfly bandage is applied in the middle of his eyebrow. The attendant tells Dad he'll need to get stitches later. Members of the emergency crew say they have to get Mother to the hospital right away; they will send another ambulance for the three of us when they get back. They place our mother on the stretcher and start the slow climb up the hill. My sister and I stand with our arms around each other watching, wondering if this is the last time we will see her alive. I want to go with her, to hold her hand and let her know she is loved. I don't want her to die in a strange place with people she doesn't know, but all I can do is stand there silently watching with my arms around Rosemary, tears brimming in my eyes.

Daddy looks at us and then at Mother. "Go with Mommy," he says, applying the name we haven't used for our mother in years. "I'll be all right."

Instantly, we climb the hill that proves to be steeper than it looks and follow our mother's stretcher into the ambulance. When we are inside, the doors slam shut, and the driver speeds off with sirens wailing. Mother manages a weak smile and whispers, "I have such brave girls."

The ride is rough along the two-lane highway, and Mother grits her teeth against the sounds that betray her pain. It takes nearly an hour to get to town, whizzing past farmhouses, orchards, fields, and rural mailboxes. For miles and miles, it seems we are traveling on the only paved road in the area, intersected here and there with rutted red-clay byways that kick up dust from the farm trucks bucking their way toward us. After what seems like an eternity, we enter a small town with a half dozen traffic lights, and the ambulance swings into a hospital parking lot. The white attendants jump from the vehicle, swing open the back doors, lift Mother's stretcher from the rear, and race into the hospital. Rosemary and I trail behind. A flurry of activity commences when nurses and doctors appear to roll Mother into the emergency room and tell us to wait outside. We find a bench in the hallway and sit praying, as curtains are drawn across the other side of a glass wall. The hall is empty now except for us.

Several minutes pass before a doctor comes out to ask if we are hurt. I show him the cut on my foot, and he gives me a tetanus shot. Then he cleans and bandages it right there in the hall. Afterward, he kneels down in front of us and tells us that our mother is very badly injured. She has lost so much blood that if she had been brought in fifteen minutes later, she would have died. Since she is in and out of consciousness, he says, he needs to have us answer some questions. He asks her full name, her address, where we are headed. He asks for her blood type and her age. When we tell him she is thirty-four, he asks if we're sure. Then we realize he has come to question us because she looks too young to be that age. She is so youthful-looking that no one ever believes our mother is as old as she really is. We assure him that she *is* thirty-four, but we can tell he doesn't believe us any more than he believed her when she told him. Then he asks about Daddy, and we tell him our father is still at the site of the wreck. He returns to the emergency room.

Rosemary and I remain quietly seated as nurses and doctors rush in and out of the room where Mother is being treated. I thank God for getting her safely here, but as I give thanks for her life, I am seized by the fear that something terrible could befall Dad. I am old enough to know how vulnerable a Negro man is searching alone in a ravine on a southern road, and I am frightened for him. I fight back tears as I contemplate life without either of my parents. Rosemary and I remain in the hot hallway on that hard bench for all the hours that Mother undergoes surgery, waiting for a word of hope. We wait so long that Daddy finally walks down the hall toward us. As soon as he sees us, he asks where Mother is. We point toward the emergency room, and he finds room beside us on the bench. No one utters a word. After an interminable amount of time a doctor emerges.

"J. T.?" he says to Dad, refusing to move beyond the derogatory way whites address Negroes by their first names, even in the midst of this catastrophe. Dad stands up and moves away from the two of us to speak with the doctor. After they have talked, the doctor returns to the emergency room, and Daddy comes back to where Rosemary and I are seated. He tells us that Mother has suffered a multiple compound fracture of the pelvis and can't be moved under any circumstances. She will have to spend three or four months convalescing here in Gaffney. After letting us know the extent of her injuries, he goes to a pay phone down the hall to call our paternal grandmother, Dear.

"Hello, Mama? It's J. T.," I hear him say. "We had a car accident."

He goes on to tell her about Mother's injuries and to assure her that the rest of us are all right. It is the only time in my life that I sense my father's need for his mother. He seems so alone standing at that pay phone talking, fighting back the pain of his distress and his inability to do anything about the situation. When he finishes talking with her, he hangs up and walks farther down the hall away from us. After composing himself, he returns to the phone to call our maternal grandmother, Madre. When the two of them have spoken, he comes back to tell us that Madre will be taking the first train she can get out of Atlanta to Gaffney.

That had to have been one of the most difficult calls of his married life. Even though the situation between him and our grandparents remains strained, their interaction with one another has softened since my sister's and my arrival. But in spite of that softening, Aunt Louise tells me later that she is thankful Mother was driving when the accident occurred, because Madre would never have forgiven Daddy if he had been at the wheel.

The doctor comes back into the hall to let us know Mother has been moved into a ward. The three of us follow a white nurse through the hallway and down a ramp at the back of the hospital. At the bottom of the ramp is the basement where the colored ward sits. A wooden desk at the bottom of the ramp is the nurses' station. A screen door to the right of the desk denotes the main entrance to the colored section. Another screen door at the end of the hall marks the back door. The first Negro hospital personnel we see are four nurses standing at the nurses' station. One of them motions for us to follow her past a tiny nursery and several rooms, including the men's ward on the left. The women's ward is across from it on the right. We follow her inside the women's ward and hear a woman speaking in a deep southern drawl from the men's ward on other side of the hall. "Who is that beautiful woman? What happened to her?" We can tell she is referring to our mother.

Walking past an empty bed, we approach Mother's bed next to a window. Her hips are in a canvas sling suspended by heavy metal chains and pulleys; her exposed legs are covered with multiple stitches. Several of her fingers have stitches, too, and she is still in a great deal of pain. Dad immediately goes to her side, leans over, and gently kisses her.

She opens her eyes and whispers through the heavy sedation, "Did you save your thesis?"

"Yeah," he answers, struggling to conceal how much more he wants to say.

"I'm glad," she murmurs and drops off to sleep again.

While she sleeps, Dad finds his way to the nurses' station, leaving Rosemary and me to watch Mother. He asks for directions to the Negro section of town and exits the screen door.

With fresh stitches over one eye, blood and red clay dried onto his short-sleeved shirt, my father now has to venture into the Negro part of a strange town and convince an understanding Negro stranger to put the three of us up, at least for the night.

Rose and I sit waiting patiently for his return and for Mother to wake up again. A hospital cart rolls down the hall with dinner trays. Only then do we realize how hungry we are. We step outside the back door to sit and wait while patients are given their dinners. We make unsuccessful attempts to stave off hunger pangs while we wait. After the trays are collected a Negro nurse brings food out to us, and we scarf it down like refugees before returning to Mother's bedside.

It is late in the evening when Dad returns to the hospital to let us know he has found a place for us to stay for a few days. He says he has already taken our luggage to the house. Rosemary and I step out into the summer night air, while he says good night to Mother. Then he comes out to tell us we can say good night to her, too. We go back to kiss her and then leave. Walking on either side of our father, we head for the railroad tracks that mark the division between the white and Negro sections of town. As we walk along the dark unfamiliar sidewalks, I am keenly aware of the fact that as bad as things are, I feel strangely secure because I am beside my father.

The three of us venture into the Negro interior of the city, passing several houses before arriving at one with steep steps. We climb up to the home of a slightly built, elderly dark-skinned woman who greets us at the front door in a housedress and bandanna. She welcomes us and shows Rosemary and me to the front room, where a double bed with freshly ironed sheets awaits us. Dad is given a smaller room at the back of the house, and all of us are given fresh washcloths and towels. We are shown the bathroom before our host retires to a cot on the back porch, where she will sleep.

Rosemary and I take baths, brush our teeth, and get into pajamas. I crawl into bed feeling as if I have just lived the longest day of my life. My exhausted body aches, but I'm so keyed up I can't sleep. Every time I try to close my eyes, I see Mother's broken body and Daddy's bleeding eye. I smell the blood and gasoline, think of all the bad things that could have happened, and try to fight back the tears that I know will have my eyelids swollen by morning. The first rays of the sun begin to appear before I drift off to sleep.

I awake with a still-aching body and swollen eyes. After Rosemary's return from the bathroom, I force myself out of bed to wash up and join Daddy and my sister for a breakfast of bacon, grits, toast, milk, and eggs at the kitchen table of our angel of mercy. When we have finished eating and helped clear away the dishes, the three of us set out for the hospital. We enter Mother's room to find her still in a lot of pain and heavily sedated. Anxious to get close to her, I bump the end of her bed, and she lets out such a painful cry that we are all careful not to knock against it after that. Between her waking and sleeping, we rub her hands, talk to her, and bend the straw in her glass toward her lips so she can take sips of ice water in the stifling heat. Dad reads to her from the Bible until she drops off to sleep again. While she sleeps Rosemary and I step outside the back door next to her room and sit. We don't talk much. There isn't much to say. We have survived a terrible ordeal. No one wants to relive it, and we know we will not make the trip to New York that we were so much looking forward to.

When the two of us begin to feel bored, we enter the hospital and walk to the other end of the hall where the nurses' station is to look at the babies in the nursery. The morning drags by slowly, punctuated by mother's occasional moans and cries for painkillers. As soon as the lunch trays arrive, Rosemary, Dad, and I walk back to the house where we are staying, so we can eat.

Our hostess hands us the morning newspaper, which has a major story about a Negro family who was leaving Florida and headed to New York when a horrific accident occurred. It describes the car and Mother's injuries and is picked up by the Negro press in the South and in the North, including the *Pittsburgh Courier* and the *Atlanta Constitution*. We read the article while having lunch.

Then Dad makes long-distance calls to Aunt Mabel in New York and to NYU to let them know what has happened. While he is on the phone, Rosemary and I clear away the lunch plates and, at our hostess's request, join her in the backyard. There she teaches us to wash clothes in a large three-legged pot by boiling them over an open fire. When the fire dies down, she sends us to get wood from a woodpile at the corner of the house and directs us to throw it on the flames and stoke the fire with long green sticks. Heat from the noonday sun and heat from the fire soon have sweat pouring off the two of us.

As soon as the clothes are clean, the old lady shows us how to lift them, a piece at a time, with broom handles, and carry them to a galvanized tub filled with cool water, where we rinse them and wring them out before hanging them on the clothesline. While we wash, our hostess talks about slavery and how easy times are for us by comparison. We can't tell if she was actually a slave as a child or is repeating stories her parents have passed down. While she talks, she mixes up a new batch of soap made from lye. Daddy comes out and indicates that afternoon visiting hours will begin soon. The three of us head back to the hospital.

Time has a way of standing still when you are anxious, and the afternoon hours seem to drag by as we sit holding vigil over our mother. Just before dinnertime, an attractive caramel-colored woman comes across the hall from the men's ward. She has read the article in the paper and wants us to know how sorry she is to learn of our plight. She says her name is Mrs. Harris and that her son Ervin, who is in the men's ward, has just had a kidney removed. She has a flower shop near the hospital where she works between visiting hours, and she and her husband own a farm right outside of town. Mrs. Harris says she has ten children and asks Rosemary and me how old we are. When we tell her we are ten and twelve, she tells us that her youngest two children are her fourteen-year-old daughter, Mary, who is called Polly, and her twelve-year-old son Calvin, whom she hopes we can meet sometime. We ask if we can meet her son Ervin, and she takes us across the hall, where we talk for a while. Ervin is twenty years old and still weak from his recent surgery. Mrs. Harris comes back to the women's ward with us and visits with Mother and us until the dinner trays appear. From that time forward she reports to us anything that happens concerning Mother during the times we are away from the hospital—what doctors have come by, which nurses have been attentive to her, and whether or not she has had a good nap with little pain, or a fitful sleep where she has had to request pain medication over and over again.

The next few days are pretty routine, with us keeping watch at Mother's bedside, rubbing her hands, giving her ice, visiting with Mrs. Harris and Ervin, and sitting outside the back door of the hospital trying to catch a breeze in the heat. Mother is still in a lot of pain, drifting in and out of consciousness.

After about five days our parents have a heart-to-heart talk, in which they decide that Daddy must go on to New York to complete the work on his thesis. He is torn about leaving Mother, who, weak as she is, insists he go. If he doesn't turn his thesis in this summer and attend school at NYU, there will be no job to go to in Mississippi. Our entire move depends on the completion of his master's work. Both our parents can be stubborn when they feel they are right, but Mother's stubbornness wins out this time, and having prevailed she insists he take the money Papa lent them to pay for this trip and that he contribute it to Mabel's household while he is living there. This latter suggestion of hers sparks a major disagreement between them because Daddy wants to leave money for her to offset hospital costs. Rosemary and I, who hate seeing them argue, go outside to sit under a tree near her window while they have it out. When they are done, Mother has prevailed again.

Madre arrives in Gaffney to care for Mother. She finds a place to stay with Mrs. Gaffney, a fair-skinned Negro woman. When we meet her I can't help wondering if her husband's relatives were founders of the town. Most of us know that despite segregation laws a lot of race mixing takes place, especially when it comes to sexual activity. Rosemary and I move in with Madre, and Dad packs for his trip to New York and his departure from the home of the first woman who took us in.

At the hospital the next day, Mrs. Harris invites Rosemary, Dad, and me for a visit to her farm before our father departs for New York. Madre stays at the hospital with Mother, and the three of us get into the Harrises' station wagon for a ride to the outskirts of town and their large working farm with chickens, cattle, fruit trees, vegetable gardens, a lake, an outhouse, and a well with spring water. It is the first time Rose and I have been away from the hospital since the accident and the first time we have been on a large farm. Daddy, on the other hand, immediately begins recalling his days as a young boy on the Peavy plantation with his grandparents, Ellen and Lewis Bass—learning to churn butter and smoke meat, and learning how to bury potatoes in the ground under pine needles so they will keep through the winter. It is the first time since the accident that we have seen our father fully relaxed, even throwing his head back and laughing at stories the Harrises tell.

Mrs. Harris is married to a handsome brown-skinned man, and every one of their children is good-looking. Rosemary and I sit talking with fourteen-year-old Mary (nicknamed Polly) while the boys finish their chores. The oldest daughter, Dot, arrives from her home nearby as does Charles, one of the oldest boys. Then eighteen-year-old Weldon, a tall handsome hunk of a young man, washes up and changes clothes before coming to meet us, and I am immediately smitten, in spite of the fact that Polly has already told us about Weldon's girlfriend. Twelve-year-old Calvin appears, too, and he and Rosemary take an immediate liking to one another.

When the boys have all washed up for a meal of fried corn, ham, turnip greens, cornbread, lettuce and tomato salad, lemonade, and coconut cake, we sit in chairs under a big oak tree in the front yard, and both families continue sharing stories about farm life. Looking out over the land, I realize that I too am relaxed for the first time since I awoke at the bottom of that ravine, but a part of me is also melancholy as I think of Daddy's impending trip. While we sit talking, clouds gather in the distance. The sky begins to turn gray, and we gather up the chairs, oilcloth where the cake has been cut, plates and forks from dessert, and head toward the porch. By the time we take everything inside and reemerge on the front porch the storm is rolling toward the farm. Having never seen a storm roll in before, I stand mesmerized on the porch, refreshed by the cooling rain that has finally reached us. Then as quickly as it came, it is gone, and the sun is shining again. As the sun begins to sink, Daddy thanks our new friends for a wonderful afternoon.

The next day we say a tearful good-bye as our father heads downtown to take a Jim Crow bus once again to New York City where he will finally complete his master's.

# CHAPTER 11

# MEM'RIES[61]

FOR THE SECOND TIME in their marriage, my father boards a bus to leave an ailing wife. The first time he made such a trip was the summer after my birth in Cordele, Georgia, when he went to Alabama to earn extra money to make ends meet. Madre had come to the rescue that time, too, driving Mother and me to Atlanta so she could care for Mother, who was recovering from phlebitis—a condition that had kept her bedridden since the day of my birth two months earlier. This time, as my father boards the bus in Gaffney, he is leaving his wife in a segregated hospital in a strange city, where her mother will care for her. As he begins his trip alone, he looks back at the obstacles they have overcome in their thirteen years together.

It seems like light-years ago—that day he and Charles Mann rang the doorbell to Madre's in Atlanta so that they could study with Madre's sister (Aunt Maude), who was their classmate at Morris Brown College.

---

61 "The Way We Were," music by Marvin Hamlisch, lyrics by Marilyn and Alan Bergman. Recorded by Barbra Streisand.

Braxton and Mann had been going to the Thomas home to study for months, but they'd never seen Anne before that day. Maude and her husband, Brit, were living in a room in the Thomas home on the second floor ever since Maude accepted Papa's offer to her and the rest of her and Madre's siblings to finance their college educations following the deaths of their parents.

On this day when Braxton and Mann ring the doorbell, Anne answers leaving the two young men so struck by her beauty that they stand speechless, mouths agape.

"Hello," she says after an awkward few moments, "you must be Braxton and Mann."

"Ye-yes," they stammer.

"My aunt is waiting for you. I'll get her."

She invites them in and disappears through the dining room and breakfast nook. She ascends the stairs to the second floor where Aunt Maude and Uncle Brit live.

"Who was *that*?" Braxton asks Mann.

"I don't know."

Maude descends the stairs and comes into the living room to greet them. Rushing toward her, they barely manage to say hello before demanding in unison, "Who was that who answered the door?"

"My sister's daughter, Anne."

"Which sister?"

"My sister Nell Thomas."

To which both men blurt out, "Mrs. Thomas has a *daughter*?"

ANNE AT SPELMAN

After his chance meeting with Anne, Braxton became part of the growing cadre of young men my grandmother hired to do odd jobs around her home—painting, yard work, and waiting tables for her numerous dinner parties. In the midst of those Depression years, Madre preferred to hire students rather than professionals, so the students could earn extra money. Famed African drummer Babatunde

Olatunji, one of the foreign students in school in Atlanta, was often in her home and recalled many years later, "She was one of the few Negroes in Atlanta who befriended foreign students."

———

AS BRAXTON RODE THE bus leaving South Carolina bound for New York City, he remembered it was his mistreatment by a football recruiter that had placed him at Morris Brown College in Atlanta instead of Alabama State, which was his first choice.

Following his graduation from the Gillespie Normal School in Cordele, Georgia, J. T. Braxton had received an athletic scholarship to Fort Valley Junior College, but because the financial aid package only covered a few expenses he had to find work in order to pay his other expenses. Due to the fact that he had a job *and* athletic obligations, he was not able to carry a full academic load at Fort Valley. In fact, he was only able to enroll in two courses during his first year, and the second year was not much better. On Sundays he attended St. Luke's Episcopal Church across the street from the school, and in spite of his grueling schedule, he found time to fall in love. He and Elizabeth "Dolly" Peyton met shortly after his arrival at Fort Valley, and she fell for the handsome football star from Gillespie. And he was drawn to Dolly who, like himself, was a gifted athlete. They dated for years and then began making wedding plans. During that time Braxton found the rigors of work, participating in sports, and keeping up with schoolwork forced him to spend an extra year at Fort Valley in pursuit of an associate degree. He had come further than his mother ever dreamed he would when she took him to the Gillespie boarding school, and the small amount of travel he'd experienced had exposed him to the possibility of even greater opportunities. He knew that other Fort Valley athletes were headed for four-year schools after they left there, and he was sure that he was capable of competing in that arena, too.

Upon graduation from Fort Valley, and due to his outstanding athletic abilities, coaches came from all over Georgia and from neighboring states to offer John "Twinkle Toes" Braxton scholarships to their four-year institutions. Alabama State College in Montgomery offered him full tuition, and that was the answer to his prayers. It was a scholarship he really needed but one he refused to take unless his best friend, George Kendrick, could go to Alabama State, too.

Braxton and George had been friends since the seventh grade at the Gillespie boarding school. He had helped George overcome his stuttering and win roles in school plays, and George had repaid him by being one of the best football blockers Braxton ever had the good fortune to play beside. George had also taken Braxton home to Moultrie, Georgia, for every holiday season and during summer vacations, because Daddy's mother was still doing the day's work she needed to do in order to provide for her younger son, Edward.

Braxton and George had taken advantage of Gillespie's work-for-tuition plan by signing up with the Imperial Tobacco Company and working the fields in the summers when school was out; George worked in Georgia, and Braxton worked in Connecticut, where he earned money loading warehouse trucks until midnight. After work, Braxton, a nonsmoker, sold the free cigarettes Imperial Tobacco gave its employees, so he could have some spending money, because Imperial Tobacco sent everything else he made back to Gillespie to pay his tuition. When the Connecticut tobacco season ended, he hitched a ride on a company truck to North Carolina, where he worked another five weeks before riding another truck to Moultrie, Georgia, where he joined his friend George Kendrick at Imperial's local warehouse. The two worked there until the late summer when they were off to Gillespie again.

After graduation from Gillespie, Braxton and George Kendrick had entered Fort Valley Junior College, where Kendrick continued to block for him on the football field and to take him home as a member of the family during school breaks. So when the Alabama State recruiter arrived at Fort Valley with a full football scholarship for Braxton, his first response was, "What about my brother?"—meaning George Kendrick. And because the recruiter had been sent to Fort Valley to bring back one of the best running backs in the area, he knew Braxton would not accept his offer without Kendrick, so he said, "Okay, I'll take your brother, too."

Braxton arrived in Montgomery, Alabama, before George Kendrick, so he went to look for the recruiter whom he'd met at Fort Valley. But that man was out of town, and the person left in charge of recruits in his place told Braxton he had a George Kendrick on his list, but he did not have a John Braxton. Try as he might, my father could not convince the man that he had a full scholarship. Finally, having spent all the money he had to get to Montgomery, Daddy, who had arrived hungry, asked, "Could you give me a meal ticket so I can get something to eat?"

"No," he was told and turned away.

Not knowing what else to do, he waited for Kendrick to arrive. When George Kendrick heard about what had happened to his friend, he was heartbroken because he realized *he* wouldn't be in Montgomery were it not for John Braxton.

"Let me go to the dining hall while they're still serving, and I'll bring you something back," Kendrick told Dad. So Kendrick ate his dinner and then sneaked food out of the dining hall for Braxton. With a meal under his belt, John Braxton began to ponder what to do next. He was determined to attend a four-year college, so he swallowed his pride and made a collect call to Coach Billy Nicks at Morris Brown College, one of the coaches who had tried to recruit him when Braxton opted for Alabama State instead.

"Coach Nicks, this is Braxton. I'm stranded here at Alabama State. The man who offered me a scholarship isn't here, and they can't find my name on the list of new players. I was wondering if you're still interested in having me play for the Wolverines."

Billy Nicks could hardly believe his ears. Virtually licking his lips, he assured Braxton that he was still interested in coaching him and promised to wire him enough money to cover Braxton's train fare to Atlanta plus an extra ten dollars, so Braxton could buy something to eat while he traveled. John Braxton and George Kendrick said good-bye to each other, and Dad boarded the train for Atlanta, Georgia.

Soon after he left Alabama, during Morris Brown's opening game against Alabama State, John Braxton ran the opening kickoff back for an eighty-yard touchdown. His succeeding yardage gains and subsequent touchdowns in that game led to Morris Brown trouncing Alabama State. When the game was over, the recruiter who had given Braxton and Kendrick the scholarships to Alabama State turned to the man who had sent my father away and said, "That's the boy you refused to give a meal ticket." Of course the man did everything he could to get Daddy to change his mind, but it was too late.

By the time he graduated from Morris Brown College, John Braxton had amassed athletic honors as an all-league, all-conference, all-state, all-southern player and garnered a football collegiate all-American honor. Four decades later, on the occasion of his induction into the Sacramento, California, Hall of Fame, John Braxton met Coach Billy Nicks at the Sacramento airport. Coach Nicks had flown out to California for the event honoring Dad, and when he rose to speak, Nicks acknowledged, "John Braxton is the greatest halfback I ever coached."

JOHN BRAXTON AT MORRIS BROWN

Braxton's work for my grandmother and his study sessions with Aunt Maude and Charles Mann in Atlanta kept him busy, but not too busy to keep him from acting in college plays, playing in the band, or singing in the choir. As he had done at the Gillespie Normal School, Braxton took advantage of everything offered in order to improve himself. Football, basketball, track, and choir trips opened new experiences for him as he traveled to other parts of the United States and to Canada. His good looks, athletic abilities, and effervescent personality made him a popular student on all the Atlanta University campuses, and they opened the door to his frequent visits to the Thomas home to see Anne. It didn't take long for a romance to develop between Anne and John, nor for Dolly Peyton's friends in Atlanta to write to her in Fort Valley and tell her she'd better come to Atlanta and see about him. Dolly wasted little time in moving to Atlanta and enrolling at Morris Brown College, where she could keep an eye on Braxton. Her presence gave him pause, as he considered the plans they had made and the years they'd spent together at Fort Valley. In the end, though, Anne won his heart.

---

LYING IN A GAFFNEY, South Carolina, hospital bed, drifting in and out of consciousness, Anne Thomas Braxton has time to think, too. Waking long enough to get sponge baths from her mother and to eat soft food before drifting off again, her mind also wanders back over the years. The confinement caused by the accident has provided the first opportunity in years for Anne and her mother to be together. Because of the decision Anne made years ago to marry John Braxton, she and her mother only formed an uneasy truce after my birth. That truce began when a friend of my grandmother's persuaded her to make the trip from Atlanta to Cordele to see Mother and me.

"I'd do anything to have a grandchild," she had told Madre. "You have one born on your birthday and named for you. You have to go see her."

So Madre and her friend had driven to Cordele to see Mother and me.

In the twilight moments before painkillers kick in, childhood memories flood Anne Thomas Braxton's consciousness.

Anne Amanda Thomas was born in 1919 to well-to-do parents following the death of their first daughter, Haru, whose neck was broken with forceps during her delivery. Promising herself she wouldn't lose another baby, Madre had gone back to her hometown of Marshall, Texas, for my mother's birth.

NELL'S GRANDPARENTS, MADRE AND PAPA WITH
HER MOTHER, ANNE, AS A TODDLER

Little Anne Amanda lived a privileged life filled with prominent Negro people of the day. It was not unusual for her to awaken to the sounds of Roland Hays or Paul Robeson practicing their scales on the piano in her parents' living room. Nor was it out of the ordinary for her to be asked to help serve dinner to members of the Fisk University Jubilee Singers, or Mary McLeod Bethune during the days when Atlanta hotels refused to give rooms to Negroes regardless of their renown. The Jim Crow laws that all Negroes were forced to live by led Nell and Jesse O. Thomas to open their home to Hays, Robeson, Mary McLeod Bethune, and other Negro notables who found themselves in Atlanta without lodging. The Thomases also hosted white philanthropists who gave money to the Urban League, Tuskegee Institute, and other organizations the couple supported.

When important people weren't passing through or staying at their home, Anne's parents entertained members of Atlanta's Negro intelligentsia. Among their closest friends and most frequent guests were William Stanley Braithwaite, poet, literary critic, and one-time teacher at Atlanta University, W. E. B. DuBois, writer, educator, civil rights leader, and Atlanta University professor, and author William Pickens, whose book *New Negro* debuted in 1916. A student of Tuskegee Institute and Talladega College, Pickens had penned the Talladega school song and written articles for the NAACP's *Opportunity Magazine*. He was such a frequent guest in the Thomas home that Anne called him "Uncle Billum." Because her father's money protected her from the full impact of segregation, and because his home provided a welcome to Negroes and whites alike, Anne grew up assuming everyone lived the way she did.

The early twentieth century was a hopeful time for Atlanta Negroes, as lynchings that had plagued the South for years began to abate, and the city emerged as a leader in the "New South." With the Negro community coming into its own, the system of Negro colleges that made up the Atlanta University complex flourished and expanded, especially along the street that became known as "Sweet Auburn" (Auburn Avenue), where Negro businesses thrived. Banks, pharmacies, and insurance companies were part of the growth and part of the reason Atlanta looked to a proud future.

Nestled in the new Atlanta were Nell Thomas, her friend, Mrs. Shriver, William Pickens, W. E. B. DuBois, and William Stanley Braithwaite, who formed a cultural group that gathered regularly to discuss important issues of the day. Each of the five took a turn at hosting the meeting by preparing his or her special dish. Though each tried to out cook the others, the undisputed favorite dish was William Stanley Braithwaite's Boston baked beans.

In 1922 (when Anne was three years old), Nell Thomas founded a group for young mothers who were at home with small children. Taking the first two or three letters of Mothers' Social and Literary Circle she formed the MoSoLit Circle, a group that allowed young mothers to come together, socialize, and discuss current books. She also designed the group's logo. Eighty-five years after its founding, the women of MoSoLit Circle were still meeting to discuss literary works and to give one another's children gifts when they graduated from college and got married.

Anne attended the Atlanta University Laboratory School, known as Oglethorpe Elementary, and the Atlanta University Preparatory School, where she completed her secondary education in three years. She entered Spelman College at age sixteen and graduated with a degree in English at nineteen.

An only child, Anne was spoiled with gifts and special trips and taken on family trips across the country where she and her parents slept in train berths reserved for "whites only." Her father, a civil rights activist who refused to ride in Jim Crow cars, often unnerved Negroes as well as whites by purchasing the berths. Anne remembers one trip when she skipped ahead of her parents toward their berth. A well-intentioned Negro woman stopped her at the end of the "colored car." Trying to protect the little girl from an embarrassing situation in which she might be turned back, the woman put out her arm and said, "You're going too far, little girl."

To which young Anne replied, "No I'm not. We're in lower berth thirteen, and it's up ahead." Her response came as a shock to the woman, but Anne's father was so proud he nearly popped the buttons off his shirt.

Jesse O. Thomas was a shrewd businessman who had learned that superstitious white people usually avoided booking the thirteenth berth on trains, and he figured the railroad would be more interested in making money by booking that car than in losing money by letting the berth go empty, so he convinced authorities to let him have the empty berth for himself and his family. Since privacy curtains were pulled across the berths, few whites realized they were sleeping next to Negroes until they awakened the following morning. Years went by before anyone complained, though to be fair, some people may have been confused as to the race of my grandmother, who was very fair-skinned. When complaints did come, the railroad solved "the problem" by offering my grandfather a drawing room. That way the company kept the Negroes out of sight but also kept a steady customer. Since the drawing room gave the Thomas family even greater comfort and privacy, they increased their travel, bringing even more money to the railroad.

When my grandfather's work kept him from traveling with his wife and daughter, he sent them off alone, escorting them to the Atlanta railroad station and entrusting them to the care of members of the Brotherhood of Sleeping Car Porters. In 1932 Anne and Nell Thomas boarded the train to visit Nell's sisters, Gertrude and Lucille, and Anne's cousins, Yvonne and Marilouise who lived in Los Angeles, California. While there, mother and daughter attended the Olympic Games. Years later Anne could still remember the pride she felt as the Stars and Stripes unfurled and American athletes marched into the stadium. She never forgot the lighting of the Olympic torch nor the sight of American athletes on the winner's stand as "The Star Spangled Banner" played. That summer, she and her mother followed their trip to California with a trip to Mexico where they stayed with a former Tuskegee schoolmate of Nell Thomas.

Returning home to Atlanta, the two donned their best clothes and went shopping for the latest outfits. But not long afterward, Anne's maternal grandfather died, and the fun and privileges she had experienced all her life came to an abrupt end. Nell Thomas was the eldest of Professors Mitchell's offspring, and she became the surrogate mother to her three youngest siblings, whom her father had been rearing since the untimely death of his wife, Ida Anne. Now they were Nell's charges, and their arrival not only ended the cross-country trips and indulgent shopping sprees that Anne and her mother had enjoyed, they also forced Anne to give up the dance classes she loved. At first her mother had said she could choose between giving up piano lessons or dance classes, but when Anne chose to forego piano lessons, her mother decided that dance should go.

It was on the occasion of his father-in-law's death that Jesse O. Thomas promised to pay tuition for any of his wife's siblings who wanted to go to college. He had done the same thing for his own siblings after his father had died. Not only did the three youngest children—Ruby, Nelson Jr., and Louise—take advantage of the offer, but Maude Baskerville came to Atlanta from Chicago with her husband to attend college, too, and ended up at Morris Brown College with John Braxton and Charles Mann.

Anne was a generation younger than her aunts and uncles, and because of the cliquishness of her aunts, she felt isolated in her own home. Her mother was busier than ever with additional mouths to feed, and her father's long working hours left her alone much of the time. She sought friendships with youngsters her own age and became close to a number of children who lived across town in less affluent neighborhoods. Often they came to visit her, but when it was time for her to visit them, she ended up playing at home alone. Her mother refused to let her travel across town alone, and she saw no need to take time from her increasingly busy schedule to drive Anne to the other side of town to play when there were youngsters in their own neighborhood with whom she could have fun. In spite of the difficulties of getting to the other side of town, Anne formed lasting friendships with two girls she greatly admired—Gustava Williams and Jeanette Harvey. She was grateful for the friendships both girls offered, but Jeanette won a special place with her the day she stood up to Anne's mother.

Jeanette had come to visit on a particularly hot summer afternoon. At some point she seated herself in the Thomases' well-appointed living room with her ample legs spread apart. Entering the room, my grandmother made her way over to the young girl and quietly suggested she "put her knees together." Catching Nell Thomas completely off guard, Jeanette responded well above the whisper her hostess had employed, "Miz Thomas, it's *hot,* and I'm sweatin'." A mild gasp escaped Nell

Thomas's lips before she admonished, "Young ladies don't sweat. They glow." But when Jeanette stood her ground, Madre exited the room.

It was during this period of family readjustment with additional family members moving in that Nell Thomas began to suffer from severe headaches and stomach trouble. Both conditions caused my mother great concern, but she lived at a time when grown-ups did not explain their conditions to children, so she never knew the cause of her mother's ailments, and no one else ever bothered to explain them to her. It was because of the adults' silence about her mother and the early deaths of her grandparents that Anne began to fear that her mother, too, might die young.

Nell and Jesse O. Thomas set high standards for themselves and for their daughter—standards Anne strove hard to live up to by doing everything she could to make them proud. Her parents, however, were not demonstrative in their affections, so my mother grew up always wondering if they really loved her. When she came of age, they presented her to Atlanta's Negro society with an elegant debutante's ball on the grounds of their spacious lawn, and her father bestowed a lovely fur stole on his only child.

In 1939, nineteen-year-old Anne graduated from Spelman with a bachelor's degree in English and a question from her parents as to what she wanted to do next. "To work with young people in personnel guidance," she told them. Her father's response was to have his secretary conduct a survey of universities throughout the country and find the one that offered the best program in that discipline. Her search revealed Columbia University in New York City to be the best in pupil personnel administration, so Anne applied there and was accepted.

That same year Eugene Kinkle Jones, head of the National Urban League, became quite ill and was told by his doctor to take a year off to recuperate. "There's only one man I trust to run the national office in my absence," he said, "and that man is Jesse O. Thomas." Since the Urban League's national office was in New York City where Anne was headed for graduate school, Nell and Jesse O. decided to leave their home in the care of Nell's sister Maude and her husband, Brit Baskerville, so that the entire Thomas family could spend the year in New York. The three younger siblings had finished college and were off on their own, so Maude and Brit were to house-sit alone.

In New York the Thomases found an apartment at 2040 Seventh Avenue in Harlem, not far from another of Nell's sisters; Mabel and her husband, Ezra Parrott, who at that time lived down the street at 1800 Seventh Avenue. Even though the Parrotts enjoyed a view of Central Park North from their apartment, Mabel wanted to be closer to Nell and Jesse O., so she convinced Ezra to move into an apartment at 2040 Seventh Avenue, too.

Beginning her graduate school experience, Anne enjoyed the freedom of New York City, sometimes walking to school rather than taking the bus or subway. During her walks she often ran into new friends and traveled to the Columbia University campus with them. She and Braxton kept in touch by mail during her year in New York. He had graduated from Morris Brown the same year that Anne finished Spelman and had secured a job as principal of an elementary school in Robinson, Georgia.

A little before Christmas of that year, Braxton wrote Anne to say he had saved enough money to come to New York to be with her for the holidays. He spent most of his savings to get there and arrived dressed more for a Georgia winter than the snowy weather of New York. In fact, it was so cold that year that he wondered if he would ever feel warm again. But cold as the weather was, it was no match for the Thomases' reception. They had never approved of the romance between their only child and John Braxton, so when he arrived in New York they refused to let him stay in their apartment.

Alone in a strange city with nowhere to turn, Braxton appealed to Anne's aunt Mabel. But the aunt who was so mischievous as a child that she put a monkey in the flour bin would not go against her oldest sister. True to her Cherokee ancestry, she had great respect for her elders and was loyal to a fault when it came to her family. But she liked Braxton and was moved by the sacrifice he had made to get to New York to see Anne, so she made arrangements for him to stay with her friend, Mrs. Francis, on the second floor of the same apartment building.

With his living arrangements solved, Braxton and Anne took in the sights of New York City, beginning in Harlem where Christmas lights and tinsel decorated major thoroughfares and evergreens with colored lights graced boulevards. Braxton, a true romantic, sang songs along with the Victrola-generated Christmas carols that spilled onto 125th Street as the young sweethearts walked toward Lenox Avenue. Boarding a city bus, they rode down Fifth Avenue beneath beads of ice that formed strands across the branches of the trees in Central Park as they headed toward Saks Fifth Avenue. They got off the bus to enjoy Christmas store windows with ornate decorations, and then they crossed the street to see skaters on the ice at Rockefeller Center and listen to the brass and drums of a Salvation Army band before returning to the warmth of their Harlem apartments. At the end of the holidays, Braxton returned to Georgia, and Anne resumed her studies at Columbia.

The remainder of the school year flew by so fast that Anne was surprised by the sudden profusion of blossoms dotting the Columbia campus. But even more than the end of the school year, the flowers signaled Anne's need to secure a job. She had graduated from Columbia with a double-A rating and plenty of contacts through her father, so there was no way she could have anticipated the trouble that lay ahead. In spite of her stellar academic record and her connections, no one was interested in hiring a twenty-year-old. She wrote to schools across the country as well as to her father's friends, but none of them would seek work for one as young and inexperienced as she was. Eventually she heard from a small school in Sparta, Georgia, that offered her a teaching position. She took it and moved to Sparta right away.

After a year, Eugene Kinkle Jones sufficiently recuperated from his illness and returned to his job at the Urban League. Nell and Jesse O. Thomas packed up their New York apartment and prepared to return to Atlanta. Meanwhile, when John Braxton learned that Anne was going to Sparta, he resigned his position as principal in Robinson, Georgia, for a better-paying job in Sparta. But their life together there was short-lived. By Christmas of that year, they had both been fired without cause. No one knew for sure whether Anne's father had used his considerable influence and connections to bring about their dismissals in an effort to end their relationship, but the fact is they were both forced to spend the Christmas holiday season searching for work.

In 1940, the superintendent of colored instruction was responsible for placing Negro teachers throughout the state, and the man who held that position was Robert L. Cousins. He was headquartered in Atlanta, where Anne went to try to find work. It didn't take long for her to land a job in Adele (pronounced A-dell), Georgia, and as soon as she did her parents prevailed upon her not to tell anyone where she would be working.

John Braxton went to Atlanta to meet with Cousins, too, but on the way he stopped by the Thomas home to see Anne, who was staying there until the time for her to go to Adele arrived. John hoped to find out whether she had found work and if so, where. But when they talked, Anne remained faithful to her promise to her parents and told Braxton she could not tell him where she would be working.

Braxton left the Thomas home more depressed than ever. Arriving at Cousins's office, he was told there were only two positions left in the state for Negro teachers and either one was his for the asking. Not knowing where Anne was going, Braxton refused to make a decision. Cousins, who had learned of the young couple's troubles, suggested to Braxton that he take the job in Adele.

Unlike Anne Thomas, who had grown up in a home that welcomed people from all races, John Braxton had not had good experiences with white people. Work on the Peavy plantation had not been easy, and his mother's birth had been the result of the rape of his grandmother Ellen, the midwife, by a white man. It was therefore beyond his wildest imagination that a white man sitting in an office in Atlanta would know or care about the future of a young Negro couple who had been fired down in Sparta. And so he dismissed Cousins's suggestion. But the superintendent persisted, assuring Braxton that he would like the job in Adele. Braxton sat stone-faced, refusing to make a decision as Cousins continued to lobby for the position in Adele. After a while, tiring of the pressure from Robert Cousins, my father agreed to take the job, reasoning that he needed the work, regardless of where Anne would be working.

A small three-bedroom cottage had been set aside for Negro teachers in Adele, Georgia, where Anne shared the largest of the three bedrooms with Georgia Oswald, a Spelman graduate from Worcester, Massachusetts. Theirs was the only room with a fireplace, so it doubled as a common room for all the other teachers. Fannie Allen, another Spelman alumna, shared a second bedroom with a fourth female teacher, and Principal "Skinny" Smith, was paired with John Braxton in the remaining room.

Pleased as she was with Braxton's arrival in Adele, out of respect for her parents, Anne continued to write several young men she'd met in school at Columbia, but none of those friendships developed beyond casual relationships.

By all accounts it was an enjoyable year for all the teachers, and when it ended they began packing to go home for the summer. Fearing he would lose Anne forever if they did not marry, John Braxton proposed to her. It was not the first time he had asked for her hand in marriage. He had proposed more than once while they were still in college, but each time Anne had refused, reminding him that they needed to finish school, or they would have nothing to live on. In Adele when she appeared to hesitate again, he told her, "If you really don't want to marry me, I won't pressure you. I don't want to keep asking if there's no hope."

Anne was twenty-one years old, facing the wrath of her parents if she said yes. She knew Nell and Jesse O. were suspicious of Braxton's motives. She had heard other doubters who shared her parents' suspicions suggesting that he was after her father's money, and although she knew the rumors were not true, knew that he really loved her, in that moment she realized he loved her enough to give her up if that was what she wanted. There were few times in her life when she had been asked to make a decision based on what *she* really wanted. Anne Thomas loved John Braxton and felt that if she turned him down this time, she could lose him forever. She accepted his proposal and hoped that someday her parents would accept him, too. When Anne said yes, John thought—but did not tell her until many years later—*With you by my side, there's nothing that I can't do.*[62]

That evening Anne sat down and wrote her parents a letter informing them of her decision to marry Braxton and asking for their blessing. And she invited them to come to Adele and share in her joy. Their response was immediate and final. They disinherited their only child, severing her connection to the only world she had known. Nell Thomas even went so far as to tell the members of MoSoLit Circle not to send wedding gifts. Only one member of the organization defied her and sent a gift anyway.

Alone in Adele, Anne Amanda Thomas dressed in her best navy linen suit, met John Thomas Braxton, and went with him to the home of a minister who performed the ceremony. They were joined in marriage in the presence of two older women who adored the young couple enough to stand as witnesses.

---

62  Conversation with Anne Braxton, Sacramento, California, August 28, 2007.

# CHAPTER 12

# SURVIVOR[63]

THE BASEMENT OF THE Gaffney hospital sits like an after-thought, cut off from the rest of the building by long hallways, stairs, and heavy doors. White doctors and nurses use the door lead-ing up the concrete ramp to the main building to get to and from the Negro section. Negro nurses and visitors stream through the colored entrance—the side screen door near the nurses' desk. They exit through the back—also a screen door that is near the women's ward. Security is nonexistent, and the heavy dampness of the ever-present humidity permeates what little air there is.

During the second and third weeks of Mother's convalescence, I can see small signs of her improvement. The intravenous tubes are removed, more substantial food is introduced, and she is able to endure the pain of having her head and torso lightly tilted up so that she can see out of the window next to her bed that overlooks a well-kept lawn. Often when she is tilted up, the position causes pressure on her pelvis

---

63 "Survivor," written and composed by Beyoncé, Anthony Dent, and Matthew Knowles, 2001.

that is so severe that she has to be lowered after a short time. For the first time since she entered the hospital she can also see Mrs. Harris across the hall, holding vigil over her son, Ervin, or "Red," as he is called. The first time Mother is raised up, Mrs. Harris comes over to talk with her.

"How you feelin' today, Miz Braxton?"

"I'm better, thank you."

"We sure have enjoyed your girls out at the farm."

"They've had a wonderful time with you and your family. We can't thank you enough for your hospitality."

"Well, we hope you'll let 'em come back again. You know this hospital's really no place for children to be sittin' 'round all day. They need to get out and run and play with children their own age. They've been through a lot with the accident an' all."

"Thank you. I'm sure they'll enjoy visiting again."

Since Madre's arrival, Rosemary and I have begun to spend whole days in the hospital instead of coming at visiting hours. Her charm has endeared the three of us to the hospital personnel who allow us to come and stay, in spite of the fact that Rosemary is not twelve years old—the official age for visitors—and because Mother is so near the rear door of the hospital we can go outside whenever white officials come down.

Rosie, Madre, and I arrive each day after having breakfast at Mrs. Gaffney's house and spend the day with Mother. We eat grapefruit, oranges, tangerines, or peaches for lunch, and Rosemary and I finish whatever food Mother doesn't want on her tray. Sometimes if there is an extra dessert the nurses will let us have that, too. In the evenings, we return to Mrs. Gaffney's home for dinner before going to bed.

At the hospital, my sister and I take turns sitting with Madre by Mother's bed and visiting across the hall with Mrs. Harris and Red, or we walk to the nurses' station and talk with them. Returning to Mother, we tell her about the comings and goings of the hospital staff and visitors and share our concern over one of the babies in the nursery who appears to be deaf. When no one is looking we get close to it and clap our hands near its head, but it never turns in the direction of the clapping. We make noises close to its ear, but it doesn't turn to see where the noise is coming from. If we bend over the baby's face it smiles, but unless we are in its line of vision, it does not respond.

I have started to read and enjoy political cartoons, and I save the funniest ones to read to Mother, who gets a kick out of them, too. Seeing her enjoyment gives me an idea. I purchase a scrapbook, go through old newspapers and magazines, cut out the best political satire I can find, and paste them in the scrapbook for her. Over the course of her hospital stay that scrapbook brings her a lot of joy.

Every morning, Madre reads to Mother from a tract called "Daily Word." The readings seem to give her courage. Afterward, the two of them can be overheard giggling as they reminisce about happier days, giving no sign of the strain on their relationship in more recent years. Madre's sisters, Gertrude and Lucille, put together a scrapbook, too. It is one of the entire Mitchell family and has photos dating back to their childhood up to cousin Yvonne's wedding and cousin Marilouise's, too. The scrapbook sparks all kinds of fun memories between Mother and Madre and many questions from us. They answer our questions while Madre combs and braids Mother's hair in two braids that she pins across the crown of her head.

All of us share the news we receive from letters that arrive from across the country. Some come from people we know, others from those we don't know. They all write to tell us they have read about our accident in the newspapers and are praying for us. Mother's friend Clarice Biggins in Daytona Beach, who used to drive us and her sons to the airport to watch the planes take off, writes Mother to say she and her family would be happy to send for and take care of Rosemary and me until Mother has recovered. We are deeply moved by her offer, and Mother considers it for days before writing back to say she thinks it is better that we remain together.

By the third week, Mom begins to piece together events from the accident. She tells us that after a restless night of sleep, she decided to take the first leg of the trip. And when we finished singing songs and gathering the grapefruit that had fallen from the truck in front of us, Rosemary, Dad, and I drifted off to sleep. She became drowsy and started searching for a place along the highway to pull over so she could rest, too, but the road was full of curves and had no shoulders, so she continued to drive.

Entering a stretch of highway that was under construction, she nodded off. Suddenly the sound of a car horn awakened her. The shock of the horn frightened her, and she jerked awake. As she did, she felt the right front tire leave the pavement. When it dropped off the road, she looked out the window my father slept against and saw water in a gorge so deep that only the tops of trees were visible. Panicked, she struggled to turn the steering wheel and get the car back onto the road, but she overcorrected the turn and found herself headed into oncoming traffic and a sure collision with the large tractor trailer barreling toward her. Having seen the deep water on the right of the highway, she drove the car over the left side praying to God, "Please spare my family." We careened down the embankment, turning over and over as the truck sped by. The men who later bring their tow truck to the site of the wreckage to remove our car tell us, "It's a miracle anyone survived that crash." They can't even salvage the tires.

During her recovery Mother tells us, "There's a nurse here named Nurse Littlejohn who makes my bed better than anyone else." She pulls the covers tightly and smooths out all the wrinkles so there are no lumps to cause discomfort. After that, Rosemary and I wait until Nurse Littlejohn is on duty before we ask for Mother's sheets to be changed.

By early July, my grandmother, sister, and I are able to help Mother turn from her back onto one side and then the other with pillows tucked between her knees and propped against her back. We rub powder on her back and buttocks to keep her from getting bedsores, and we place towels next to her skin to try to keep her dry from perspiration in the hot basement, where there are no air conditioners. Madre stands near her bed for long stretches at a time, fanning Mother to keep her cool. When our grandmother gets tired, Rosemary and I relieve her.

One morning when we arrive at the hospital we find that a new patient has been brought into the room. Up to that time, Mother has had the room to herself. The new patient is also the victim of a car crash that has left her with a broken neck. She is heavily sedated, flat on her back in a neck brace, and experiencing a lot of pain. Through conversations with family members who come to see her, we learn that she is the sister-in-law of baseball great Don Newcomb.

Over the course of the next two months, our two families become friendly. They bring a radio into the room, so we can all keep up with

Dodger games. Now Madre can listen to her beloved Dodgers and engage in endless conversations with the family about baseball stats, players' backgrounds, and theories as to why the team has won or lost.

While Madre enjoys the ball games and her newfound friendships, the Harrises take Rosemary and me to their farm to spend weekends. There we dive into farm chores, gathering fresh produce from the garden, collecting eggs from the chicken coop, feeding animals, and learning to prepare food on their wood-burning stove. Fourteen-year-old Polly teaches us to bake pound cake, which we eat at the end of the day and wash down with glasses of homemade lemonade. The Harris farm is filled with numerous cats and dogs, and it has a stream stocked with fish and a well with the coldest water that ever filled a tin cup.

Following our second or third visit to the farm, Rosie and I begin to feel like members of the Harris family. We return to the hospital with stories of the mischief we've gotten into and the fun we have had. I tell Mother about the day I wore my favorite red sundress and got into the fenced-in area where there was a bull. Using the skirt of my dress, I begin to wave it like a cape in front of the animal. The others call to me, "Come out of there!" I ignore them, because the bull is ignoring me. But a short time later he turns, looks as me, and charges in my direction as if he is crazed. I zigzag all over the pasture, shrieking to Polly, Weldon, Calvin, and Rose to open the fence so I can get out. But they are all doubled over with laughter, and no one can open the gate. Eventually Weldon distracts the animal long enough for me to dive through the barbed-wire fence, leaving a piece of my beautiful red sundress on one of the barbs. Mother swears it is the laughter from stories like this that speeds up her healing.

When the Harris children come to visit their brother Red, they make their way around to the window outside Mother's room and meet her for the first time. Calvin (the youngest child) endears himself to everyone when he looks in the room and coos, "Oooh-wee, where in the worl' did Mr. Braxton find such a pu-urty woman?"

During the weekdays, when we are not at the farm and Mother is sleeping, Rosemary, Madre, and I walk the few blocks to Mrs. Harris's flower shop to help her with arrangements for weddings, funerals, and hospitals, and with corsages for dances. As we work together, she and Madre talk about the farm, share recipes, and share information about sewing and flower arrangements.

By early August, the nurses have taught us to raise Mother to a sitting position, lift her legs, and swing them over the side of the bed. Because of the pain she is still in, we have to move her carefully in stages. We learn how to help her on and off the bedpan, too, and to steady her as she lifts her hips up. Her roommate is also improving—healing to the point of being able to sit up.

The fact that we have made friends and that our days are filled with visits to the farm, trips to Mrs. Harris's flower shop, and picnics with the Harris family, the month of August flies by with twice the speed that June and July dragged along. We are all happy when Red is released from the hospital, as well as when Mother's roommate is strong enough to return home.

Toward the middle of August, Mother is able to stand for the first time. Once she is standing, she slowly turns and eases herself into a chair beside her bed. From there she can look out the window and talk to Rosie and to me seated on the lawn outside. After a week has passed, we help her get into a wheelchair and roll her into the hall so she can see the rest of the hospital floor and all the things we've been telling her about during the summer.

At the end of August, Daddy returns from New York. He comes straight from the bus station to the hospital and enters the door by the nurses' station and then stops short as he turns the corner leading to the hall where Mother's room is. She is standing down the hall several yards from him with crutches, nurses and a doctor standing by, and Madre, Rosemary, and me behind her. Slowly and painfully she drags one foot forward and then the other until she is in his arms. One of the doctors looks at my parents and reveals what the medical staff has thought all along.

"I bet you thought you'd never walk again," he says. To which Mother replies, "The thought never crossed my mind."

# CHAPTER 13

# MISSISSIPPI GODDAMN![64]

PRESIDENT'S MANSION

O N THE DAY WE arrive in Tougaloo, Mississippi, I can think of no more desolate place on earth to be. Gone are the golden sands, palm trees, and pastel-colored houses of Florida. Gone too are the friends we've made in South Carolina, the farm we've grown to love—and those with whom we've made promises to keep in touch. In

---

64 "Mississippi Goddamn," written and recorded by Nina Simone.

their place stands the harsh reality of our distant slave past, first and foremost being the president's mansion on the college campus.

During the days of slavery when cotton was king, the mansion belonged to John Boddie, a cotton plantation owner who had built his antebellum home with an expansive cupola to please his fiancée, who wanted to stand on it and see all the way to Jackson, ten miles south. But prior to completion of the mansion, the young woman married someone else, and Boddie lost interest in construction of the house. He had finished it with "glass fit for a palace and bricks unfit for a cabin,"[65] and he used the veranda to oversee the work of his slaves rather than view the distant city of Jackson.

The end of the Civil War had brought an end to the profit Boddie amassed from his cotton plantation, and his dwindling finances forced him to seek buyers for the land. He sold it to a former Union army officer named Allen P. Higgins, who'd been commissioned by the American Missionary Association (AMA) to locate land suitable for a normal agricultural school for newly freed slaves. Higgins bought five hundred of the two-thousand-acre Boddie plantation in 1869 for $10,500 and began what would become Tougaloo Southern Christian College.[66]

So we leave our brand-new house in Daytona Beach, Florida, the jungle gym we'd swung on in the middle of a Florida hurricane, our log cabin playhouse with so many happy memories of baked mud pies, grass-onion salad, our dog, Thunder Mike, and all our friends. We leave them to come and live on a former slave plantation.

There is no nearby swimming pool in this new place, there will be no trips to the Dairy Queen or to the beach, and drive-in movies are

---

65 Clarice T. Campbell and Oscar Allan Rogers, Jr., *Mississippi: The View from Tougaloo* (The University Press of Mississippi, 1979), 6, 10.

66 Ibid. 7.

nonexistent, at least for Negroes. There's no city bus, no cab company or grocery store. There isn't even a traffic light, just five hundred acres of campus and two thousand more of agricultural land populated by Negro families. A few juke joints selling moonshine whiskey (that the dry state of Mississippi ignores the illegal consumption of) speckle the surrounding area, and sundries can be purchased at small country stores. But groceries, drugstores, bakeries, and department stores are several miles away on Highway 80—the road that leads from Tougaloo to Jackson.

A railroad track runs along Highway 80 (referred to by Negro locals as "eighty highway") next to a sign that announces the existence of the school: Tougaloo College, 1/4 mile. Going over a railroad track past the sign toward the college, one notices a community post office on the left. It houses a switchboard that connects most of the community unless one is lucky enough to have a private phone line. It was once a station house for the Illinois Central,[67] but by the time we arrive the IC has been replaced by a freight train that local automobile drivers try to outrun as they race along the strip of highway toward the capital city of Jackson.

The road that crosses the railroad track leads to the college and is just wide enough for two-way traffic. Small trailers and wooden A-frame houses populate the side where the post office sits, and a wooded area with moss-laden oak and hickory trees grows wild off to the right. There is a wrought-iron gate at the end of the road that leads onto the college campus. The top of the gate forms an arch with letters that read, Tougaloo Southern Christian College.

Tougaloo is an Indian word that means "at the fork in the stream" or "between two rivers." Both terms perfectly describe the area, because

---

67  Ibid. 6.

it lies at a point where two brooks come together. Tougaloo also lies between the Pearl and the Yazoo Rivers and straddles two counties, Hinds and Madison, so neither county has jurisdiction over the college or the community that surrounds it. Today Tougaloo is part of the city of Jackson, but in 1954 when we arrived, it was still seven miles north of the capital.

Cotton fields to Tougaloo's north are worked by sharecroppers, many of them the descendants of workers who were tricked into farming the fields by slave owners like L. F. Thomson, who convinced his former slave, Luther Mills, to work the land on which Mills had labored during slavery. Because Mills could neither read nor write, Thomson signed the agreement for both of them—an agreement that left the descendants of Luther Mills still working the land in 1954,[68] buying "seed and staples on credit," paying the storekeeper when the crop was sold and risking the loss of their home, their way of earning a living, and supplies to keep their family fed and clothed[69] if they crossed the landowner. The Mississippi Delta lay roughly fifty miles northwest of Tougaloo. There one could still find field workers, stooped over from the weight of heavy cotton-filled sacks slowly moving between the rows dragging their sacks behind them.

When we arrive at Tougaloo from Gaffney by way of Atlanta, the first order of business is to get our semi-invalid mother settled. Rosemary and I help Daddy assemble their bed and make it up. Then, following his instructions, we place pillows against the bed board for her to lean on and roll others lengthwise to put under her knees in order to relieve any pressure that might be placed on her back when

---

68 Thomas J. Ladenburg and William S. McFeely, *The Black Man in the Land of Equality* (New York: Hayden Book Company, 1969), 77, 80.

69 Ibid. 81.

she is sitting up. Once she is settled, we help put our own beds together in the back bedroom the two of us will share. When our beds are made, we unpack pots, pans, plates, and glasses. New neighbors bring over chicken, greens, rice, lemonade, cake, and eggs to welcome us to Tougaloo. Our father uses a campus station wagon to go to a nearby shopping mall for staples. We place what we don't eat right away in the deep freeze on the screened-in back porch.

Within days of our arrival, Dad is on the football field setting up a practice schedule for a new crop of football players, so the cooking and housekeeping fall to my ten-year-old sister and me. We have never cooked before, so we sit at the edge of Mother and Daddy's bed and get instructions from her on how to prepare food.

When we aren't cooking and unpacking boxes, we comb Mother's hair, give her sponge baths, and help her get on and off the bedpan. Once or twice a day, we lift her legs from the bed and swing them over the side so she can practice walking down the hall toward our room and sit on the toilet in the bathroom, which is next to our bedroom. The most difficult part of caring for her is our inability to relieve her pain. It seems absurd today, but back then she never received any physical therapy or instructions on strengthening the muscles around her pelvis. She wasn't even given crutches when she left that segregated hospital in South Carolina. The makeshift bed board (wood planks Daddy has had cut by campus carpenters) are an invention of our father's, fashioned to give Mother support. Dad's knowledge has come from the health education training he received in graduate school.

In addition to caring for our bedridden mother and unpacking all the things that have been shipped from Florida (including the money Mother packed in a dresser drawer and now has to send to Papa as repayment for the advance he gave her), we have a whole new set of cultural, political, and social rules with which to cope.

Our arrival in Mississippi has come three months after the May 17, 1954, Supreme Court decision in which Chief Justice Earl Warren declared segregation of white and colored children in public schools to be detrimental to colored children, noting that the condition could affect our hearts and minds in ways unlikely ever to be undone.[70] When the decision is announced, Mississippi State Senator James O. Eastland tells his constituents that the Constitution of the United States has been destroyed, and they are not obliged to obey the ruling.[71] "Whites' anger over the ruling has fueled violent segregationist backlash in which gangs have committed beatings, burnings, and lynchings—murder by mob. The Supreme Court decision leads to the formation of a new hate group in Mississippi composed of urban middle-class whites determined to fight desegregation. Many of them are prominent bankers, lawyers, doctors, and politicians who call themselves the Citizens' Council. This racist organization is created by the state's Sovereignty Commission for the sole purpose of preserving Mississippi's 'sovereign right' to maintain a segregated society, and it funnels $5,000 in taxpayers' money into the organization on a monthly basis."[72]

The state legislature is also incensed by the Supreme Court decision and passes a law abolishing compulsory school attendance.[73] With an outraged sense of having had their state's rights ignored and trampled on by the federal government, Mississippi whites turn on

---

70 Williams, *Eyes on the Prize*, 34.

71 Ibid. 38.

72 Ibid. 211.

73 The Southern Poverty Law Center, *Free At Last: A History of the Civil Rights Movement and Those Who Died in the Struggle* (Montgomery, AL: The Civil Rights Education Project, 1969), 13.

the Negro population, increasing racial tensions and vowing to "get Tougaloo,"[74] the only integrated spot in the entire state. They begin by discontinuing the college's A and B ratings through the Southern Association of Colleges and Secondary Schools by intentionally failing to inform the school of changes in standards. They then send notification that the school's approval rating will terminate because of deficiencies. President Warren (a white man) phones the American Missionary Association to find out why his recent letter from them has not mentioned the new requirements. That is when a secretary informs him that she wrote at Christmastime, but she was also "pretty busy." American Missionary Association Secretary Philip Widenhouse (also white) then calls the AMA's Mississippi office to find out what has happened only to have the same secretary tell him, "Well that's the college that has both Nigras and whites on the faculty."[75]

Widenhouse and Warren quickly produce evidence that shows AMA support is equivalent to an endowment in excess of the required amount and that Tougaloo is spending sufficient funds on its library to have received approval. Faced with the evidence, the Southern Association claims "an error has been made" and drops its harassment,[76] but Tougaloo and the national board note the legitimate deficiencies pertaining to faculty salaries that require immediate steps to correct.

Daddy is among the professionals President Warren recruits during a search for faculty members with advanced degrees to fulfill the requirements of the Southern Association of Colleges. Our father joins the faculty as head coach of football, basketball, track, and tennis, and as associate professor of health education and head of the

---

74  Campbell and Rogers, *Mississippi: The View from Tougaloo*, 177.
75  Ibid. 177.
76  Ibid. 177.

Physical Education Department. To assist him with football, he calls on two recent Bethune-Cookman graduates, Andy Hinson and Wilbert Owens, who along with the college chaplain, John Mangram, set about rebuilding the sports program at Tougaloo. It will be an awesome task. The football team hasn't won a game in over a year, losing one game by a score of 99–0. The basketball and track teams have fared only slightly better, and the tennis program is in such disarray that the courts are overgrown with weeds and strewn with trash.

The house we live in and the one next door to us sit on an acre of land. Our house has a front lawn almost large enough for softball or for badminton or volleyball courts. And since our visit to Tougaloo a year earlier, the school has refurbished the seedy-looking place and turned it into a lovely space with full living and dining rooms, three sets of refinished French doors, a large country kitchen, and newly sealed hardwood floors. And the side porch has been screened in, making it an ideal place for Rosemary and me to use as an entertainment area when friends come to play. The back and front porches have new screens, and my sister and I decide we can use the basement with its outdoor entrance as a bomb shelter if the Russians ever attack us. Our neighbors on both sides are white. The Palmers, with whom we share the half-acre front lawn, are to our left. They have two children. Lea Lou is seven, and Randy is five. The space to our right is vacant and wooded, but the Bogles live at the front corner of our front yard at a right angle. Their first baby, Heather, a little blond-haired girl, is born soon after our arrival. When I look back on our arrival in Mississippi, it seems totally incongruous that our first experience in Negro-white living began in the heart of the old Confederacy. That is because the faculty is made up of Negro and white professors, and all of them (and their families) live on the college campus.

One of the first visitors to welcome us to Tougaloo is a portly, balding white man with a twinkle in his eyes. Dr. Ernst Borinski is head of the Sociology Department, chairman of Social Science, and a professor at Tougaloo. He is one of a group of Jews who managed to escape Nazi Germany and find refuge at a Negro southern college in a Depression economy that exhibited discrimination in hiring Jews at Ivy League schools. The practice has forced people like Borinski to work at Negro colleges like Tougaloo and Talladega in Alabama, schools that offer a genuine community in America where local whites consider the newcomers Marxist agitators or Nazi spies. Negroes, on the other hand, "view them as kindred souls..."[77]

We develop a close relationship with Dr. Borinski, who is a frequent guest in our home. He derives joy from surprising Rose and me with gifts like chiming Christmas angels propelled in a circle by the heat of four lit candles. He also enjoys giving us and other faculty children free German and speed-reading lessons on Saturday mornings, during which time he also shares stories about his native Germany.

Tougaloo is a striking counterpoint to life in the rest of Mississippi. The campus is calm—serene even—compared to other parts of the state; an oasis in a racist desert where Negro and white faculty members live next door to one another, go in and out of one another's homes with regularity, and attend lectures, receptions, church, ball games, recitals, and dances together, in spite of the fact that mixing of the races is strictly prohibited by the state. Rosemary and I make friends with other

---

77 Samuel G. Freeman, "Finding Their Refuge in the Segregated South," *The New York Times*, January 29, 2001. Based on a PBS program directed by Lori Cheatle, "From Swastika to Jim Crow."

faculty brats, even though nearly all the white children attend all-white schools in Hinds or Madison County, and all the Negro children attend segregated schools in the same areas. Should anyone forget and take the integrated experience for granted, it only takes a quick trip into town to remind us that Tougaloo is the exception, not the rule. As soon as local whites discover that we live at Tougaloo, they call us "uppity Nigras."[78] They call whites from the college "traitors" or "Nigger lovers."

Settling into our new life, my sister and I make beds, wash dishes, sweep, dust, and perform other household chores while Mother recuperates. Dad combines the demands of a new job with the heavy cleaning and waxing of hardwood floors, doing family laundry, and washing our hair. To help Dad out with the latter chore, my sister and I take turns kneeling on the floor next to the bathtub with our heads under the faucet while Daddy gives us shampoos. Afterward Rosie and I comb each other's hair. Continuing to set up the household, Daddy strings up a clothesline in the backyard on which to hang clothes that we wash in the washing machine on the screened-in back porch. That's when some of the men on campus begin to tease him for doing "women's work." Undaunted, our father shouts back at them, "This is *my* house and I take care of it the way *I* choose. You can do what you want in yours."

By the time school is in full swing and football season underway, Mother is able to walk by herself inside the house with the help of two sticks. Since the hospital in Gaffney discharged her without crutches, Dad has cut the handles off two broomsticks and placed rubber tips on the ends for her to use. On good days she can climb the four or five steps from the sidewalk outside to the front porch of our house, but she will have to wear a heavy back brace for at least another year.

---

78 The term *Nigra* is as close as whites can get to calling us *Nigger* to our faces, and they use the word as often as they can.

Money is tight after my parents repay Papa the loan from the summer, but Daddy has to buy a new car out here in the middle of nowhere, because it is the only way he can shop and drive us to our new school in Jackson. It is the Jackson State College Laboratory School, and in order for us to attend, Dad has to take his turn in a car pool with the Frasers, the Owens, and the Randalls, all Tougaloo families whose children travel the ten miles into Jackson in order to attend the lab school.

At Jackson Lab, Rose and I immediately are faced with school loyalty issues. Every schoolmate who is not from Tougaloo is a rabid Jackson State College sports fan. Being the daughters of the coach at the rival school, my sister and I naturally pull for Tougaloo. But we are surrounded by the children of Jackson State faculty members—the daughter of the Jackson State band director, Phyllis Walton, and Bonita Merritt, Tellis Ellis III, and Sonia, Craig, and Joey Gillam (who later becomes one of the National Football League's first Negro quarterbacks) are all the children of Jackson State College football coaches.

All of us children begin the year with satchels full of new loose-leaf notebooks, pencils, erasers, paper, and plastic rulers, but our textbooks are hand-me-downs from white children who no longer have any use for them. Seated in our respective classes, we cover the old textbooks with precut brown paper to protect them for next year's students, in spite of the fact that they are outdated and have already been discarded by whites. We know Mississippi white schools are terrible compared to white schools in other states and that Negro schools in Mississippi are in even worse shape, but we also know that using old books and having poor equipment doesn't mean white children have better values than we do or that they are more capable of learning than we are. We know this because our teachers tell us so and make us feel we can achieve anything we want to.

I enter the seventh grade as a twelve-year-old. My classroom is shared with the eighth grade in this four-room schoolhouse. Rosemary's class is in another room shared with the fourth and fifth grades, and the first- through third-grade classes are in a third room. The fourth room of the old schoolhouse is reserved for assemblies. Toilets are outside and around the corner of the building—a place no one relishes going when autumn turns to winter, and the weather dips to freezing temperatures because they are unheated. Mr. Williams is our principal and teacher of both the seventh and eighth grades. He is a strict disciplinarian but relaxes enough toward the end of the week to allow us to hold talent shows on Friday afternoons.

We begin each morning with the Pledge of Allegiance, followed by songs very different from the patriotic postwar songs of Bonner Elementary School in Daytona Beach. In Jackson, we sing lullabies and nonsense songs like "John, Jacob, Jingle Harold Smith," but I miss the spirituals we used to sing in Florida. They gave me pride and reassurance in the survival of my ancestors from slavery to the segregated times of today.

As a seventh grader, I have escaped the Confederate version of Mississippi history, but Rosemary gets a full dose of it and has a difficult time accepting what she's being taught. One of the most glaring insults comes when she sees the word *Negro* spelled with a lowercase *n*. We have been taught that if the word *Caucasian* is spelled with a capital *C*, the word *Negro* should to be spelled with a capital *N*. My sister, who has always been a rebel, finds herself aligned with another precocious classmate named Marion Alexander. Together they refuse to accept the spelling of Negro or to swallow whole portions of Mississippi history without questioning what they are learning. Marion says she knows portions of books that describe the slaves as happy are untrue because one of her ancestors was a slave, and her mother has told her how the woman tried to escape slavery with her children, only to be apprehended by slave catchers and tied to a whipping post. She was stripped of her blouse and beaten until she fell unconscious. The story she tells in class later becomes the basis of her mother's book, *Jubilee*.[79] As the daughter of a renowned poet, with a grasp of historical facts, Marion comes by her skepticism of Mississippi's version of history honestly. She is the eldest of the four Alexander children and is not afraid to share other stories she's heard at home. Encouraged by Marion's challenges, Rosemary begins to relate stories she's heard at home and those she remembers from Mrs. Bethune. Before long, others of their classmates are sharing versions of history that contradict the writings in their textbooks.

Mrs. Lottie Thornton, teacher of the fourth, fifth, and sixth grades, encourages her students to share their stories and to challenge the textbook information. She is required by law to teach Mississippi history, but like many Negro teachers of her day, she is wise enough to use the material she has been given to expose the racism that brought about the segregated conditions under which we live. Young as they are, her students understand why she encourages them to arm themselves with additional data to share.

It is during one of these periods that Rosemary discovers Marion's mother's poem, "For My People," and decides to learn it with the same fervor she learned "The Creation." When she has mastered the poem, she goes to Margaret Walker's home and recites it for her, asking for suggestions on interpretation. Later, she gives public performances in which she shares her interpretation.

---

79 Margaret Walker, *Jubilee* (Boston: Bantam Books, 1977), 143.

During recess we sometimes play "Stonewall Jackson," reenacting his death over and over again. At other times, I gather the first graders together and teach them ballet positions or enter into a game of hopscotch with my classmates. Rosemary and I also join the Girl Scouts and travel with Melanie, Earlene, Dorothy, Lula, Phyllis, Falvia, Camille, Maria, and Shelton Ann to those meetings after school. At the height of Mississippi's racial hostilities, we enter the front of the city bus and sit in the first set of seats every week on our way to our Girl Scout meeting, fully aware of the fact that we are breaking Jim Crow laws. The same white bus driver greets us each week and chats with us all the way to our destination without ever once telling us to move.

Settling into the school year, I become friendly with six girls in the seventh and eighth grades, all of whom are, or soon will be, thirteen years old. Every day after lunch we gather outside the girls' bathroom and harmonize the latest rock-and-roll songs. A couple of months into the school year, we decide we are good enough to perform in one of the Friday afternoon talent shows. Wearing white blouses, poodle skirts over yards of crinoline petticoats, wide elastic cinch belts, and snow-white bobby socks, we announce that we are the Lucky Thirteens. We stand in a straight line, swaying to and fro, crooning, "Sincerely (wee-oo, wee-oo), Oh-oh yes, sincerely (wee-oo, wee-oo) 'cause I love you so dearly..."

Gail Skinner, a member of the group, is six months older than I am and a year ahead of me in school, but we become the best of friends, sharing the joys and secrets of our emerging womanhood. We complain about our menstrual periods and the size of our breasts. We meet in the restroom each morning to stuff Kleenex in our bras, so we can appear more womanly. We talk endlessly about boys and spend hours on the phone in the evenings discussing what to wear to school the next day and how to comb our hair, even though Gail always wears a ponytail and (at my parents' insistence) I still wear two thick braids.

Gail introduces me to *True Confession* magazines, which I read under the bedcovers with a flashlight after everyone else has gone to sleep. I share my allowance with her so she can buy the magazines and pass them on to me after she's finished with the stories. Later we discuss the girls "in trouble" and the women whose love lives have gone astray. Gail also teaches me the latest dance steps, and as our friendship grows, she comes to Tougaloo for football games and sleepovers. Her older brother, Howard, plays football for Tougaloo Prep, so when she comes out to visit, we walk over to the football field to watch him play in the high-school games that precede the college games.

With Howard on the field for Tougaloo Prep, Gail, Rosemary, and I sit in the stands and cheer, "Howard, Howard, he's our man, If he can't do it, nobody can!"

At night we move a rollaway bed into our bedroom from the side porch for Gail to sleep on. She and I lie awake talking long after Rosemary has fallen asleep. Often we lament the fact that we are barely into size 32A bras, while Gail's classmate Virginia looks like she wears a C cup. Virginia is also said to have an eighteen-inch waist, which she accentuates with a wide elastic belt. She wears tight skirts and the collars of her blouses turned up against hair that is cut in a boyish bob. She has long feathery eyelashes that she bats at drooling boys until she has them eating out of her hand, and then she spins on the heel of her penny loafer and saunters away. You would think we'd be envious of her, but we secretly admire her. Everybody does because as cute and provocative as she is, she is also friendly and fun to be around. Besides, Gail's beauty and sweetness attract her own share of admirers. I don't mind the competition because the object of my affection is her sixteen-year-old brother, Howard.

On afternoons when the Tougaloo Prep school bus leaves the campus to take the Jackson city kids back home it passes our car, filled with day students. On my way home to Tougaloo from the Jackson lab school, I look from inside our car to see Howard in the middle of the bus, laughing and talking with his friends.

Except for the fact that he is nearly six feet tall, he and Gail look very much alike. They have the same keen noses, bright eyes, beautiful white teeth, and flawless brown-sugar complexions. Gail's hair is fine and straight, whereas Howard's is thick and tightly curled. He wears a Negro version of the pompadour the white boys sport. The Negro version is called the "bush." Like all brothers and sisters, he and Gail have their spats, but theirs are never serious. They help each other with household chores and cover for each other if one of them gets into trouble with their parents. They adore each other, and watching them together makes me wish I had an older brother. The feeling is especially strong on the day I visit their home and find myself sitting in the living room with them watching television. Engrossed in a program, I soon become aware that the two of them have moved away from me and gotten very quiet. I look up to discover them standing arm in arm at the front door, watching a beautiful sunset. At that moment I wish I had an older brother for Gail to love, so the four of us could share these kinds of times forever.

At Tougaloo, Dad has set up his coaching staff and contacted coaches throughout the state asking them to be part of his fall football schedule. Given the school's lousy record, everyone he contacts agrees to play him. Due to the fact that Mother is unable to walk outside the house, Daddy comes home on game days and drives the three of us over to the football field, even though it is only a block away. He parks behind one of the goalposts so Mother can see the game because she can't climb into the bleachers. Rosemary and I stay in the car with her to keep her company.

Having moved to Tougaloo from Bethune-Cookman where Daddy coached winning teams, it is difficult at first to understand why students filing into the stands at Tougaloo look so dejected. Even faculty members seem to have a sense of doom as they take their seats. The band plays, and the pep squad tries to drum up spirit, but little energy comes from the crowd. The opposing team scores early in the first half of the first game we attend, and they continue to score as if Tougaloo's defense doesn't exist. Then near the end of the game, Tougaloo slowly makes its way down the field toward the goal near where our car is parked. Three attempts to gain a first down fail. With very little time left close to the end of the game, Tougaloo decides to go for a fourth attempt at scoring rather than give the ball up. That's when a Tougaloo player manages to break free and stagger across the goal line a few feet in front of our car. Mother begins blowing the car horn. Rosemary and I get out of the car, jump up and down, and yell at the top of our lungs. At first the crowd in the stands doesn't seem to realize what has happened. When they finally see that Tougaloo has scored a touchdown, a cheer goes up that sounds as if we've won the game. Even players on the bench jump up and hug one another. Tougaloo loses the game but has scored its first touchdown in a long time, giving everyone hope that change is in the air. During his first year as head football coach, Dad takes the team to four wins, five losses and one tie, and in the eight years that he is coach, he brings Tougaloo four football championships, six basketball championships, three tennis conference championships, and over twenty track championships, seven of them conference championships. In fact, Dad is so successful at Tougaloo that Coach "Monk" Wilson at Jackson State (Tougaloo's chief rival) once remarked, "Brax does more with *nothing* than anybody I've ever seen." He made such a statement because Tougaloo was the school that attracted students with higher intellectual abilities than physical prowess, while Jackson offered more lucrative athletic scholarships. Because of Tougaloo's athletic success that first year, Dad has a tough time getting the schools that were eager to play him when he arrived to agree to play him during the second year. No one wants to lose to a team that has been an underdog for so many years and is now turning that losing streak around.

NELL'S DAD AT HIS DESK, TOUGALOO COLLEGE

Once football season ends and basketball season begins, the school year seems to fly. Before we know it, it is May, and we are awakened by Dad's shouts that we have all overslept and missed worshipping at St. Mark's Episcopal Church in Jackson on Mother's Day. Now he says we have just enough time to get to the Congregational church on campus. Rosemary and I bolt out of bed, race around the house, pulling out socks, dresses, and gloves. We quickly wash ribbons for our hair, remove the lampshade in our room, and wait for the light to get hot. When it is heated we "iron" and dry our wet ribbons by pulling them across the hot light bulb before tying them in our hair.

Dad takes the corsage he has bought for Mother out of the refrigerator while muttering under his breath that we are missing worship at our own church. The four of us drive across the campus to Woodworth Chapel, since Mother can't walk fast enough for us to get there on time. We enter the chapel and follow Dad up the aisle to a front-row pew. I am annoyed with him for going all the way to the front of the church and self-conscious about sitting there. Since I am not familiar with the Congregational service, I would much rather sit behind someone who understands it so I can follow that person. Now all eyes are on us, and I'm sure they are all wondering why we are here instead of at St. Mark's.

The topic of today's sermon is "God Wants Women, Too," and because it is exactly one year after the Supreme Court decision outlawing segregation in public schools there is talk of this week being touted as "Annual Freedom Week" when NAACP branches all over the country mark the first birthday of Brown v. Board of Education. Following his sermon, the minister solicits support for the organization by indicating that the offering will be given to the Fighting Fund for Freedom. He asks that everyone be as generous as possible.

After the collection is taken up, a member of Omega Psi Phi fraternity (the frat to which my father belongs) stands and begins talking about Mother's Day and the importance of mothers. He ends by saying, "Each year the fraternity honors a woman who exemplifies the spirit of motherhood. This year," he continues, "we have chosen Mrs. Anne Thomas Braxton as Omega Psi Phi's Mother of the Year." Daddy helps our stunned Mother to her feet and up the aisle to receive a bouquet of flowers and a plaque, while Rosemary and I sit in disbelief. Mother manages a bewildered, "Thank you," and one or two other words before returning to her seat. That is when, looking at the satisfaction on Daddy's face, the three of us realize Dad has planned the entire morning, right down to our oversleeping, in order to surprise her.

In Mississippi the school year ends in May so that the children of sharecroppers can help their parents in the fields. Those of us who do not have such responsibilities make dates with one another to swim at the Negro pool in Jackson, or go off to Girl Scout camp in June.

One Saturday, Rosemary and I invite twenty friends to come to Tougaloo for an all-day picnic. We play softball in the front yard, take hikes around the campus pointing out historic sites, tour Brownlee Gymnasium, and walk down a dirt road to the Tougaloo water tower. On the way back, we shake pecans from trees and eat them all the way home.

Back at our house, we spread blankets under the trees, drink homemade lemonade, and eat sandwiches, brownies, and potato chips. Then we set up card games, checkers, jacks, and listen to rock-and-roll music on the Victrola. When parents begin to arrive to collect their children, no one wants to leave. The day has been so much fun that we promise to do it again soon, but our lives change so drastically by the end of the summer that we never do.

In August, when Girl Scout camp ends, we return home. In the last lazy days before school starts, Rosemary and I stretch out under the famous Tougaloo oak with our friend Charlette Randall, whose mother is an elementary-school teacher and whose father is superintendent of buildings and grounds at Tougaloo. Charlette has always been more precocious than everyone else in our group, and on this day she begins to relate a story she has read in the newspaper. As she talks, an icy chill runs down my spine. She tells us she has read about the murder of a Negro boy who either spoke to or whistled at a white woman. She says his name is Emmett Till. Rosemary and I leave her under the tree and immediately go home to read the article for ourselves. The information is still sketchy, but it confirms everything Charlette has said.

As I put the paper down, I am gripped by a fear I cannot shake. For the first time in my life, I realize Negro children are not safe. Before this day, I thought we were innocent victims in an adult dispute; I thought adults would go after one another, but they wouldn't hurt children. In all the time we've been growing up, I have never thought of myself as living in danger, but now the unthinkable has happened—to a fourteen-year-old boy close to where we live—and now I know that in Mississippi, *anything* is possible.

Emmett Till had come from Chicago, Illinois, to Money, Mississippi, for a visit with relatives. On August 28, 1955, he and his cousins had driven to a country store to buy candy. Before entering the store, he reportedly accepted a dare from one of his relatives that led him to utter, "Bye-bye, baby," to the white woman inside the store. The kids left without any further thought about the incident. Four days went by. Then at midnight on the fourth day, a carload of white men drove to the unpainted cabin of Till's uncle, Mose Wright. Two of the men,

Roy Bryant and J. W. Milam, got out of the car, went to the door of the cabin, and ordered Wright to "get that boy who done the talkin'."[80] Mose pleaded with them to leave young Till alone, telling them the boy was from up North and didn't know the ways of the South, but the men dragged Till outside, shoved him into the backseat of their car, and drove off. Joining a mob of like-minded vigilantes, Bryant and Milam proceeded to the Tallahatchie River where they forced Emmett Till out of the vehicle. They made him carry a seventy-five-pound cotton gin fan to the riverbank and then strip naked. They tortured him, shot him in the head, crushed his skull, gouged out an eye, and tied his body to the cotton gin fan with barbed wire before dumping it in the river.

Days later when investigators pulled his corpse up, it was so badly mutilated that his uncle, Mose Wright, could only identify him by the initialed ring his nephew wore. The boy's casket was sent by train to his mother in Chicago, who collapsed on the station platform when she saw the remains of her only child. She decided to leave the casket open so the rest of the world could see what had been done to him.

On the day of his wake, thousands of people lined the Chicago streets to pay their respects. *Jet* magazine, a national Negro weekly, ran a photograph of his mutilated body on their pages, causing the outrage of the throngs of people who saw it. Most sent record-level contributions to the NAACP's "fight fund." Reported nationwide, the Emmett Till murder alerted the world to the horrors of life in Mississippi.

Even with photographs, state law enforcement officers tried to deny what had happened, claiming that the body they fished out of the river was too decomposed to be positively identified. Having made the declaration, they refused to do any real investigative work, preferring

---

80 Williams, *Eyes on the Prize*, 42.

to go through the charade of an investigation by appointing a special prosecutor, to whom they gave no funds or assistance. Further complicating matters was speculation as to whether any Negro witnesses would testify against the white men who had murdered Emmett Till, and that speculation included doubts as to whether or not Till's cousin, Curtis Jones, would return to Mississippi for the trial, since he had fled the state right after the murder. In the end, he did not return because he was afraid that as a Negro testifying against a white man in Mississippi, he'd be signing his own death warrant.[81]

Five Mississippi Delta lawyers agreed to represent Roy Bryant (the husband of the white woman Emmett Till reportedly spoke to) and his brother-in-law, J. W. Milam, both identified as the ones who took Till from the cabin. White people in Mississippi closed ranks and spread the word through the Negro community for people to keep their mouths shut.[82]

Mose Wright refused to go back to his home after his nephew's kidnapping and murder, for fear the men would come back to kill him, too. His wife never went back, either, asking her son to get a corset, a couple of slips, and some dresses for her.[83]

When Roy Bryant and J. W. Milam were indicted for the murder, Mose Wright received anonymous warnings to leave the state with his family before they were all killed. He refused to be intimidated, deciding instead to become a witness for the prosecution. His testimony marked one of the few times in Mississippi history that a Negro man pointed to white men as the killers of a Negro. He said later that it was the first time in his life that he'd had the courage to accuse a white man

---

81  Ibid. 45.
82  Ibid. 45.
83  Ibid. 45.

of any crime, "let alone something as terrible as killing a boy. I wasn't exactly brave..." he said, "I just wanted to see justice done."[84]

His testimony encouraged other Negroes to come forward, including Willie Reed, the son of a sharecropper, who testified to seeing Till in the back of a passing truck at six o'clock on the morning of August 28. Reed had been on his way to buy meat for breakfast when he saw the truck drive to a shed on the plantation where he worked. Hearing cries from the truck, he went to his aunt's nearby home where he could hear the sounds that became wails and then pained moans of "Mama, Lord have mercy, Lord have mercy." Reed asked his aunt who the men were beating in the shed at just about the same time J. W. Milam came from the shed and headed to the well for a drink of water. A gun was in his holster. Three other white men then emerged from the same shed and joined him. The four backed their truck up to the shed and got three Negro men to help them roll something wrapped in a tarpaulin into the back of their pickup. Reed testified that he later saw the Negroes washing the back of the truck as the blood-red water soaked itself into the Mississippi dirt.[85] Willie Reed's aunt, Amanda Bradley, testified to hearing the sounds of someone being beaten coming from the shed. Following their testimony, all witnesses for the prosecution were hurried out of the state.[86] The Negro men who assisted Milam and Bryant never came forward for fear that they would be killed for testifying to what they had seen and done.

An all-white jury deliberated little more than an hour before returning a not-guilty verdict, provoking NAACP Executive Secretary Roy Wilkins to proclaim at a Harlem gathering that month that the state

---

84  Ibid. 48.
85  Ibid. 48.
86  Ibid. 48–52.

of Mississippi had decided to maintain white supremacy by murdering children. "The killers of the boy felt free to lynch because there is in the entire state no restraining influence of decency, not in the state capital, among the daily newspapers, the clergy, not among any segment of the so-called lettered citizens."[87]

When the killers are freed, I think the federal government will step in and seek justice for Emmett Till. I don't know that Milam and Bryant have become local heroes to like-minded whites. Thinking the feds will arrest them, I imagine they are on the run, possibly headed for Tougaloo to continue their killing, making examples of me and any other Negro youngster they think needs to be taught a lesson. They have gotten away with murder in one of the country's most high-profile cases, and I am convinced they are hiding out in the woods near our home to continue their killing. I am so terrified that I'm afraid to take the trash out in the evenings after dinner or to bring in dry clothes from the line, but at thirteen years of age, I am too ashamed to tell my parents of my fears. After everyone has gone to sleep, I lie awake in bed for hours, listening to the sounds of the woods, convinced the killers are outside, and I begin a battle with insomnia that will continue to plague me for decades. Emmett Till's murder steals my innocence, awakening me to the horrors of life in Mississippi, and I don't know how to become normal again.

Those who contend that the murder of Emmett Till "had a powerful impact on a new generation of Blacks"[88] are right. They say his lynching had a tremendous effect on my generation of teens because we became the "generation that would soon demand justice and freedom in a way unknown in America before."[89]

---

87 Ibid. 52.
88 Ibid. 57.
89 Ibid. 57.

# Chapter 14

# Darkness on the Delta[90]

I T IS THE FALL of 1955 and the beginning of a new school year. What would ordinarily be the routine anticipation of another new semester still feels awkward in the wake of Emmett Till's murder. To make matters worse, it is the first time my best friend and I will be attending different schools, and I have a real need to see her, so I keep after Mother and Dad to let me spend a weekend at Gail's. She has graduated from the lab school and is attending a new high school in her neighborhood, so I won't get to see as much of her this year. In fact, I haven't seen her since the beginning of the summer—a lifetime for friends who are usually on the phone with one another daily. Finally, weary of my constant pleading and wanting to help me return to some sense of normalcy in the aftermath of the Emmett Till murder, Mother and Dad relent and drive the fifteen miles into Jackson and over to the Skinners' home, so I can spend a couple of nights there.

---

90 "Darkness on the Delta," by Marty Symes and Jerry Livingston, 1932.

At last, Gail and I are together again. Attempting to shake off the horrors of the summer, we don't talk about the murder. None of us kids do, as if to talk about it will bring it closer to us. Instead we go about our lives and try to find joy in the things we used to delight in before our world was turned upside down.

Gail and I go out to dance in the Skinner family store that Friday evening. The store is about twenty-five yards from their home and set back farther from the street than the house. If one faces the house, the store stands back and slightly to the right in a spot that allows Gail and me to exit a side door of the house and enter it. Upon entering the store one immediately faces the area where groceries are sold. The next room is entered through a wide doorway. There's a jukebox in the middle of the second room and a dance area where teenagers hang out. The room also has a front door facing the outside, which is the door most people enter. On the other side of the room with the jukebox is an adult lounge with booths where grown-ups play cards, smoke cigarettes, and listen to the music. Entering the room with the jukebox and dancing to the music blaring from it makes Gail and me feel better after the tense few weeks following the racial unrest of Till's high-profile murder. But we aren't in the store long before she tells me, "We have to get dinner ready now. We can come back later and have more fun."

In the kitchen of their house, chicken sizzles as Gail drops it piece by piece into a pan of hot oil on the stove. Filling a pot with water, she starts the rice. In another pot she puts some ham hocks, salt, pepper, and prerinsed lima beans to boil.

"Get a knife from that drawer"—she points to the drawers near the kitchen sink—"and cut up some tomatoes for salad." I follow her instructions and cut up tomatoes and lettuce.

"Should I make lemonade?" I ask.

"Uh-huh," she says, nodding.

I fill a pitcher with water, squeeze lemons, and add sugar. When the food is ready, we leave the warm pots on the stove for later and go back into the store again. We let Mr. Skinner, who is behind the counter, know we have come back. Then we head straight for the jukebox, where we punch in our favorite song. The forty-five record drops onto the turntable and begins to spin as we join other teenagers on the dance floor.

"You be the girl, and I'll be the boy," Gail says as the opening lines ring out. "Life could be a dream (sh-boom) if I could take you up to paradise up above (sh-boom)." We are in the middle of swinging out and twirling around when a heightened level of excitement overshadows the whole room. It's almost as if the music and everything else is suspended as brothers Freeman and Alex McNeil saunter in. They are local high school football heroes who are neighborhood heartthrobs, and we can't believe they have deigned to drop by the store. Gail, who tries to cover her excitement, has a crush on Alex, the younger brother, and *everybody* has a crush on Freeman. Well-built and good-looking, they look over the girls on the dance floor and those standing against the wall. Then each brother takes a partner and leads her onto the floor. One or two couples continue dancing as the rest of us stand paralyzed, watching the brothers dance with their chosen partners. When the song ends, Freeman and Alex exit as quickly as they came, and the dancing slowly resumes. One or two girls rush to the door to see where the brothers have gone, then return to the dance floor. It's funny how such seemingly insignificant occurrences create such a big stir in a small segregated town, but having the McNeil brothers drop by the store has generated the only real excitement of the afternoon.

At sunset, Mrs. Skinner, who has returned from work, calls Gail and me inside for the dinner we cooked earlier. We eat and carry on small talk with Gail's seven-year-old sister, Jerel, then clear the table and wash the dishes. Afterward, we head for the back bedroom, where we sneak out the latest issue of *True Confession* magazine that Gail has been hiding under her mattress. We read the questions from lovelorn girls and women who've written in and debate whether or not the advice given to them is advice we would give. We sympathize with the girls who can't afford to go away and have their babies, and we wonder what we would do in their situation, even though at thirteen and fourteen years of age[91] neither of us has experienced sex or has any intention of doing so until we are married. "Gail!" Mrs. Skinner calls as she heads out the front door for another shift as a nurse at a nearby facility. "Get the couch in the living room ready for Howard, and take care of Jerel."

The living-room sofa bed is where Gail's big brother, Howard, will sleep, and she needs to prepare it for him. Late afternoon has turned to dusk when Gail and I slide the magazine back under the mattress and start getting the sofa bed ready for Howard, whom I adore. We don't bother turning on the living-room light when we enter because we can use the stream of light from their parents' adjoining bedroom to see what we are doing.

Suddenly Gail remembers that seven-year-old Jerel has been in the bathtub since before their mother left, and she bolts from the room to get her baby sister out of the tub and ready for bed. Silently Howard enters the living room (*Where did he come from?* I wonder) and begins helping me make his bed. I'm so unnerved by his presence that I can hardly breathe as we pull and tuck the sheets.

---

91 Gail, who is six months older than I am, turned fourteen that fall, but I won't be fourteen until the spring.

Moving to a corner of the bed to arrange the covers, I suddenly feel the heat from his body. Placing an arm around me, he guides me to him. "Come here," he says. "There's something I've been wanting to do for a long time." As he takes me in his arms and kisses me, I don't have a clue about what I'm supposed to do, but it doesn't take me long to realize I am not doing something right. My suspicions are confirmed when he steps back and holds me in his gaze. "This is your first kiss, isn't it?" Embarrassed and flustered, I manage a nod. "I thought so when you kept your mouth closed." Now I am completely rattled. I feel stupid, too mortified to utter a word. "It's okay," he says. "I'll show you how."

When he takes me in his arms again, my lips part, and his tongue slides inside my mouth; I become light-headed as he pulls me closer to him. Just as I begin to wonder how long I can hold my breath, Gail reenters the room, talking a mile a minute. Walking from a lighted room into the darkened one, she doesn't immediately see the two of us, but as her eyes become adjusted to the darkness, she turns in my direction and blurts out, "What's going on? Haven't you finished making this bed up yet?" Howard makes a hasty retreat toward the kitchen, as she and I finish readying the sofa bed. When we are done, she and I go into the adjoining bedroom, where the two of us will sleep. It is regularly the bedroom her parents sleep in, but with both of them working, she and I will use it tonight. Closing the bedroom door, we get into our pajamas, and I whisper to her about Howard kissing me. I'm speaking softly, because I don't know where he has disappeared to, and I don't want him to overhear me.

"I feel so stupid," I tell her. "I didn't even know what to do when he kissed me. Now he's probably never going to kiss me again."

"Yes he will. He likes you," she reassures me.

"Really?" I answer hopefully. I hope she isn't just saying that to make me feel better.

After we are in bed, I toss and turn all night long, and I can hear Howard tossing and turning on the couch in the next room, too. I wonder if he is as nervous about our first kiss as I am.

By morning, my stomach is so upset that I have to struggle to keep my breakfast down. Howard sits across from me at the breakfast table and eats as fast as he can. Then he hurries out to the store to help his father. When Mrs. Skinner leaves for work, I help Gail with her chores. Then I sit at the kitchen table chatting, while she starches and irons Howard's denim jeans and dress shirts. She chats away about her new school and the difference between public and private schools. Half listening, I lapse into daydreams about one day being the woman who irons Howard's clothes and takes care of his home. "Hey, where's your mind?" Gail says. I'm so lost in my dreams of a future with Howard that it takes me a moment to actually comprehend the question she's asking. I smile, and when she has finished the ironing, I help her fold the ironing board and put it away. Then we wash and dry breakfast dishes, put them away, sweep the kitchen, and make the beds. I'm too nervous to go into the store where Howard is, so Gail and I sit at the piano and play "Chopsticks," "Heart and Soul," and other duets. We are still playing when Mother and Daddy arrive to take me home. Except for the acknowledgment that I had fun, I ride in silence all the way back to Tougaloo, reliving my first kiss over and over again in my mind, and in the weeks that follow I lie in bed at night hugging my pillow, pretending it's Howard kissing me.

On November 6, when Dad goes to scout a football game between Lincoln University from Missouri and Jackson State College, Mother, who is walking better with her sticks but still not well enough to climb stadium steps and sit for hours on hard bleachers, stays at home. Rosemary and I accompany our dad, hoping to find schoolmates from the lab school attending the game. We usually sit with them so we can enjoy the halftime battle of the bands together, but we don't see our usual crowd as we climb the steps to the middle of the bleachers with Dad. I look around to see if Howard is there and find him just as I turn toward the field to sit down. He's standing near the football field in front of our seats, watching the game from behind a cyclone fence that separates the Jackson State College bench from the crowd, but I can't tell if he knows I have arrived or not.

As the game begins, Daddy talks to us about how he scouts teams. He says he notices the reaction of players along the offensive line who may not touch the ball at all during a play, and he keeps an eye on the center and the quarterback. He tells us that many times a player who never puts his hands on the ball will telegraph a play by making a motion, and that player will make the same motion every time a certain play is called. When Dad prepares his team to play against Lincoln, he will tell them about the player who makes a certain move every time a specific play is called. One of his linesmen will watch for the move and be ready to stop the forward movement of the opposing team.

At halftime, Dad leaves us in the stands and goes to talk with the coaches from Lincoln University. As soon as he's gone, Howard comes into the stands to sit with me. I am thrilled, because I'm not allowed to date yet, and this is one of the few chances I'll have to be with him. I sense that he is shy around my father and maybe even a little fearful of him, so I am happy he has waited for Dad to leave before coming up to sit with me. I am still embarrassed about flubbing our first kiss, which he seems to sense, because he makes a comment about my being special because I haven't "been around." We make idle conversation before he says good-bye and returns to the place behind the cyclone fence where he has been standing all night watching the game. Soon Daddy is back beside us in the bleachers.

"Daddy, may I go buy a hot dog?" I ask.

"Yeah," he says, digging into his pocket for money. I leave the stands to get the food. I'm not really hungry, I just need an excuse to pass by Howard and speak to him again.

"Hi," he says as I approach.

"Hi."

He walks me over to the hot dog stand, and I give him a message to give Gail when he gets home. It isn't anything important, just an excuse to prolong our conversation. My food comes, we part company, and I head back into the stands to eat with Rosemary and Dad.

The game moves to a brutal conclusion as a Jackson State player is tackled by his opponent near the sidelines where the yardage chains are. Taking exception to the manner in which he's been stopped, the player comes up swinging. A Jackson State student on the sideline who is holding the yardage marker suddenly pulls the metal pole attached to his end of the chain out of the ground and begins hitting the Lincoln player with it. In those days, heavy metal (rather than aluminum) poles were used to mark the yardage because the metal was strong enough to support the weight of the heavy chains needed to pull through mud and snow on wet and soggy grass fields. Being hit with one of those poles could cause serious injury.

Seeing the chain holder beat his teammate incites a player from Lincoln, who snatches the pole from the hands of the chain bearer, bends it into the shape of a U as if he is Hercules, and wraps it around the Jackson State player's neck. The commotion takes place near Jackson State's team bench, causing their entire team to pour onto the field for a melee. Then Lincoln's bench empties, too, and a free-for-all explodes with chains and metal pipes flying.

A dozen white policemen (there were no Negro policemen in those days) reluctantly walk to the edge of the playing field, feigning breaking up the mayhem as the fighting continues. Seated in the stands with my father and sister, I find myself extremely upset. I've been attending football games all my life but can't ever remember seeing a brawl like this. The Jackson College band behind us tries to restore order by playing the national anthem. As the opening chords begin, every white cop on the field stops, stands at attention, and salutes the flag, while the fight between the Negro gladiators rages on. People in the bleachers and those encircling the field stand silently facing the field, stunned by the spectacle. Then the players slowly begin to recognize the strains of the national anthem and cease fighting. Pretty soon they are all standing silently facing the band, and some semblance of order is restored. At the end of the anthem, people in the stands sit down. Not sure of what else to do, the band plays on, switching to a love song called "Wake the Town and Tell the People." By this time, I have lost all interest in the game. Winning by either team seems fruitless in the aftermath of the bloody battle that has just ended on the field.

When the game is finally over, Rosemary, Dad, and I leave the stadium and silently walk toward our car. Usually when I'm with Dad, I feel safe. From the time I was a little girl, he's been my knight in shining armor—the strongest man I know. But on this night as we walk toward the car, I feel jittery. I try to throw off the sensation, telling myself it is due to the fight that broke out on the field.

As we approach a nearby street corner, I suddenly relax. My eyes meet Howard's. His tall, athletic frame leans against a streetlight that casts a romantic glow across his face. *How did he know we would pass this corner at this very moment?* I wonder. He smiles and says, "Good night" as we walk by. I smile. We all say, "Good night." I look back over my shoulder and blush to find his eyes following me up the block.

It is late by the time we arrive at home, so Rosemary and I go straight to our room to get ready for bed. Dad sits down next to Mother on the couch and begins telling her about the game. At about midnight, I get out of bed and go back to the living room where my parents are engrossed in *The Steve Allen Show*. My uneasiness has zeroed in on Howard, and I go to them with an unusual request.

"May I call Gail?" I ask.

"Call Gail?" Mother says. "It's after twelve o'clock. It's too late to call anyone."

"I know," I say, pushing my luck, "but I have the strangest feeling that something is going to happen to Howard tonight, and I want to make sure he got home all right."

"Something like what?" Mother wants to know.

"I don't know. Like maybe he's not going to get home safely."

"I'm sure he'll be all right," she says. "Go back to bed. You may call Gail in the morning."

I go back to bed, but I don't go to sleep until long after Mother and Dad retire.

The next morning our front doorbell rings unusually early, and in my drowsiness, I recognize the familiar voice of our neighbor and paper boy, Charles Jones. He is speaking in such hushed tones that I think one of our kittens has been run over by a car. I pray it isn't our newest kitty, Smokey Joe.

I hear my father say, "Thank you," and close the door. He goes into his and Mother's bedroom and speaks with her before heading down the hall to our room. When he enters, his voice is gentle. "There was an accident last night at the Skinners' store, and both Mr. Skinner and Howard were shot." His words seem to come from far away.

"Is Howard dead?" Rosemary asks. *Of course he isn't,* I think. I am angry with her for even asking such a question. *Doesn't she know the difference between being shot and being killed? Dad distinctly said shot.* But before I can complete the thought, Dad answers, "Yes."

I dissolve into tears. My father hugs me tightly to him, as if by doing so he can take the pain from my broken heart into his own strong chest. Suddenly my mind is flooded with a thousand images—memories of our first kiss, of Gail and Howard watching the sunset, of Howard playing football with his teammates, of him climbing into the bleachers to sit with me. I remember the way he looked at me from beneath the street-light, and I think of the message I gave him to give Gail—a message I could not then, and cannot now, remember. I wonder if it's my fault that he's dead, if he went out into the store to deliver my message to Gail and got shot. I think of the phone call I wanted to make last night and wonder if it might have saved his life—if he might have been talking on the phone to me instead of being out in the store. Why wasn't I allowed to make that one phone call? Now I'll never see his face again, never feel his arms around me, never kiss his lips again. He is gone.

Mother comes down the hall and into our room. "Let's get dressed so we can go to church before we visit Mrs. Skinner and the girls," she says. Dad lets go of me and heads back down the hall. Rosemary and I take turns in the bathroom getting cleaned up. Then we dress slowly and silently. When we finish, I look in the mirror. Nothing about me seems real. Not my swollen red eyes, dripping nose, quivering lips, or ponytail hanging askew.

The ten-mile ride into Jackson for church is a silent one. I wipe away tears during the whole trip. By the time we arrive at St. Mark's Church, news of Howard's death has spread throughout the city. Getting out of the car, I realize it is the junior choir's Sunday to sing. As a member of the choir, I head toward the choir room to put on my robe as Rosemary, Mother, and Dad enter the front door of the church.

Everyone stops talking when I walk in. Choir members watch me dress in silence before we process in, singing. During the service, Father Keeling offers a prayer for the Skinner family. That's when the tears I've been fighting back since arriving at church fall freely. Phyllis, who is seated beside me, opens the *Book of Common Prayer*, turns to the Twenty-Third Psalm, and places it in my hands. Knowing she cares helps me get through the remainder of the Sunday morning service. When church is over, I go back to the choir room, take off my robe, and head out to our car where Mother, Daddy, and Rosemary are waiting.

We arrive at the Skinners' home to find Mrs. Skinner under the covers in the front bedroom. She is lying in the bed Gail and I so often slept in when I spent a weekend. Mr. Skinner is still in the hospital. Mother and Dad sit in chairs next to the bed and speak quietly with Mrs. Skinner. She looks up at me. "Gail's in the back room, Nell. You know where it is."

I lead Rosemary down the hall to the room where Gail and I so often went to sneak peeks at *True Confession* magazine. When I see her, all the pity I have for myself evaporates. She is lying facedown in the dim room wearing a plaid shirt, dark skirt, bobby socks, and penny loafers. She has been sobbing for so long, her face is swollen. We embrace before all three of us sit down on the bed. No one speaks for a long time.

"I saw the whole thing," Gail finally says.

"What happened?" Rosemary asks, realizing this is something Gail needs and wants to talk about. Through sobs she tells us that she'd taken a nap around six o'clock the previous evening and gotten up at about nine. She'd gone into the store, thinking the rest of the teens in the area would have arrived by that time. She entered, unaware that while she slept, her father had stopped two Negro boys in the neighborhood from fighting. Both had bottles in their hands. Mr. Skinner told them to drop the bottles, saying there wasn't going to be any fighting in his store; if they wanted to fight they'd have to take it outside. The boy named Johnny obeyed and dropped his bottle, but J. C. drew his bottle back and brought it forward in an effort to hit Mr. Skinner. Gail's father caught J. C.'s hand as it held on to the bottle and hit the boy in the jaw; then he told J. C. to leave. When the boy had exited the store, Mr. Skinner rejoined his friends in one of the booths the adults usually sat in. I try to picture J. C. because I don't know him or Johnny and can't remember if either of them hung out in the store when I came to visit.

A few hours after the incident, and after Gail had entered the store, Howard returned from the football game at Jackson State and went to let his mother know he was home. She sent him into the store to tell Gail it was time for her to come home. Howard entered the store just as J. C. was returning. J. C. bought a bottle of antiseptic from Howard, who had stepped behind the counter to wait on him. J. C. drank the entire bottle of antiseptic before entering the room where folk were dancing.

Howard walked behind J. C. on his way to tell Gail, who was among the dancers, that it was time for her to go home. As Gail's partner swung her out, J. C. brought the back of his hand across her face. The impact was so hard, it knocked her to the floor. From the floor, Gail turned and looked up just as J. C. pulled a gun from his pocket. Suddenly there was an explosion and then a burst of blue light. In the same moment, Howard saw J. C. lift the gun and aim it at Mr. Skinner. Howard lunged toward J. C. and attempted to knock the weapon from his hand. The gun went off. A bullet hit Howard in the stomach, and he fell to the floor. Before anyone else could react, J. C. turned, aimed the gun at Mr. Skinner again, and fired. That bullet entered the back of Mr. Skinner's neck, exited his mouth, and struck a woman in the knee. A third shot from the same gun, intended for Gail, hit a male customer in the arm. J. C. was obviously angry at having been put out of the store earlier by Mr. Skinner and had returned to make the whole Skinner family pay for it.

Gail scrambled over her brother's body and crawled out the store door. Running into the house, she screamed to her mother, who called an ambulance and then rushed into the store where pandemonium had erupted. Mr. Skinner lay on the floor in a pool of blood. People ran around in a state of hysteria trying to get someone to take him to the hospital. Unsure whether an ambulance would come into their Negro neighborhood, people placed him in a car and drove away. Howard lay wounded on another part of the floor as patrons suggested they get him to the hospital, too, because he was hurt. Friends carried him out to a neighbor's car and rushed him off to the hospital, his mother and Gail in the car with him.

After he was admitted, Gail and Mrs. Skinner sat in the hall of the Negro section of the hospital. They had barely taken a breath when a doctor appeared to tell them Howard was dead. He had bled internally and died ten minutes after being placed on the operating table. Now his mother and sister began to weep. The same doctor told them that Mr. Skinner was bleeding so profusely they were having a difficult time stopping the blood.[92] Nurses hurried in and out of the emergency room, delivering blood for transfusions and testing Gail and her mother for their blood types. When Mr. Skinner was finally rolled out, Gail and her mother stood next to the gurney where he lay with tubes hanging from stands, pumping fluids into him. "Please don't die," they begged of him. "We couldn't stand it if you did. You've got to live." Seeing all the machines with tubes running into her wounded father, Gail wanted to tell the staff, "Leave him alone; stop causing him pain."[93]

Back inside the Skinner bedroom where Rosemary, Gail, and I are seated, everything grows quiet. As Gail becomes silent, the three of us start to cry. We cry for a long time before controlling ourselves again. Rosemary and I are seated on either side of my best friend, stroking her back as she struggles to continue. "The thing is—he didn't bleed. If he'd just been able to bleed maybe he wouldn't have... Oh, God! Why?"

Howard died from internal hemorrhaging. The one ambulance the hospital used for Negroes was out on another call when the call came in from the Skinner residence, and hospital dispatchers refused to send the empty ambulance it used for white people to pick up a Negro. By the time folks in the Skinners' store decided to use a private car to get him to the hospital, too much time had elapsed to save him.

"Where's Jerel?" we ask Gail.

---

92 Gail McGrady (née Skinner), "My Loss," a paper written for Dr. Carl Schneider's course on "Birth and Death," October 23, 1979.
93 Ibid. 5.

"She's staying with friends until funeral arrangements can be made."

Mother and Dad come down the hall and tell us they and Mrs. Skinner have agreed that Gail may come stay with us after Howard's funeral. Then Mother says it is time for us to go.

"Go say good-bye to Mrs. Skinner," she says.

It seems as if we've just arrived, and already we are leaving. This wasn't nearly enough time to console ourselves or one another. I want to stay, to be with my best friend for as long as she needs me, but Rosemary and I obediently rise and go to Mrs. Skinner's bedroom. She holds her hand out to me as I enter. I take it, moving closer to her bed.

"He loved you," she says.

Then she tells me she cradled his head in her lap in the backseat of the car as it sped toward the hospital. "He knew he was dying, even though I told him he'd be all right as soon as we got to the hospital. He said he wasn't afraid to die, and I shouldn't be afraid, either. Nell," she continues, speaking from her deep religious faith, "you mustn't hate the boy who did this. He's sick. I've forgiven him, and you have to, too. If you don't, Howard will have died in vain. You and Gail—all of us—have to pray to God to forgive him."

I nod my head but don't think I can ever forgive him, and I wonder how she can be so strong with her only son gone. I kiss her and say good-bye. Then I walk out to the car where the rest of my family is waiting.

For days all I can do is cry. I can't eat or sleep, and I refuse to watch westerns on television. I no longer want to see the simulation of death. Death is real. I know it is. It has taken Howard from me.

Music, like prayer, is the only thing that soothes my soul. The song that brings me greatest comfort is Al Hibbler's "He." I listen to the last two lines over and over again, remembering my promise to Mrs. Skinner, "Though it makes Him sad to see the way we live, He'll always say, 'I forgive.'"[94]

Mother and Dad insist that I come to the table and eat, even though I tell them I have no appetite. When I do eat, I can't keep anything down. Don't they understand the depth of my pain? Or are they like other adults who tell me that what Howard and I felt for each other was "just puppy love"? Does that mean I'm not supposed to hurt like I do?

On the day of his funeral, people fill the church and spill out onto the sidewalk. The service reaches deep into the Skinners' Baptist roots, allowing mourners to cry out in anger and in pain. It draws people from every aspect of the family's life: teachers and students from Tougaloo Prep, neighborhood friends, faculty members from Tougaloo College, and folk from all over Jackson. At times, weeping inside the church becomes so loud, the minister cannot be heard, and one girl after another is carried, sobbing, from the church. At the end of the service, ushers begin to motion each row forward to view the body. As I approach his casket and look down on his peaceful face, the strangest thought crosses my mind. I am going to get older, but Howard will always be sixteen. I weep because we'll never be together again. I weep because I want to die, too—to be with him.

I head back to my place in the church as ushers help Gail to her brother's casket. As she looks on his face, a wail comes from deep inside her, and she throws herself across his body. Elders lift her up and carry

---

94 From a Gospel song, "He Can Turn the Tides," words and music by J. Richards, R. Mullan, and B. Feldman, published by EMI Music Publishing (source: Metrolyrics).

her out, while she sobs his name over and over. They place her in a limousine where she waits for the rest of the family.

Inside our car, my family follows a long line of other cars to the cemetery, where we are directed to the Negro section in back. *Even in death,* I think, *white people refuse to be near us.* The graveside ceremony is subdued until the casket is lowered into the ground. As it touches the bottom, Gail leaps forward and attempts to jump into the earth with her brother. I turn away and sob on Daddy's shoulder as funeral attendants restrain her.

A few weeks later, Gail comes out to Tougaloo to spend time with us. She and I sleepwalk our way through normal activities—walking around the campus, visiting friends, attending ball games—but a sadness is always with us, forming a void where he used to be. At night I can't fall asleep. Gail goes to sleep right away, only to awaken screaming from the nightmares that visit her. Each time she awakens, Rosemary and I get out of bed to sit beside her and try to bring her some comfort. Sometimes Mother comes down the hall to soothe her, too.

One night as we sit with our arms around her, she says, "He always bought the nicest Mother's Day gifts, like a heart-shaped apron that said, 'To Mother.' I don't know where he found them. I could never find anything like that." On another night she sleeps through the night until morning. When she awakens, she tells us she dreamed she saved Howard's life by ripping his shirt off and forcing him to bleed.

A few more weeks pass before I go out to the Skinners' to spend time with her. When I arrive, she is wearing one of her brother's shirts—one I used to love seeing him in.

"Today," she says, "Jerel asked where Howard is. We told her again that he's dead, and she said, 'You mean he's never coming back?' When we told her no, she started to cry. I still don't think she understands."

After a long convalescence, Mr. Skinner recovers, but he speaks from that day on with a speech impediment. J. C. is arrested and jailed. The Skinner family store is closed and never reopened.

Some days as Rosemary and I wait for Mother to pick us up after Girl Scout meetings, while my sister plays off in the distance with friends, I lie on a grassy hill looking up at the clouds, forming images with them the way I did when I was a little girl. I see Howard's face in the clouds and wonder if he can see me, too. I wonder if he is happy, and I long to know what people do when they go to heaven. I think about how, in his sixteen years on earth, he showed us how to live *and* how to die, when he gave up his life for his father's.

After his death I lie in my bed at night, after my sister has fallen asleep. I cry into my pillow and fumble with the radio between our twin beds until I find WDAI in Memphis, Tennessee. Then I lie back and listen to Lee J. Hooker, Faye Adams, B. B. King, Bo Diddley, and Bobby Blue Bland. The blues speak to my pain.

# CHAPTER 15

# GUIDE MY FEET WHILE I RUN THIS RACE[95]

T HE REST OF NOVEMBER drags sadly by. When we sit down to Thanksgiving dinner I feel there is little for which to be grateful. December sneaks in, bringing with it the starkness of leafless trees that mirror the bleakness of the place inside me that has died. I struggle to imagine myself entering Tougaloo Prep next fall without Howard and wonder when the pain of losing him will end.

Then on December 1, five days before the one-month anniversary of Howard's death, the photograph of a woman named Rosa Parks is flashed across the television screen. This attractive woman seems calm and composed, in spite of the fact that she has just been arrested and fingerprinted for refusing to give up her seat to a white man on a segregated Montgomery, Alabama, bus. The bold stand she takes begins to pull me out of my depression and to give me something, besides the pain in my heart, to focus on. Her refusal to stand while a white man sits is the start of a boycott of city buses by Negroes in Montgomery. It

95 Traditional Negro spiritual.

exposes an ugly side of segregation to the rest of the nation and initiates protests that grow stronger each day. Tentatively at first, I begin to make a point of turning on the television every day when I arrive home from school so I can catch a glimpse of an action that has never happened in the country before—southern Negroes publicly taking a stand against segregation.

White officials in Mississippi must think something terrible is going to happen in Montgomery, because they run daily accounts of the protest without ever blacking out news about it. This is so unlike the past when people working at the local television station scrambled the signal or displayed a PLEASE STAND BY sign whenever a Negro face appeared. I've grown accustomed to seeing Mitch Miller introduce Leslie Uggams on his variety show and then have our television screen (which has been perfect up to that time) suddenly develop confetti-like dots that fall like snow. When Ms. Uggams has finished singing, the television picture clears up again. The same thing happens when Negro basketball players are given the ball during ball games because most players these days are white. Every time a Negro catches or dribbles the ball, the screen goes dark, or white dots rain down. The only time we get a clear picture of a Negro's face is when he is arrested. Even our newspapers are segregated. The *Clarion Ledger* reports the news of white people on regular newsprint, while news about Negroes appears on a green newsprint insert. But with the Montgomery bus boycott, a running account of the protest appears on television every day without interruption. Jackson's local officials are obviously oblivious to the strength Negroes in Mississippi are beginning to feel as reports of the boycott stream out of Alabama. That is, unless they are hoping that something will go terribly wrong, and scores of Negroes will be killed as television cameras follow the horror. And so I am lifted up by the protest and by the signs that begin to appear: DON'T RIDE THE BUSES TODAY. DON'T RIDE THEM FOR FREEDOM.[96]

Negroes in Montgomery are filmed silently walking to work with lunch pails in their hands. A few are seen waiting in idling cars at the stops where they have agreed to meet older people to drive them across town to work. At the end of the day, the same people are filmed walking wearily home, while reports of the firing of protesting maids and custodians are aired. City buses can be seen going to and from town with a smattering of white folk on them, but the Negroes keep walking, holes visible in the soles of their shoes, determination on their faces.

A few days into the protest, Montgomery reporter Joe Azbell covers a mass meeting where twenty-six-year-old Martin Luther King Jr. speaks. It is the first speech of this young preacher, but Azbell describes it as setting the people who pack the church "on fire for freedom (with) a spirit no one (can) capture..." He goes on to say it is "the beginning of a flame that (will) go across America."[97] White bigots in Montgomery must feel the young preacher is a figure to be reckoned with, too, because on January 30, 1956, they firebomb his house, as if the act will end the bus boycott. If that's what they think, they are mistaken because the boycott continues as strong as ever.

And as if the boycott isn't enough for Alabama to deal with, three days later, on February 3, a Negro girl named Autherine Lucy is admitted to the all-white University of Alabama in Tuscaloosa. Her acceptance into the graduate study program less than one hundred miles from Montgomery touches off riots that have been feared for a long

---

96  Williams, *Eyes on the Prize*, 72.
97  Ibid. 74–76.

time,[98] as white Alabamians gear up for a fight at the school. Invoking their infamous "states' rights" cry, white rioters cause the situation to become so volatile that state authorities respond by declaring the 1954 Supreme Court decision nearly two years earlier (the decision under which Lucy was admitted), to be "null, void, and of no effect."[99]

President Eisenhower could take the high road and support Lucy's admission by upholding the '54 decision, but he remains silent, thereby giving tacit approval to the mobs of students who taunt Autherine Lucy on a daily basis as she travels to and from class. The campus uproar leads university officials to suspend *her* (rather than the troublemakers) for reasons of safety to herself and the school, they say. On February 29, 1956, a federal district court orders the University of Alabama to reinstate Autherine Lucy, but the board of trustees votes to "permanently expel"[100] her. The school does just that and remains segregated for another seven years.

Between the bus boycott in Montgomery and school integration attempts in Tuscaloosa, my life seems small and insignificant. It has been three months since Howard's death, but changes in the country are coming faster than I can make sense of them, and the ache in my heart for him seems to be unwilling to move at all.

By this time, Mother has done away with the walking sticks Dad made for her and can now climb the steps to our front porch as well as the stairs to the stage in the gymnasium near Daddy. She sits through basketball games on a pillow placed on a folding chair. To my amazement, she has also gotten behind the wheel of a car again to drive short

---

98  C. Vann Woodward, *The Strange Career of Jim Crow*, second revised edition (Oxford University Press, 1966), 155.
99  Ibid. 156–57.
100  Ibid. 163.

distances and on occasion to drive the seven miles into Jackson as part of the car pool that takes Tougaloo faculty children to the Jackson Laboratory School, but she will never again drive on long highway trips.

Since Howard's death, I've been struggling to get back into a familiar rhythm. Then one day while searching radio stations for rock-and-roll music, I stumble upon Frankie Lymon and the Teenagers singing, "Why Do Fools Fall in Love?" Their new song and clean-cut looks have begun to change the negative view most adults have of teenagers, and I am immediately pulled to them. Before they arrived on the scene, dressed in crewneck sweaters with "letterman Ts" on the front, the word *teenager* conjured up images of black-leather-jacket-wearing hoodlums ready to fight at a moment's notice. But Frankie Lymon and the Teenagers create an image so positive that I start to feel positive about myself as a teenager. I go and buy the forty-five of "Why Do Fools Fall in Love" and play it until it is worn out. I cut pictures of the group from *Ebony* magazine and tape them to the wall over my bed. Their photos are soon joined by a slew of other teenage idols of mine: Johnny Mathias, The Platters, Paul Anka, Fabian, and Sam Cooke—and Elvis Presley, until Daddy reminds me that Elvis has said he doesn't want any "Nigra" girls swooning over him. I rip Elvis's picture from my wall and refuse to buy a single one of his records. But Mississippi rednecks applaud him for the statement. It is exactly what they want to hear from a boy from Tupelo.

---

BY THE TIME SPRING arrives, I've learned to live with the heartache I know will always be with me following the loss of my first love. Then in May, Gail calls to say her parents are separating, and she, her mother, and Jerel are leaving Mississippi to begin a new life in Chicago. She and I weep together over the phone as we face the end of our constant companionship. We promise to keep in touch by mail, which we faithfully do, but we won't meet face-to-face again for another six years.

In June, Mother, Dad, Rosemary, and I prepare to return to New York for the summer. Mother has been awarded a study grant at NYU, and Dad will take courses there and help Aunt Mabel in her new venture as a candy store owner. She has begun the enterprise after the French mending and weaving shop at Grand Central Station, where she spent so many years, closed. Rosemary and I will spend time between the candy store on the corner of Seventh Avenue and 118th Street and Aunt Mabel's apartment in the middle of the block between 117th and 118th Streets.

On the way to New York, we stop in Atlanta to load our car with the usual packages Madre is sending to Aunt Mabel and Aunt Louise, and we stop with the Harris family in Gaffney, South Carolina, to share a meal and catch up on the year we have been apart since the accident. We leave a batch of Madre's homemade fudge and Mother's brownies with the Harris family, and Mrs. Harris stocks us up with ham, fried chicken, fruit, and homemade cake to last us for the rest of our trip.

Having done all the driving, Dad is exhausted when we reach Kiptopeke, Virginia. So he stretches out across the front seat and goes to sleep while Mother, Rosemary, and I go up to the top deck of the ferry for fresh air, as we've done in the past. When we sight land ahead, the three of us head back down to the car where Daddy is waking up, and several hours later we are in New York, a few blocks from Aunt Mabel's apartment.

Waiting for a red light behind a city bus, I am already envisioning myself sitting in my aunt's living-room window watching people on the street below. All of a sudden Daddy starts blowing the car horn. The light in front of us is still red, so I can't understand why he is honking so frantically. Mother turns to ask what we all seem to be wondering, "What's the matt—" WHAM! People on the sidewalk scream and scatter in all directions as our car is rammed from behind by another car and sent headlong into the New York City bus ahead of us with such force that the bus slams into the car in front of it, both of which were stopped for the red light, too. Everyone inside the car is pitched forward. I look back through the rear window and see a car whose front grille is a mess of metal, and steam is now pouring from beneath the hood. The driver is slumped back against the seat, but his passengers stumble out. Daddy had seen the car in the rearview mirror racing toward us at twice the speed limit, and that's when he began blowing the car horn, hoping the driver would pay attention to him and swerve around us.

The city bus driver jumps out of the bus and starts yelling at Dad for ramming into him. Dad doesn't say a word but points to the car behind us. A bystander heads for a pay phone, presumably to call the police. Dad, the bus driver, and the driver of the car in front of the bus walk over to the driver who caused the accident to speak to him, but he is so drunk, he can't communicate with anyone.

People on the bus file off looking for bus passes to get onto another bus, while everyone else waits for the police to arrive. Someone comes over to our car to see if anyone is hurt. Fortunately, no one is. The police soon arrive and take information from everyone involved in the wreck, then take the drunk driver into custody. Placing him in the back of their cruiser, they drive away. Dad gets back into our car and drives it, with all its damage, to Aunt Mabel's, where he parks.

We ring the doorbell downstairs, but no one answers. We keep ringing, but the follow-up ring we are expecting that will let us in does not come. After a significant amount of time passes, a neighbor leaving the building recognizes Dad from the summer he spent there attending school at NYU and lets us in. Exhausted from the trip capped off by the accident a few blocks away, we climb the stairs to Aunt Mabel's third-floor apartment. Upon reaching her front door we are greeted with a handmade sign that reads, Do Not Disturb. Ball Game. Ignoring the sign we ring the bell, knock on the door, and call out to her, but no one answers. We keep the racket going for so long that Mrs. Murphy, her next-door neighbor, opens her front door to tell us, "Mrs. Par-ROT doesn't want anybody disturbing her while the Dodgers are playing."

"Yeah, we know," Dad tells her, "but we're her family from Mississippi, and we just got into town."

Mrs. Murphy goes back inside and calls Aunt Mabel on the telephone. Within minutes Aunt Mabel flings open her front door and throws her arms around each of us. After we've used the toilet and told her about the accident, she comes downstairs to help us unload the car. As soon as the car is empty, Aunt Mabel gives us something to eat, assures herself that we are all right, and returns to her beloved Dodgers and their game.

A few days later, while our car is being repaired, we begin our summer routine—Mother goes to school, Dad works in the candy store and takes a few classes, and my sister and I move between the candy store and Aunt Mabel's apartment, where we watch television. Some few weeks into the summer, Mother tells Rosemary and me to take baths at midmorning and get dressed in our green-and-white seersucker mother-daughter dresses by noon. We follow her instructions and wait excitedly for her return from school.

That afternoon she walks us to Lenox Avenue and 116th Street where there is an opening in the sidewalk with steps leading down into the ground. I wonder why I've never noticed this place before. Rosemary and I are entering a New York City subway for the first time. We follow Mother to a booth, where she purchases tokens from the station attendant. She slips a token into a slot for each of us. The three of us push through the turnstile and wait for a train on the platform. Almost immediately one speeds in, faster than anything I've ever seen, and screeches to a halt. Everyone on the platform where we are standing rushes into one of the cars as riders inside rush off. The doors slam shut, and we speed off into a dark tunnel that has traffic lights like the ones on the street above.

It isn't until after we've found places on the rattan seats that I feel the hot air being blown around by ceiling fans. Leather straps hang in loops from white bars, and high up on the sides of the car are ads for Broadway shows and a photograph of Miss Subways. At Fifty-First Street, we get off the train and climb steps to exit the station. On the sidewalks above we stroll along until we come to the windows of a large theater, where we stop to admire photographs. Rosemary and I recognize Pearl Bailey in one of them, because we have seen her on *The Ed Sullivan Show*, but we don't know any of the other people. Mother tells us the Negro man is Peg Leg Bates, a tap dancer "who can dance better with his one wooden leg than most people who have two legs." Knowing of my love of dance, she points to the women in another photograph and says they are the world-famous Rockettes, known around the world for their high kicking. We continue along the sidewalk admiring photos until we arrive at the corner. There, we follow Mother inside. She picks up tickets and leads us into Radio City Music Hall.

For two young Negro girls who have only seen the inside of "colored" movie houses, entering a theater with crystal chandeliers and a sweeping staircase is like stepping into wonderland. We climb the stairs to the mezzanine, sinking into the plush red carpet, and are given programs by ushers who lead us to our seats. The movie that afternoon is *Young Bess* starring Jean Simmons and Stewart Granger and is about the life of Queen Elizabeth I when she was a young girl. It is one of the best movies I have seen, and when it is over Rosemary and I thank Mother for the treat and stand to leave. "There's more," she tells us, then asks if we want to get candy from the lobby.

"More?" we say. "Yes, we'd like some candy." We go to buy candy, return to the theater with it, and sit down again to wait for what, we cannot imagine. Then the curtain rises, and we are enthralled. Pearl Bailey sashays onto the stage, waving a handkerchief and wiping her brow. In an aside to the audience, she complains about her aching feet. Then she launches into a medley of songs that end with her signature, "Won't You Come Home, Bill Bailey." When she exits, Peg Leg Bates dances on stage to the roar of the crowd. I've never seen anyone move like he does, jumping and tapping on his peg leg with as great agility and enthusiasm as he does with his real one. I am speechless when he finishes, and I jump to my feet with the rest of the crowd until he returns for two encores. Then the Rockettes appear with a series of routines that end with their line of high-kicking dancers. Rosemary and I talk about the show all the way back to Aunt Mabel and Uncle Ezra's, and then we start all over again as soon as we see Daddy. The summer flies by. Soon we are headed back to Mississippi, stopping to drop off packages for Madre from Aunt Louise and Aunt Mabel.

Arriving back home in Mississippi, I discover that the Montgomery bus boycott has continued through the summer with no sign of city officials giving in. Montgomery's Negroes have grown tired but are still resolute in their determination to change the system. I've lived in the South all my life and never dreamed that it would change, so as far as I am concerned, they're waging a losing battle.

TOUGALOO PREPARATORY SCHOOL

In September, I enter the ninth grade at Tougaloo Prep, which is one of the best prep schools in the state, if not the country. Prep's sixty-five-member student body is made up of local Negro youngsters as well as boarding students from cities throughout Mississippi and one or two from outside the state. Secure in its warm environs, I am one among twelve members of the freshman class—six girls and six boys. The two-story white wooden schoolhouse is located down the road from our house, approximately fifty yards on the far side of the Palmers, our next-door neighbors. The college infirmary is on the other side of their house, and we children of faculty members never get to pass it without Dr. Ting, a tiny Chinese woman who is the college physician, beckoning to us with a crooked finger and urging, "Come here, come here." Leading us inside, she checks our ears, eyes, throats, hearts, and lungs, and during the early fall, she gives us influenza shots before letting us go. The prep school is across the gravel road from the infirmary and would ordinarily be a five-minute walk from home if Dr. Ting did not waylay us.

As my freshman year begins, the school eliminates the prep-school football program due to financial constraints. In some respects the absence of football is a blessing, because it is one less reminder of Howard, who used to play for Tougaloo Prep.

Robert Calhoun is the only classmate from the Jackson Laboratory School who attends Tougaloo Prep with me. He and our paper boy, Charles Jones, from down the road are the only classmates I know. Assessing my new class, I find myself immediately drawn to a pretty olive-complexioned girl with warm brown eyes and soft brown curls. She is sweet and friendly and the only girl in the ninth grade who is taller than I am. Her name is Alyce Faye Wattleton. The two of us sit next to each other in all our classes as well as study hall and soon become the best of friends.

Our civics teacher, Mrs. Mahalia Smith, teaches us to spell the names of states by breaking them into syllables that are easy for us to remember. She tells us we can remember the correct spelling of Connecticut by first writing the word *connect* and then the word *cut*, and she says we should remember that the two words are separated by the letter *I*, Connect-i-cut. She makes civics as easy as she makes spelling, causing us to wish we could take her class every day rather than every *other* day. Mrs. Susie Jones teaches English and starts the school year by having us practice loops and circles of cursive writing until our papers look like the script in our writing manuals. Mr. Townsend is the science teacher, and Mr. George Jones, the husband of our English instructor, teaches us algebra. The Joneses are parents to Charles, our classmate and to his sisters, Norma (called "Boo") and Sue, who also attend Tougaloo Prep. Mrs. Annie F. Davis (a fair-skinned and blue-eyed woman whom I first mistake for white) is the school principal. Miss Redmond teaches gym in Brownlee Gymnasium, where Daddy's office is and where basketball games are played. Brownlee is also where both the college and the prep school hold dances. Music is taught in a combined ninth- and tenth-grade course by Mr. Aurelius Marcus. To get to his class, we walk across the college campus to a study room inside Woodworth Chapel (next to the gymnasium). It is the same chapel where Sunday church services and special concerts are held—the one where Mother was surprised with the Mother of the Year award on Mother's Day. The combined class of music is all the incentive I need to earn an A in music. I am not about to be embarrassed in the only class I have with Edward, a tenth-grade boy I'm beginning to become attracted to.

I first noticed Edward Harris Jr. in the spring prior to my entering high school, on our drives home from the Jackson lab school. Seated in the back of the car, I'd see him walking beneath the Tougaloo College archway just as our car entered the campus. Edward is a finely chiseled young man with beautiful chocolate-brown skin that's as smooth as velvet. He has black wavy hair, sensitive brown eyes, a keen nose, and luscious-looking lips. He often wears a V-neck sweater over a dress shirt or the dress shirt without the sweater, the sleeves turned up, and shirttail tucked into dark pants. Ambling along the road toward "eighty highway," lost in thought, he hardly ever notices me. But each day when I see him, I feel more and more drawn to him, and every day I look forward to glimpsing him on the road. By summertime, I have developed a crush on him. That's when I realize my heart is opening up to love again.

A few weeks into the school year, I say to Faye, "I have a crush on a boy in the tenth grade, but I don't know how to let him know."

"Want me to tell Duck?" she asks. "Duck" is the nickname by which Claiborne Rhone is known, and he is one of Edward's close friends. If Faye tells Duck, he will tell Edward, and if Edward doesn't already have a girlfriend, maybe he'll start to speak to me, so I tell her yes.

She confides in me that she has a crush on Bob Harrison, the son of our family dentist. Since our families are friends, it's easy for me to get that message to Bob, an eleventh grader, who lives forty-five miles away in Yazoo City and is one of prep school's boarding students.

Only four instructors teach the academic subjects at Tougaloo Prep, so each student gets called on every day in class. In algebra, half the students go to the blackboard one day, and the other half the next day. Mr. Jones, the algebra teacher, chooses students at random and gives us problems from our homework assignments to work out at the blackboard in front of the entire class. When we are finished, we must explain the problem we have done, answering questions from class-mates who don't understand the steps we've taken to reach the solu-tion. The first time I make a mistake at the board, Mr. Jones says, "You were at my house last night, were you not?"

"Yes," I say, because Rosemary and I were there visiting his daugh-ters, Boo and Sue, the previous evening.

"If you didn't understand the assignment, why didn't you ask me at that time?"

When I don't respond, he calls on another student to show me how to solve the equation.

Of course on the first day Edward speaks to me in the hall on my way to algebra, Mr. Jones sees us. And that *would* be the day I make another mistake in an algebra problem.

"You can't get it courting, my friend. You can't get it courting," Mr. Jones tells me as I return to my seat, humiliated.

During the first weeks of school, two of the boys in my class are noticeably absent, gone for nearly a month before returning and diving into the work as if they have never left. I thought they had left school, but when they return I ask other classmates where they've been and am told they are the sons of sharecroppers who left school to help their parents bring in the heavy haul of cotton the landowner demanded. Their sacrifice makes me realize how lucky I am to only be required to attend school and complete my classwork.

When Mr. Marcus, the choir director, holds choir auditions, Faye and I decide to try out. We are thrilled to be among the students chosen, although in truth Mr. Marcus can make singers out of nearly anyone. He teaches us to breathe from our diaphragms, and to pronounce the tees and esses at the end of phrases as if the entire choir is one voice.

"Ladies and gentlemen," he admonishes, "I don't want to hear hissing throughout the choir when there is an S at the end of a phrase. I want you to sound like a single voice when you pronounce that ess. Enunciate. Enunciate," he commands with precise diction.

On the afternoon when we get our first report cards, Faye and I stroll across the campus toward my house to watch Dick Clark's *American Bandstand* on television. Talking idly we walk past Mrs. Davis, the school principal, who asks to see our grades. First she looks over Faye's card, filled with As and Bs and congratulates her. Then she looks at mine, also filled with As, Bs, and one C.

"You have a C in algebra," she says.

"I know," I respond feebly. "I have trouble with math."

"A C is average," she tells me, "and you're not average. I don't ever want to see another C on your report card."

"Yes, Mrs. Davis," I promise.

Faye and I say good-bye and continue our walk toward my home.

"What am I going to do?" I ask Faye in a panic. "Mrs. Davis says I can't make another C in math."

"I'll help you," Faye, who is a whiz at math, promises. And she does.

After that we go to my house every day after school and study algebra after we've watched Dick Clark. She takes me through algebraic equations over and over, patiently explaining the process for each one the same way Madre taught me my multiplication tables the summer I stayed with her. When Faye thinks I understand the process, she has me explain the formula to her until I can do it without a mistake.

Since I am skilled in English (a subject in which Faye has received a B), I help her diagram sentences, explaining why certain words and phrases are connected to others and why whole prepositional phrases can sometimes be used as nouns. It is often early evening when we finish our homework. Mother and Rosemary have returned from school in Jackson, so we invite Faye to stay for dinner. She is the only friend I ever had who cared as much about my grades as she did about her own.

This school year, Tougaloo College welcomes a new president and first lady. Samuel and Mrs. Kincheloe have come to the school while we were in New York to replace President and Mrs. Harold Warren, and an inaugural ball is being planned. It will take place in the Brownlee Gymnasium, and everyone in the community (including the high-school faculty and students) is invited. To my delight, Edward asks me to go as his date.

To get ready for my first dance, Mother and I venture to the shopping center to buy the first evening gown I'll ever own, a white sleeveless lace dress with a blue taffeta cummerbund. I also purchase a pair of long white gloves, a pearl evening bag, and a pair of white high-heel shoes. Then we go to the hosiery department so I can buy my first pair of hose. Mother chooses a color she thinks will look nice on me, but when she attempts to place her hand inside the top of the stocking to check the color like the white customers do, the clerk refuses to let her. Instead the white clerk slides her own hand inside the stocking and says to Mother, "See?"

"Yes," my mother responds. "It looks nice on you. Now let's see how it looks on me."

The woman is caught so off guard that she opens the top of the stocking and lets Mother slide her hand inside. The shade we decide on is called "South Pacific," and we stock up on several pairs of nylons in that color to keep on hand because the largest orders in most stores are for shades that will be sold to white customers.

As I grow older, I will discover that whenever the store runs out of the South Pacific shade, clerks are quick to recommend another shade called Red Fox to every Negro woman who shops there, regardless of the customer's complexion. Since pantyhose have not yet been invented, we try to buy the same shade of hose each time. That way if we should rip one stocking from an old pair we can match it with a stocking from the new pair. Unimportant as it may seem, no one wants to have a right leg the color of a warm South Pacific shade and the left leg a glaring Red Fox color.

When we approach the cosmetics counter, I am ready for another challenge, but Mother says Charles of the Ritz has a counter where all the customers are seated under special lights, and a salesperson blends face powder to match each one's complexion. Because of this policy, I will always buy my makeup from Charles of the Ritz.

At the same mall we find a white clerk who allows us to go into the changing room and try on clothes as long as she accompanies us inside, and for the rest of our years at Tougaloo, we will give her our business. The mall where we shop is located between Jackson and Tougaloo, but inside the Jackson city limits the only place Negroes can try on clothes is at Negro-owned stores like Lula Belle's Fashion Center on the first floor of the Masonic Temple.

On the night of the presidential inaugural ball, Dad is away with the football team, so Mother walks with Edward and me over to the gym for the affair. I am in my white lace gown with all the accessories,

Edward is in a tuxedo, and Mother looks beautiful in a floor-length strapless taffeta gown with velvet bodice and sparkling amber jewelry.

We enter to music and a big glass ball turning from the ceiling, throwing sparkling light around the room. Edward leads Mother and me to seats at the edge of the dance floor and then brings us punch. He and I sit and talk. Schoolmates mingle and dance until Miss Tougaloo is crowned and her court introduced. After he crowns Miss Tougaloo, President Kincheloe addresses the crowd; when he is done, dancing resumes. That is when Dr. Borinski (the professor who escaped Nazi Germany and who was the first person to welcome us to Tougaloo) breaks every law in the state of Mississippi governing mixing of the races and walks across the floor to ask Mother to dance. As he leads her onto the floor, I can hear muted gasps from several onlookers. Edward takes my hand and leads me onto the floor filled with couples, and we begin a slow drag that has my heart racing. I feel as if I'm in dreamland. The only thing about this night that's not perfect is the fact that Faye isn't here to enjoy it with me. Her mother has said she may not attend any school dances, so she has made me promise to remember everything that happens and share it with her in school on Monday. Mrs. Wattleton is a Church of God minister who refuses to allow Faye to attend school dances or go on school trips due to her religious beliefs.

At the end of the evening Mother, Edward, and I walk home together. My first date has been a magical evening. Nearing the front door, Mother walks ahead of Edward and me and ascends the front steps. She climbs the steps and opens the French doors to the living room just as Edward brings my hand to his lips and kisses it.

"Good night," he says.

"Good night. I had a wonderful evening." It was a perfect ending.

On Monday, while Faye and I make our way to Brownlee Gymnasium for gym class, I tell her all about the dance. At the end of the school day, she and I return to the gym to try out for the basketball team. Neither of us has ever played basketball, so we are excited when we're chosen for the second team.

Home games are fun, with the girls playing their games before the boys begin. The guys sit in the stands and cheer us on during the first half of our game. Then at the girls' halftime, they go to the boys' locker room to get ready for their game. When our game is over, we take showers, get dressed, and climb into the bleachers to cheer for the Tougaloo Prep boys. Even though it is fun to play basketball at home, everyone looks forward to the road trips. When that day arrives, I can't wait to share it with Faye, but just as with the dance, Mrs. Wattleton says Faye cannot go on the road, because she can't play in any games that are not at Tougaloo. Disappointed, I prepare to make the trip without her. I've heard that during the ride home from games on the road couples sit together on the bus and kiss, and the anticipation of my first kiss with Edward has me both excited and nervous. What if I've forgotten what to do since a year ago when Howard kissed me?

Riding along the highway after the game, schoolmates Gloria and Charles Wilson keep all of us in stitches playing "the dozens," which we call, "talkin' 'bout people's mommas." Gloria and Charles are siblings, so when they start to talk about each other's mother, it's funnier than it would be between friends.

I sit next to Edward hoping he will kiss me on that first trip, but nothing happens. On the bus home after the second game, he and I find seats together near the back of the bus, in front of Boo Jones and her boyfriend, Roscoe Williams. Gloria and Charles Wilson begin by keeping the whole busload laughing as they talk about each other's mother. Then another group of kids join the fun and start teasing one another. After a while the bus quiets down and people start falling asleep. That's when the couples wrap themselves in each other's arms and start kissing. Edward and I sit quietly holding hands while couples all around us "make out." It isn't until we pass the sign that reads, TOUGALOO COLLEGE, 10 MILES that Edward puts his arms around me and kisses me. I part my lips and feel his tongue slide inside my mouth as I melt into his embrace. Suddenly a hand comes from the seat behind ours between our faces and tries to push us apart. Teammates cough and clear their throats, but Edward and I are so rapt we hardly hear them. The hand comes back between our faces again so strong that it pulls us apart. We pull back and Edward looks back at Roscoe, who is responsible for separating us.

"What's going on?" he says.

Roscoe leans forward and whispers, "The lights came on while you were kissing, and Mrs. Jones walked back here and saw you." Mrs. Jones, our English teacher and Boo and Sue's mother, is also the chaperone for this trip. Edward and I are so embarrassed at having been seen that we don't touch each other for the rest of the ride home. Weeks later when Edward and I board the bus for our third game away and head toward the back of the bus where we again hope to kiss, Mrs. Jones stops us at the second row of seats.

"Sit right here," she says. "This is where you will sit on every trip from now on."

That ended kissing on the bus for the two of us. The only thing sitting in second-row seats allows Edward and me to do is talk about our families.

"Do you have sisters other than Albertine?" I ask as the bus pulls off. Albertine is the sister who is immediately older than Edward, whom I know because she is one of the princesses in Miss Tougaloo's court. I remember that the sister who is older than Albertine is Lauretta, but he tells me Maude is the oldest of his four sisters, and Atlanta, the one born after him, is the youngest. Atlanta is a student at the Daniel Hands Elementary School on the Tougaloo College campus. Edward's father owns a convenience store on Highway 80, but he doesn't say much about his mother, who I assume is a homemaker. There isn't much to tell about my family. Everyone knows Coach Braxton and his wife and daughters, but Edward and I do exchange funny stories about our siblings before falling silent.

I look through the bus window across the fields at sharecroppers toiling in the sun or take note of the prisoners we pass along two-lane highways dressed in black-and-white-striped uniforms, swinging picks or laying tar. Some are virile young Negro men, others tired and old, their muscles obviously aching and sweat dripping from them in the heat. Their ankles are chained together with heavy-looking manacles, and one of the students inside the bus whispers loudly enough for most of us to hear, "Chain gang." White prison guards with guns stand over them barking orders as we roll by. Often thereafter I see the chain gangs and sharecroppers on the road; I'm saddened and become very quiet.

During the year when I discover Daddy has given my allowance to basketball or football players who have run out of money, I decide to ask our friends, the Arzenis, if I can babysit for them to make a little extra money for myself. Joan Arzeni is married to Dr. Charles Arzeni, the biology professor. When he is hired at Tougaloo, his wife finds a job in Jackson as a receptionist for a local white doctor, but the job doesn't last long. Mrs. Arzeni, who even calls her Negro housekeeper "Mrs. Snowden," refuses to call Negro patients by their first names the way southerners do. She refers to them as "Mrs." or "Mr." just as she does the white patients. This enrages the doctor who hired her, so she is fired. Undaunted, Mrs. Arzeni takes a job at Tougaloo as secretary to the Negro dean of students, Dr. A. A. Branch. The Arzenis live near us, and sometimes when they go out in the evening, they need a babysitter. I decide that the nights when they are away from home would be a good way for me to earn extra money, so I offer to take care of their new baby, Paul.

Prior to coming to Tougaloo, the Arzenis lived in Africa. They returned to the States with beautiful books and artifacts from the continent, and one of the things I love about being in their home is the opportunity to browse through their African books and collections while baby Paul sleeps. Their collection helps me reclaim a part of the African history I have longed to know about, a part I have felt sure existed, but one to which my Jim Crow world has denied me access. Now, in the living room of the Arzeni home, I can study African pieces of art and pore over African books that confirm the richness of a heritage I have long suspected existed.

November 1956 marks one year since Howard's death. It also marks the month that the Supreme Court outlaws segregation on Montgomery buses. Negro protestors have won their struggle to desegregate city buses, and the announcement makes me feel like we've all been lifted to a new level. It also makes me begin to believe in something I once thought impossible—that there could be real change in the South one day.

At Christmastime, Madre sends us the latest in aluminum Christmas trees. It comes with a four-color rotating cellophane wheel of blue, green, red, and amber lit underneath and reflected against the tree. It is the first artificial tree we've ever owned. We decorate it with shiny green and red ornaments and then sit and watch the colored wheel change it from green to blue to red to amber. We celebrate New Year's Eve with eggnog in front of the television counting down the time as we watch the ball drop in Times Square.

After Christmas, the school year really flies, and before long we are studying for exams. How Mr. Marcus comes up with the music test, I will never know, but as we walk in and take our seats, he begins to play the piano, instructing us to sit down and write on a clean sheet of paper whether the songs are written in harmonic or melodic scales. "Ladies and gentlemen, do not forget to identify whether or not there are sharps and flats." When that part of the test is over, he says we are also to note whether the pieces he has played are written in major or minor keys. Then we are to write our names on the papers, turn them in, and leave. That's it. That's the midterm test.

Sometimes Faye comes home with me to have lunch with Daddy. Other days she goes back to her family's mobile home for lunch, and I eat with Dad alone and then return to school and wait for her to come back or for Edward to return from having his lunch off campus. One day while I wait for them to return, I decide to go around to the back of the schoolhouse to see what the tenth-grade boys in Edward's class are doing. I find them back there playing mumblety-peg, which I haven't played since we moved to Mississippi from Florida.

"May I play?" I ask.

"Yeah. Sure."

When I played back in Florida we threw the knife into the ground, but these guys are throwing it into the side of the wooden schoolhouse, because recent rains have made the ground too soft to hold the knife. We are having a great time until, during one of my turns, I let go of the blade and send the knife sailing through the principal's window. Everyone scatters as glass rains down inside her office, and for the remainder of the day, I wait to be called to Mrs. Davis's office. But nothing happens.

That night I'm a wreck, wondering when she's going to call and tell my parents what I've done. I'm sure she has seen me through her window, and I'm so riddled with guilt about it that I decide to overcome my fear and tell Mother. After confessing, I wait for the tongue-lashing I know is coming. To my surprise and relief, she bursts out laughing. Catching her breath she says, "Tell me what happened again."

When I repeat the story, she laughs even harder. I've never been in trouble in school in my life, and she can't get over the fact that I've done something so outrageous. Relieved but puzzled I go back to my room, vowing never to play mumblety-peg again. Strangely, the broken window is never mentioned except by the tenth-grade boys, who can't wait to tell Edward.

While I enjoy high school, Rosemary is ending her year at the Jackson lab school. She and Mother have been traveling back and forth to Jackson together, Mother dropping Rosemary off at the lab school before continuing to her new job as guidance counselor at Lanier Junior-Senior High School. Her position has come through Daddy who, during one of his trips to the school to scout seniors for his basketball and football teams, learned that the principal, I. S. Sanders, has been looking for a credentialed Negro guidance counselor for the school. He tells Dad that he has not been able to find a single one in the whole state of Mississippi. "My wife is a credentialed counselor," Daddy tells him.

Mr. Sanders has been searching for so long he can hardly believe his ears. "Are you sure?" he asks.

"Yes, her credentials are from Columbia University," Dad reassures him.

"Well," says Sanders, "my only other requirement is that the person be under forty years of age."

"She is," Daddy tells him.

A graduate of Tougaloo College with a postgraduate degree from Columbia himself, Mr. Saunders immediately puts the wheels in motion to hire Mother, but officials at the Mississippi Board of Education claim she is not qualified. Mother contacts Columbia University for verification of her standing. In no time, the Mississippi Board of Ed has a letter from New York stating, "Anne Thomas Braxton's double-A rating from Columbia University covers anything the state of Mississippi requires." The board backs off, and Mr. Sanders hires Mother as the first Negro guidance counselor in the state of Mississippi.

NELL'S MOTHER AT LANIER HS

My first year of high school continues to roll along with a new best friend and a new boyfriend. As the winter fades away, I blame spring fever for the day Faye and I go home for lunch and then decide to experiment with makeup. I go to my room, get out the drugstore eyeliner and mascara I have smuggled into the house, and the two of us draw on eyebrows with a black pencil, layer on mascara, apply lipstick to our mouths, and rub it on our cheeks for rouge. Afterward, we head back to school. Entering Mrs. Jones's English class, we pull out our books and begin to work. As is her custom, Mrs. Jones walks up and down the aisles through the rows of chairs checking each student's paperwork. On this day, when she gets to Faye and me (sitting across the aisle from each other), she stops dead in her tracks. Taking a long look at the two of us, she announces to the rest of the class, "In the ninth grade, girls should be like rosebuds, just starting to grow. In the tenth grade, they should be like blossoms beginning to open. By the eleventh grade, they should be starting to bloom, and by the twelfth grade, they should be in full bloom." With the rest of the class now in rapt attention, she looks down at us and continues, "But two members of this class have budded, blossomed, and bloomed in the course of a one-hour lunch."[101] Faye and I slump sheepishly down in our seats and pray for the floor to open.

Few pleasures in my teenage life can compare to a soft spring breeze on evenings when the smell of honeysuckle permeates the air and the magnolias are in bloom. On Friday nights during the spring I look forward to school dances and the thrill of melting into Edward's arms as the Five Satins sing, "In the Still of the Night" or the Penguins croon, "Earth Angel." In the magic of these evenings, I never want the dances to end, but like everything else, they do. School dances are held on

---

101 Faye Wattleton, *Life on the Line* (New York: Ballantine Books, 1996), 52.

Friday evenings upstairs in the auditorium of the prep school. They end when Mr. Townsend plays, "Good Night Sweetheart, Well, It's Time to Go." That's when the soft lights are turned up, and we dance the last dance before I descend the stairs to the front door of the school with Edward and our friends for a casual walk home. I always look forward to a kiss at my front porch before going inside. On one of those nights Edward removes a silver ring from his finger and gives it to me—a sign that he wants me to be his steady girlfriend. I wear his ring on a silver chain around my neck tucked inside my blouse so Mother and Dad won't see it, because they think I'm too young to go steady.

At St. Mark's, Rosemary and her friends have been preparing for confirmation all year, gathering after school with Father Keeling to learn the same creeds, prayers, rites, and history of the church that I learned in Florida. But when the day of their confirmation arrives, Bishop Duncan Gray Sr., the Bishop of Mississippi, refuses to come to St. Mark's. In fact, he does not set foot in our church (the only Negro Episcopal Church in Jackson) during the entire eight years we are in Mississippi. A white bishop comes down from Michigan to confirm Rosemary and her class, and no one ever receives Mother into the Episcopal Church after she gives up the Congregational Church she grew up in. She will have to wait until we move to California for that to happen.

During the afternoons that Rosemary and Mother stay late in Jackson so that my sister can prepare for confirmation, Faye and I complete our studies, and she heads home. Alone in the house at Tougaloo, I raid Dad's LP collection. It is a small amount of time that I have the house to myself until Daddy gets back from football or basketball practice. I go through my father's albums and pull out Nat King Cole, Ella Fitzgerald, Dinah Washington, Nina Simone, Sarah Vaughan, Dave

Brubeck, Louis Armstrong, Errol Garner, Duke Ellington, and Dizzy Gillespie. Then I lie back on the couch and make up stories in my mind to go with the songs on every album.

Having acquired our father's love of music, Rosemary and I beg Mother and Dad to let us take piano lessons. It takes a lot of pressure from us before they buy an upright piano and enroll us in Mrs. Princess Jones's beginners' class. We are such enthusiastic students that we cover two years of work the first year and are performing in recitals within months of starting classes. I spend hours playing everything from Mendelssohn and Strauss to boogie-woogie and blues, and as I had dreamed of doing when I was a little girl, I sometimes sit at the piano with Dad playing duets.

This is the year I also add a new set of photos to the ones already on my bedroom wall. Poring through Dad's discarded *Sports Illustrated* magazines, I cut out pictures of Althea Gibson, Oscar Robertson, Sugar Ray Robinson, Ezzard Charles, "Big Daddy" Lipscomb, and Bill Russell. In another year I will add Johnny Unitas and Lenny Moore, and two years after that, Wilma Rudolph, Rafer Johnson, and Cassius Clay (now known as Muhammad Ali).

Soon the school year is ending, and final exams are upon us. Mr. Marcus's music exam is by far the toughest of all our tests. For the final, each student has to compose a song on the music sheets he distributes when we enter the class. Before the hour ends he collects the compositions we have written, and without saying whose they are, he sits at the piano and plays each one. The class is asked to judge which are real tunes and which are not. We are graded accordingly. Faye and I each earn an A in music, and true to my promise to Mrs. Davis, I do not get another C.

A few days before the end of the school term, the student body is called to a special assembly in the auditorium on the second floor. Mrs. Davis doesn't mince words. "I am sorry to announce that Tougaloo Prep has not been able to raise enough money to continue another year. After twenty-five years, you will be the last students ever to attend Tougaloo Prep. Eleventh graders who pass the accelerated test will be allowed to enter Tougaloo College in the fall, but ninth and tenth graders will have to look for new schools."

The student body sits in stunned silence, many with tears rolling down our cheeks. We pay little attention to the rest of what Mrs. Davis says. Our carefree days are over, and so is the best high-school education most of us have known or will ever know. Many students will say in later years that Tougaloo Prep prepared them better for college than any school they attended thereafter. I know Faye and I have always felt that way.

The senior graduation is held in Woodworth Chapel. With tears streaming down our faces, the Tougaloo Prep choir gives a final concert. Sounding every T and S as if we are of one voice, we sing a medley of songs that we love; then it is over. The school year has ended, and I am losing another best friend. Faye and her parents are moving to Texas where her mother has accepted a ministerial position with a congregation in Houston. She and I say a tearful good-bye and promise to write. We stay in touch for years, and then our correspondence dwindles and finally stops. More than twenty years go by before we are reunited in New York City after she has become the first woman, the first African American, and the youngest person ever to head the Planned Parenthood Federation of America.

# CHAPTER 16

# GO 'WAY FROM THE MISSISSIPPI[102]

W E WON'T BE RETURNING to Girl Scout camp in Canton, Mississippi, this summer. Mother has found a new camp outside the state. Camp Atwater in East Brookfield, Massachusetts, will give us relief from the toll our Jim Crow life is beginning to exact from Rosemary and me. We pack for our first airplane trip. We will fly from Jackson to Atlanta, where we'll meet Madre who will travel with us by train as far as New York City. There Rosie and I will board a bus for Massachusetts, and Madre will spend the summer with Aunt Mabel.

On the day my sister and I are to leave, Mother, Dad, Rosemary, and I wait in the segregated section of the Jackson airport while I wonder if there will be segregated seating on the airplane. I don't have long to ponder the question, because Mother and Dad are soon kissing us good-bye. Rosemary and I walk across the tarmac and up a flight of rolling stairs; we board the small propeller plane bound for Atlanta.

---

102 A line taken from "Old Man River," from the musical *Showboat*, lyrics by Oscar Hammerstein, music by Jerome Kern.

Stewardesses show us how to strap ourselves into our seats, seeming almost too kind to be white southerners. Welcoming everyone aboard, they hand out free chewing gum and free sample cigarettes in a small box. They tell us to chew the gum in order to clear our ears during take-off and landing, then show us how to use the air bags in case we get sick to our stomachs during the flight.

Our plane taxies down the runway and begins to rise as I look out the window at the blue and orange flames shooting from the propeller. In a panic I wonder if the plane is catching fire, but no one else seems alarmed, so I force myself to relax. I feel nauseated as we begin our ascent, and I pray to God to keep me from throwing up. Gripping the arm of the seat, I chew a wad of gum and take deep breaths to brace myself as we lift into the sky. Rosemary and I are the only Negroes on this flight. When we level off white people get up to enter and leave the restroom while I sit pondering whether or not the toilets are segregated. I decide I won't use them, because I don't want to be embarrassed by being told I can't go in. There will come a time when Rosemary and I won't be the only Negroes on a plane, and I will observe Negroes and whites using the same toilet, but on my very first trip, I'm not taking anything for granted. I limit my intake of fluids so that I can wait to use the toilet until we get to Madre and Papa's home.

Trays of hot food are brought, and I eat slowly so as not to upset my stomach again. Rosemary and I talk and read magazines until our plane begins its descent. Soon we will be the ones emerging from the aircraft like the people we used to watch when we lived in Daytona Beach and stood at the airport with the Biggins boys. We set down in Atlanta shortly after the sun has disappeared. Descending the stairs, we spot

Madre standing in a dark suit, white gloves, and black hat, with her feet in one of the five ballet positions. We hurry toward her excitedly.

"There are my little darlings," she coos, giving each of us a big hug. "I always enjoy flying at night," she continues as we walk toward the baggage area. "From the sky, the city looks like a big bowl of jewels."

I can't begin to imagine what a bowl full of jewels looks like, but I like the image her remarks conjure up. A few days after our arrival Papa drives Rosemary, Madre, and me to the Atlanta railroad station. The three of us are decked out in suits, hats, and white gloves for our trip to New York. Redcaps meet us when we arrive and help with our luggage.

"Good afternoon, Mr. Thomas," they say to Papa, as they ease our bags from the trunk of the Buick onto the baggage trolley.

"Good afternoon," Papa answers. "Mrs. Thomas and our grand-daughters are traveling to New York. I know you will take good care of them."

"Yes, sir."

We hug Papa good-bye and follow a redcap onto the train and into the drawing room our grandfather has booked for us. Porters help us get settled as Madre inquires about each man's family. I can't tell if she actually knows the families of these men, or if she's just carrying on polite conversation. At any rate, they respond as to the welfare of their wives and children or their mothers as if my grandmother knows all of them.

"Will you let us know when the train approaches Gaffney, South Carolina?" Madre asks in the cultured tone I've heard since childhood. "Some friends will be waiting to meet us on the platform there."

"Yes, ma'am, Mrs. Thomas," the porter promises, backing out and thanking her for the crisp new bills she has just pressed into his hand.

Settling into the cushioned seats of the Pullman (Madre facing my sister and me), the three of us pull out newspapers and magazines to read. A daydreamer by nature, I allow my eyes to wander to the window and the backyards of the houses we pass along the way. Houses where women hang laundry, men chop wood, little girls jump rope, and barefoot boys swing on tires hanging from ropes beneath sturdy trees. When our train speeds by their houses, the children stop playing and run alongside us, waving. We wave back until the train leaves them in the dust of their villages.

A gentle rap on our door startles me from my reverie. "Come in," Madre calls out. A porter opens the door and leaves a tray of sodas. We drink them with the fried chicken and rolls we have packed in a foil-lined shoe box wrapped like a mailing package. Riding under the Jim Crow laws that apply to train travel, we will not be allowed in the dining car until we've crossed the Mason-Dixon Line. After we finish our supper, Madre unwraps homemade fudge for each of us to enjoy. The sun has long ago gone down by the time the porter knocks at our door again to say we are approaching Gaffney. He and the other porters make sure the Harrises are standing where our compartment stops on the darkened platform, so we will not waste time searching for them.

We exchange hugs and kisses amid exclamations of how much everyone has grown since last summer when we stopped with Mother and Daddy on our way to New York. Calvin and Rosemary walk away from the rest of us to talk alone quietly. The two of them and Polly and I have been writing one another during the two years since we left Gaffney. While Mrs. Harris and Madre visit, Polly, Weldon, Red, and I talk about our summer plans.

"All aboard!" the conductor calls as we exchange neatly tied boxes of goodies. Time always passes quickly when I wish it would stand still, and this is no exception. Madre leaves her divinity and fudge candies with the Harrises, and they give us food that will last the rest of our journey. The time we've had together has been much too short, but we are consoled by the fact that we'll see one another again on our trip home, when Rosie and I will share camp experiences.

"Good-bye!" we call from the train as it chugs its way along the track. It slowly picks up speed as we watch and wave from inside until darkness enshrouds them, and all that's left is the night.

Returning to our drawing room where beds have been prepared with crisp, clean sheets turned back, we brush our teeth, wash up, and get into pajamas. Rosemary and I say our prayers before climbing into the double-bunk berth. Madre, from her bed across the floor facing us, turns out the light and raises the window shade, so we can see the stars. Lying there in the dark, I count the telephone poles that whiz by, and enjoy the rocking that will soon lull me to sleep. Somewhere at the edge of sleep, between awareness and semiconsciousness, I wonder if there's a little girl in one of the houses we roll by who's lying in her bed like I once did in Jacksonville, dreaming of the day when she will board a train and travel to places she's never been before.

Sunlight streaming through the window awakens me early the next morning. We all rise, wash up, brush our teeth, and change back into traveling suits before eating a breakfast of fruit and ham that Mrs. Harris has packed for us. Around noon a porter knocks on the door to let us know we will soon be pulling into Washington, DC—the invisible line that marks the end of our Jim Crow travel. When the train leaves the nation's capital, Rosemary, Madre, and I enter the dining car to have lunch. Madre speaks to us in Spanish to make it difficult for the people around us to understand what she is saying. Rosemary and I don't speak Spanish, but we understand enough of it to respond as she talks with us.

Before long our train is entering New York's beautiful old Pennsylvania Station with its magnificent 150-foot vaulted ceiling. When we get off the train, we spot Aunt Mabel and rush toward her to exchange hugs and kisses. After claiming our luggage, we follow the redcap outside to a big yellow Checker Cab. While the bags are being piled into the trunk, Rosie and I get into the back of the taxi and pull open the jump seats, so we can ride backward all the way to Harlem.

The fact that Mother has straightened our hair before we left home doesn't matter to Aunt Mabel, who has already made appointments for Rosemary and me to get it done again at the beauty parlor on 116th Street. Madre goes with us to tell the beautician to make our hair as straight as hers is—as if *that's* possible. For the life of me I cannot understand why it is so important to have straightened hair for camp when one of the first things the counselors demand is that we get into the pool. Even if that were not the first thing on the agenda, our hair is not going to stay straight for the entire month anyway, and I know from our days in Florida that the bathing caps we have brought are not going to keep the pool water out of them. Nevertheless, Rosie and I board the bus for Camp Atwater with freshly straightened hair. At camp we will be joined by other middle- and upper-middle-class Negro girls from across the country, all sent to spend one month together at Atwater before the start of the boys' season in August.

Camp Atwater is set on Lake Lashaway amid manicured lawns and immaculately laid stone paths. The scenic setting is worlds away from the rustic 4-H Girl Scout camp in Canton, Mississippi, where we sat around a made-from-scratch campfire roasting marshmallows. Here, among complete strangers, we begin the camp season with a talent show. Seated in the audience, watching one talented girl after another perform, I'm relieved that I haven't volunteered to play my flute. These girls take to the stage as if they are born to it. They offer piano and violin sonatas, scenes from plays, and a finale in which one girl dances to a version of "Slaughter on Tenth Avenue"—a scene right out of a Broadway show. Compared to the way I've been brought up, and the little plays we've put on, these girls look like professionals.

As the season begins, Rosemary and I make friends easily, but Rosie is also homesick and within days she is at a pay phone near the administration building making a collect call home begging Mother and Dad to let her come home. They try to convince her to give the camp a try while I stand next to her asking her to please stay. With all three of us working to convince her to stay at camp, she finally agrees and tries to settle into the daily routine.

I have always enjoyed being with younger children, and it takes very little time for me to discover that my true interests are working with the youngest campers and taking dance classes. So those are the activities I sign up for. There is so much to do at Atwater that the month seems to fly by. At the end of the session we board a bus and head back to New York City, where we take the train back to Atlanta with Madre. In Gaffney we stop again to visit with the Harris family, who are waiting on the train platform with goodies for us to eat during our journey. Back in Atlanta we board a plane for the short flight to Jackson, where we are met by Mother and Daddy.

At home, Rosie and I tell Mother, "Camp Atwater was a nice change from camp in Mississippi, but we don't want to go back. It was too bourgie." Bourgie is shorthand for bourgeois.

"I'm glad you told me," Mother says. "The last thing I want you girls to become is snobs."

Less than a month after we are back at home and in bed, the crack of gunshots echo through the night. Within moments of the shots being fired there is banging at our front door. Dad opens it to find a student, who has crept across campus at fast as he could to our front door. He reports breathlessly, "Coach, white people are shooting through the windows of the girls' dorm!"

The boy says Tougaloo students are terrified that white people from Jackson have come to invade the campus. The students are crouched down inside their dormitories screaming, while a car filled with white people drives back and forth firing rounds.

"Dean Branch is out of town," the boy continues, "so they told me to come get Coach!"

From the time my father was a young man, he has stood up to racist white southerners. In fact, shortly after he and Mother were married he nearly beat a young white man to death, because the man called him a nigger and refused to pay him for the work Dad had done. At the time Dad was teaching school in Cordele, Georgia, during the day and working at a filling station at night to earn extra money to support himself and his new bride. He had never really had positive experiences with whites until he entered graduate school in New York, so his expectations of them were quite low. It took his friendship with Jim Metress, a white student at NYU, to change my father's condemnation of all white people.

People at Tougaloo have long known that "Coach isn't afraid of anybody." And they know if they call him for help, he'll come. So they look for him whenever there is trouble, which is why in the middle of this 1957 summer, when white people are shooting up the campus, a young Negro student has knocked at our front door. Dad quickly goes for the gun he has been keeping and starts across the darkened campus to investigate. He makes his way to the gymnasium and enters. Brownlee Gymnasium sits several yards across the road from the girls' dormitory. Inside the unlit gym, Dad crouches down and waits for the car with the shooters to return. Before long he hears their automobile coming down the road crawling through the front gate of the campus—the wrought-iron gate with the arch that reads TOUGALOO SOUTHERN CHRISTIAN COLLEGE. Slowly the car moves along the road toward the gymnasium where Daddy is waiting. As the vehicle approaches the gym, my father theorizes that this is the carload of whites that has been terrorizing the students, so he eases out of the gymnasium and makes his way behind a tree on the lawn in front of the gym. Crouched down behind the tree, he waits for the car to pull even with it. When it does, my father spots five white teenage boys inside. He yells to them, "Turn that car around and get off this campus!"

The driver of the car continues to creep slowly forward, then turns the automobile around and backs up even with the tree.

"Nigger," he shouts back, "if you want us off, *put* us off!"[103]

Daddy raises the gun, points it over the top of the car, and fires two shots.

The car with the teenagers inside catapults forward and with tires screeching races toward the wrought-iron campus gate, sailing through

---

103 Interview with John Braxton, summer 1988.

it so fast that the car almost clips the side of the archway. Moving at breakneck speed, the driver careens down the narrow road between the A-frame houses and trailers on one side and the moss-laden oak and hickory trees on the other. It roars past the post office where the pavement rises to meet the railroad tracks and then goes airborne. Sailing over the tracks, it bounces down onto "eighty highway," makes a sharp right turn, and peels off toward Jackson.[104]

On Monday, the sheriff comes out to Tougaloo to meet with Dean Branch, who has returned from his trip. He knows nothing of the weekend events. The sheriff knows all about what has happened, though, and he wants to meet with the dean to discuss the incident. Dean Branch stands inside his office facing the sheriff with the door ajar. That's when he receives news from the sheriff that "somebody at Tougaloo did some shootin' over the weekend, and I wanna know who it was."

"I don't think any shooting took place here," Dean Branch states confidently.[105]

At that very moment my father happens to be walking past the dean's office and realizes the men inside must be talking about him.

He knocks and enters, then says, "I'm the one who did the shooting. Some white boys came out here last weekend and fired shots on this campus. When I intercepted them and told them to leave, they refused, and I fired two warning shots over their car."

"That was a var' dangerous thang to do," the sheriff responds. "S'pose you'd a hit one of 'em?"

---

104 Ibid.
105 Ibid.

"If a group of Negroes came into your neighborhood using profanity and firing guns, how would you greet them?" Dad responds. "My family lives on this campus, and I don't intend to have anybody come out here and injure any one of them. Besides, if I'd meant to hit somebody, I wouldn't have shot in the air. I'd have aimed at the car."

"Well," says the sheriff, "I've talked to the boys, and they admitted to bein' here, but they say they jus' set off firecrackers."

In spite of the sheriff's claim, at his insistence, two of the boys do something unheard of in Mississippi in those days. They come out to Tougaloo and offer a formal apology.[106]

In September with Tougaloo Prep closed for good, Rosemary and I are enrolled in Holy Ghost Roman Catholic High School in Jackson. There, white nuns in spit-polished black lace-up shoes and flowing black habits teach classes.

Entering the tenth grade I take geometry, world history, English, and religion, which is the toughest class to master, because I don't believe everything I am being taught in the Roman Catholic religion classes. Daily mass is required for Roman Catholic students, but non-Catholics have to attend chapel, too. However, we are relegated to the hard wooden benches in the dimly lit room surrounded by burning candles, religious icons, and crosses, while our Catholic classmates kneel at the altar and receive Communion. It is here during this boring time in a dimly lit room that I begin to exchange handwritten notes with a girl named Tommie Ann Johnson.

Meanwhile, in the neighboring state of Arkansas, the Little Rock school board has declared the city's intention to comply with the US

---

106 Ibid.

Constitution's desegregation requirements "as soon as the Supreme Court outlines the methods to be followed."[107] But one hundred thousand residents are still following the rules of segregation, and Governor Orval Faubus has announced that 85 percent of the people polled throughout the state are opposed to integrating the schools. An old-fashioned segregationist, Faubus declares he will not be "party to any attempt to force acceptance of change"[108] in spite of anything the Little Rock school board has said.

Nevertheless, nine Negro teenagers are scheduled to enter Little Rock's all-white Central High that fall, and their parents, who have filed a federal suit claiming the color of their children's skin is the only basis for Central High's rejection of their children, are looking to the NAACP for counsel.[109]

Governor Faubus's response is that, "Blood will run in the streets if Negro pupils attempt to enter Central High."[110]

I watch the drama on television from one state away with the same fascination that I watched Autherine Lucy in Tuscaloosa, Alabama, and with the same fear for the nine students that had me trembling after the lynching of Emmett Till. Hearing Governor Faubus's threat, I have no doubt that his prediction of blood flowing in the streets will come true. There's no difference between white folks in Arkansas and white folks in Alabama and Mississippi, I tell myself. And since President Eisenhower refused to protect Autherine Lucy in Alabama a year ago, he's not going to intervene in Arkansas. But I am wrong.

---

107 Williams, *Eyes on the Prize*, 92.
108 Ibid. 94.
109 Ibid. 94.
110 Ibid. 100.

With the eyes of the whole world on Little Rock, the president has no choice but to enforce the 1954 Supreme Court ruling,[111] so he sends federal troops into the city in order to permit nine Negro students to begin their first day of school. Walking toward Central High they are surrounded by a convoy of jeeps and soldiers behind machine gun mounts and holding rifles. Helicopters hover overhead and paratroopers strain to hold back the hostile mob that has formed to throw debris and hurl racial epithets.[112]

Back in Jackson, I stand in the schoolyard at Holy Ghost with my classmates talking in hushed tones about Little Rock as we wait for the school bell to ring that will begin our day. No one says it, but we know our fate is tied to the fate of the Little Rock Nine. We enter the classroom and sit quietly in our seats. Not one nun mentions Little Rock—not even in our history or current events classes. How different these white nuns are from Mrs. Lottie Thornton, the Negro teacher at Jackson Lab who taught Rosemary and her classmates to think outside the curriculums she was given to teach. At Holy Ghost, it is as if not mentioning the events means they're not happening, means that the South is not being reordered in some way, that even *their* lives are changing. Or do they think that if they don't say anything, *we* won't notice?

For the second time in as many years, I rush home at the end of the school day to watch television and see Jefferson Thomas, Carlotta Wills, Gloria Ray, Elizabeth Eckford, Thelma Mothershed, Melba Pattillo, Terrance Roberts, Minniejean Brown, and Ernest Green—the Little Rock Nine—face angry mobs the same way Autherine Lucy did in Tuscaloosa, Alabama. These nine students and Autherine Lucy are not

---

111 Ibid. 106.
112 Ibid. 110.

the old, uneducated domestics, nor the middle-aged Negro professionals of Montgomery, Alabama, defying a city's transportation system. These are young people my age going through the worst humiliation imaginable in order to guarantee the education our government has promised to all of us. If they succeed, maybe even in Mississippi I'll succeed. So I watch every day—watch them absorb racial slurs and humiliation from the angry mobs they encounter entering and leaving school.

"We don't want to go to school with no niggers!"

"Two, four, six, eight, we don't want to integrate."

I feel every taunt as if it is hurled at me personally, as if each insult is an indictment against the whole Negro race. The courage these nine teenagers show inspires me and puts my experience at school into perspective. Just as I realized a year ago how lucky I was to be able to go to school and not have to pick cotton in the Mississippi Delta like two of my schoolmates, I realize now how lucky I am not to have to face a hostile white mob every morning on my way to school. Every morning these nine brave young people face the possibility of death. By comparison, attending a Roman Catholic school is easy. I vow to make friends at Holy Ghost and get good grades, so I will be in a position to take advantage of future opportunities that may come my way, even though I do not delude myself that schools in Mississippi will see integration come anytime soon.

Through the notes we've been passing during Holy Communion, Tommie Ann and I have become friends. She is a tall, slender, brown-skinned girl with long, wavy hair who has been attending Holy Ghost since elementary school, even though she is a Baptist. Like Faye Wattleton, my best friend at Tougaloo Prep, Tommie Ann is an only child with parents who lay down very strict rules—no dating, no makeup, no sleepovers, and no after school dances. Tommie's mother is a homemaker, her father, a barber. The first time I spend a weekend at her house, I am awakened by the most god-awful screams imaginable. Bolting upright in bed, I demand to know, "What's going on?"

Tommie Ann rolls over from the other side of the double bed we are sharing and says sleepily, "That's a little boy getting his first haircut."

Slowly she raises the blinds of the window over the headboard of the bed where we've been sleeping, and the two of us raise ourselves onto our elbows high enough for our heads to peek into her father's barber shop in the adjoining room. In the barber's chair sits a little boy about three years old, squirming and screaming his lungs out. His father holds him down, and Mr. Johnson's electric shears send swirls of beautiful black curls onto the shop floor. The men are carrying on conversation above the tot's screams as if nothing else is happening.

Having been completely awakened by the shrill cries, Tommie Ann and I get up, make the bed, bathe, and get dressed. After breakfast, we run errands for Mrs. Johnson and then return to listen to rock and roll on the radio. Looking back now, it seems odd that those of us living in the segregated South carried on such normal teenage lives in the midst of all the violence taking place, but that was the only way we knew to live. These were the very things our parents and teachers were struggling to keep us from accepting as a way of life. It is why they worked so hard to bring us up as normally as possible even in the midst of the brutality of the times. Had they allowed the violence and hatred to consume us, we would surely have become emotionally and mentally stunted.

Searching for a good music station, Tommie Ann and I stumble upon Aretha Franklin singing, "It Won't Be Long." Laughing and singing along with her, we can hardly believe we've found a station that plays "race music," and we break into gales of laughter when Aretha belts out, "Baby, here I be, by the railroad track, waitin' for my baby. He's a'comin' back. Comin' back to me on the five-o-three and it won't be long, no, no it won't be long." Hearing someone sing in the Negro vernacular on the radio for the first time causes us to sing over and over for the rest of the day, "Baby, here I be by the railroad track..." like it's some secret code the grown-ups don't understand.

At Holy Ghost, I'm starting to resent Catholic school rules. Rosemary and I have grown up shooting marbles, playing football, dodgeball, and mumblety-peg with boys throughout our young lives. At Holy Ghost, girls have to sit on one side of the classroom and boys on the other. When we attend school dances, the nuns take a ruler and measure the space between each boy and girl while we dance to make sure we are at least twelve inches apart, and we are closely watched if we try to talk with the boys during recess time. Rosemary and I tell Mother and Daddy that the rules of not associating with boys make us uncomfortable.

"What's wrong with being with boys at school?" we want to know. "It never mattered before."

"Nothing's wrong with your being with boys," Mother says. After a few private words with Dad, she concedes, "I guess you might as well go to public school; they are the people you'll have to get along with when you go out into the world anyway." So after six weeks, we leave Holy Ghost and are enrolled at Lanier Junior-Senior High School, where Mother is a guidance counselor and Uncle Dynamite is an American history teacher. Our great-uncle has moved to Mississippi from Los

Angeles and begun teaching at Lanier High. He is living with us until he can find a place to live in Jackson.

At Lanier, I am assigned to Mother's vocational exploration class (all tenth graders have to take the class), to Miss Thompson's French class, Mrs. Young's biology class, Mrs. Granville's English class, and Uncle Dynamite's class in American history. Band satisfies my music requirement, and art and geometry round out my courses. On my first day of school, my homeroom teacher, Mrs. Dorothy Young, embarrasses me by announcing to the rest of the class that I have transferred from Holy Ghost with straight As, except for an A-minus in religion. As the new student, all I want to do is blend in, and I fear Mrs. Young's announcement will make it seem as if I think I'm better than the other students. I'm shocked when they show admiration for my accomplishments and reach out to make me feel welcome. I appreciate their friendliness, but I miss Tommie Ann, miss the opportunity to have another best friend like Gail and Faye.

In this new school, Rosemary and I gain instant recognition and acceptance because we are Mrs. Braxton's daughters. We are among a number of schoolmates whose parents also teach at Lanier—the Bracey kids, the Hollys, the Jacksons, and Lynette Anderson. We find ourselves in many of the same classes (based on a tracking system) and governed by test scores, grades, and aptitude tests. We are all the children of educators who have demanded the best from us, and so we find ourselves in the fastest tracks that make up the Lanier Junior-Senior High of seventh- to twelfth-graders. There are roughly twenty-five students per class—twice the size of the classes at Tougaloo Prep and with at least five more students per class than at Holy Ghost.

Lanier has an orchestra and a marching band that Rosemary and I join. Her clarinet and my flute are taken out and played for the first time since we left the band in Daytona Beach, Florida. Mr. Holly, the band director, orders new maroon-and-white uniforms for the two of us and assigns us places in both the marching band and the orchestra.

Fellow band members Benny Mullen, Walter Evege, Robert Harrion, Anthony Coyt, and Jacob Moore form a combo they call the Blue Notes, and they are so good that they play for all our high-school dances and for dances throughout the city. Beatrice Thompson is the group's singer. When my artistic talents flourish under the tutelage of Mr. Willie Kyles, I go to the group's drummer, Benny, with an offer I hope he'll accept. I offer to paint blue notes on the combo's wooden music stands if he will teach me to play the drums. He agrees and a great new friendship begins.

I try out for the basketball team and am chosen for the second string. But going on road trips with Lanier's team isn't nearly as much fun as traveling with Tougaloo Prep was. For one thing, Gloria and Charles Wilson aren't with us to play the dozens, and for another I don't have a boyfriend to sit with on the long trips away. Edward has entered school in Madison County, and he and I have begun to drift apart. But there is at least one trip I will never forget, and it doesn't have anything at all to do with a boy.

On that basketball trip we got the surprise of our lives when our bus pulled up to the front of a beautiful new brick schoolhouse set back on several acres of land. Everyone on the bus was so sure the driver had come to the wrong place that we refused to get off the bus. Our coaches even insisted that the driver go inside to make sure this was where we were supposed to be. The driver got off, entered the school, and returned.

"Yeah, this is the right place," he said.

So we got our gear and exited the bus. Inside we found a state-of-the-art gymnasium, a science lab, and an Olympic-size swimming pool. When we asked how such a beautiful school came to be built for Negroes, we were told that local contractors mixed up the blueprints for two schools being built at the same time. The specs that should have gone to the white part of town went to the Negro section and vice versa. By the time the error was discovered, construction for both schools was too far underway to make any changes, so Negro children got a state-of-the-art school with secondhand books and broken and outdated equipment, while white children got the latest books and equipment in a school that was designed for Negroes.

In the evenings on the Tougaloo campus, I take modern dance classes with Miss Redmond, who is the school's girls' physical education teacher. Like Dr. Borinski, who spends Saturday mornings teaching us German and speed-reading, Miss Redmond offers the children of faculty members dance classes for free. During stretching and leaping to music, I acquire a new sense of grace. Difficult movements force me to push myself to the limit, and that gives me a whole new sense of confidence. In a short time, I am a good enough dancer to perform at the halftime of the Lanier boys' basketball games. After the girls' basketball team has played, I shower, change into my costume, and sit in the bleachers until halftime of the boys' game. Then I take to the floor and perform. My life becomes so full that the school year that term whizzes by. In the spring, one of the most popular boys in school asks me to be his date to the junior-senior prom. I am overjoyed with his invitation, because he is such a hip guy that all the kids call him "Cool Breeze." But Mother says I can't go to the prom because it is for juniors and seniors, and I'm just a sophomore. (Sometimes I really don't understand my parents at all, especially since they allow Rosemary to attend the prom the following year when she's a sophomore.) Turning down Cool Breeze's invitation is the lowest point of the school year, and just as I fear, the word gets out that Mrs. Braxton's daughter either can't go anywhere or is "too good" to go out with the rest of the kids.

As my tenth-grade year draws to a close, the Little Rock Nine complete a tumultuous time of mental and physical abuse. They have been escorted to and from school by armed soldiers, shadowed by paratroopers encircling Central High, and followed by helicopters for the last nine months. They've entered school each day with soldiers carrying bayonets and attended their classes with bodyguards, but their white schoolmates had tripped them up, poured hot food on them, and hit them in their faces, and they couldn't hit back. They had to keep going in spite of the taunts and name calling, because they'd been instructed not to retaliate.[113] Graduation exercises for the only Negro senior, Ernest Green, took place with a mostly white audience that applauded each graduating white student enthusiastically,[114] but when Green received his diploma there was only silence.

"Nobody clapped," he remembered later. "But I figured they didn't have to, because I had accomplished what I had come there for."[115]

That summer Orval Faubus won reelection to a third term as governor, declaring he stood where he'd always stood, "in opposition to integration by force or at bayonet point."[116] True to his word, Faubus closed the city's public schools the following fall and assisted segregationists in setting up a private school corporation to which he leased segregated

---

113  Ibid. 108–109.
114  Ibid. 118.
115  Ibid. 118.
116  Ibid. 118.

public-school facilities.[117] Half the white children in the city of Little Rock enrolled in those private schools the following term. Another third went to schools outside the city. The rest (both Negro and white) were left without a school to go to at all, including the remainder of the original Little Rock Nine. And in a 1958 Gallup poll, "Americans selected (Governor Orval Faubus) as one of their ten most admired men."[118]

It is not until one year later, August 1959, that Little Rock's public school system reopens to Negroes and whites, and it only opens then because "the United States Supreme Court rules that 'evasive schemes' (can) not be used to avoid integration."[119]

Determined to get Rosemary and me out of Mississippi for another summer, Mother has spent the better part of the winter looking at new camps. Hearing of one in upstate New York, she has written this letter.

*Tougaloo Southern Christian College*
*Tougaloo, Mississippi*
*December 7, 1957*

*THE LITTLE RED SCHOOL HOUSE*
*196 Bleecker Street*
*New York, New York*

*Dear Sirs,*
*I am writing to get some information about Camp Woodlawn (sic). I understand that you can give me the information that I need or that you can direct me to the persons who can.*

117 Ibid. 118.
118 Ibid. 118.
119 Ibid. 118.

*Our daughters have had some very enjoyable camp experiences in Massachusetts. However, we should like them to have the experience of camping in the Catskill Mountains, famous in legend and history, where we understand Camp Woodlawn is located. We should like them to have this experience this summer. Because we know that applications must be sent in early, we should like to get all of the necessary information now.*

*Could you please give the opening and closing dates for camp, the cost for the full season or half season, requirements for admission, etc.*

*Any information you are able to give will be greatly appreciated. I would be grateful for a prompt reply.*

*Very truly yours,*

*(Mrs.) A. T. Braxton*

Based on her letter, Rosemary and I receive scholarship aid for the full two-month period at Camp Woodland and begin helping Mother sew name tags in our clothes according to camp regulations. We pack footlockers and duffel bags to the brim, shocked that we need jackets and heavy sweaters for the summer months. We've never been anywhere during the summer where warm sweaters were needed. And we certainly haven't lived anywhere where we've needed them. In fact, everywhere we've lived we have had to turn off the lights inside the house at night and open the doors to keep the house cool. Now we need jackets, heavy sweaters, and insulated sleeping bags in the middle of summer.

At the end of June, Mother and Dad drive us to Atlanta. We prepare to travel to New York City by train with Madre once again, unaware that this camping experience will change our lives forever.

# CHAPTER 17

# THIS LAND IS YOUR LAND, THIS LAND IS MY LAND[120]

W̶E GET OUR HAIR straightened on 116th Street in New York and prepare to spend two months at a new camp. On the first of July, we hail a cab in front of Aunt Mabel's apartment and ride with Madre down to Eleventh Street near Second Avenue, where we find a chartered bus parked in front of the Downtown Community School waiting to take Negro, white, and Puerto Rican campers to the Catskill Mountains. Amid the good-byes to relatives and friends, Rosemary and I kiss Madre and shove our footlockers and duffel bags into the bus's holding area. Then we board with other campers and look for two seats together. But a white girl with dark curly hair asks Rosemary to sit next to her before we've gone more than three rows in, so I sit in the seat behind them next to another white girl—with bobbed dark-brown hair.

"Hi, my name's Joan. What's yours?" my seatmate asks.

---

120  Composed and recorded by Woody Guthrie, copyright May 30, 1956.

"Nell," I respond timidly, somewhat overwhelmed by this instant friendship.

"Where are you from?"

"Mississippi."

"Really? Is it as bad as they say?"

"Yes."

I hear the girl who has invited Rosemary to sit with her say, "My name's Katy. What's yours?"

"Rosemary, but you can call me Rose or Rosie."

A redheaded girl with freckles and a chipped tooth bounds onto the bus holding hands with a boy sporting a crew cut and horn-rimmed glasses. They are followed by two other redheads with guitar cases and several other teens who make their way to the back of the bus laughing and talking animatedly. The redheaded girl who was the first of this group to enter the bus bites into a peach as she passes me and extends it, offering me a bite.

"No, thank you," I say, with surprised apprehension. I don't even share fruit that has been bitten into with members of my own family. The bus fills quickly and begins pulling away as teenagers wave good-bye to parents and relatives standing at the curb. Before we've driven a full city block, guitars and banjos come out of cases and campers begin to sing. A couple of camp counselors sit in the front seats of the bus talking, but the kids are left alone to sing, eat, and move around without interference. Neither of the counselors says to sit down, be quiet, or stop eating on the bus. Coming from a culture in which rules and laws govern everything I do—from the books I read to the toilet I use and the water I drink—and where even Negro adults dictate how I am to behave in public, I don't know what to make of the total freedom with which the kids are allowed to move about and have fun. Phoenicia, New York, where the camp is located, is approximately two hours outside New York City, and kids laugh, sing, and talk all the way there.

Within a couple of miles of the campsite, we come upon a sign that reads, Camp Woodland for Children. Our bus drives past it and moves alongside a bubbling creek. Then it turns onto a road that winds up a hill before veering off to the right and creeping down a dirt road, where it finally comes to a stop. This is work camp, where Rosemary, her seatmate, Katy, my seatmate, Joan, and I, and about forty other campers, will spend the summer. Everyone on the bus (except the dozen or so kids seated at the back) gets off and begins unloading luggage. Girls are directed into the two-story white wooden building in the middle of a patch of grass a few yards away, and boys are sent around to the back of the building and up a path to tents with wooden platforms for floors and electric light bulbs hanging from the tent tops. The counselors-in-training (CITs), still seated in the back of the bus, wave good-bye to us as they chug up a long rocky hill on the bus toward upper camp where the CIT tents are located.

Rosemary and I walk over the grassy front lawn with the other girls, enter the two-story building, and go up the stairs. The first-floor living room that we crossed upon entering is where work campers will gather on this and future evenings for meetings. To the right of it is a dining room, and behind the dining room, a kitchen. At the top of the stairs Katy, Joan, and I discover we are roommates in the last room down the hall. It is the room closest to the back door, which has a screen at the top and a hook on the wood at the bottom to lock it after closing the outside door.

There is a small half bath with a basin and toilet between our room and that of one of the counselors who was on the bus from New York City with us. The rest of the girls along the hallway share a bathroom near the showers midway down the hall. All of us take showers in the same shower stalls. As Katy, Joan, and I open our trunks and begin unpacking, Rosemary comes down the hall to join us. At first the counselors don't want Rosemary and me to be in the same room, but Rosemary puts up a fuss about their decision, and they relent. Staking out cubbyholes for our clothes, we fill them up. Since there is one bunk bed and two lower ones, Katy says we should rotate sleeping in the top bed by flipping a coin so that everyone spends two weeks on the top bunk. I pull the first two-week rotation.

This is the first time Rosemary and I have had white roommates and white counselors. It is also our first coed camp. And as if that isn't enough, it is the first environment we've been in where kids curse and are not called to task for it by the adults. In our southern culture, kids can be called to task for saying "hell," but on this first day of camp counselors don't even blink at the occasional "damn" being uttered.

After our beds are made, we place toiletries in the bathroom that we share with the counselor. Then we push our empty footlockers under the beds and start to get acquainted. Katy has a copy of *LIFE* magazine on her bed, opened to a picture of a man standing in front of a charred cross. Leslie, the counselor, enters our room through the small bathroom that connects our two rooms and introduces herself. She's new at Camp Woodland this year, too, she says. It turns out that everyone gathered in our room is new except Joan.

Spying the open magazine on Katy's bed, Leslie asks, "Is that your father?"

"Yes," Katy answers.

Picking up the magazine, Leslie looks more closely at the photo.

"I've read about Levittown," she says. She and Katy begin to talk about the incident that has led to the article as the rest of us sit listening. I've never known anyone whose parents were in a magazine, so I listen attentively to hear why Katy's father is featured in this article.

It turns out that during the months when I sat at home in front of our television watching the drama unfold over the desegregation of Little Rock's Central High, Katy Wechsler's family was immersed in a racial conflict in Levittown, Pennsylvania. It began when a Negro family moved into their white middle-class neighborhood and set off a storm of violent reactions that pitted neighbor against neighbor and friend against friend.

The first time Daisy Meyers showed up at the house next door to the Wechslers, most of the neighborhood people assumed she was "the help" coming in to clean for the new owners. But when a mailman knocked at the door to tell her he had a letter for Mr. Meyers, she took it, informing him that she was Mrs. Meyers. That's when all hell broke loose. An article appeared in the *Levittown Times* announcing, "First Negro Family Moves Into Levittown."[121]

The story of Bill and Daisy Meyers's move to Levittown, Pennsylvania, went on to grab national headlines, because developer William Levitt (for whom the town was named) had advertised and offered his houses on a "whites-only" basis, and a number of people had moved to the town for the express purpose of getting away from Negroes in Trenton and Philadelphia.[122] But Katy's parents were

---

121 Lewis Wechsler, *The First Stone: A Memoir of the Racial Integration of Levittown, Pennsylvania* (Chicago: Grounds for Growth Press, 2004), 2.
122 Ibid. 2–3.

members of the Human Relations Council and were working to challenge segregated housing in their neighborhood, so they welcomed Bill Meyers, an engineer, and his wife, Daisy, a professor, as well as their two young sons and brand-new baby daughter.

In August 1957, the Wechslers awoke to discover a cross had been burned on their front lawn—the same charred cross we are now looking at in the *LIFE* magazine photo. And that September, the White Citizens' Council and the Ku Klux Klan began harassing the Meyerses and anyone who extended a welcome to them, including children. Because of Katy's and her parents' friendship with the Meyerses, Katy's best friend's parents refused to let their daughter spend time with her anymore, and the Wechslers feared their ten-year-old son, Nicky, would be beaten up going to and from school. Anonymous callers leveled abusive threats, and hate mail began to arrive at the Wechslers' home. Every time they went out, they were forced to run "a gauntlet of racist and anti-Semitic abuse."[123]

The FBI took over an empty house in back of the Meyerses' and hung a Confederate flag in full view while they played "Old Black Joe" all night on a hi-fi. A neighbor named his a black dog "Nigger" and then unleashed the dog whenever Bill or Daisy Meyers went outside and called to the dog, "Here, nigger, come here, you nigger."[124]

There were accusations by some neighbors that the Wechslers led the Meyerses to purchase the home in order to help the Communist cause,[125] a highly inflammatory suggestion to make in the wake of the McCarthy witch hunts.

---

123  Ibid. 51.
124  Ibid. 65.
125  Ibid. 63–64.

Listening to Katy share parts of this story, I think of white people in Mississippi who have endured similar abuse because of the stands they have taken—Dr. Borinski, who was a member of the NAACP and hosted interracial conversations at Tougaloo, and Mrs. Arzeni, who refused to call Negro adults by their first names—but Katy is the first white teenager I've ever known who is proud to be part of the struggle for equal rights. As she comes to the end of her explanation of the magazine article, Leslie suggests we go downstairs because it's time for the director of work camp to welcome us.

Camp Director Larry Goldberg greets the girls and boys of work camp in the living room after we and the work camp counselors are all assembled. He lays down the rules:

1. We will go hiking once a week.
2. We will sort dirty clothes and bed linens that we are to leave in pillowcases and personal laundry bags at a designated spot each week on laundry day, which is also hike day.
3. We are to sign up for work projects on the sheets posted on a corkboard attached to the front of the bunkhouse, and on and on.

There's a reason they call this work camp, I realize. Larry continues, "There will be a two-week canoe trip with a limited number of spots, and anyone who wants to sign up for it—first come, first served—must be a strong swimmer."

Other information includes the annual folk festival, weekly folk dances in upper camp, trips into the town of Phoenicia to the movies and summer stock productions at the Phoenicia Playhouse, trips to Folkerts where we can build our own ice cream sundaes at the counter (*and eat them seated next to white people*, I think). And he announces there will be a "mock Olympics" during Olympic Week when each camper is assigned to one of four teams, each team representing a different country. During that week, campers will research and share information about the country they represent, and the entire camp will eat food from each of the four countries while we gather data about the culture, sing songs, and perform dances from each country. Larry also announces that there is a camp orchestra that is open to anyone who has brought an instrument. That's when I discover that in addition to all the guitars and banjos, some campers have brought recorders, clarinets, saxophones, violins, and flutes.

Now Larry introduces the work camp counselors, Susan, Leslie, Bruce, George, and a husband and wife named Mack and Clare, whom campers immediately dub "Clack" and "Mare." Coming from my southern culture, it is really difficult to get used to calling adults by their first names, even at camp. Bruce and George are the only Negro counselors in work camp, but most of the kitchen staff are. They are older Negro women and boys from colleges in the South or from New York City.

At the end of Larry's welcome and orientation, guitars and banjos appear and a sing-along begins. A mixture of folk songs, blues, and country songs bring back memories of my childhood when our family sang on car trips, as the country sounds of Texas blend with Mississippi blues and Louisiana zydeco. Even though they are fans of the Weavers and Pete Seeger, Woodland campers who've been here before sing the blues just as easily as they sing folk songs, because Folkways Records (which promotes Seeger and the Weavers) also features Leadbelly, whose songs campers know well. We sing "Hang Down Your Head, Tom Dooley," "The Rock Island Line," and "The Klan Song" before moving on to "If I Had a Hammer," "House of the Risin' Sun," and "This Land Is Your Land." It's the first time I have ever heard "This Land Is

Your Land," and it suddenly makes me feel as if this country is as much mine as it is anyone else's, a feeling I never experienced growing up in the segregated South. Dinner follows the singing, and then the girls go upstairs, and the boys go to their tents. It has been a long day filled with new adventures.

Immediately after breakfast the next day, I go out to the corkboard attached to the front of the bunkhouse to sign up for a job, but when I get there, nearly all the jobs have already been taken. Everyone has gotten up early, signed up for tasks, and are already headed off in groups of threes and fours to begin their workday. The only job left is gardening around the bunk, so I place my name beside the task and spend the mornings of the first two weeks of camp weeding and planting, hating every minute of it. Next time I'll know to get up early, so I can get one of the better morning jobs.

In the afternoon work campers walk through the woods to a clearing everyone refers to as "the museum site." There we swing picks and shovel dirt that begins the process of digging ditches for the foundation of a folk museum, the dream of the camp director, Norman Studer. Norman loves the Catskill Mountains and its folklore so much that he has decided to build a permanent museum to house memorabilia from the area, and we are the ones who will help make that dream a reality. We pull up tree stumps and set the foundation without the least idea that construction will continue for many summers, but Norman's dream will never come to pass as he envisions it. The artifacts he hopes will be part of the Catskill Mountains eventually end up in the hands of his daughter, Joan Levine. But in this my first summer at Woodland, we campers swing picks and dig holes for Norman's museum.

While working, I ask fellow campers for recommendations for jobs I should consider signing up for during the next two-week cycle. Someone says that if I like young children, I could work as a counselor assistant in upper camp, where everyone is younger than the work campers. Upper camp is also where we meet each Sunday morning for Sunday Meeting in the outdoor amphitheater to hear Norman Studer tell folk stories or present singers from the Catskill region or the Deep South or modern dancers from New York City.

Since I love children, I take the advice of seasoned campers, and at the beginning of the second two-week work cycle, I sign up as a counselor assistant. Rosemary, who is called "Rose" at camp, is determined to go on the two-week canoe trip, so she takes swimming lessons and learns to swim well enough to be among those chosen for the trip during the second week. Campers who have attended Woodland for years reach out to those of us who are new, sharing folklore and the history of camp. They are especially welcoming to those of us from faraway places like Mississippi, North Carolina, and California.

When laundry day rolls around, Katy, Joan, Rose, and I strip our beds, get our washcloths and towels from the bathroom, and place everything in a pillowcase outside our bedroom door along with our laundry bags of dirty clothes. Then we pick up brown-bag lunches that the kitchen staff has prepared, fill our canteens with water, and go downstairs to get onto the flatbed trucks that will take us to the foot of the mountains we've been assigned to climb, while the staff back at camp sweeps and hoses down our bunks.

It doesn't take long for me to discover that I dislike hiking even more than I do gardening and swinging a pick at the museum site. My hiking group is driven to the foot of Mount Tremper, where two counselors get out and announce, "We will climb to the top of that mountain by noon."

I want to sit down and cry right on the spot, but I look around at other campers and mimic what they do—strap on my knapsack, sling my canteen over my shoulder, and fall into line. The top of the mountain seems miles away as we climb the path. The steeper the climb, the more I hate it, but Chuck, a chubby blond boy with a crew cut, is the only camper who complains out loud, moaning all the way up about how hard it is, and asking, "Can't we stop and rest?" To my surprise I notice some of the kids actually seem to enjoy the hike, taking pride in their ability to climb. Thanks to Chuck's whining, we take several rest stops along the way, sitting for a few moments and gulping down swigs of water before continuing. As far as I can tell, the only good thing about hiking is that I might wear out the blood-red oxfords I hate and be able to buy new school shoes when I get home. Some of the other campers are wearing oxfords, too (so-called "sensible shoes") and some are in work boots. It's the first time I've been among teenagers who wear the same kind of shoes that I wear. No penny loafers or tennis shoes (which these kids call "sneakers") for the hikers on this trail.

Halfway up the mountain, I get so hot that I peel off my work shirt and tie it around my waist before continuing in my T-shirt and jeans. I climb slowly, conscious of the difficulty of my upward progress in this, my first hike, but when we arrive at the top, the splendor of the view and my feeling of accomplishment give me a sense of exhilaration. The air is cool, and the town below as serene as a watercolor painting. Taking it all in, I flop down, unpack my bag lunch, and devour the sandwich and fruit inside. After a brief rest, we begin our descent down the opposite side of the mountain—a lot easier task than the climb up, in spite of gnarled tree stumps along the way. At the bottom we sit and wait for the camp truck that brought us to the mountain to take us back to camp. When it arrives, we climb in and sing folk songs all the way back.

Arriving at work camp, I drag myself up the stairs to my room and fall across the lower bunk bed I now sleep in. I'm exhausted, but it is a good kind of exhaustion. Katy is already back from her hike up Mount Hunter and is sitting talking about it with Joan. Rose has left for the two-week canoe trip. The dinner bell rings, and I slowly pull myself up, walk across the floor to the bathroom, and wash my face and hands for dinner.

After we've eaten, I sit with campmates singing songs until teenage couples start to pair off and wander away. Joanie, Katy, and I make our way upstairs to our room, where we unwrap the brown paper that seals our fresh sheets. The packages were left at the foot of our beds when we were out hiking. We make up our bunks, then shower and collapse into bed, sharing experiences from the day. We whisper long after lights-out, beginning a pattern of late-night conversations that will go on until the end of camp. I'm missing Rosemary, but I feel good about getting to know Joan and Katy better.

Later in the season during these late-night conversations, the four of us will find ourselves discussing issues of race, and Joan and Katy will ask Rosemary and me about how it is living in Mississippi. We'll tell them how we feel at Tougaloo, living next door to white people and then leaving the college campus and going into town to segregated schools. We'll talk about the inferior books we have to use and the fact that the state doesn't require Negro teachers in most of Mississippi to have more than a high-school education. We're surprised to hear about Regent exams and anti-Semitism, because in our black-and-white world, all white people are white. It has never occurred to me that white people discriminate against one another, so when Katy tells us her family was once turned away from a restaurant, I ask why.

"Because we're Jewish," she says.

"How did people at the restaurant know that?"

"Because our name is Wechsler. When my father called to make reservations, they said, 'We don't serve Jews.'"

With this new revelation I find my mind racing to understand how people know Lew Wechsler is Jewish when Billy Eckstein is not. Why Ella Fitzgerald sounds like she's Irish but *she's* not. Like most Negroes, these entertainers carry the names of their former slave holders, so I've never given much thought to the meaning of surnames and didn't know a person's race could be identified by one's last name. Listening to Katy and Joan, it begins to dawn on me that Mr. Rodriguez, who owned the candy store near the Negro movie theater in Daytona Beach, was Cuban like my fourth-grade classmate, Carmen, but they both lived in the Negro community because of Jim Crow laws. I think of people at Tougaloo now, too. Dr. Arzeni must be Italian, Dr. Borinski, Jewish. But there is a camper down the hall who is so fair-skinned, I assume she is Jewish, too. Now I think about her again because her name is Peggy Delany, and I will discover before the end of the summer that she comes from one of the most well-known Negro families in New York City.[126]

---

126 Peggy's aunts, Sadie and Bessie, became famous forty years later when their book, *Having Our Say: The Delany Sisters' First 100 Years*, was published, Sarah and A. Elizabeth Delany with Amy Hill Hearth, Kodansha America, 1993.

Peggy Delany, Nell and Rosemary at camp

During other lights-out conversations, Katy and Joan say they are atheists. Having grown up in the Bible Belt, where everyone goes to church and religion is taken for granted, the thought of someone not believing in God is almost incomprehensible. We have friends at home whose parents take religion so seriously that they won't even allow their children to play cards or dance on Sunday. *So how do kids my age not believe in God?* I wonder. The four of us spend many nights discussing the existence or nonexistence of God.

"What do you do when you're afraid?" I asked. "Who do you pray to for help?"

"I don't pray. I depend on myself."

"Isn't that scary?"

"Sometimes."

Once, at the end of one of our conversations about God, just as I begin to doze off, and voices flow in and out mixing with the sounds of the night outside our window, I hear a very soft whisper that is barely audible concede, "Sometimes I wish I did believe."

Every Friday after dinner, work camp girls get dressed in peasant blouses, wide, flowered skirts, and sandals, and boys dress up in plaid shirts, loafers, and jeans. Then in groups of threes and fours or in couples, we walk together up the dirt road that leads from work camp to the social hall in upper camp for the weekly folk and square dances. They are called by old-time fiddlers who live in the mountains or by camp counselors. CITs (who are technically campers, too) join us on these Friday evenings, but they are allowed the privilege of staying later and continuing to dance with the counselors after we have left for work camp. I love these Friday evenings—getting dressed up and walking to upper camp the way Rosemary and I walk onto the main part of the campus at Tougaloo for special events. Upon our arrival in upper camp, fiddles are already humming, the fingers of gray-haired men skipping rhythmically along the frets, towheaded younger men moving bows back and forth in rapid precision across the strings, nimble fingers picking at banjos.

There is a caller at the microphone. "Swing yer partner 'round an' 'round, back in place, now do-si-do. Swing that gal across the floor, now back to the one you had before."

As soon as that dance is over we form a circle to dance the hora, moving faster and faster until the music comes to a stop, and we are spent. Catching our breaths at the sides of the room, we mop perspiration from our foreheads and sip cool sodas and lemonade. Then another caller approaches the microphone and begins a new round of songs. Sometimes the songs tell stories of the hillbillies from these mountains; sometimes they are played for their melodies alone.

After several dances, Norman Studer walks onto the social hall stage and places a chair in the middle. He raises the microphone and starts to introduce a real old-timer by the name of Mike Todd, who looks to my sixteen-year-old eyes as if he is eighty years old. In reality he is probably in his late sixties or early seventies, but his leathery skin and wrinkled, callused hands make him appear older. For some reason it occurs to me that the dirt beneath his short nails comes not so much from filth as from Todd's being a man of the earth, a man for whom the soil is as much a part of life as the air he breathes. His hair is straight and white, covered by a worn leather hat that has seen better days. He wears faded jeans and a plaid shirt with a well-worn, tattered denim jacket.

Following his introduction, Norman helps Mike Todd walk onto the stage and gets him comfortably seated, and then he lowers the microphone and stands off to one side, leaving the bulk of the stage to Mike. With the room appropriately quiet, Mike begins to tell stories of his early days in the Catskill Mountains, his speech laced with an old mountain twang. Now and again the stories are interrupted by Norman Studer, who adds a detail Mike has forgotten or an explanation to help the rest of us understand the context of the story. Applause follows Mike's musings, and Norman thanks his guest before helping him down the steps from the stage.

"Play 'Boil That Cabbage Down,'" someone yells from our crowd, and we join the chorus.

> *"Boil that cabbage down,*
> *Make those hoe cakes brown*
> *Onliest song I ever heard was*
> *Boil that cabbage down!"*[127]

When the evening of dancing and singing is over, we walk back down the hill to work camp for a good night's sleep. On Saturdays we enjoy free time in the evenings after dinner—playing tether ball, badminton, or softball, or just sitting around work camp singing. One Saturday evening, Michael Meeropol comes to camp for a visit. Michael is the elder son of Julius and Ethel Rosenberg, who were accused of being Russian spies and executed by the US government in 1954, the year we drove through Atlanta on our way to New York, and I found Madre crying about their deaths. Michael's brother, Robbie, is a camper in middle camp, and the boys' adoptive parents, the Meeropols, are camp counselors. Most of us know who Michael and Robbie are, in spite of the fact that their last name has been changed, but we go out of our way to keep them from knowing we know. On this particular Saturday, Michael and some of the CITs come down to work camp to sit outside our bunkhouse with guitars and banjos and sing camp songs.

---

127 According to musicologist and folklorist Alan Lomax, "Boil That Cabbage Down" was originally associated with African slaves brought over from Niger.

Billy Levy, Johnny Gruzen, Paula Blum, Jeannie Blumenfeld, and others sit on the grass with him in front of the bunkhouse with instruments and lead the sing-along.

Michael has a quiet charisma that seems to draw others to him, one that makes me want to know him better, but I can't figure out how to become friendly during such a short evening. However naïve it may be, I fantasize that since we have both gone through difficult experiences, maybe we can talk about how hard it is being a teenager when your reality is so different from that of other kids. I don't know what makes me think a conversation like that is possible, but I want to share my Mississippi experience—the deaths of Emmett Till and Howard, the humiliation of segregation—and I want to hear about how hard it's been for him to grow up without his birth parents, what it feels like to face each day knowing the country he lives in has taken them from him. But I know I shouldn't intrude on his privacy or his need for anonymity, and so we speak briefly of simple things and sing folk songs. Michael visits camp several more times that summer but hangs out with the CITs more than he does with work campers and never again spends as much time sitting and singing with us as he did that first evening.

At the end of the first two-week work period, I go to upper camp to begin work with the youngest group of campers, the ones in junior-A. They are the six- and seven-year-olds, many of them the siblings of older campers or the children of counselors who are working in camp. Junior-A's head counselor is a Negro woman from Raleigh, North Carolina, named Irene Scales. Her son Clark is in work camp, and another son, Frederick, is in senior camp. One daughter, Tommie, works at the infirmary, and another, Laurie, assists in the administration office. Irene's assistant is a young Jewish woman named Joan who comes from New

York City. The counselors-in-training (CITs) at junior-A are Jeannie Blumenfeld and Bob Kurtz, also New Yorkers.

An attractive nineteen-year-old Negro girl named Judy Coleman is the head counselor next door in the junior-B bunk, where the seven- and eight-year-olds are. Judy and her twelve-year-old brother, "Topper," have been campers at Woodland since they were young enough to be in the junior-A bunk. And their father, Gerald, built the jungle gym on the lawn when Judy was five years old. She is an exceptional counselor and a great athlete who becomes a role model for me at camp. She works especially hard with a little boy named Charlie—a child given to unprovoked tantrums so outrageous that no one but Judy can handle him. The junior-B bunk is to the left of junior-A, and the two share the lawn where the jungle gym built by Judy's father is the main attraction.

Across the road from the bunk at a right corner to junior-A is a gravel road where the administration building is located. It is next to the upper camp dining room and the social hall that is transformed into the square-dancing space on Friday nights. One of my duties as a counselor assistant is to take two youngsters from junior-A across the road to the administration building each morning to get the American flag. We return to the bunk area, where there is a flagpole surrounded by large whitewashed stones. The rest of the children have gathered there while we were getting the flag. When we return, we unfold the flag and hook it to a rope on the flagpole and then raise it. All of us then place our hands over our hearts and recite the Pledge of Allegiance. Following the pledge we cross the road to the dining hall for breakfast in a small room off the main dining hall next to the kitchen, where we sit at miniature tables in miniature chairs. Waiting for the food to be brought to the counter from the kitchen, we sing, "Itsy Bitsy Spider,"

"Abiyoyo," and other favorites of the smallest children in camp. After breakfast, campers clear the tables, and we begin the day's activities of arts and crafts, music, swimming instruction, and athletics, followed by lunch, story time, and nap time. In the afternoon there is free time, free swim, and at the end of the day, the lowering and folding of the American flag. Then two campers and I return it to the administration office.

There are wonderful children with strong personalities in the junior-A bunk, Negro, Jewish, and Puerto Rican children, some of whom have come to camp for a one-month stay rather than for the two-month period. They've been sent by New York City's Hospital Workers Union 1199 to get away from the heat of the city and enjoy an interracial camping experience.

One morning I arrive at junior-A to discover two of the children—a girl and a boy—have mixed their feces in one of the bathroom sinks to see if they can make a baby. If children at home in Mississippi had done such a thing, they would have been punished the way Sonya and I were punished in the fourth grade for drawing a naked man and woman. But here at camp, counselors talk about the best kind of conversation to have with the children in order to let them know this is not the way babies are made. The discussion with counselors expands my thinking in terms of how adults respond to the curiosity of children.

Hike days with junior-A campers consist of trips to the petting zoo at the Catskill Game Farm, or walks through the woods to eat lunch by a stream. We take a ride to the spot where Rip Van Winkle is supposed to have slept for a hundred years. There we read portions of "The Legend of Sleepy Hollow," have lunch, and sing, "Michael, Row the Boat Ashore," "This Little Light of Mine," "The Mockingbird Song," and other favorites, accompanied on guitar by Joan, the assistant counselor. My two weeks as a counselor assistant with junior-A go by much too quickly, and soon I'm bidding farewell to the children there and beginning another new camp job.

# CHAPTER 18

# SOMEWHERE[128]

O N SUNDAY MORNING WHEN everyone gathers in upper camp for the Sunday meeting, youngsters from junior-A (where I've just ended my two-week work time) come over to where I am seated with work campers and find a spot beside me on the grass, or they sit on my lap. The bonds we have forged are so strong, they can't be severed simply because my work time with them has ended. Joan Schneer, who is in a room down the hall from me in the work camp bunkhouse, succeeds me as a counselor assistant in junior-A. She returns to work camp in the evenings with stories of how much the children miss me. It's only now that I begin to appreciate the freedom and acceptance I'm receiving at camp and to realize that this kind of acceptance could happen anywhere in the world, were it not for bigotry. I think about my friends in Mississippi and about the kind of summer they are having (at segregated camps, in the cotton fields, swimming in segregated pools), while Rosemary and I form

---

128 "Somewhere," a song from the musical *West Side Story*, music by Leonard Bernstein, lyrics by Stephen Sondheim.

new friendships across racial lines and sing songs of protest and of peace.

"We are Black and white together, we shall not be moved."

"If I had a hammer, I'd hammer out love between my brothers and my sisters all over this land."

"Last night I had the strangest dream...to put an end to war."

But we are having other experiences, too, and they clash so forcefully against the backdrop and customs of the South that they present dilemmas that are sometimes difficult for me to make peace with. On our first overnight, Rosemary and I hike up a mountain with fellow work campers and counselors "Clack" and "Mare." At the top we pitch a tent, cook, and eat dinner around the campfire, sing songs, and tell stories before washing the pots and pans, dousing the fire, and going to bed. My first shock comes when the counselors retire to their small pup tent and leave all the campers to sleep in the big tent—boys and girls together. This is the first time my sister and I have ever been left to sleep in the same space with boys, and we are really uncomfortable. The two of us move as far to one corner of the tent as we can get without being outside and snuggle together in our wool "mummy bags," which is what the sleeping bags we have brought to camp are called by the other campers. Almost everybody else has insulated sleeping bags that are much warmer than ours, but the wool ones our parents have bought are the ones they could afford.

One girl says she is cold in her sleeping bag, so Chuck (the same guy who hated climbing up Mount Tremper), who has an air mattress and a super warm sleeping bag, says she can sleep with him if she wants. Without a moment's hesitation, she crawls out of her sleeping bag and into his. No one else in our tent blinks an eye, but Rosemary and I can hardly believe it. I wonder if Mother knows what kind of a camp she has sent us to. The other campers get into their sleeping bags and once inside undress themselves, telling us we should take our clothes off, too. They claim that if we do we'll be warmer in the morning when we put them back on, but all I can think of is having to get up and urinate in the middle of the night and trying to find my pants and shirt. Rosemary and I keep everything on but our shoes and sweatshirts. Then we get as close to each other as we can in our woolen mummy bags. We twist and turn on the cold, hard ground, trying to find a comfortable spot among the rocks, but my ever-present insomnia, the coldness, and uneasiness about sleeping a few feet away from boys work together to keep me from sleeping most of the night. In the morning, I wake chilled to the bone. I wiggle into my sweatshirt. Then I get out of my sleeping bag and put on my shoes. I go out to brush my teeth and wash my face in the cold water before stoking the campfire Clack and Mare have already started, and then I pitch in to help make breakfast. I can't wait for something hot to drink to warm me up. Eggs, toast on the end of a stick over the camp-fire, and cocoa help get my circulation going again. After breakfast we wash the pots, clean our metal dishes, forks, knives, and spoons, douse the fire, and break down the tent. When everything is rolled up, we fill our knapsacks and start down the mountain, at the bottom of which we will be picked up and driven back to camp in one of the Woodland trucks.

Mock Olympics begin this week, and everyone gets into the spirit of friendly competition. On Sundays when the whole camp gath-ers on the slope behind the social hall in upper camp, the junior-A kids who are on the same team that I'm on come to share the points our country, Japan, has accumulated. We add the points Japan has earned in work camp with the ones it has gotten in junior camp and try to figure out how many more have been accumulated in middle camp and senior camp to see if we are ahead. We talk about the foods we like from the country and share a little bit about what is happening in that part of the world. We sing songs from the four Olympic countries, then together belt out, "Everybody Loves Saturday Night" in the four languages of the Olympic teams. Pete Seeger, Geoffrey Holder, Odetta, and other artists and musicians join us on these Sundays, performing and leading us in the singing. Mesmerized would be an understatement of my sense of awe the first time I see Geoffrey Holder and Carmen De Lavallade dance. I have to pinch myself to believe I'm actually sitting this close to the first professional dancers I have ever seen, two whom I have watched on television in Mississippi.

"Nell!" Mother and Dad would call in unison each time Carmen De Lavallade came on TV. It was the only time either of them called me away from my studies. I'd rush into the living room, find a spot on the floor in front of our black-and-white console, and watch her leap across the stage, soaking in the moment and dreaming of the day when I would dance before people the way she did. She's the first Negro dancer I remember seeing on television. And I've never in my life heard a voice like Odetta's. I feel a great sense of pride in Norman's having brought her to us. And everybody loves Pete Seeger.

As a new work week begins, Joan Schneer, my successor at junior-A, sits next to me at dinner and asks about Bob Kurtz, the male CIT who works with the kids. She wants to know what he was like to work with when I was a counselor assistant. I figure she's asking questions because her roommate, Penny, likes Bob, and I think Joan is planning to share whatever I tell her about Bob with Penny, so I tell her I found him easy to work with and fun to be around. She's surprised.

"He says I don't do anything right," she confides. "He compares everything I do to the way you did it."

Now I'm the one who's surprised. Joan and I have become pretty good friends over the camp season, and I want her to succeed at junior-A, so I try to help her think of ways she might fit in better. That Friday night at the weekly square dance, I talk with Bob about the kids in junior-A. He tells me how much they miss me, and I admit to missing them, too. I also say I hope he'll help Joan have a good experience. We dance together as callers sing out for us to "do-si-do" and "swing yer partner," and then I say good night and head back down to work camp with the rest of the work camp group. That's when I start to get a strange feeling—one I've not been aware of before. "It can't be," I say to myself. "I can't be attracted to a white boy, especially one I know Penny likes." I'm afraid to breathe a word of my feelings for him to anyone, but that night when we turn out the light and get into our bunks, I have such a difficult time falling asleep that I confide to Katy, Joan, and Rose (in one of our many nighttime talks) what I'm feeling. The four of us get out of our bunk beds and sit on the floor, and I pour my heart out. I tell them of the sense of panic I feel at the realization of my attraction to Bob. "I've never been attracted to a white boy before," I say, knowing that except for them, I have to keep these feelings to myself because nothing can ever happen between Bob and me.

"Why don't you tell him how you feel?" Katy whispers.

"I can't do that," I whisper back.

Even with my crush on Edward Harris when I was in the ninth grade, I had asked Faye to tell Edward's friend Duck that I liked him rather than tell him myself, and I certainly wasn't going risk having a white boy think I'd lost my mind by telling him I liked *him*.

"Why not?" Katy persisted.

"I just can't." How do I explain a cultural gap this wide?

"But he might like you, too," she insists.

"He couldn't."

"Why not?"

"Because I'm Negro."

"That doesn't matter," Joan chimes in.

"Yes, it does," I whisper, not wanting Leslie, the counselor on the other side of our bathroom, to overhear us.

"Well, if he lets that stop him, he doesn't deserve you!" Katy shoots back.

*She's so idealistic*, I think as we sit in the quiet that follows.

"Shh," Joan says, "I think I heard something outside." Getting up from the floor, she goes to the window and puts her face against the screen.

"Nothing's out there," Rosemary insists.

"There is, too. Who's there?" Joan whispers, trying to keep the counselor who shares the adjoining bathroom from overhearing.

"It's Bob. Bob Kurtz. Is this Nell Braxton's room?"

"See. I told you," Katy whispers to me as she and Rosemary get back onto their bunks.

"Yes, she's here," Joan says, climbing back onto her bunk, too.

Careful not to make noise, I go to the window.

"Hi," I manage to utter.

"Hi." A moment goes by before he continues. "I'm so stupid," Bob says. "I've been taking things out on Joan, not realizing I was doing it because I miss you. I really grew to like you in the time you worked with us."

"I grew to like you, too," I surprise myself by admitting.

"Really?"

We're silent as the realization of our mutual confessions sink in. For a split second I think back to the movie *King Solomon's Mines* and the African girl and white prospector. Maybe it really *is* possible for people of different races to fall in love.

After what seems like a very long silence, Bob begins again. "I was moping around the bunk, being obnoxious to everyone. Irene Scales—she's a wise woman, you know—took me aside and suggested my ill-humor might be due to the fact that I was missing you."

We whisper back and forth a few moments more, promising to meet again and continue our conversation. After that night we spend all our free time together, and Joan's situation at junior-A improves.

As Bob's and my love for each other grows, I realize he is the boy with the dirty-blond crew cut and horn-rimmed glasses whom I saw bounding onto the bus that first day of camp, holding hands with the redheaded girl who offered me a bite of her peach. He is a tall, good-looking sixteen-year-old who lives on McGraw Avenue in the Parkchester section of the Bronx, a neighborhood that is half Jewish and half Irish Catholic with Italians to the north and east. He attends the Bronx High School of Science and is a member of the cross-country track team. He plans to become a doctor and has a serious way of questioning nearly everything, which I think will serve him well as a physician.

One evening while we are sitting on the rail of the small back porch outside the girls' bunkhouse at work camp, Bob tells me he believes in Darwin's theory of evolution. It's a theory I'm slowly coming to accept, too, but one that I believe God caused to happen. I also believe a force greater than man controls the universe, and I tell him so. We go back and forth about this and the "missing link" but never come to an agreement about how the world began and how human beings were created. We discover we both like music, literature, and history, and we both have a passion for justice. We each have younger siblings at camp, and our mothers are both teachers. Bob's father works for a newspaper, but I don't know enough about New York City to ask which paper it is.

Like most young people who fall in love, we want to know and share everything, and in many ways we reveal more of ourselves to each other than we ever have to anyone else. But there are things we don't share, too. It is odd that I can see myself talking to Michael Meeropol (Rosenberg) about Mississippi but feel I can never explain the humiliation of living there to Bob. I think I can tell Michael because he has lived through the kind of nightmare this country can bring upon a child and can probably understand the fear I felt over the lynching of Emmett Till. If I really allow myself to be honest, I think I can't tell Bob because I love him and feel a lot more vulnerable with him than I would possibly feel with Michael.

It will be thirty years before I learn how much Bob has kept from me and how much he truly sympathizes with Michael and Robbie.

"As much as I loved you, there is one part of me I was warned never to discuss with anyone. It is a secret about my father's line of work."[129]

Bob's father was a member of the International Telecommunications Union (ITU), a powerful organization at the time. And from 1937 to 1957, Mr. Kurtz worked as the foreman of a printing company that had a private existence. He was a printer for a Communist newspaper, *The Daily Worker*. So Bob was more aware of the times we were living in than a number of young people our age, because the year before he and I met at camp, the IRS had shut down *The Daily Worker*, allegedly for tax evasion.[130] By the time of the shutdown, Mr. Kurtz had enough experience in printing to gain entrée to other New York newspapers, including the *Herald Tribune*, the *New York Times*, and the *New York Daily News*. Following stints at those newspapers, he became a proofreader and compositor at Fairchild Publications, publisher of *Women's Wear Daily*, among others. But in 1958, Communists were considered enemies

---

129  Interview with Dr. Robert Kurtz, New York City, summer 1994.

130  Although it is a mystery how the government could shut down a paper that shouldn't owe taxes since it had no right to exist, as Bob would tell me during my 1994 interview with him.

of the state and were forced to "fly under the radar," and according to Bob, his father had "a reputation in his union as a 'Red.'"[131]

The summer of 1958 was a very repressive time in American history. In addition to Klansmen terrorizing people in the South, there was the recent memory of Joe McCarthy's witch hunts throughout the country, and the fear of communism was still palpable among the American people.

So in addition to discussing evolution, history, and music, Bob and I talk about the Rosenberg boys. Their parents' execution has left an indelible scar on us both, and it isn't hard to empathize with them. Robbie, the younger brother, is in camp, and Bob's group of CITs is the group Michael hangs out with when he visits camp. Bob can remember vividly the night their parents were executed, because his mother took his brother and him to a restaurant to keep them from hearing the news on the radio or seeing it on television. But Bob knew what was happening, and after that night he had what he described as "daymares," in which he visualized his own parents being carted off and murdered.

I remember the day the Rosenbergs were executed, too. It was the day I found Madre crying in her living room, saying she couldn't understand how a country could take the parents of two innocent children. No one in my family was a member of the Communist Party, so they would therefore likely have escaped interrogation by the House Un-American Activities Committee (HUAC),[132] but my grandparents' friends Paul Robeson and W. E. B. DuBois were said to be Communists, and my parents belonged to the NAACP, an organization often accused of having

---

131 Ibid.

132 A group created to investigate people the committee members identified as subversive, including people accused of being Communists. The HUAC was associated with McCarthyism and the blacklisting of actors, musicians, people politically left of center, and numerous others.

Communist ties, so I knew a little of what it was like to have that "Red" paintbrush come near. I remember thinking when the Rosenbergs were executed, *If the country can accuse and kill white people, what won't it do to Negroes?*

Bob said that once, when he was younger, he'd made the mistake of telling a friend what his father did for a living, and when he told his parents about the conversation, they said he must go back and tell the boy that he couldn't believe the friend had really swallowed "the joke" he told him about his father. Bob dutifully obeyed, and when he did, his friend chuckled and said, "Aw naw, I didn't believe it. I knew you were kiddin' me."[133]

But the lesson Bob learned from that experience was that there are some things you cannot share even with your closest friends, and his father's membership in the Communist Party was something that could not be spoken about with *anyone* ever again.

Years later I will learn that there were a number of kids at Camp Woodland whose parents were either Communists or Communist sympathizers. "Red-diaper babies," they were called, and they all lived with the fear of having their parents dragged off and killed by the US government, leaving them orphans like the Rosenberg boys. But communism was not what drove Camp Woodland. Peace and justice were the things the camp stressed, and the backgrounds of Norman (a Quaker) and Hannah (who was Jewish) as educators made *those* things real and important to us. Civil rights and freedom were camp's most important lessons, not Communist ideology.

And so even though Bob and I are aware of the dangerous times we are living in and of Michael and Robbie being in our midst, we don't

---

133 Interview with Dr. Robert Kurtz, New York City, summer 1994.

speak about them except to acknowledge that they are at camp. We talk instead of the other camps we've attended and of the summer homes we've enjoyed. I tell him about the Engrams' place at Volusia Beach where Rosemary and I romped along the shore with Carol, George, and their boxer, Princess Anne. He shares memories of his family's place on Mohegan Lake, "a refuge for Lefties from New York." We both swear that the Woodland summer is the best we've ever known.

One evening after we begin seeing each other, work camp counselors announce that shooting stars will be visible that night. The oldest kids in camp (work campers and CITs) will be allowed to go to the athletic field to see them. After dinner we take our blankets and sleeping bags to the athletic field to see the show. Bob finds me among the work camp kids and takes me to a more thinly populated area of the field where we unfold my blanket and sit down.

"Have you ever seen shooting stars?" he asks.

"No," I confess.

Soon he is pointing out stars that appear to be part of a meteoric shower, and I am awed. We concentrate on the stars for a long time before he takes me in his arms and kisses me, sweeping me away amid the shower of stars, the magic of the night, and our newfound love. Then his hand begins to move slowly up the outside of my blouse toward my breast. I grab it and pull away, stopping him the way every girl I've grown up with has done for as long as I can remember.

"What's the matter?" he asks.

"Don't touch me like that."

"Why?"

"I don't want you to."

"But why? I love you."

"Because I don't want you to."

"Why not?"

"Because where I come from girls don't let boys touch them like that. If they do, the boy will lose respect for them."

"What?" he says, a look of surprise crossing his face.

"If I let you touch me, you won't respect me."

"Where did you ever get an idea like that?"

"It's the way I was brought up."

"I never heard of anything like that before. Maybe boys feel that way where you come from, but that's certainly not the way we think up here. At least it's not the way *I* think."

He takes me in his arms again and begins moving one hand toward my breast. I move away, taking both his hands in mine. Now instead of looking at shooting stars and kissing like couples all around us are doing, we get into a discussion about northern and southern customs. Stuck at a stalemate, I turn my attention back to the stars, but before the night is over, Bob has convinced me to let him slide his hand over my blouse to my breast.

Years later he confesses, "I wanted to make love to you that summer. I really did, but I saw at a certain point that it would scare you or hurt you. And even though I thought you probably wanted me, too, I also thought it was stupid to carry a condom. I thought it was a sign of somebody who just wanted to go around screwing all the time. I knew you were scared, and I knew I couldn't push you beyond a certain point, but I certainly did want to."[134]

He was right not to push me. Bob was only the third boy I'd ever kissed, so his having a rubber wouldn't have made any difference. I was much too naïve about sex to have even considered making love that summer. Letting him touch my breast through my blouse was already beyond anything I'd ever done or imagined doing with a boy.

While shooting stars fall our kisses become more passionate, but kissing is as far as we go. Other couples lie on blankets and sleeping bags, making out all over the field while counselors sit talking. This is another place where my two worlds clash. Here I am under the stars, hugging and kissing a white boy, with counselors paying us no mind at all, but a little more than a year ago, Mrs. Jones was insisting that Edward and I sit behind her on the team bus because she had caught the two of us kissing.

When the meteor shower comes to an end, counselors say we should prepare to return to work camp. Bob and I fold my blanket and meander down the hill with a crowd of other campers. He takes my hand in his as we walk past the infirmary and remembers a funny story.

"One evening," he says, "I was walking down this road with Thomasine." Thomasine is Irene Scales's daughter who works at the infirmary. "We began running toward the infirmary and somehow I lost my footing. For the first and last time in my life," he continues, "I flipped head over heels in the middle of the air and amazingly landed on my feet."

The two of us fall out laughing at the image.

---

134  Ibid.

Then he says, "While I was flipping I scraped a patch of skin from my side, so Tommie and I went to the infirmary where the nurse cleaned and bandaged me." We are still laughing so hard we scarcely realize we have made it back to work camp. Lingering at the back door of the girls' bunkhouse, we let other girls pass us and go inside, and we grab a few more moments alone. Here alone at the back door of the bunkhouse, we drag out our kisses for as long as we can. A soft murmur begins inside the bunk, but I'm much too swept away in Bob's kisses to let it distract me. Suddenly the back screen door swings open and Sue, one of the work camp counselors, grabs me by the shoulders and yanks me inside. I'm so startled I let out a shriek loud enough to bring the other girls from their rooms. Since my room is closest to the back door, my bunkmates are beside me in a flash. They put their arms around me, and the four of us go into our room. Meanwhile, Bob refuses to leave the back porch, demanding to know what's going on.

Rosemary, Katy, Joan, and I stand huddled together in our room listening to him become more and more agitated. I am bewildered, but Joan and Katy are shaking with rage over a racist comment Sue uttered before yanking me inside. Now I move toward my bed, tears welling up in my eyes because of the way this beautiful night has ended. This is the first inkling I have of grown-ups at camp being upset by our relationship. Within days of this night, counselors question the two of us about our friendship. We ignore them.

*So this is the way they do it up here,* I think. *At least in the South there are signs—bold signs that everybody understands—but here you go along thinking everything is all right, and then suddenly you're knocked flat by a wall you didn't even know was there.*

NELL, KATY, ROSEMARY AND JOAN OUTSIDE OUR
BUNK (COURTESY OF JOAN FAULKNER)

Later in the week, during our time off, Bob and I walk down to the
work camp creek. Seated on a large rock, we watch the water rush over
rocks and tree limbs while we throw in stones and get into a conversation about Christian traditions—how Episcopalians sprinkle water
over the heads of babies at christenings, but Baptists do full immersion
of adults. I tell him about the Sundays I have spent at Pilgrim Baptist
Church in rural Mississippi with my friend, Tommie Ann, from Holy

Ghost High School. How once a woman in church got so filled with the Spirit, she nearly hit me in the head with her pocketbook. I had to duck to avoid the heavy bag headed toward me like a missile. In ducking her bag, I almost fell off the bench and onto the floor. Laughing, the two of us stand atop a big rock and start to hold a mock revival. Then we splash around in the creek conducting a mock baptism. *This is one of the reasons I love my Church; we know how to laugh at ourselves,* I think.

But within days of that innocent fun Bob and I are summoned to my bunkhouse by Larry, the director of work camp. There he reprimands us for our "baptismal service," which apparently another counselor saw. Larry scolds us for our antics, saying some people could view what we have done in an unfavorable light because we were "treading on people's sensibilities."

I'm speechless. In this place where half the people are atheists, the director of work camp is telling me, a Christian, that I have offended Christian sensibilities. Larry goes on to say that at Woodland we live in "a microcosm," and we have to be careful not to offend others. Bob looks surprised. He tells me later that all he could think was, "Larry's a teacher, but he's not using that word right. He's trying to say that we live in an atypical community at Woodland, not a microcosm, because a microcosm is the world in miniature, and if we're living in a miniature world, what is there to complain about? If Woodland is the world in miniature, then what we're doing is okay."[135]

After more nonsense, Larry gets around to what I realize is the real reason he has called the two of us before him. He says Bob's and my relationship is an example of something that might be tolerated at camp but not outside of camp. Within days of that conversation the senior

135 Ibid.

camp director is adding his two cents' worth, trying to convince me that Bob's and my relationship should end, but his and Larry's disapproval—and the disapproval of some of the other counselors—only strengthens our resolve. Like most teenagers, we see ourselves as "us against the world."

"I'm not about to stop seeing you," Bob declares. Bolstered by his declaration, I make the same vow.

Amid the craziness of adults trying to break us up, camp activities continue. One evening work campers are given a special night down at the creek with a campfire and pizza. It is the same creek where Bob and I held our mock baptism. Rosemary and I, who have never tasted pizza before, ask what it is. Our surprised campmates assure us that we'll love it, so we sit singing folk songs and rolling 6-12 Insect Repellent over our bodies waiting for the pizza to arrive.

"You've never had anchovies either?" Margie Gruzen gasps when I ask what they are. "You have to have a slice with anchovies."

And so I bite down into my first slice of pizza. In doing so I take something into my mouth so salty, it makes my flesh crawl (an anchovy). Not wanting to disappoint my friends, I force the pizza down, only to have another slice thrust in my hands. I ask if this one has anchovies on it, and when I'm told it doesn't, I bite down, but I don't like it any better than I did the first slice. It's just too salty for my taste. In fact, after that first night at the creek, it will be years before I acquire a taste for pizza, but I love another new treat that we have that night—"s'mores," those tasty graham cracker, toasted marshmallow, and chocolate sandwiches that I can't get enough of.

This week, Katy leaves for her canoe trip, and the same evening the older work camp girls are called together by a female counselor and told we've been chosen for a special treat. She says she and one other counselor are planning to take us skinny-dipping that night in a part of the creek where the waters run deep. I've never heard of skinny-dipping, and when I discover what it is, I can't understand why anyone would consider it a treat. For the first time in my life, I thank God that I have my period. I'll use it as an excuse to bow out. A couple of the girls try to convince me to wear a tampon so I won't miss the "fun." I decline, not knowing how to explain to them that where I come from, virgins don't use tampons; however mistaken we may be, we think tampons will break our hymens, and since we're expected to remain virgins until we marry, we don't wear them. Still, I can't understand why getting naked and plunging into an ice-cold creek by the side of a country road is considered a treat, but I go along anyway to watch "the fun." I figure the counselors insist that I come along because they are convinced that once I see how great it is, I'll want to take off my clothes and jump in, too. No way!

On the day Katy returns from her two-week canoe trip, Joan, Simon, Rose, and I gather around her and hang on her every word. She describes the excitement of the adventure to such an extent that other girls come from down the hall to hear her, too. Katy has gotten tanner on this trip than any white person I have ever seen. So tan, in fact, that one of the girls from down the hall exclaims without thinking, "Katy, you got black!" Another girl who has entered our room joins in, seemingly without an awareness that Rosemary and I are there. "You surely did! Are you sure you're not part Negro?"

Now the girls are acutely aware of the fact that Rose and I are present. The room becomes deadly silent. I hold my breath waiting for Katy to answer. This girl has asked a question that almost always sparks vehement denial or leads to an all-out argument, but it slides off Katy like water off a duck.

"I don't know," she says offhandedly, "most of us probably have a Negro somewhere in our family."

Now the two girls are looking sheepish. Moving their eyes from Rosemary to me, they quickly agree. "Yeah, I probably have a Negro somewhere in my family, too."

"Me, too."

Katy goes on with her description of the canoe trip, answering questions and comparing her experience with Rosemary's as if the intrusion never occurred.

The first parents' visiting weekend is coming, and our campmates look forward with excitement to welcoming their mothers, fathers, and siblings. Rosemary and I grow quiet watching them prepare for the visit. How can we get excited when no one is coming to see us? Visiting weekend lasts from Saturday morning to Sunday evening, and on the Friday before it begins, Katy invites us to join her and her family. "Are you sure it's all right?" we ask.

"Yes," she assures us, so we accept, but I'm melancholy thinking of Mother and Dad so far away. This is a camp I know they would love coming to, and they have sacrificed so much to send us here. For the first time since leaving Mississippi, I'm homesick.

Saturday morning arrives, and we leave our room with Katy. We go downstairs and watch the parents walking up the hill toward work camp. I am completely baffled by the sea of adults dressed in shorts, T-shirts, sneakers, and sandals. A few of the women are in flowered skirts, but most are much more casual. Every other person appears to be carrying an ice chest, a beach chair, or a canvas bag.

I have never in my life seen so many adults in shorts. No adult at home even thinks of wearing shorts outside except for Daddy and his assistant coaches when they go to the football field. Mrs. Arzeni, who is thin and well-proportioned, is the only woman I can think of at Tougaloo bold enough to wear shorts around the faculty housing area, and tongues wag when she does. The closest anyone else back home comes to being this casual is when they don Bermuda shorts with knee socks. Yet here come adults of all sizes and shapes in various lengths of shorts, T-shirts, and sandals with dress socks, or sandals with no socks at all.

While I am taking in the sight of all these adults in shorts, Rosemary bursts past Katy and me and runs down the hill and through the sea of visitors. All of a sudden she throws her arms around Madre, who is making her way up the hill with the other adults wearing her signature seamed stockings, black high-heeled shoes, a navy-blue sleeveless dress, white gloves, and a wide-brimmed navy hat. Rosie jumps on her with such enthusiasm that she almost knocks our grandmother down. Madre steadies herself and the basket of food that hangs from the crook of her arm, and then she and Rosemary continue climbing the hill together. By this time I have made my way down the hill, thrown my arms around my grandmother, and inhaled the sweet smell of her Jean Nate perfume.

Katy's family also emerges from the faces in the crowd, and after exchanging hugs and kisses, her father, Lew, and brother, Nicky, go ahead of us to find a place to picnic down by the creek—one spacious enough for all of us to sit and eat. Bea Wechsler walks with Katy, Madre, Rosemary, and me to the chosen spot, and after everyone is seated, introductions begin.

"Hello, Mr. and Mrs. Wechsler," Rosie and I say when introduced to Katy's parents.

"Don't call us 'Mr. and Mrs. Wechsler,'" they tell us. "We are Bea and Lew."

*I can't call them that!* I think. I can't call anyone's parents by their first names, but every time I say "Mr. or Mrs. Wechsler," one of them corrects me. We introduce Madre, and the adults hit it off right away. As she's always done with our friends, our grandmother insists that everyone call her "Madre."

Katy's paternal grandmother, Rae, joins us, too, announcing in her thick British accent that she's found a lovely place to spend the weekend called Cherokee Pines. She says a gracious couple runs the bed and breakfast that welcomes visitors headed to Woodland for parents' weekend. Nearly a year will go by before we discover that the couple who owns Cherokee Pines is the only Negro couple in the area, because Rae has only said that Katherine Drayton is a great cook and quilter, and her husband, Fred, is a gracious host who works with wood.

In the weeks that follow, we will learn that the sight of our two families eating together that first visiting weekend confuses many campers. Madre, looking for all the world like a Jewish grandmother, and Katy's mother, Bea, coming straight from Lake George where she and Lew are spending the summer, has a tan even darker than the one Katy got on the canoe trip and in the words of her husband, Lew, "looking like a beautiful Indian princess."

We invite Mrs. Miller, the mother of David, a work camp friend, to join us, only to discover that she and Madre have driven up to camp together from New York with another set of work camp parents. Woodland has done a wonderful job of pairing parents who don't have transportation to camp with those who do, making it possible for family members like Madre to come up from New York on visiting weekend.

The Wechslers open their cooler of food and share lox and cream cheese on bagels—something Rosemary and I have never tasted before. When I bite into the sandwich, the bagel is so tough I'm sure I'm going to lose a tooth, and I don't think I'll ever be able to chew it up enough to swallow it, but I keep working at it until I do. And they have kosher pickles (I only know dill and sweet ones), cheeses of all kinds, and herring—all new tastes, as are the different varieties of rye bread and mustard—my first venture beyond French's mustard, a southern staple. The Wechslers welcome us into their lives as if they've always known us, reminding me of old friends we've spent time with in the past like the Engrams and Bigginses in Daytona Beach.

Madre unpacks fried chicken, fresh peaches, ham sandwiches on whole wheat bread, deviled eggs, devil's food cake, carrot sticks, and fudge. As usual, everyone goes wild over her homemade fudge. I have eaten new foods like lox and bagels provided by the Wechslers that surprised me. Now it is our turn to surprise them. When the watermelon is cut, Rosemary, Madre, and I sprinkle salt and pepper on our slices. The Wechslers have never seen anyone eat melon with salt and pepper, but where we come from, we've never seen anyone eat it any other way.

Other work camp parents and their children continue eating near us at the creek, the one with babbling water rushing toward the Ashokan Reservoir—the creek where Bob and I held our mock baptism. Later in the afternoon, we head up the hill to join families from the entire camp on the athletic field where shooting stars fell one magical night. It is the middle of the afternoon now, and after everyone finds a place to sit on the grass, all the parents, relatives, and friends are welcomed to camp by the director, Norman Studer. Then we sing folk songs, while families and friends continue meeting one another or getting reacquainted. Some of the children from junior-A bring their parents to meet me, and Bob comes to meet Madre and the Wechslers before taking me to meet his parents, who are very cordial.

A week after parents' visiting weekend, Madre sends Rose and me a package with letters and, unaware that she is breaking a camp rule, a box full of fudge for us to share with our bunkmates. Camp rules prohibit treats from home. We are supposed to hand them over to the counselors when they arrive, but Katy says, "There's no way we're giving Madre's fudge to counselors. All they'll do is eat it themselves."

She pulls her footlocker out from under her bed, opens the lid, removes the small tray on top, lifts her recently laundered towels, and lays the fudge sealed in waxed paper and scotch tape between the towels. For the next few weeks, the four of us say good night to Leslie, the counselor who shares our bathroom, then brush our teeth and turn out the light. Gently we close the bathroom door, ease Katy's trunk out from under her bed, unfold the towels, and take care not to rustle the waxed paper as we remove scotch tape. We sit on the floor in our pajamas, eating fudge and whispering into the night. On one of those nights, Joan tells us about a cabin in the woods called "Copacetic." She says that counselors and CITs refer to it as "Cope," because it's the place counselors go to make out. Cope is off-limits to campers, so Joanie isn't sure exactly where it is, but for the rest of the summer we lie in bed or sit on the floor eating fudge waiting to hear stories about the comings and goings of couples at Cope, especially if they involve work camp counselors.

During the coming weeks, the CITs perform in a summer stock production of *Green Grow the Lilacs* at the Phoenicia Playhouse. We work campers go to see them one Saturday night dressed in our square dance clothes (the most dressy outfits we have) and riding together in the back of a couple of the camp trucks. When the play is over, Bob, whom I couldn't take my eyes off during the performance, meets me outside the playhouse. He takes me by the hand to ask Leslie, the counselor, if I may ride back to camp in the CIT truck with him instead of with the work campers. When she says it's all right, I joyfully hop on the flatbed.

Bob and I sit next to each other in a corner of the truck, talking softly while the rest of the kids sing songs. "I'm head over heels in love with you," he tells me.

"I love you, too, Bob."

"I don't know what it is, but I've never felt this way about anybody before."

I listen quietly, hanging on his every word.

"I've never met anybody I've had these kinds of feelings for," he continues. "You're sweet, intelligent, and"—he stops and looks into my eyes—"you're beautiful, and you're interested in me."

He says we're from the same kind of background, which is important to him. The chill of the cool night wind blowing into the truck makes me shiver as we huddle together, talking. I haven't brought a jacket to camp that's dressy enough to wear with my pretty skirt, and the sweater I have on is suited more for southern evenings than the Catskills' mountain air.

"You're cold," Bob says, removing his Bronx Science jacket and placing it around my shoulders. "I don't know what makes me feel the way I do about you," he continues. "Maybe it's the way you look at me, or the way you laugh at my jokes. Maybe it's all those things."

I slide my arms into the sleeves of his jacket, take his hand in mine, and put my head on his shoulder.

Too soon, the sign announcing CAMP WOODLAND FOR CHILDREN appears, and the driver shifts gears to climb one hill and descend the one leading to work camp. Bob removes a silver chain bracelet from his wrist and fastens it on mine. "A token of my love," he whispers.

I start to take his jacket off to return it, but he says, "Keep it for the rest of the summer."

"Really?" I ask, a smile creeping across my face.

"Really, and when we get back to New York, I'm going to ask my parents to get tickets for us to see *West Side Story*."

I've never seen a Broadway show and can't imagine what *West Side Story* (or Broadway) is like, although I've heard kids at camp singing "When You're a Jet" and "Officer Krupke," and I've heard them talk about actors in *West Side Story*. If Bob wants to share the play with me, I want to experience it.[136]

Our future talks lead to discussions about marriage and children. We each have one sibling and decide we want to have more than two children; three would be ideal, we say. We know there will be problems for an interracial couple, but we are young and idealistic, and here in this idyllic setting, even with our detractors, we believe there is nothing that we can't conquer together.

---

136  The movie version of *West Side Story* will not be made for another three years.

NORMAN STUDER AND AN OLD-TIMER AT A FOLK FESTIVAL.

In August, preparations for the annual folk festival begin. It takes place at the foot of a mountain in the town of Phoenicia. Old-timers come and play their banjos and guitars and tell stories about life in the mountains. They teach us tunes from their past, and as the sun sinks behind the mountain, we cherish the things we've learned, and we will take them home with us when we leave, sharing them with our parents and one another whenever we remember camp.

The end of camp arrives too soon, and I find myself walking the familiar road to junior-A to say good-bye to the little campers who've meant so much to me. Making my way along the rocky road, I think of how easily Rosemary and I have slipped into the integrated freedom of Camp Woodland, how we've adapted to its way of life as if the free-dom we've found here is our God-given right. Woodland has made me

believe that freedom *is* my God-given right and the right of every Negro
trapped in a cotton field or on a tobacco farm or sugarcane plantation.
It is the right of every Negro in the South—this feeling of liberty and
justice.

I say good-bye to the youngest campers and return to work camp.
Rose and I promise friends we'll return next summer. I feel guilty even
making that promise, because it has been difficult for Mother and Dad
to send us to camp this year, and I don't think I should ask them to come
up with that kind of money for another summer.[137] But our friends are
all returning, and they're anxious for us to come back, too.

"You're coming back next year?" They nod anxiously.

"Yes," I respond. How can I tell them we don't have the money?

In the room we've shared, Rosemary, Katy, Joan, and I pack trunks
and duffel bags and then help one another carry them downstairs to
load in the hold under the bus that will carry us back to New York City.
There are more good-byes as we climb aboard the bus and promise to
meet under the arch at Washington Square Park in Greenwich Village
the following Sunday. I don't even know if Madre and Aunt Mabel will
let Rosemary and me go to Washington Square Park alone, but we
promise to be there anyway.

Riding the bus back to New York, campers pull out banjos and guitars
to sing the songs we've come to love over the summer—"Scarborough
Fair," "St. James Infirmary," "Kisses Sweeter than Wine," "Ticky-Tacky
Little Houses," "Marching to Pretoria." Again counselors sit in the front
seats talking, making no mention of our noise. This time their behavior
doesn't seem strange to me. In fact, it pains me to think of returning

---

137 Even with the scholarship aid my parents received from the camp, due to the
low salaries the state of Mississippi pays Negro professionals I don't know if they can
come up with the extra money for camp two years in a row.

home, where the rules between Negro adults and Negro young people are so stern. I'm going back to a world where those rules prohibit me from singing on a bus at all, a world that will be even stricter and more repressive following this summer at camp. So for now, I'll let go of that world and sing and laugh with my friends. For now, until the reality of it is thrust upon me, I won't think of the other world.

# CHAPTER 19

# TO EVERYTHING
# THERE IS A SEASON[138]

W HEN WE ARE WITHIN blocks of the Downtown Community
School, everyone on our bus begins hugging and saying good-
bye, and as the school comes into sight, the reality of our not seeing
one another for a year can no longer be ignored. Tears flow as the bus
comes to a stop in front of the school. Parents who've sent their children to camp for the first time, who have been standing with the more
seasoned parents on East Eleventh Street anxiously waiting to welcome
us home, look perplexed. They're expecting to welcome children who
are happy to see them again like the ones they saw on parents' visiting
weekend.

"Why are they crying?" these new parents want to know. "What's
happened to our children that they've come home in tears?"

The bus stops, and the door swings open as parents who have been
through this scene before explain to the newer ones that their children

---

138 Words from the book of Ecclesiastes, music and additional words to the song by
Pete Seeger, 1954, copyright, 1962, renewed, Melody Trails, Inc., New York, NY.

have had such a good time at camp they don't want to leave one another. Still sobbing, we say our good-byes and promise to meet under the arch in Washington Square Park on Sunday.

Rosemary and I kiss Madre hello and unload our gear while she hails a cab. The driver places our trunks and duffel bags into the trunk of his cab, and the three of us head uptown to Aunt Mabel's. We get our hair washed and straightened the next day. Then on Sunday, we walk to the subway station at 116th Street with Aunt Mabel, who rides with us to Washington Square Park. There, we run screaming toward camp-mates, who are screaming and racing toward us with outstretched arms. We embrace as if we haven't seen one another for years. Aunt Mabel says good-bye and heads home. Taking Rosemary and me by the hand, our campmates run with us across the square to where other Woodlanders are playing banjos and guitars and singing folk songs. We join the singing and spend the rest of the afternoon there. Only as the sun begins to go down do Rosemary and I say good-bye and board the train with Katy for Aunt Mabel's apartment where Katy's parents, Bea and Lew, will pick her up.

By the time the Wechslers reach Harlem, Katy, Rose, and I have already had dinner with Madre, Aunt Mabel, and Uncle Ezra. A warm visit between our grandmother, Aunt Mabel, and Bea and Lew takes place before the Wechslers prepare to leave. That's when five-foot, ninety-eight-pound Aunt Mabel insists on walking them to the subway station to "protect" them. Rosemary and I go along too and then return home with our aunt to take baths and get ready for bed.

A few days later Bob comes to visit, disappointed because his parents have not gotten the tickets for *West Side Story*. But he still wants to go out with me, he says, so remembering how much Rosemary and

I enjoyed Radio City Music Hall, I suggest we go there. He readily agrees, because he's never been to Radio City. I'm shocked to discover that someone who lives in New York hasn't seen the great music hall. He and I say good-bye to Madre and Aunt Mabel and head downtown, bringing Rosemary along, because my grandmother and aunt are not about to let me go out alone in New York City with a boy they barely know. Bob and I hold hands throughout the movie and stage show and then return to Harlem. We say good-bye and promise to write each other during the year. Next year, we'll come back to Woodland and be together again, we promise.

Rosemary, Madre, and Nell outside Aunt Mabel's apartment in NYC ready to take the train to Atlanta (courtesy of Katy Dawley)

After a few days Madre, Rosemary, and I are boarding the train and preparing to visit with the Harrises in South Carolina on our way back to meet Mother and Dad in Atlanta. In the car on the way home from Atlanta to Tougaloo, Rosemary and I bubble over with stories of camp, our friendship with Katy, Joan, and others, and the hope that we can return to camp next year. When we've told all we can think of to tell, we sing the camp songs we've learned. Then we drift off to sleep. I sink into a long, deep sleep before coming into a semiconscious state and a numbing sense of claustrophobia. This feeling is so heavy, I can hardly breathe. I move my head around on the backseat of the car in an effort to get more air. Then I open my eyes. It is dark outside, but somehow I know.

"We just crossed the Mississippi state line, didn't we?" I say.

"Yeah," Daddy says.

I will have this sensation of fighting to breathe every year when we drive from Atlanta to Tougaloo and cross the state line on the way back from camp in New York. Every year I will awaken, struggle to breathe, and confirm with Daddy that we just crossed the Mississippi state line. It is as if an invisible shroud envelops me each time we return following that first summer at Woodland—a shroud warning me to keep my true feelings in check until we are back in the Catskills again next year.

At home we unpack camp clothes and load them in the washing machine. Melancholia settles in as I think of my summer and compare it to the school year ahead. I take my film to the drugstore at the shopping center to get it developed, then worry that processors there will destroy it when they see photographs of Negro and white kids together with their arms around one another. I'm shocked when I pick up the photos and find the pictures unharmed.

A new family has moved in next door during the months that we were away at camp. The Barnabys have replaced the Palmers, and in Lea Lou and Randy's places are three Barnaby boys—a thirteen-year-old, a ten-year-old, and a baby less than a year old. Mrs. Barnaby has driven to Tougaloo from New England alone with the three children, leaving her husband to close up their home. Somewhere along the Atlantic coast, she realizes she cannot handle the drive all by herself, so she teaches her thirteen-year-old to shift gears and steer, and he relieves her on the long drive. This gutsy woman and her thirteen-year-old son make the whole drive from New England to Tougaloo depending on each other, while the younger boys wake and sleep on the backseat of the car.

The Barnabys are vegetarians, but the oldest boy loves to fish and hunt, making us the recipients of everything he catches or traps. Going out into the woods alone, he returns home and shows up at our front door with a string of fish or a rabbit. Once he brings Rosemary and me a snake that we add to our menagerie of chickens, tortoises, cats, and dogs. We nickname the Barnabys' oldest son "Huck Finn," because of all the trapping and fishing he does.

My entrance into the eleventh grade on the heels of my Camp Woodland experience marks the beginning of a determination to change the lives of people in my area of the country. I don't know how I'm going to do it, but I'm determined to share the feeling of Woodland with Negro people in the South. The first step toward making that change, I decide, will be to get signatures on a formal petition requesting the federal government to bring pressure on the state of Mississippi to force it to uphold the 1954 Supreme Court decision. I sign the petition first and then ask Mom, Dad, Rosemary, and Uncle Dynamite to sign. They all do. Then I go to teachers at Lanier, starting with the history teachers, and ask each one of them to sign.

"Do you know what you're doing?" the first one asks me. "If people downtown[139] find out I signed something like this, I'll lose my job."

To a person, all the teachers say something similar.

"What about our right to an equal education?" I'm tempted to ask. "What about standing up for the things we believe in?" But I have never challenged an adult in my life, so I walk away more disillusioned than angry with adults who are afraid to put their names on a slip of paper that will go to Washington before it ever sees the light of day in Mississippi. Growing up with parents and grandparents who aren't afraid to stand up to injustice, listening to Mary McLeod Bethune and Medgar Evers speak out forcefully at their own peril, I don't understand how professional Negroes can allow white people to have that much power over them. I end up mailing the petition with only seven signatures (two teachers signed it in addition to me and my family members), telling myself it's better to send in a few names than none at all.

Letters from Bob begin to arrive, full of protestations of love and longing for me. My letters to him are much the same. In one letter he asks me to send him a tangible token of my love, something similar to the bracelet from him that I'm wearing. I mail a silver necklace in a letter filled with love. I tell him about the courses I'm taking and the activities in which I am engaged. He writes about New York and family dinners, and he asks questions about Mississippi. All our camp friends want to hear firsthand about life in Mississippi—something I'd just as soon not talk about. Living here is an embarrassment, and I don't even want to relive it for my friends. On the other hand, I know people

---

139 By people downtown he meant the all-white Mississippi school board.

outside the state will never know the truth if I don't tell them how awful Mississippi is for Negro people.

One day a letter from Bob arrives describing a dinner he and his family have enjoyed at a restaurant. He tells me that during dessert he was so melancholy his father said, "A penny for your thoughts."

"I'd been thinking about you," he relays. "I guess my father realized that because when I didn't answer, he said, 'Well, whatever they are, I'll bet there's a train in them somewhere, and that's not worth a penny.' Whereupon I returned his money," Bob wrote.

Of all the things he could have written, I wonder why he tells me this story. *Is he having second thoughts about us? Does he think I'm not worth a penny too?* a strange feeling causes me to wonder.

A few weeks later another letter arrives, telling me he is under pressure from his father to end our relationship. He is asking him questions like, "What kind of future can you have if you continue to see each other?"

He tells him I'll never come back to New York, and he'll never travel to Mississippi so, he asks, "What sense does it make for you to continue? Where's it going to lead? If you get married, where will you live?"

Reading these letters one after the other, all the fears that plagued me on the night that Joan, Katy, Rosemary, and I talked softly in our bunkhouse come flooding back—all the reasons I said a relationship with Bob would never work. If it had been my parents asking the questions I would have kept those conversations to myself, never mentioning them to Bob, because whatever my folks said to me about him wouldn't have mattered. Nothing would have made me give him up. I would have followed my heart the way my mother had followed hers when she chose my father over her parents' objections, and I hoped he would do the same. I hoped he would stand up to his parents and fight for us, fight for me. But he had to do that on his own. If I had to ask him to go against his family, then how I could I trust that he'd stand with me against the rest of society? Besides, asking him to fight for us was like asking him to love me, and either he loved me, or he didn't. Either he was strong enough to face the reality of life with a Negro, or he wasn't.

So I wait and pray for the letter to arrive that says, "I don't care what my family says, I won't stop loving you," the way he did at camp when counselors objected to us. But that letter never comes. Instead more letters arrive with new arguments from his father about why our relationship will never work, and it is becoming clear to me that Bob does not plan to stand up to him. When the letter finally comes that says, "I think my father is wiser than we are and knows more about the world than I do," I see the futility in continuing. I write back and say, "Maybe you should listen to your father."

Even as I drop my letter in the mailbox, I hold out hope that Bob will write back saying he loves me too much to give me up, that he's not ready to end it all. Instead I get a package with the silver chain he begged me to send him as a tangible expression of my love, along with a note asking me to return the bracelet he gave me. I refold the letter, put it back in the envelope, lie across on my bed, and sob. I weep because I'm hurt and embarrassed that I've allowed myself to believe in us, to believe our love was different, strong enough to withstand the poison of society. And I cry because all of the reasons I laid out to Joan and Katy that warm summer night about not wanting to open myself up to Bob have come true. Because the hope I felt with him at the window that night has been dashed. But I cry most of all because his father has said I'm not good enough, and it seems he believes that too—that I'm not good enough because I'm a Negro. I pack up his bracelet and return it, then throw myself into the schoolwork that I hope will make time fly swiftly.

In the spring Woodland offers me a spot as a CIT (meaning Mother and Dad only have to pay half of what it cost to send me to work camp), and Rosemary receives scholarship assistance for her second year as a work camper. That same spring Dad gets an offer from Camp Meadow Spring in Lenhartsville, Pennsylvania, to work as athletic director there, but he isn't sure he wants to go. Rosemary and I jump at the chance to return to Woodland and begin planning what clothes to take, and she, Mother, and I beg Daddy to take the offer in Pennsylvania and get out of Mississippi for the summer. If he does, it will be the first "vacation" he and Mother have ever had, and it will place him in close proximity to us at Woodland. Each day when we get home from school, we ask Dad if he's made up his mind. He says no. We keep urging him to fill out the papers and finally put so much pressure on him that he agrees to send in the application.

At the same time Mr. Smith, the industrial education teacher at Lanier High School, approaches Mother to say the boys in his auto mechanics class want me to represent them in the Queen of Trades beauty pageant. It's a state contest that moves on to higher levels if the queen wins the first level. That's the last thing I want to do after a painful breakup. I am more down than I have been in a long time, struggling with low self-esteem, so I don't want to accept their invitation. Besides, everyone knows beauty contest judges (even the Negro ones who will judge this pageant) lean toward light-skinned girls with naturally straight hair, and I'm brown-skinned with hair that has to be straightened. I'm not ready to put myself through another rejection so soon after being rejected by Bob, and I don't want to let the shop boys down by having some light-skinned girl with straight hair win out over me. But Mother knows I'm depressed, even though I haven't told her why, and she convinces me to give the contest a try. I reluctantly agree, mainly because I don't want to talk to her about Bob.

I start walking around with books on my head the way Madre taught me to do when I was a little girl, and Miss Redmond (the physical ed instructor at Tougaloo College) helps me create a new dance routine for the competition. The state contest takes place in Jackson on a night when Mother and Daddy have another commitment, so they ask Miss Thompson, my French teacher, to accompany me to the competition.

Contestants model bathing suits and evening gowns and display talent; then they wait in the wings for the judges' results. When the second and first place runners-up are announced and my name isn't called, my heart sinks. I turn to Miss Thompson and say, "Let's go." I already know what has happened, and I don't want to endure the humiliation of not having placed at all. But Miss Thompson says, "No, let's wait." Not wanting to disrespect her, I stand beside her in the wings and prepare myself for the inevitable.

Then comes the announcement: "And the winner of the Miss Mississippi Queen of Trades contest is Nell Anne Braxton!"

I can hardly believe my ears. I grab Miss Thompson and scream, "I won! I won!" She smiles, turns me toward the stage, and gives me a gentle shove to get me moving. I float onto the stage in a haze of excitement and disbelief. Standing there with bright lights in my face and applause from the crowd embracing me, I am crowned, photographed, and asked questions by reporters. I can't remember a word I said. Nor can I remember the last time I was so happy. I've just turned seventeen, and this is the best birthday present I could ever have hoped for.

Nell being crowned MS State industrial education beauty queen 1959

It's raining when Miss Thompson and I leave the Jackson State College auditorium to head for Lanier High School where Mother and Dad will pick me up. I say good-bye to one of my favorite teachers as my parents drive up, and I climb into the backseat of the car with the hood of my raincoat pulled over my head. No one says anything about the pageant, which I suspect means my parents think I haven't brought home the crown. We talk about everything but the contest as I slip my raincoat hood off. Just then Mother turns to look at me. When she does she catches sight of the tiara and exclaims, "She won! She won!"

In the rearview mirror I can see a broad smile creep across my father's face.

In the weeks that follow, boys from the industrial education and shop classes make a point of thanking me for representing them so well, and they wish me good luck in the regionals.

To help me prepare for the regional contest, Mother arranges for a white professional dance instructor in Jackson to critique my routine. She and I drive into town together and enter the first dance studio I've ever seen—a real studio with mirrored walls, a ballet barre, and a piano in the corner. Taking it all in, I can't help but compare what white kids have to use, while I've rehearsed and performed in Negro auditoriums and gymnasiums with a Victrola and records. I walk to the middle of the room and warm up, then hand over the record I've brought of the song "Malaguena." The music begins, and I leap and spin with all the energy and grace I possess.

When I'm finished, the instructor turns to Mother and says, "I can't recommend anything she can improve on, except maybe getting a little more height on her leaps."

With that declaration, he has confirmed what I have felt all my life. That in spite of segregated gyms, and rehearsals sandwiched between physical education classes, sporting events, sock hops, and school assemblies, Miss Redmond and all the dance instructors before her have taught me as much as any white instructor could have, with their state-of-the-art music systems, mirrored walls, and ballet barres. The breakup with Bob left me despondent, but this new challenge has given me a positive direction for those negative energies. Through dance I am finding purpose again and beginning to see blue skies where there were only gray.

Then on April 25, a single headline from the newspaper shocks me back to the reality of Negro life in Mississippi. The body of Mack Parker is dragged up from the Pearl River and photographed. Parker, a twenty-three-year-old Negro living near Poplarville, Mississippi, was arrested a few days earlier and thrown into jail because a white woman accused him of rape. White people in Poplarville got riled up over the accusation, even though Parker is said to have been out with friends on the night the woman cried rape. In what has become a pattern in Mississippi, a lynch mob forms, this one made up of men that include Parker's jailer, a Baptist minister, and a former sheriff. They, along with others, enter the jail he is in a few days before his scheduled trial, drag him from his cell, and take him to an undisclosed place where they beat him and shoot him through the heart before dumping his body in the river. Parker is missing ten days before FBI agents find his body and pull him out.

Following what has become a familiar chain of events, no one is indicted for the murder, and no one ever will be. The outraged call for justice from Negro civil rights leaders, which began before the body was ever recovered, creates such an unbearable situation for the dead man's mother, Liza, that she flees the state before her son's body is discovered. Governor J. P. Coleman's response to the lynching is that he hopes Mississippi will not be "punished by civil rights legislation"[140] as a result of the incident. As expected, letters from friends at camp pour in asking for the inside story. But Mississippi news is so slanted that I can't give them much more than they've already read.

A week after the sight of Parker's bloated body appears in newspapers, Mother and I arrive at Southern University in Baton Rouge, Louisiana, for the regional industrial trades beauty pageant. At a time when I should feel the excited anticipation of competing, I feel only embarrassment to be here representing the state of Mississippi. I am torn between representing a state where such heinous crimes take place without prosecution and representing the shop boys who have placed so much faith in me. Somehow I summon the courage to compete, telling myself that the white people in Mississippi don't represent me, nor I them. I've come to Baton Rouge to represent Negro people, to be a role model for them, and to prove that even though we are down, we are not out.

The contest is covered by Negro magazines and newspapers from across the country, including the *Atlanta Constitution* and *Pittsburgh Courier*. To my utter surprise, I win the regional industrial trades contest over contestants from North Carolina, South Carolina, Alabama, Louisiana, and other southern states, but that is as far as the competition will allow me to go. Jim Crow customs won't let Negroes from southern states compete in the national trades contest. The situation causes some in the Negro press to label me "National Queen of Trades," which means "National *Negro* Queen of Trades."

---

140  The Southern Poverty Law Center, *Free At Last: A History of the Civil Rights Movement and Those Who Died in the Struggle* (Montgomery, AL: The Civil Rights Education Project, 1969), 47.

At the end of the pageant, Madre enters my dressing room. I had no idea she'd be here in the audience. The appearance of my grandmother, the charm-school teacher, makes me proud that I have won, in spite of the fact that I have represented Mississippi. I am so happy to see her, I can hardly contain myself.

"Baby, I'm so proud of you," she tells me. "I kept a scorecard just like the judges, and I had you ahead of the other girls, too."

NELL AFTER BEING CROWNED REGIONAL BEAUTY QUEEN 1959

This is a sweet reunion with my grandmother, made all the sweeter because it is so short. That same night Mother and I head back home, and Madre leaves for Atlanta. There isn't any place in this town for us to get a room and spend more time together because we are still Negroes in the Jim Crow South.

After Mom and I are back in Jackson, Lanier High plans a special assembly so that I can model my bathing suit and evening gown and perform the dance that has won me the title. In honor of my accomplishment, the school commissions a portrait of me to be taken at Beasley Studios. It is hung in the entranceway of the school over the athletic trophies, where it remains for decades. Finally, the school wraps it up and sends it to me in New York. Today it hangs over my husband's chest of drawers.

From the day that I win the contest in Louisiana, Uncle Dynamite, who teaches history at Lanier, calls me "Miss Grease Monkey." His nickname for me comes from the fact that auto mechanics is part of the industrial trades department, and auto mechanics are called grease monkeys. Every time he yells through the hall, "Hello, Miss Grease Monkey!" a smile creeps across my face. It makes me proud to remember my accomplishments, but I know it is also my uncle's way of reminding me not to take the win or myself too seriously.

Springtime smells of honeysuckle and magnolia give way to the heat of summer as Rosemary and I prepare to return to the Catskills. I am happy to be leaving. There have been times when it felt to me as if a Negro body came up from a river every time I tried to return to normal life, and it is still difficult to shake the image of Mack Parker's bloated body from my mind and come to grips with his vicious death. That's why, with summer approaching, I am more anxious than ever to get out of Mississippi, back to the mountains in New York where I have felt freedom.

In June, Rosemary and I board the train in Atlanta with Madre and head for New York, making our usual stop in Gaffney to visit with the Harrises and exchange Madre's fudge for sandwiches and cake. This summer, Mother and Dad leave Mississippi, too, and drive to Camp Meadow Spring in the Pennsylvania Dutch country, where Dad has accepted the position we pushed him so hard to take.

Katy Wechsler returns to Woodland as a CIT this summer, too, and she and I are once again bunkmates, this time in a tent with wooden steps leading up to a wooden floor platform. We place our beds at right angles to each other so we can talk at night like we did the year before. We will continue discussions about the existence of God, and I will question for the first time whether there is a God. There will also be times when, in the stillness of an afternoon with a few hours off from our campers, we'll lie on our bunks looking at the patterns of leaves splashed against the tent top, and I'll tell her about what happened between Bob and me. It will be the first time I've shared that pain with anyone else. One night as we lie in bed with the rain beating against the tent flaps I tell her about one of the counselors I have a crush on—a crush that remains a secret (except for Katy) because counselors and campers are not allowed to fraternize.

Joey Grossman, another friend from work camp, a hunk whom girls drool over, returns as a CIT, too. Over the course of the summer, he and I become close friends, closer than I ever imagined I could be with a boy with whom I am not romantically involved. Joey is a bit of a loner by nature and, as the only Negro CIT, I sometimes feel as if I'm alone, too. He and I find ourselves together a lot during the summer, sharing confidences and enjoying each other's company. Joey is the first person with whom I share my dream of becoming a dancer. He talks to me about his mother, who used to work as the camp nurse before Rosemary and I came to Woodland. He and I usually meet in the evenings just as the sun begins to sink. Sitting on a large rock looking at the sun, we share our dreams and failures of the past year. I tell him the full story of what happened between Bob and me, and he tells me of his breakup with Jeannie.

"I don't think her parents thought I was good enough for her," he says.

"That's what happened with Bob and me, too."

We talk about pain and love as well as ambitions and dreams. Sometimes we get depressed thinking of the racism each of us will face when we return home after camp—I to the blatant racism of Mississippi, Joe to a more subtle form in Leonia, New Jersey. We conclude that Woodland may be the only place where we can truly be friends.

"It's so schizophrenic moving between here and Mississippi," I say. "Sometimes I wonder how long I can take it."

"I wondered about you when I was reading articles about what was happening there," he tells me. "I always wonder how far you are from what is happening and if it's affecting you."

A little before the second month of camp begins administrators approach me to say the Phoenicia Playhouse is looking for a Negro female to play the role of Tituba in Arthur Miller's *The Crucible* in this year's summer stock production. They encourage me to take the part, so I do. Now, each afternoon I am driven into Phoenicia for rehearsals. In accepting the part, I haven't thought about the fact that I'll be separated from my fellow CITs and from the kids in junior camp. I haven't considered how much this new schedule will set me apart from my friends, or how lonely I will be with all the white adults at the playhouse. During the run of the play, I get to know professional actors and hear stories about other plays and other actors and directors. And for a fleeting moment, I flirt with the idea of becoming a professional actor. But deep down, I know this is not the life for me.

On opening night, I am a nervous wreck. My fellow CITs come out in force to give me support, and they send flowers to my dressing room. The play has a good run, but I am totally unprepared for what happens during parents' visiting weekend. As soon as I step onto the stage there is wild applause, even before I utter my first line: "Me Betty be hearty soon?" When the play is over and the house lights come up, I look out into the audience and see the Wechslers. It is then that I understand the reason for the applause when I first stepped onto the stage. Mother and Dad are also present, having driven in from Pennsylvania where Dad is working. It is the first meeting between my parents and Katy's and the beginning of a lifelong friendship between them.

After removing my stage makeup, I go out to meet my family and the Wechslers, who have come to the play with Katy and Rosemary. "We've got a great restaurant to take you to," Katy, Rose, and I tell our parents. It's an Armenian restaurant in the mountains that we kids have come to love, and even though my parents have never had Armenian food, Rosemary, Katy, and I are sure they'll like it. They do, and because they do, the magic of the night continues.

On Sunday during parents' weekend, Mother and I leave the group for a short while and walk down to work camp together. There we sit in a swing on the front porch of the girls' bunk.

"I want to tell you what happened between Bob and me," I say.

"All right."

My eyes fill with tears as I relate the pain of receiving his letters, describing his father's words and my final decision to let go. When I am finished she says, "I wish I could have talked to that father. I wasn't any happier about your friendship with his son than he was, but you are children. You weren't talking about going off and getting married. You had a friendship, and you had a right to end it the way *you* wanted to, when *you* decided it was over."

"Thank you for understanding," I say as we get up from the swing and start back to upper camp.

I don't know why it is such a relief to have shared this painful experience with my mother. But I have been carrying a lot around inside for a long time, and it's beginning to feel like too much to handle alone. I need to hear the mature thoughts of an adult I trust, and her words mean more to me than she'll ever know.

There are days when I return from rehearsals at the Phoenicia Playhouse looking for companions my age, only to find that the CITs are still at work, or they are all away on a trip together. These are lonely, isolating days, days when I climb a mountain overlooking the camp and sit listening to the wind or to tunes played on a distant recorder in camp below. This is when I feel most alone. Sometimes I wander through the woods and sit on a log, where I can secretly watch the handsome Negro counselor on whom I've developed a crush, the one I've told Katy about. Often he's out by himself shooting basketballs into an outdoor hoop or playing one-on-one with another counselor during their time off from the boys in senior camp, where they are both counselors. His name is Bert Gibson, and he comes from the Bronx. During the summer his light skin has been toasted a golden brown, his hair bleached auburn by the sun. I've seen him with several female counselors over the summer, but the one he finally settles on is the dance counselor, Fay Berrios, who is from Spanish Harlem.

I haven't breathed a word to anyone about the time I spend watching him from this secret spot in the woods, not even to Katy. At night when she and I lie talking on our bunks, I tell her, "I'm crazy about him, but he doesn't know I exist."

"What's the matter with him?" comes Katy's rhetorical question, because we both know counselors have been sent packing for dating CITs like us, because we are technically still campers.

Summer moves along at a slow pace between acting time and time at camp. Rosemary (a counselor assistant in senior camp this summer) and Katy develop close relationships with several youngsters among the senior campers. One little boy adores Katy. He is Puerto Rican, comes from the Bronx, and is called "Papo." Rosemary, Katy, and I are all charmed by a gifted twelve-year-old dancer from Brooklyn named Michael Peters.[141]

Folk singer Odetta is at camp teaching American folk songs and singing at the weekly Sunday morning meetings. Woodland has many outstanding artists, including a gifted sculptor named Inge Hardison (whose little girl, Yolande, is in my junior-A bunk). Inge teaches art at camp and during the summer is commissioned by the camp to sculpt a statue of Sojourner Truth.[142] The enormous sculpture of Sojourner

---

141 Mike goes on to dance with the Alvin Ailey Company, on Broadway in Hello, Dolly with Pearl Bailey, and in Purlie with Melba Moore and Cleavon Little. In the early days of MTV he becomes a kind of icon with his choreography of Michael Jackson's "Thriller" and "Beat It" videos.

142 Years later, Inge's miniature sculptures of famous African Americans will be featured on television and in Ebony magazine.

Truth, which she completes that summer, is later placed in the city of Hurley, New York, where Sojourner was born. On the day it is unveiled at Woodland, Rosemary recites Truth's famous women's rights speech, "Ain't I a Woman?"

Too soon the summer comes to an end, and it is time to pack for home. Because of the evenings I've spent acting in summer stock, I've been robbed of time with my fellow CITs and with the kids in the junior-A bunk. Boarding buses for New York and waving good-bye to the counselors who will stay behind to close up camp, we prepare to leave another summer behind. As our bus begins to pull away, Katy, who is in the seat beside me next to the window, lets the window down and yells to Bert Gibson, who is standing next to his girlfriend, "Nell likes you. Write her!"

At Katy's words, Bert looks shocked. His mouth drops open, and he stammers, "Huh? What?" as our bus chugs off down the hill. I'm so embarrassed, I slide down in the seat and try to disappear.

Soon we are back in New York at Aunt Mabel's. A few days later, Katy comes to Harlem with her brother, Nicky, bringing standing-room-only tickets her parents have bought for the four of us to see *A Raisin in the Sun*, starring Claudia McNeil with Diana Sands, Ruby Dee, Sidney Poitier, and Ivan Dixon. It is Rosemary's and my first Broadway show, and it blows me away. Not even in the movies have I seen Negro family life portrayed so honestly. Members of the Younger family are portrayed so realistically on stage that I feel as if I'm part of their family. Mama Lena's dreams are so much like those of my parents that it could be my life unfolding on stage. Sister Beneatha's aspirations to leave the States and go to Africa are feelings I've had for years, beginning with the days I sat in the Arzenis' home thumbing through their

African books; and Beneatha's brother Walter's pain is the pain of every young Negro man who faces life in racist America. The triumphant ending sends Katy, Nicky, Rose, and me straight for the stage door in search of an autograph from Sidney Poitier.

As we step into the alley that leads backstage, Ivan Dixon (who played the part of Beneatha's African suitor, Asagai) emerges, looking so handsome that I literally stagger backward, sighing, "Asagai." Shoving my Playbill toward him, I ask for an autograph. He graciously obliges, signing everyone's program before heading down the block under the gaze of our admiring eyes. At the end of the block, he disappears around a corner.

Claudia McNeil emerges and signs Playbills, as do other members of the cast. Finally, Sidney Poitier appears. Barely able to speak, we stretch out our Playbills and ask for an autograph. He smiles, talks to each of us, and signs his name. Signatures in hand and a line behind us awaiting for autographs, we glide back toward the sidewalk and down the block toward the subway station where we board the train that takes us back to Harlem.

A few days later, Katy takes Rosemary, Nicky, and me, along with a friend from camp named Leslie Rosenfeld, to see *The Diary of Anne Frank*, where the claustrophobic sense of enclosure Anne and her family experience in the Gies family's attic seems to leap from the screen. With every knock on the attic room door, their fear becomes mine. I finally see the human faces of the people in Europe that were missing from my World War II history classes when I learned of the Japanese internment and the bombing of Pearl Harbor. In the darkness of that movie theater, I come to understand what the Holocaust was about and am moved to tears. In fact, we are all teary as we exit the movie.

On Sunday, we all meet again at Washington Square Park, where we sing songs from camp before saying good-bye for another school year. Mother and Daddy return from Pennsylvania a few days later, and the four of us begin our drive home, sharing stories of Woodland as they share news of their Pennsylvania summer.

We get a kick out of the fact that Dad was the only Negro counselor at Camp Meadow Spring, and campers fell so in love with him they wrote letters home about "John." Being innocent children, they never mentioned in their glowing letters the fact that John was Negro, so when their parents arrived on visiting day with the excited expectation of meeting "the wonderful John," they were stunned to make Dad's acquaintance. Mother and Dad mimic the expressions on the faces of parents who, upon meeting John, gape speechlessly before extending an overzealous handshake and greeting, "John, we didn't know you were—I mean...what a pleasure to meet you."

After sharing news of the summer, Rosemary and I find comfortable spots on the backseat and fall asleep. Hours later, in what has become routine, I awaken to ask, "Did we just cross the Mississippi state line?" When Dad confirms that we did, I close my eyes again, wondering how many Negro bodies are at the bottom of the river this year.

# CHAPTER 20

# I WISH I KNEW
# HOW IT WOULD FEEL
# TO BE FREE[143]

ROSEMARY AND I BEGIN the fall semester at a newly constructed high school that is closer to Tougaloo than Lanier, where
we've been students for two years. Those of us who are seniors ask the
Lanier administration, "Please let us finish Lanier High School where
all our friends are," rather than be sent to Brinkley out in the boonies.
We love Lanier and don't understand why we can't finish our senior
year there, but our pleas fall on deaf ears. Mother is moved to Brinkley,
too, as one of the new guidance counselors. Mr. Obie Graves, the father
of two of Rosemary's classmates from the Jackson lab school, is the
other counselor.

I dislike Brinkley from the minute I see it. It's out in the country,
where there's no grass yet and no trees—only dust blowing around. I've

_____

143 Words and music by Billy Taylor and Dick Dallas. Recorded by Nina Simone,
1967.

never seen half the kids who are here and can't imagine where they've all come from. It feels like a consolation prize when teachers tell us we can choose the new school colors and the mascot. Royal-blue and red are the colors we choose, and we opt for the eagle as our mascot. The facts that Tougaloo is known as the "Eagle Queen," and her colors are royal-blue and red, cause people at Brinkley who want a different mascot and other colors to spread the rumor that Rosemary and I led kids to vote the way they did. The truth is that no one really likes the other color options—orange and red, or black and gold. Every rural Negro school in the state of Mississippi shows up in black and gold, and the red and orange just looks tacky.

Our new band director is a recent graduate of Jackson State College and, being one of the youngest teachers at Brinkley, spends hours transposing popular songs into band pieces for us to play. In addition to the regular marches, we learn to play Ray Charles's "What'd I Say," "Love Potion Number Nine" by the Clovers, and the Coasters' "Poison Ivy." When we rehearse, Mr. Burgess demands that we learn dance steps to perform along with the songs, and he embarrasses the heck out of students who can't keep step by yelling, "What kind of Negroes are you that you can't dance and play at the same time?" That gets everybody in lockstep dipping and spinning to the music. Before long our ragtag band is marching onto fields at the halftime of football games dressed in red sweaters and blue slacks, looking like anything but a school band. But because of our hip music, we are touted as the coolest (Negro) band in the state, and everyone wants to sit near us in the bleachers so they can dance in the stands when the popular tunes are played. Football season will be halfway over before our real band uniforms arrive, because they couldn't be ordered until we voted on school colors. But none of that matters when we strut onto the field to a special drum beat we call the "eagle walk," named for our mascot. As soon as the drums start, people in the stands go wild!

Being a new school, we can't have a homecoming because there are no alumni to come home. We therefore hold a "premiere classic," and our band rocks the stadium. At the end of our halftime performances during every game, the band forms a single line and exits the field doing the eagle walk. During the premiere classic when we exit the field, the crowd goes more crazy than ever—so crazy that even those of us on the field turn around to see why they are screaming; it's obvious something more than our regular eagle walk has set them off. All of a sudden I catch sight of Jimmy, the tuba player, at the end of the long line of band members improvising on the eagle walk with extra twists, dips, and turns, prancing and bowing as he struts off the field. From that game forward, Jimmy and his famous strut become the signature ending to our halftime show.

By the time our uniforms arrive we are flying high, and nearly everyone has heard about the band from Brinkley High. Our football team doesn't fare as well, though. The new group of boys wins very few games that first year, but the school has great team spirit and a band that plays "What'd I Say" every time a touchdown is made, regardless of the score; it turns out *we* (the band) are what make football games enjoyable during the first year of the school's existence.

Letters from Bert Gibson, the counselor I had a crush on at camp, start to arrive, inquiring about news from Mississippi. He wants me to verify information he is reading in the New York newspapers, and he asks a series of questions. These are not the kinds of letters I was hoping to get from him, but I answer his questions just so that his letters will keep coming.

In November, Rosemary receives a letter from a campmate named Greta, indicating that some of the kids from Camp Woodland have gotten together and raised enough money to pay for a plane ticket for her to travel to New York for the Christmas holidays. Greta asks Rose to come early enough to go to the winter hootenanny and camp reunion in the city. Mother and Dad agree to let her go and stay with Carol Litt, the daughter of a couple that the camp put our parents in touch with during parents' visiting weekend, with whom Mother and Dad have become friendly.

One month later, Rosemary and Madre get on a plane to New York, where Madre will stay with Aunt Mabel while Rose becomes the houseguest of the Litts. My sister takes gifts of candy corsages for the girls and candy boutonnieres for the boys who have raised money for her trip. When she arrives in the city, she calls home to let us know she has gotten there safely. She shares news about mutual friends and, with great excitement, lets us know it is snowing at Christmastime.

A few days later she calls again to say she has attended an off-Broadway play with Katy Wechsler, Carol Litt, and Ruth Wallach, and that she will be the guest of honor at a party to which more than twenty campers have been invited. The Litts take Rosemary and Carol to the Gaslight for dinner, and she writes home raving about the food. I'm envious of all the fun she's having, even though I am enjoying being an only child for a change. Toward the middle of her first week in New York, Mother gets a call from a college acquaintance, Carolyn Powell, whose husband, John, was Dad's roommate at Morris Brown. During their college days, Carolyn was a close friend of Daddy's former girlfriend, Dolly Peyton. But with Carolyn's marriage to John Powell and Dad's to Mother, a new friendship between the two couples was forged. Carolyn and John are the parents of a five-year-old boy. She calls Mother and Dad to ask if she may sponsor me as a debutante for Shreveport's Christmas Cotillion. Mom says yes, and before I know it, the three of us are off on a drive to Louisiana for a Christmas as exciting for me as the one Rosemary is having in New York.

As a five-foot-nine-inch seventeen-year-old, my biggest worry about the ball as we travel in the car toward Louisiana is whether or not Carolyn will find an escort who is as tall as I am. I needn't have worried. She has managed to get a good-looking six-foot-three-inch boy, Jack Estes, to take me to the ball as well as to all the pre-deb parties and dinners. He is a great date, an attentive escort, and a wonderful dancer, who seems to delight in squiring me around town.

I debut with nineteen other girls in a beautifully decorated auditorium with a winter wonderland theme—sleds, snow-covered Christmas trees, snowbirds, and snow people. On the night of the ball, I walk from the wings to the center of the artificially snow-covered stage and descend the stairs to take the arm of my father, who is waiting at the bottom. I feel like a fairy princess as the two of us walk between the row of fathers and daughters and take our place—I'm on the side with the debs, and Dad is opposite me with the fathers. When all the debutantes have walked through the line of fathers and daughters, we waltz and then are given over to our escorts. It is a magical night from beginning to end.

Jack and I spend the remainder of the ball together, and afterward I meet his mother. When the ball has ended Jack takes me back to the Powells' home, where I change clothes for the after parties that will follow. He returns to pick me up after he has gone home and changed clothes, too. Then we drive off to join other debs and their escorts at a special breakfast before stopping by several parties.

On the day we are to leave for home, Mother, Dad, and I are packing our bags when the doorbell rings. It's Jack with a gift for me from his mother, who is a furrier. I invite him in and open up the gift his mother has sent—a beautiful mink collar. Surprised, I gasp and offer profound thanks. He and I sit and visit for a while, exchange addresses, and say good-bye; then I get back to packing for our trip home. Back at Tougaloo, I write Jack's mother a warm thank you note, and Jack and I keep in touch by mail into our freshman year at college.

At the beginning of basketball season, I am elected captain of the Brinkley High School team. We end the season with a fifty-fifty record, which is a decent showing for a team so new. During the last game of the season, Brinkley plays Natchez High School, and our friends the Wests drive up from Natchez, Mississippi, for the occasion. Their oldest son, George, plays basketball for Dad at Tougaloo, and their second son, Eddie, plays for Natchez High. Rosemary and I know George and Eddie's sister, Diane, from our Girl Scout camp days, and there are two other brothers whom we've not met before. Our two families get together at our house before the games begin, and the parents decide they will go to the Tougaloo game to see George play. The youngsters (except for the baby boys) all agree to attend the high-school game where Eddie and I will be playing. Uncle Dynamite comes out to the house from Jackson where he lives and drives Rosemary, Diane, Eddie, and me to the high-school game. This is the last game I will play at Brinkley, and I have an extraordinary night right up to the last minute. I go up for a rebound and come down with such force that I land on one ankle instead of both feet. Pain shoots up through my whole body, and I scream so loudly that both boys' basketball teams empty their locker rooms. Rosemary runs down from the bleachers and halfway onto the court as Uncle Dynamite helps to carry me into the girls' locker room. There a trainer gives me an aspirin and bandages my ankle. I hobble into the shower after the other girls have finished taking theirs and then get into my street clothes. I manage to emerge for the boys' basketball game and find Rosemary and Diane West in the stands. We watch Eddie play, but I'm in excruciating pain and can't wait for the night to end. Coaches carry me to Uncle Dynamite's car, and I stretch out across the backseat. Rosemary, Diane, and Eddie get onto the school bus for the ride back to Tougaloo. The bus will bring other students home who have traveled from Tougaloo to Jackson to watch the game.

My five-foot-four-inch Uncle Dynamite pulls into our driveway alongside the hedges and lifts my five-foot-nine-inch frame onto his back. Then he carries me from his car along the sidewalk and up the front steps to our house. Both sets of parents jump to their feet when we enter the front door. Uncle Dynamite explains what happened, and Dad rips the bandages off my ankle to examine my injury. After applying heat and ice, he tapes my ankle the way I've seen him do for so many of his injured players through the years. The West kids and Rosemary arrive just in time to tell everyone about the high-school games and to ask about how George's game for Tougaloo ended. When everyone has settled down, we have something light to eat before the West family heads back to their home in Natchez.

The following day, Dad and I go to the doctor in Jackson so my ankle can be X-rayed. The doctor tells us I have a torn ligament and that I should continue wearing the wrap Dad has made and use the crutches that he provides.

Hobbling from class to class with friends carrying my books is not the way I have envisioned ending my senior year, but I have no other choice. I graduate from crutches to a cane and finally begin limping along on my own as the school year draws to a close.

In the spring, James Bracey, a former classmate at Lanier High, asks me to be his date for the senior prom. I am thrilled to be back among the friends I've missed during my senior year at Brinkley. Lanier is where I feel most at home and most appreciated, and I haven't been with this group of friends since I attended the prom as a junior with Wilbert Hillard.

When my Brinkley High School prom rolls around I ask Jimmy Armstrong, a freshman at Tougaloo College, to be my escort, because he is one of the best dancers I know. Jimmy and I double-date with Rosemary and her boyfriend, E. B. Nelson, and the night flies by. When it is over we make a brief stop at an after-party. Then we rush home, because Rosemary and I were not supposed to attend the after-party.

Facing the uncharted waters of college, I feel excitement and sadness to be leaving my high-school days and everything that is familiar. Part of me is sorry that I've been such a "goody-goody" throughout high school because I am the daughter of the guidance counselor at Brinkley and of Coach Braxton at Tougaloo. I'm a senior in high school and have never broken a single rule. That's when I make up my mind to get into a car with classmates and leave the school grounds. Getting into the car breaks the first rule, and leaving the school grounds breaks a second. My friends and I don't have anything planned; we just want to prove we can get away from school and get back without being caught. So we drive around and try to smoke cigarettes.

"How do you get smoke to come out of your nose?" I ask. Before, when I tried to smoke, I made the smoke come through my nose by sending it from my mouth to my nose without ever inhaling.

"Okay, take smoke in your mouth, and then take a deep breath. Let the smoke go down before you blow it out."

I do exactly as I am told and get so dizzy and nauseated that I have to hang my head out of the car window to keep from throwing up. Now the driver of the car has to keep circling around until I'm no longer sick to my stomach. When my light-headedness has gone away, we head back to school.

Just as we park the car, one of the younger teachers sees us and comes over to admonish us, "Get out of that car right now and go to your classes."

That was it. No "What are you doing in a car?" No "Where have you been?" No "Why were you off school grounds?" No "Braxton, I'm going to send you to your mother." Just "Get to your classes." I don't know why he let us off without having us pay any consequences, but we consider ourselves lucky as we rush off to our classes.

During the last weeks of school, our homeroom teacher, Mrs. Rogers, asks Shirley Wells and me to step out of class and into the hall with her. This starts everyone to whispering about why we are being called out. Shirley is one of the most respected girls in the school, and she was not with the group I slipped off campus with, so I'm pretty sure Mrs. Rogers has not found out about that. When the two of us are in the hall with Mrs. Rogers, she tells us we have the highest grades in the graduating class.

"You barely edged Shirley out for top honors," she tells me, "by something like a tenth of a point, and so you will be delivering the valedictory address." Shirley and I hug each other and offer congratulations. I am speechless. This feels just like the time I won the biology award in tenth grade without having had any idea there would be competition for the top spot in that class. There are so many things about public school life that I've been ignorant of; I would have worked harder for them had I known. Even with my A average, I could have been a much better student (bettered the B in Math and added pluses to the As) had I known about the prizes. It never occurred to me to strive for the best grades in the class, but now I can see that other kids were working toward that end all along. I just got lucky.

Graduation does not come without its drama. A few weeks before we are to receive our diplomas, seniors get word that one of our teachers has asked a student from another high school to write our farewell song. Some of us have already written our good-bye song and are incensed to hear the rumor. We enter the auditorium to practice for graduation night, and the teacher at the piano plays the chords to the song we've been given to sing, the song we've heard a student from another school has written. We stand mute. This is the first protest I have ever participated in, and I like the feeling of power we have in challenging authority, even though it isn't a well-organized protest. A few of us decide just before entering the room that we aren't going to sing a song written by a student from another school, and everybody else follows suit.

"All right, ladies and gentlemen, let's act like mature young men and women and sing the song," the teacher says. "If you don't sing, you will put your graduation in jeopardy."

The introduction is played again. Some students begin to sing, but most of us do not. Another attempt is made with the introduction, but only a few members of the class sing. Someone begins to sing the song *we* have written: "We'll be seeing you in all the old familiar places..."

"Just a moment now," the teacher interjects. "We're not going to have this. Let's try the introduction again, and this time sing the *right* song." The introduction is played again, but only a few students comply.

"Everybody dismissed," the teacher says, closing the lid of the piano.

For the next few days, rehearsals do not fare any better. Senior rehearsals for graduation become battles of will between teachers and the senior students, with everyone unsure of what will happen on graduation night.

When the night arrives, Mrs. Arzeni, one of the few white people present, is seated in the audience next to Mother and Dad. I step to the microphone deliver a valedictory speech that challenges my classmates to denounce the disenfranchisement that the state of Mississippi has forced on Negro people and seek full participation as citizens, because this is our constitutional right.[144] I return to my seat, and the whole class rises. The introduction to the farewell song we did not write is played, and just as happened in rehearsal, the majority of us stand mute while a smattering of seniors sing the song. School officials are horrified. In the car on the ride home, I wait to see what my parents' reaction will be to the protest and am relieved to find out they support the students who refused to sing.

I have high hopes of attending Oberlin College where Katy Wechsler's father, Lew, went to school and where Katy is planning to go, but my hopes are dashed when I receive a letter of rejection from Oberlin. It is the only school I really wanted to go to. Katy, Rosemary,

---

144 True to the times we are living in, there is no response from students, parents, or teachers to my speech, and the white board of education officials sit stone-faced. Mrs. Arzeni is the only person (besides my parents) who makes a point of telling me it was a good speech.

and I have all promised to go to the same college, but now that won't happen. Tougaloo College awards every Negro high-school valedictorian in the state of Mississippi full tuition, and their offer is in my hands. With nothing else on the table, how can I turn them down without seeming ungrateful? Mother and Dad have struggled to send us to camp for two years. To ask them to send me somewhere else to college when I have a full scholarship in my hands seems unfair, especially since I don't have another offer or a second choice for college. Ever since Rosemary and I were little girls sitting in the audience at graduation exercises, I have dreamed of going away to college—enjoying college life and living in a dorm. Now, with Oberlin out of the picture, I have no choice but to stay at home. My parents have not discussed anything with me regarding college; they have left everything to me. They knew I was applying to Oberlin, and since it is no longer an option I decide to accept the scholarship to Tougaloo. But what I really want to do in the wake of missing out on Oberlin is take a year off from school. Yet what would I do? My family can't afford to send me anywhere for a year, and there is nothing for a Negro girl with a high-school education to do in Mississippi except scrub floors. Besides, I know that what is expected of me is to follow in my mother, grandmother, great-grandfather, and father's footsteps and attend college.

Summer arrives, and Mother and Dad head back to Camp Meadow Spring in Pennsylvania. Rosemary and I return to Camp Woodland. Katy and I are both junior counselors this year, and Rosemary is a CIT. I'm the new assistant counselor for the junior-A bunk along with a young Jewish head counselor. After many years as a fixture in junior-A, Irene Scales has decided not to return, and this is both a shock and a disappointment to me. I have learned so much about counseling small children from her.

All counselors arrive at camp early for orientation, and then several of us return to the Downtown Community School in New York City to accompany the campers on the buses back to Phoenicia. I ride with the five- and six-year-olds, who are to be my charges for the summer. The seven- and eight-year-olds, who will be next door in junior-B, are on the same bus with their counselors. They were my kids a year ago. A handful of adults pull out their guitars and begin singing the songs we hope will keep the children happy on the way up to camp. It never ceases to amaze me that the kids who are the least homesick always seem to be the youngest ones. More often than not it's the twelve-year-olds who try to run away from camp once everyone has arrived.

Before we know it, the bus is chugging its way up the hill to upper camp and stopping in front of the administration building. I step off and start to turn around to help my five- and six-year-olds get off the bus when Sara Gordon, one of my little campers from a summer ago, leaps into my arms and smothers me with kisses. As the child of camp counselors, she has arrived early with her parents, and she has been waiting for my return. I lift Sara up as she kisses every part of my face, and I give her a long hug and kiss. Remembering my new charges, I put her down and whisper that I will visit her in her new bunk later that evening. Wise little soul that she is, she understands as I turn to help the new children off the bus. My new group of children is terrific, and I come to love each one of them as I loved the group I had the previous summer when Sara, Beth, Valerie, and Yolande were among my favorites.

Yolande Hardison, Sara Gordon, Beth Lewis circa 1960.
Sara sobbed when she thought of Nell being mistreated by
whites in Mississippi (photo courtesy of Beth Lewis)

Judy Coleman, who worked in the junior-B bunk during several of
my years with the kids in junior-A, has been moved to middle camp
with Charlie, the problem child whom no one else is able to handle.
Nine years is the age at which the boys are separated from the girls,
and Charlie is nine years old. It is also the age when male counselors take the boys and female counselors take the girls. But because
of Judy's skill with Charlie, this summer she becomes the first and
only female counselor ever to be assigned to an all-boy bunk. Peggy
Dammon, a new Negro counselor from New York City, is in charge
of teenage girls in senior camp. She, Judy, and I become close friends
during this summer, choosing the same days off so we can spend
time together. Each week on our day off, we walk or hitchhike into

Woodstock to shop, or we walk to Phoenicia to buy ice cream or go to craft fairs.

A couple of new kitchen boys have arrived from Virginia and North Carolina and are part of the regular crew of kitchen guys who come from New York City. It is the first summer that I'll be able to date counselors, and members of the kitchen staff are in that category. I've looked forward to Bert Gibson's return this year, but he doesn't come back. A very pretty Negro girl named Angeline Butler, a student at Fisk University, has been active in the Nashville student movement along with Diane Nash, James Bevel, and John Lewis, and she is one of the new counselors at Woodland this summer. The Nashville students have gained respect from students around the country with their nonviolent demonstrations, and we all want to be like them. They and the A&T students[145] have staged some of the country's first student sit-ins.

Joel Melton and Gus (McGustavus) Miller are part of the kitchen staff who hail from the South. One evening they join Angeline for an upper camp assembly to present a reenactment of the 1960 A&T College sit-ins at the Woolworth counter in Greensboro. The whole camp, with the exception of work camp down the hill, sits in the social hall to learn about what happened in Greensboro. The dramatization by these students is real and riveting. White actors simulate crushing cigarette butts on them and pouring hot coffee over their backs as they remain nonviolent, and we in the audience cringe. Actors from the staff, dressed as policemen, stand idly by during the abuse. Suddenly hysterical sobbing begins behind me, and it

---

145 Students from North Carolina Agricultural and Technical College in Greensboro, North Carolina.

becomes so loud that people start turning around to see what is happening. It is little Sara Gordon, the camper who smothered me in kisses when I returned with new campers from New York City. She is crying so loudly that no one can quiet her. Her counselor holds Sara on her lap and whispers in her ear, but eventually she has to be carried out of the room. The production, which has momentarily come to a halt, picks up again and moves to its conclusion amid muted applause. Everyone realizes that we have just witnessed a reenactment of something real and troubling. Afterward, campers are encouraged to ask questions about student demonstrations, and the actors answer them as best they can. Songs of freedom follow the presentation before we all file out and go back to our bunks for the night.

I take my kids back to the junior-A bunk and begin putting them to bed, but I am interrupted by one of the counselors from junior-B next door.

"Will you come over and talk to Sara Gordon?" she asks. "She is upset about the play, because she thinks all the things that happened to the students on stage can happen to you."

Sara can't be more than seven years old, but she understands that the actions of whites against Negroes in the South means that I could be threatened the same way the Greensboro students were treated if I stand up to the racists. That realization is what sent her into hysterical sobbing during the reenactment. I read bedtime stories to my campers and quiet them down for the night before I go next door to sit with Sara on the steps of her bunk. I talk to her about Mississippi and tell her that my state hasn't had any student protests, so I have not been in the kind of danger we witnessed on stage earlier.

"Promise me that you'll stay safe," she begs.

I have never made a promise to a child that I couldn't keep, so I say to her, "Nothing like that has ever happened to me, but I can't promise you that it never will. All I can promise is that I'll be very, very careful to keep myself safe."

She seems to understand why I cannot make the kind of promise she's asking me to make, and I think she even appreciates the fact that I don't do what is most expedient but am truly honest with her. We say good night, and I kiss her before she goes inside her bunk for the night. Afterward I look for her mother, Millie, to discuss the matter further. Millie tells me about the time she took Sara and her older brothers to see the movie *South Pacific*. "When the song 'You Have to Be Taught to Hate' was sung, Sara cried so loudly that I had to carry her out of the theater," Millie says. "She feels injustice very deeply." Millie and I agree that together we will continue to reassure Sara that I am not in any danger, so she won't be overcome with fear and worry.

Judy Coleman, Peggy Dammon, and I begin dating three members of the kitchen staff. I go out with Joel Melton, Judy with Gus Miller, and Peggy with Manny (Emanuel) Taylor. Manny is the only one of the three who lives in New York City, on 118th Street, around the corner from Aunt Mabel where Sugar Ray Robinson used to go to visit a friend.

MANNY TAYLOR, AND PEGGY DAMMON WITH WHOM I
HAD POLITICAL DISCUSSIONS AT AL'S SEAFOOD BAR. THEY
ARE SHOWN WITH TWO UNIDENTIFIED CAMPERS

In the evenings when we girls have put our kids to bed and the
night counselor is on duty, the six of us walk the two or three miles
from camp into Phoenicia to Al's Seafood Bar and Restaurant, where we
order fried onion rings, shrimp salad sandwiches on rye, sloe gin fizzes,
and lime rickies. These are the days when the drinking age in New York
State is eighteen, and we can all legally drink. We sit at a table in the
back of the restaurant eating, drinking, and debating. We talk about
the independence struggles taking place in African countries—Zaire,
Dahomey, Upper Volta, Senegal, and the Ivory Coast.[146] All of them have
won or are winning their independence this summer, and we discuss

---

146 Many of these African country names are different today. For example Dahomey
is Benin, Upper Volta is Burkina Faso, and the Ivory Coast is Cote d'Ivoire.

the connection between our struggles here on US soil and theirs across the Atlantic. Around midnight we pay the bill, say good night to Al, the owner, and began our moonlit walk back to camp. Gus and I usually walk ahead of the other four, harmonizing popular songs, while our friends continue their discussion of national and international politics.

Many of our thoughts this summer are focused on the civil rights movement, because it is the first year that students have challenged the laws of the Jim Crow South; and (even with my promise to Sara) because of the new student challenges taking place, I am beginning to wonder when my time to stand up for equality is coming.

I find myself struggling with a personal clash of cultures, too. Most of my friends declared their independence when we were in our early teens, but Rosemary and I came so close to losing Mother in that South Carolina ditch that we drew very close to her during those years. Now I am eighteen and feel the need to assert myself. My first act of defiance is to shave my legs. I have always hated the hair on my legs in spite of the fact that southern Negro boys think shapely, hairy legs are sexy, and they love the kind of legs I have. When I return home from camp after this summer away, Mother discovers my smooth legs. An argument ensues, but I refuse to give in. This summer I also enter a more challenging internal struggle, one that brings my entire upbringing, including my religious convictions and cultural values, into question. The inner turmoil I am experiencing involves my chastity. The church I love and have grown up in teaches me that sex is a sacred gift from God, to be shared between a husband and wife. My parents have reinforced this teaching, and my southern culture supports the fact that I have come of age in a time when "nice girls" tolerate their boyfriends' dalliances with the "fast girls" because they expect to marry virgins like me.

I share the struggle I am having with Katy, who says she doesn't believe anyone has to wait until marriage to have sex. She and I spend many nights discussing this dilemma, just as we spent nights in our bunks in work camp discussing the existence of God.

Finally Katy says, "You should talk with my mother about it."

"NO!" I shriek. "I'm not sharing my feelings about sex with *any* adult, not under any circumstances, especially someone's mother." But at the end of summer, when Rose and I go to Levittown to spend a weekend with Katy and her family, Katy finds an opportunity to get her dad, brother, and Rosemary out of the house so Bea and I can have "the talk."

Bea begins by saying, "I know you and Katy have talked about sex during your time at camp." I am so embarrassed I can hardly look at her, but she presses on. "Sex is a beautiful experience between two people who really love each other," she says, "but sexual relations should never be entered into for the sake of sex alone. Sex should be based on a couple's love for, respect for, and commitment to each other. If you decide to become sexually active," she tells me, "you must really love the boy and be responsible enough to protect yourself against an unwanted pregnancy."[147]

I have grown up believing all adults look down on young people who have sex outside of marriage, but this conversation with Bea helps me see sex as a natural part of life. When the weekend with the Wechslers ends, Rosemary and I return to Aunt Mabel's to prepare for another long drive back to Mississippi with Mother and Dad.

---

147 In the fifties and early sixties, sexually transmitted diseases were neither as prevalent nor as feared as an unwanted pregnancy, even though Bea did tell me it was important to protect myself against getting a venereal disease, which is what we called STDs back then.

# CHAPTER 21

# WAIST DEEP IN THE BIG MUDDY[148]

B ACK HOME AT TOUGALOO, the 1960 Rome Olympics capture my attention. My whole family sits glued to the television as a host of talented Negro athletes win gold medals—Wilma Rudolph, Rafer Johnson, John Thomas, Wyomia Tyus, and Cassius Clay. After Clay wins his boxing match, he jumps on the ropes and begins talking nonstop about becoming heavyweight champion of the world. Living in the harsh realities of Mississippi, I can hardly believe his brash presumptuousness.

On September 22, Mali becomes the tenth African country to gain independence. Nigeria follows on October 1, and hope for new freedoms in this country start to seem more possible to me. I desperately want the United States to live up to its promise of liberty and justice for all, and I look to the independence struggles in Africa for hope.

I enter my freshman year at Tougaloo College, and we welcome a new president, Dr. A. D. Beittel, and his wife, Ruth, from Beloit College

---

148 Words and music by Pete Seeger, TRO, 1967, Melody Trails, Inc., New York, NY.

in Wisconsin. My buddy from Holy Ghost High School, Tommie Ann Johnson, is a freshman at Tougaloo, too, and the two of us become so inseparable again that we're dubbed "the Gold Dust Twins." A number of my elementary school friends from Jackson Lab, as well as high-school friends from Tougaloo Prep, Holy Ghost, Lanier, and Brinkley enter Tougaloo as freshmen, too. I declare English as my major and physical education as a minor—the fields of both my parents' areas of concentration. Like them, I hope to become a teacher.

Every freshman is required to participate in an orientation that includes the history of the founding of Tougaloo beginning with *Amistad*, the slave ship that was overthrown and that gave birth to the American Missionary Association. The AMA in turn gave birth to Tougaloo "and her five sister institutions": LeMoyne (now LeMoyne-Owen), Talladega, Straight (now Dillard), Tillotson (now Huston-Tillotson), and Fisk University. As the story of Tougaloo unfolds, I remember how Rosemary and I, as young girls, admired the dramatic portrayal of the *Amistad* on a wall of the Talladega College library during our trips to the school with Dad and his teams. The AMA established more than five hundred schools in the South for "free illiterates regardless of color."

Listening to the *Amistad* story gives me a sense of pride and a sense of responsibility because of the AMA's founding of so many Negro colleges. Based on this history, I don't want to waste the opportunities I've been given. Even so, readjusting to segregated life in Mississippi after another summer of freedom in New York makes me more aware than ever of how much I have to accommodate myself to what has become for me an alienating Jim Crow culture.

All freshmen are assigned to Daddy's health education class (a required course for incoming students), and one of the areas he covers is mental health. In one session he says, "People think nothing of going to the doctor when they feel something is wrong with their bodies, but they shy away from seeing a therapist when they are emotionally upset." I think about that a lot as I struggle to find my way back into Mississippi life. The racial tightrope I've been walking is growing more difficult to navigate, and I wonder how long I can teeter between the two cultures before I lose my balance and fall into the abyss.

At camp I have had the freedom of walking into town with friends, sitting in an integrated restaurant, and talking politics over drinks. I've been part of a summer stock play—the only Negro in an otherwise white cast—and gone on integrated overnight camping trips. I've seen firsthand what the South has denied me, and I know what life *can* be compared to what my life is. The more I leave Mississippi and return, the more convinced I am that white folk in this state will not change during my lifetime.

Remembering what Dad has said about taking care of our emotional health, I tell Mother, "I'm having a hard time settling back into life at Tougaloo, and I think it would help if I could talk to a therapist." She takes me to a Jewish therapist in Jackson who listens to me but who seems more interested in getting information about my parents than in helping me understand my struggle, so I don't go back. I struggle along, hanging out in the co-op with Tommie Ann dancing to Ike and Tina Turner's "I Think It's Gonna Work Out Fine" and Mickey and Sylvia's "Love Is Strange."

In November, after a series of historic television debates, John F. Kennedy is elected president over Richard M. Nixon by one of the slimmest of margins in history. The election of the first Roman Catholic president, a man who has said, referring to the student sit-ins, that

Negroes have shown, "the new way for Americans to stand up (is) to sit down,"[149] is a momentous occasion. Then, when I hear that he called Coretta Scott King when her husband was arrested in Atlanta, Kennedy becomes a bona fide hero in my eyes.

In December, Madre presents Rosemary as a debutante in Atlanta, Georgia. Katy Wechsler and Mike Peters (the dancer we all adored from senior camp) prepare to come down for the ball. Madre has called the dean of Morehouse College and asked him to recommend young men from Atlanta's best families as escorts for Rosemary, Katy, and me. Dean Brazeal sends Robert Saxon for Rosemary, Paul Golightly for Katy, and Julius Coles for me. Rosemary and Bobby make the rounds of rehearsals and pre-deb parties before Katy and Mike Peters arrive, and Julius and Paul come by Madre and Papa's house on Christmas Eve to meet Katy and me, not realizing she hasn't arrived yet.

My grandparents have razed their original home at 212 Griffin Street and replaced it with a new residence on the same site, numbered 220 Griffin. The formal living room, dining room, bedrooms, and a full kitchen are upstairs. A den, a soda fountain and bar with barstools, and Papa's office are downstairs. Papa uses the den to host his regular bridge games, but when we visit them, the area is turned over to Rosemary and me as an entertainment area for us and our friends. There are also apartment houses in back of the new house on the site where the tennis court once was. The rentals are called the Nell-Rose Apartments, named for my sister and me. They were built to bring income to our grandparents in their later years.

Julius, Paul, and I spend Christmas Eve talking about family Christmas traditions, and somewhere during the conversation Julius,

---

149 Williams, *Eyes on the Prize*, 135.

who is also Episcopalian, says, "My family used to go to midnight mass on Christmas Eve when I was a kid."

"Really? I've never been to midnight mass," I tell him.

"Would you like to go?" he asks.

"Yes."

So he and I take out the phone book and begin looking for a church in the area that might be holding a midnight mass. When we have trouble finding one, Julius says, "The cathedral probably has a mass tonight."

"Yeah, but that would mean integrating the cathedral downtown," Paul counters.

"What other church do you know of that's holding a midnight mass tonight?" Julius asks.

"You're talking about integrating the cathedral?" Paul asks, incredulous at the thought.

It is now eleven o'clock, and we're hard pressed to think of anywhere else to go, so we decide to go to the cathedral, even though we don't know if the ushers will let us in. We say good night to Mother and Dad after I get permission to attend, and we head for downtown Atlanta. The fellows are wearing dark suits, and I'm in a purple-and-teal-plaid wool dress with a matching mantilla-like shawl that I will use to cover my head. These are the days when no Episcopal young woman dares to show up in church with her head uncovered and without gloves. I am wearing black leather ones.

The three of us arrive just after the service begins. An usher greets us, gives us service leaflets, and then leads us up the center aisle to seats near the middle of the church. A priest reads the opening collect, and in the bishop's sermon the familiar story of Mary and Joseph seeking room in an overcrowded inn unfolds. Then the strains of "God Rest Ye Merry, Gentlemen" and "Silent Night" echo through the church. As Eucharistic prayers begin, I wonder if we'll be passed over at the altar by the priest and bishop or be forced to intinct[150] when the Communion cup comes to us. I wonder if I will have the courage to walk out of the church if we are not allowed to drink from the common cup like everyone else.

Sliding out of our pew, we move up the aisle, approach the altar rail, and kneel. The bishop moves from one communicant to another, placing a wafer in each one's outstretched hands, uttering the familiar and reassuring words:

> "The Body of our Lord Jesus Christ, which was given for thee, preserve thy body and soul unto everlasting life. Take and eat this in remembrance that Christ died for thee and feed on him in thy heart by faith with thanksgiving."[151]

A small round wafer is placed in my hand as he moves past me to Julius.

"The blood of our Lord Jesus Christ which was shed for thee,"[152] says the priest who follows the bishop, placing the Communion cup to my lips. I take a sip and rise. The three of us walk back to our pew one behind the other, then slide in to kneel in prayer. It has been a beautiful service, made all the more so for me because of the acceptance of the three of us at this Christmas Eve service.

---

150 Dip the wafer into the Communion cup, rather than drink from the cup like the others.

151 John Wallace Suter, Custodian, *Book of Common Prayer* (New York: The Church Hymnal Corporation, 1945), 82.

152 Ibid.

When the service ends, we walk to the rear of the cathedral, where we are invited to a reception in the parish hall. We thank the usher but decline the invitation. We have come to worship, and we've done that. But once we are inside the car we all let out a collective whoop. It wasn't our intention to make a statement, but we can't help being excited about having successfully integrated Atlanta's Episcopal cathedral on Christmas Eve.

Katy and Mike arrive a few days later, and our drive around town is eased considerably by the assumption of local friends that Katy is a fair-skinned Negro. Mike Peters is a biracial child whose Negro father's family lives in Atlanta. As a dancer, he has remained close to Fay Berrios, the dance instructor Bert Gibson dated at camp. The two of them have stayed in touch since the close of camp, so I pump him for information about her and her relationship with Bert. "Are they still seeing each other?" I want to know.

"Yes," he confirms. In fact, he says, "I think they are planning to get engaged."

Crestfallen, I force myself to let go of any thoughts of winning Bert's love. Instead I concentrate on having a good time at Rose's deb ball, and I reconcile myself to the idea of marriage between Bert and Fay.

At our dinner table, Katy and Mike bow their heads for grace, even though they are atheists. They do so without objection, just as Rosemary and I have dug into our food without objection at the Wechslers' without having the food blessed. At those times I have said a silent grace to God.

The deb ball is wonderful, and Rosemary, Katy, and I have a great time with our dates. It is only after the ball when Madre invites a few girls from Atlanta's middle- and upper-middle-class Negro families for an evening of socializing that the conversation about race moves to an uncomfortable level. Some of the girls who are visiting start to make disparaging remarks about white people in general, unaware that Katy is white. After several comments from them, Rosemary and I say, "Katy has experienced what it is like to be hated by white people, too, because her family stood up for a Negro family who moved next door to them in Pennsylvania."

"What do you mean?" one of our guests asks.

"She knows what it's like for white people to make life difficult for other white..."

"What do you mean?" another girl asks.

"Katy is white, and her family befriended the first Negro family that moved into her neighborhood."

There is dead silence—almost as dead as the silence at camp when a white girl asked Katy if she was sure she wasn't part Negro. After a few silent strained moments, conversation begins again, and we girls make feeble attempts at overly polite talk. Soon our guests start to depart one by one.

At the end of the Christmas season, Mike and Katy return to New York, and we go back to Mississippi to a bundle of Christmas cards that have arrived in our absence. Many are from friends at camp. In my pile of cards is one from Bert Gibson. It is signed, "Love, Bert."

*What does that mean?* I wonder. I know nearly all our friends from camp sign their cards and letters with love, but somehow this doesn't seem like an appropriate closing from someone who's engaged to be married. I write him a letter thanking him for his card and explain that we were in Atlanta when it arrived. I share news about Atlanta and Jackson, and then I say, "I understand you and Fay are engaged. When is your marriage scheduled for?" Within weeks I have a letter back from him saying, "Fay and I are not engaged and, in fact, we have broken up."

For one of the few times in my life I throw caution to the wind and write back telling him I have loved him for two years.

In Bert's next letter to me he says, "If you're going to be in New York next summer, let me know, and maybe we can see each other." I promise myself and him that I will.

Our next-door neighbors, the Barnabys (with their three sons—including "Huck Finn" the trapper and fisherman who gave us rabbits and fish he'd caught) left Tougaloo at the beginning of the school year. They were replaced by another white family. Collins and Helen Bell and their children become as good friends and neighbors to us as the two families who preceded them. Mrs. Bell works as a secretary at Tougaloo, and Dr. Bell is professor of speech and drama. Of all the theater professors Tougaloo has had, Dr. Bell is the master at producing sweeping dramas (like Sophocles's *Antigone*) on a small stage with almost no budget. Using the old Tougaloo Prep School auditorium where dances and assemblies were held when I was in ninth grade, Dr. Bell abandons elaborate set designs and period costumes. He sets up simple columns on the stage and places actors in modern clothing. He dresses actors in tuxedos and actresses in pastel chiffon gowns with Empire waists. When he learns of the role I had in New York summer stock a year earlier and of my small parts in high-school plays, he casts me as Portia in Tougaloo's spring production of *Julius Caesar*. Ernest McBride, the handsome president of our freshman class, plays the role of Brutus, the man to whom Portia is married. George West (the basketball player whose family drove up the year before from Natchez when I got hurt in my last basketball game) is cast as Marc Antony, Ruth

Thompson (a campus beauty queen) gets the role of Calpurnia (wife to Caesar), and Daddy is cast in the title role.

Playing opposite Ernest McBride is a dream role for me. I have been drawn to him since the school year began because of the way he carries himself. Even as a freshman, McBride wears tweed jackets, carries a pipe, and loves the classics. He is the heartthrob of several girls in the freshman class, including me, and so I am a bundle of nerves playing Portia opposite his Brutus. A couple of weeks into rehearsals, Dr. Bell pushes me to give a solid performance by indicating that what I've been doing is giving him a Debbie Reynolds version of Shakespeare. "Portia was one of Shakespeare's most beautiful women, the daughter of royalty," he says. "Make us believe that."

It is all the motivation I need to move myself to the next level. Dr. Bell is pleased, and following another few weeks of rehearsal, he says he wants a kiss between Portia and Brutus. Nervously I move toward Ernest McBride. We embrace as I wait for his line that begins, "You are my true and honorable wife..." As I prepare for a stage kiss, I am knocked off my feet when his tongue parts my lips. I'm also excited to be kissing the boy nearly every girl in class wants to kiss, so I go along with it. *Julius Caesar* runs several weeks and is a huge success. At the end of each performance I walk to the middle of the stage on the arm of Brutus and meet Calpurnia and Julius Caesar (Daddy) as the two of them enter from the opposite side. At center stage I take my father's arm and the four of us bow together to thunderous applause. It is one of the most special times of my life, playing opposite a school heartthrob and my father in the title role.

In March I decide to go over to the girls' dorm to study for exams with the boarding students who are gathered in Norweida and

Clintoria's room, and it is here that Norweida teaches me to smoke. For years I have puffed on cigarettes at camp without inhaling, but I am determined to become as cool as my classmates so I can shed my goody-goody image and be part of the in crowd. To further help that image, I meet Tommie Ann in the co-op nearly every day to dance to records by Ike and Tina Turner and Jerry Butler as we practice new dance steps.

When the beatnik social takes place in the gymnasium, Tommie Ann, Doris Carter (a friend from Lanier High School), and I are determined to be as cool as can be. Everyone dresses like beatniks—even though none of us play guitars or banjos—and we all have a great time.

LEFT TO RIGHT TOMMY ANN JOHNSON, DORIS CARTER, AND
NELL AT THE BEATNIK SOCIAL, TOUGALOO 1960

As the year moves to a close, we are expected to make a formal report in one of our classes, but the book we are to report on is on reserve in the library, because it is the only copy. By the time I get to sign up for it, my name is close to the bottom of the list, and it doesn't come to the top before class reports are due. In fact, there are a number of us who do not get to use the book before our reports are due. The instructor begins the class by saying that Carrie Lapsky has made one of the best reports on the topic, and she is asked to read her report aloud. When she finishes, students ask her how she got the information, because we don't remember seeing her name on the reserve book list in the library. In her sweet little Mississippi drawl she says, "I got it from the library."

"But your name wasn't on the list at the library," someone reminds her.

Again in her sweet country voice she says, "Not the school library, the library downtown."

"You mean the Jackson public library?" another student asks incredulously.

"Uh-huh," she responds.

We are all so flabbergasted that no one else says a word! It will take some time before we put together what probably happened. Carrie, with her light skin, brown curly hair, and surname (Lapsky), was probably mistaken for being Jewish when she checked out the book. After all, no self-respecting white Mississippi librarian would ever imagine that a Negro would walk up the front steps of Jackson's segregated public library and check out a book, then reenter the same way to return it. The irony of segregation laws is that so often people can't tell who is Negro and who is white, be they Negroes, like the girls in Atlanta who thought Katy was one of us, or white, like the librarian who allowed

Carrie to walk in the front door of the segregated library downtown and check out a book.

Nevertheless, toward the end of March there is an intentional entering of the same Jackson public library when Meredith Anding Jr., Sammy Bradford, Alfred Cook, Geraldine Edwards, Janice Jackson, Joseph Jackson, Albert Lassiter, Evelyn Pierce, and Ethel Sawyer stage the first read-in at the same municipal library on State Street. All nine are arrested for their actions. I learn of their arrest in class that day and fear for them. Part of me is really upset that I didn't know they were going. Whether or not I would have been brave enough to go I couldn't say, but I hated the fact that it was out of my hands, because I didn't live in a dorm but with my parents on a road behind the dorm. The courage of the "Tougaloo Nine" (as they have come to be known) marks the beginning of civil rights protests in Mississippi and—after Freedom Summer and voter registration drives that summer—will lead to the desegregation of public facilities in the state of Mississippi.

Immediately following the arrest of the Tougaloo Nine, I begin receiving letters from friends at camp. Bert Gibson writes to say, "I see where your state and your home of Tougaloo are getting into the press. Are you involved? I have one clipping from the *New York Post*, 3/31 that I am enclosing. I thought you might want it. I'll send you all the clippings that I can find if you'll let me know how it's going down there." I write back thanking him and telling him that I wasn't involved in the arrests because I hadn't known of the plan, and I share as much as I know about what is happening.

On April 3, 1961, I receive a letter from him including an article with the headline: NAACP GOES 'ALL-OUT' IN MISS. DRIVE. It states that the NAACP has launched an "all-out and continuous" campaign to wipe out discrimination in Mississippi. NAACP Executive Secretary Roy Wilkins says the organization will mail appeals to every NAACP member in the country asking for funds to mount an attack on "the nation's most backward state." The appeal of Mr. Wilkins is occasioned because of the use of billy clubs, tear gas, and police dogs to attack Negro demonstrators protesting the arrest of the Tougaloo Nine. Wilkins says the NAACP will use its influence to support a campaign to wipe out discrimination and segregation in Mississippi where only eight thousand of eight hundred thousand Negroes in the state are registered to vote.

The school year ends with excitement around the Tougaloo Nine and with relief for me that I will soon be headed for New York as the head counselor in junior-A. I have also talked Daddy into coming to Woodland as athletic director, because the director of athletics, who has been there for years, is not coming back. Near the end of May, Bert sends me another article, written by Ted Poston, titled, NEXT BUS STOP MISSISSIPPI. It is about the Freedom Riders who are headed for my home state. Judy Coleman and Peggy Dammon, my counselor buddies from the previous summer, are excited to be coming down to participate in the rides, but I can't wait to get out. The long, hot Freedom Summer is gearing up, and all I can think of is the freedom of Camp Woodland and another integrated summer in the Catskills. Mother will be one of the work camp counselors this summer, and Rosemary will complete her second year as a CIT. For the first time in years, the four of us will be in the same place during the summer. To my regret, nearly all the friends I hoped to spend the summer with are headed straight for my hometown as Freedom Riders.

When we get to New York, I call Bob Kurtz with the hope of doing exactly what Mother had said we should have been allowed to do—bring closure to our relationship on our terms; at least that's what I tell myself. I tell Bob I am at Aunt Mabel's, and he says he'll come by. It isn't long before the doorbell rings, and I go to let him in. There he stands, tall, tanned, and handsome, and there I am, my heart pounding as strongly as ever at the sight of him. I'm wearing a white blouse, straight navy skirt, and sneakers.

"You had turned into the most lusciously gorgeous woman I could remember seeing," he would say years later. "The most beautiful I had ever seen you, and I was floored. I thought, 'Good God, what an idiot I was. What have I given up?'"

But neither of us shares the thoughts that are in our hearts that day. Instead I manage to utter, "Hi, come in." I lead him into the living room, where we talk about everything but us—school, summer jobs, Freedom Summer, family, and friends from camp. At the end of that visit, we go our separate ways, each falling in love with other people and getting married, both making our homes in New York. In time we both have daughters who compete in the same Colgate Women's Games at Madison Square Garden, where the most talented women and girls in track and field vie for trophies and scholarship money. It will be thirty years before we meet face-to-face again.[153]

I call Bert, who comes over to meet my family. Shaking hands with Daddy, he calls him "sir" and makes a lasting impression. I take him into the kitchen to meet Mother, who is seated in a chair next to the kitchen stove getting her hair straightened. He endears himself to her when he takes her hand in his and says, "I see where Nell gets her beauty." Then he and I return to the living room to get acquainted. Although

---

153 By this time, Bob is a respected surgeon who has become best known as the doctor who saved the life of the woman known as "the Central Park Jogger," and I am interviewing people for the writing of this book.

we've been exchanging letters, this is the first time we've been alone together. We sit talking for a long time before finally reaching an awkward silence. That's when Bert invites me to come up to the Bronx and meet his family. He doesn't tell me until much later that his Aunt Dora wants to meet the girl who has loved him for two years without even seeing him. When he received the letter in which I professed my love for him, he went to his aunt and said, "I haven't seen this girl in two years, and she writes me a letter telling me she loves me. What do I say to her?" So she must have been the one who suggested he offer to see me when I returned to New York.

Leaving Aunt Mabel's apartment, Bert takes me by the hand and leads me toward the subway. We enter a train that makes its way out of Manhattan and above ground to the elevated tracks in the Bronx. Bert begins to explain the history of the places we are passing. I'm impressed. I've never known anyone who could rattle off so many facts about his city, and I try to think of all the places my family has lived and whether I could tell a visitor that much about any of those cities. I can see that he loves New York and takes pride in sharing information about its history. But I also notice that he's not the only New Yorker who loves the city or knows lots about what is taking place in it. All along the route to his home in the Bronx, people are talking about what's going on in the city, and they have opinions on everything from the mayor's latest decision and union strikes to Russia's Nikita Khrushchev. Even the junkies we pass on the street are arguing over politics. I've spent my whole life living on college campuses among professional people, and I've never heard the kind of political debates I hear on street corners this afternoon as we make our way to his home in the Bronx.

At his apartment on Union Avenue, I meet his Aunt Dora, his grandmother, Irene Gibson, his father Bert Sr., his cousin, Veronica Fabian (Dora's daughter), and Dora's gentleman friend, Willie Mays Sr., father of the legendary baseball player. Mrs. Irene Gibson is a West Indian woman who comes from Tarpum Bay in the Bahamas. In the early days of her marriage, she and her husband, Lorenzo, lived in Key West, Florida, but when Bert's father was born, they took a ship to New York and have lived here ever since. Lorenzo has died by the time I meet Irene. Bert Sr. is their oldest child, followed by Dora, Lorenzo Jr., and Leroy. Bert's cousin, Veronica, called Ronnie, and Bert were reared by his Gibson grandparents as siblings following the death of Bert's mother (Dorothy) when he was a toddler and the divorce of Ronnie's mother (Dora) from Ronnie's father. I spend a lovely afternoon getting to know them before Bert takes me back to Manhattan.

At Aunt Mabel's, the two of us climb the stairs to the first-floor landing, where I hope Bert will kiss me, but he continues to the second floor and up toward my aunt's third-floor landing. Before we reach the last few steps he turns, takes me in his arms, and gives me a kiss that melts my whole body. I've never been kissed like this in my life, and when he steps back, I feel as if I'm floating up the rest of the stairs. "Good night," he whispers as I ring the doorbell. "Good night," I manage to whisper back.

Katy returns to camp for another summer as a counselor. Gus and Manny come back for another stint in the kitchen, but Judy and Peggy, their girlfriends from the year before, are headed to Mississippi to participate in Freedom Summer. Bert comes up to visit me during the July parents' visiting weekend and returns two weeks later in order to spend as much time with me as possible before he and his cousin, Ronnie, make their first trip to Nassau, Bahamas, to visit relatives. During his second trip to camp, we sit at the work camp creek exchanging family histories.

His paternal grandfather, Lorenzo, was a steward in the US Navy when he met Irene, who had come to Key West to visit her brother. Lorenzo was so taken with Irene's beauty that he wasted no time in winning her heart. Bert's mother was a member of the Arrington family, who traced their lineage back to the Civil War. His grandmother, Ella Arrington, was the only girl in a family of boys. I listen to him, noting how self-assured and confident he is, much more so than other boys I know. He plans on finishing college and becoming an accountant. He wants to work for a large accounting firm before entering politics. He is upset that the City College of New York (CCNY) dropped him from its rolls when he contracted mononucleosis, and he is working to get back into school there. At the time he withdrew from CCNY, he hadn't known there was a procedure he needed to follow in dropping out, so when he tried to return to school he was told he could not come back because he had withdrawn illegally. Now he is fighting to be reinstated. He comes to camp again in August to see me and says he has given up his trip to the Bahamas in order to work as a relief counselor at camp, so he and I can be together for the rest of the summer. I've never had anyone make that kind of choice for me, and I believe that is the moment I decide he's the man I want to marry.

When I have my hands full with five- and six-year-olds, and he has time off from work as a relief counselor, Bert spends time with Dad on the athletic field assisting in any way he can. He and Dad spend hours together doing sports with campers and during their time off sit under the bridge near the athletic field and talk. A year later Bert will spend time with a young Cuban counselor named Hector Angulo who teaches the kids at camp a new song that catches on like wildfire. It is called "Guantanamera," and after Hector teaches it, folks can hear the song being sung all over camp. When Pete Seeger comes up to sing at the annual folk festival and for the camp kids at the Sunday meeting, the youngsters tell him, "We have a new song to teach you," and they sing "Guantanamera." After the kids teach Pete the song, Hector shares its history with Pete, who later teaches it to the Weavers. It goes on to become a hit record by a group called the Sandpipers.

HECTOR ANGULO (LEFT) AND BERT GIBSON AT CAMP, C.1962

Bert and I arrange to have the same day off and spend that time talking about our future together. We want to get married one day and have a son, whom we'll name Bertram Maxwell Gibson III, and a daughter, whose middle name has to be Anne, the family name we women have kept in every generation to honor our Cherokee ancestor, Missouri Anne. We also consider making love, but we don't want to rush into it. I'm nineteen years old and still conflicted about sex. He, on the other hand, does not feel there is anything wrong with sex outside of marriage and carries condoms because, he says, he doesn't want to have any children until he's married. During one of our days off we decide to spend the night at the top of a mountain in back of camp. That night when we make love under the stars, I truly understand what Katy's mother meant when she said, "Be sure you love the man you give your heart and body to."

At the end of camp, when my family returns to Aunt Mabel and Uncle Ezra's, Bert meets me in Harlem and takes me out. First we go to his Aunt Dora's liquor store on Amsterdam Avenue and 158th Street. There, Willie Mays Sr. stands at the back door in a private area behind the store. Willie is standing over a stove cooking and gives us each a plate of food when we enter the room. After we've finished our meal, Willie gives Bert the keys to his red Pontiac Bonneville convertible and tells us, "Have a good time."

As we are driving through the streets, Bert keeps up a running commentary, pointing out Yankee Stadium and then LaGuardia Airport as we drive along the highway. At last we arrive at the site where the New York World's Fair is to be held. He parks the car and takes me on a tour to see the buildings being constructed. After seeing the construction, we return to the car and head back to his aunt's liquor store, where he returns Willie's car. Then he takes me back to Aunt Mabel's on the subway.

The time is approaching for my family to return to Mississippi, but not before Bert takes me to the Apollo for a movie and show. He also invites our younger sisters to come along—Rosemary and his half sister, Debbie. It is a night I'll never forget, because the entertainment is as riveting as anything I remember seeing at Radio City Music Hall. The movie is forgettable, but the performers on the show are Nipsy Russell, the Coasters, who sing their hit "Searchin'," Gladys Knight and the Pips, and James Brown, who closes the evening on his knees draped in a satin cape singing, "Please, Please, Please."

Coming back to Mississippi after a summer as wonderful as the one I've had is more depressing than ever. This year it feels as if the life is being choked out of me, as if all my hopes are being trivialized. Because Camp Woodland doesn't stomp on my dreams the way Mississippi does, I feel myself sinking into a depression so deep, I fear I won't come out of it. I have a heart-to-heart talk with Mother to tell her I don't think I can survive another year in Mississippi. She makes a call to Atlanta to see if Madre can make some calls to Spelman and get Rosemary and me into school there at this late date. It is almost September, but Madre and Papa go to work to get us enrolled. Within a week, I am saying good-bye to Tommie Ann and heading to Atlanta, completely unaware that I am jumping out of a Mississippi frying pan into a blazing-hot Georgia fire.

# CHAPTER 22

# MIDNIGHT TRAIN TO GEORGIA[154]

I WALK ALONG THE FAMILIAR cracked sidewalks of my childhood, past steps that lead to the porches of houses whose spacious lawns are covered with leaves. As I return to Madre and Papa's from enrolling at Spelman, a flood of memories rush back. I remember passing these same front porches years earlier with Rosemary, speaking to neighbors watering their front lawns with hoses in the days before sprinklers came into vogue and fanned the water from side to side or sent it spiraling into the air, creating rainbows in the sun. I walk by the home of the elderly gentleman who always got a kick out of calling from the rocker on his front porch, "Hello, little boys," to my blue-jeans-clad sister and me in the days when proper little southern girls wore dresses.

Rosie and I always indignantly responded, "We're not little boys; we're little girls."

---

154 "Midnight Train to Georgia," written by Jim Weatherly, recorded by Gladys Knight and the Pips.

He'd chuckle at having once again gotten under our skin as we continued our walk home. I breathe in the autumn air and see myself and Rosemary, little girls again, standing in the bathroom door watching Papa shave in the old house and seeing Madre serve up bountiful meals, while family members gather around the table at the damask cloth, each one in front of his or her embroidered name. The koi pond teems with fish outside the solarium, and the tennis court awaits our arrival. In another scene, I see Dad seated at the piano playing and singing songs, and Mother sewing in the basement with her aunts who fill the air with laughter.

Today my grandparents are older. Papa uses a cane on his morning constitutionals and seldom asks what Rosemary and I have learned in a day. He is content to listen to the news we volunteer or to debate us on an issue. Recently he and I have had a running disagreement over the use of the word *Negro* versus *colored*. Because he has traveled the world, *colored* doesn't hold the kind of negative connotations it does for me, so he prefers it to *Negro*. Whether or not it's my attempt to assert my independence, I do not know, but I contend that *Negro* is more acceptable, because it's not the word that bans me from segregated restrooms and drinking fountains.

These days, following many of our breakfasts, my grandfather excuses himself and goes to his office in the basement of their new home where he continues to work on his autobiography, *My Story in Black and White*. Both my grandparents have given up driving, but Madre engages a local cab driver named Mr. MacDowell, who takes her wherever she needs to go and drives Rosemary and me to and from Spelman during the first weeks of school until dormitory rooms become available. Because of our late registration, dorm rooms for us are not yet ready, so we live with Madre and Papa until the rooms can be found.

Madre still teaches charm at the Blayton School of Business, sharing the information she learned years ago at the John Robert Powers School of Charm in New York City. Her infrequent dinner parties are smaller and less extravagant than they used to be, and she and Papa seem happy to have us in their home again. Madre especially relishes the squeals that come from the bedroom Rosemary and I now occupy whenever we open a letter from Mother. She usually writes at the end of a day before leaving her office at Brinkley High School and driving back home to Tougaloo. We can hardly contain our excitement at the receipt of one of her newsy letters.

*My Dears,*

*Hope you have some plastic rollers to put your hair up at night, as I heard Madre say that bobby pins used for pin curling break the hair off, and I can see how this could easily happen.*

*Received both your letters today. I have already answered your questions about football in Jackson, Nell. Your daddy will have to tell you who traded whom. This I don't know...*

*I believe* Bullfinch's Mythology *will prove very helpful to you in English Literature as there is so much reference to mythology...*

*A package will be in the mail this weekend with something for each of you. Aunt Mabel sent your skirt, Rosemary, and Nell, the sweater I mentioned will be in it also.*

*I can hear the band practicing, and it sounds pretty good. Naturally it would sound better if you were in it. Sounds like I heard the "eagle walk" beating a cadence outside. It is almost time to go home now. Have been writing this in bits and pieces. Hope it makes some kind of sense when you read it. This Thursday Lanier*

*and Brinkley play, so you know not to call us on Thursday night
(smile).*

*My heart is with you both, and my prayers are constantly for
your welfare. God has been so good to bless us in so many different
ways that I remind myself that I must continue to count my blessings. And, among all that I have you are my greatest and choicest
blessings! My jewels beyond great price!!*

*Well, enough of being a "mother." Remember ALWAYS, I love
you with ALL my heart. If I can help you in ANY way, don't hesitate to let me know. Love to Madre and Papa. Good luck in ALL
your work.*

*Love always,*

*Mother*

*P.S. Looking forward to our visit at Thanksgiving. Miss you!
Miss you! Miss you!*

The memory of Brinkley's eagle walk being done by new high-
school band members sends a wave of nostalgia over me as Rosie and I
fold the letter and put it back in its envelope. We will read it again and
again until a new one comes to replace it.

By October, a room becomes available in one of the freshmen dorms
for Rosemary, and one in Morgan Hall (the sophomore dorm) for me.
During our first evening on campus, Rosie and I sit on the floor of the
Spelman gymnasium with other new students, learning school songs.
I strain to make out the words of one song set to the tune of "Are You
from Dixie," a southern song I've never learned. The words have been
changed to make it uniquely collegiate.

*"Are you from Morehouse, I say from Morehouse, well the bell on Graves Hall beckons to you...I'll see you, I say I'll see you. That's the place I'm longing to be..."*

The song goes on to say the good-looking boy we are singing about is "tall, handsome, and what's more, he is the pride of the South." As the singing moves from one song to another, I look across the gym at my sister, who is making friends quickly and easily. I'm happy for her because of the two of us, she is the one who used to call home from every camp we were sent to (except Camp Woodland), begging Mother and Dad to let her come home. While she was crying on the phone to my parents, I was busy making new friends. Now I'm the one having trouble fitting in. My classmates have had their entire freshman year to bond with one another, and I'm the outsider.

Our dorm mother, Miss Taylor, does all she can to make me feel welcome. Miss Taylor is a slightly built, caramel-colored woman with tightly pursed lips, gentle dark-brown eyes, and dyed black hair pulled straight back into a bun at the nape of her neck. Her hands are delicate and are almost always clasped at her waist like those of a nun. Her black ankle-length skirts brush the tops of her lace-up shoes, and her long-sleeved black blouses reveal a touch of white at the neck. She speaks in a quivering little voice as she welcomes me to Morgan Hall, and I sense right away that she likes me. Sizing her up, I suspect she is at least sixty years old, someone who, because of my youth, I would refer to as a spinster. In reality she's probably in her forties, in spite of the fact that the word *spinster* is an apt title for her.

Morgan Hall stands on the right side of the main road leading from Spelman's front gate. The kitchen and dining room that feed the entire school are on the first floor of Morgan Hall; residence rooms make up the second and third floors. Climbing up to the second-floor landing of the dorm, the first thing I see at my immediate left is a check-in desk and chair. Behind the desk is an open parlor where girls are to entertain male callers on weekday evenings and on Sunday afternoons. In back of the parlor is a small, dim television room that all the girls in the dorm are to share. Down the hall from the check-in desk is a public phone booth that everyone on the second floor must share. This pay phone and the one of the third floor are the only phones in the entire dorm for residents. Local phone calls cost a dime, but most students save every dime they can by sticking a safety pin in the rubber telephone cord and running it along the metal cradle until a dial tone can be heard. That's how we make "free" phone calls.

My room is on the third floor to the right of the door at the top of the landing. I have been eagerly looking forward to my first dormitory experience, but now that I'm here, I feel melancholy and wonder if living with Madre and Papa might not have been better. The rules of dormitory life are stricter than any our grandparents have imposed on us, rules that seem not to have changed since Mother was a student here.

1. No whistling in the halls. If heard whistling, young ladies will receive demerits.

2. No men on campus except at assigned visiting hours. Young men may only visit in the parlor on the second floor.

3. Young ladies must sign out when leaving the dorm.[155]

---

155 This rule applies even if one is visiting a friend or relative across campus or going to the library.

4. At the time of sign-out, young ladies are to estimate the time of their return and record it. If they return later than the estimated time, they will receive a demerit for each minute they are late.[156]

5. Young ladies are only allowed to wear pants on campus on Saturdays.

6. Young ladies may go bare legged or wear socks to class during the week but must wear stockings on Sundays.[157]

7. Young ladies are expected to attend vespers every Sunday afternoon.

8. Young ladies must have special permission to leave the campus.

9. Young ladies are not allowed to ride in cars without permission from home.

10. Young ladies are not to socialize with married students.

As if to reinforce the severity of breaking these rules, there is a ten-foot-high ivy-covered brick wall surrounding the school—a visible reminder of the "sanctuary" to which our parents have entrusted us.

Since I haven't made friends with anyone in my dorm, I spend a lot of time alone in my room, studying. One afternoon while sitting and reading, I become aware of a group of girls tiptoeing down the hall. Glancing up from my book, I catch several of them peering around the door peeking into my room.

---

156 After a certain number of demerits, a student receives a warning; if she incurs additional warnings, she is placed on campus probation and is unable to leave the campus to attend ball games, visit family members, or shop. If she accumulates additional demerits, she will be placed on dormitory probation and be unable to leave the dorm except for classes.

157 My class is the first to demand and be granted permission to go bare-legged to classes and wear blue jeans on Saturdays, a precursor to the student movement protests that dominate the sixties and seventies.

"Is that your new roommate?" one asks Delores, the girl with whom I share this room, who is also in the hall.

"Uh-huh," she responds.

"What kind of shoes are those she's got on?" another snickers, referring to the oxfords I've always hated wearing. Before anyone answers her, they enter the room en masse.

"Hi," one of them says.

"Hi," I respond and return to my book. My feelings have already been hurt by girls I don't know, and I'm in no hurry to make friends with any of them.

One girl pulls the chair out from my roommate's desk and sits. Others join Delores on her bed.

"Where are you from?"

"Mississippi."

"Where in Mississippi?"

"Tougaloo."

"Where?"

"Tougaloo. It's near Jackson," I say, turning back to my books.

"How did you end up being my roommate?" Delores asks.

"I don't know. I registered late and had to wait until a space became available." For some reason the question makes me wonder if someone else was moved from this room to create space for me. I never learn whether or not this is true.

"They say you come from an important family in Atlanta," someone else says.

"Well, my grandparents have lived in Atlanta since my mother was born, and they are well known. I guess that's what they mean." I am more uncomfortable than ever now. I have never liked being "the daughter of..." and I thought leaving Mississippi would help me escape that label. But here in Atlanta, I've become "the grand-daughter of..." When you're the daughter or granddaughter of peo-ple who are well known, there's pressure to live up to expectations. And I feel I can never be rid of all my family baggage. Once I com-plained to Mother about always having to live up to her and my father's name.

"You ought to be proud to be 'the daughter of...'" she said. "Do you know how many people would love to have something or someone to live up to?"

Still, I wonder if there will ever come a time when I have my own identity.

I continue to read my book while the girls discuss the Spelman/Morehouse mixer that is coming up. It will be held in the Spelman gymnasium.

"I can't wait till the mixer this weekend."

"Me, either. Can't wait to lay my eyes on Sippy again. Umph, is he fine."

"Sippy *and* Tex."

"Yeah, Tex, too. Who's he dating?"

"Don't know. Never see him with anybody."

"And they're so tall. Especially Tex. He must be at least six foot four."

I pretend to be studying, but I can't help being curious about these two guys who are so fine. At least I'll have some handsome boys to look for at the dance, even if I don't get to meet them. I have no hope of get-ting near either Tex or Sippy, since so many girls are looking forward to seeing them and maybe dancing with them, too.

By the end of the week, I run into Marsha Goodwin, an acquaintance from Camp Atwater in Massachusetts, and Louisa Bell Stewart, a childhood friend from Austin, Texas, who make me feel a little more welcome. Other childhood friends from my summers in Atlanta are at Spelman, too. Marie Thomas, the friend with whom I made doll clothes in Madre's basement; Carol Ann Jackson, who lives across campus in the "honor dorm," the dorm reserved for girls who've proven themselves trustworthy enough to live together without a dorm mother; Bunny Foster, with whom I attended Oglethorpe Elementary School in the summer, whose grandfather is president of Atlanta University; the Brazeal girls, whose mother works at Spelman and whose father is dean at Morehouse; and Carol Henderson, with whom Rosemary and I spent one memorable Christmas Eve playing board games and singing "Santa Baby" along with the Eartha Kitt recording.

Just as I begin to ease into the rhythm of the semester, I am singled out and called to be at a photo shoot, which makes me uncomfortable again. Miss Taylor summons me to her office to say that all members of the "Granddaughters Club" are to dress in white and meet outside on the lawn for photos that afternoon. The Granddaughters Club is composed of girls whose mothers and/or grandmothers attended Spelman. Belonging to it should make me feel like I'm part of a sisterhood, but instead it feels like a way of making girls whose mothers and grandmothers did not or could not attend Spelman feel less worthy than the rest of us, and that embarrasses me. Nevertheless, I obey Miss Taylor and join Rosemary and other childhood friends on the main lawn to take photographs that will document the arrival of the club's latest members.

The weekend arrives, and excitement about the Spelman/ Morehouse mixer comes with it. Many of the girls in my dorm meet their dates on the second floor in the parlor behind the check-in desk; then they leave together for the gym. Not having a date, I stroll to the gym alone, passing classmates escorted by young men from Morehouse, Clark, Morris Brown, and Atlanta University. I enter the gym and stand at the edge of the dance floor with a slew of other girls to watch dancers moving to the music.

All at once a deep sigh emerges from someone behind me. "Ooh, there's Sippy."

When I look in the direction she has just pointed I see Emory Jackson, the older brother of Charles and Joseph Jackson, two of Rosemary's classmates from the Jackson lab school. Their mother is the home economics teacher at Lanier High School in Jackson, Mississippi, and Emory is a gifted artist and champion swimmer. So *that's* the famous Sippy—and I already know him. Then I realize he's probably acquired the nickname because he comes from Mississippi. He *is* cute; always has been. While I am marveling at the fact that I actually know one of the guys the girls are swooning over, a tall, good-looking, light-skinned fellow with black curly hair comes up and asks me to dance. Stunned, I accept. The last thing I expected at this first mixer of the school year is to be asked to dance. In fact, I don't expect to be noticed at all. But the two of us walk onto the floor and move together as the Marcels' recording of "Blue Moon" begins to spin.

Halfway through this slow dance, my partner looks down at me and says, "You don't remember me, do you?"

The best I can muster is a quizzical look.

"We've known each other a long time," he says. "From childhood."

I take another look at him but still can't place him, and I can't figure out what he's talking about. By the time I arrive at Spelman, my family has lived in so many different cities that I don't even know which one to think back to. Yet he seems too genuine for this to be a pickup line, so I try to place him.

"I'm Jim Murray."

"Jimmy!" I shout. It's Jimmy Murray, my "big brother" from Austin, Texas, the friend who beat up neighborhood bullies to protect Rosemary and me; the friend who pretended to eat mud pies in our log cabin playhouse and searched through the grass with us for four-leaf clovers; the son of the Episcopal priest with whom I got into trouble in church seated in the front pew while his father preached; Jimmy Murray who pretended not to notice the hideous scab on my face that long-ago Easter Sunday after I fell off my bike. He's a senior at Morehouse now and as tall and handsome as he ever was.

"Jimmy!" I scream again.

"How long have you been here?" he asks.

I relate the almost overnight decision that has brought Rosemary and me to Spelman. I later discover that Jimmy is "Tex," the other guy the girls have been drooling over.

"Have you been to church lately?" he inquires, escorting me off the dance floor when the song ends.

"No," I admit somewhat sheepishly.

"Come to evening prayer at Canterbury House this Sunday."

"Okay," I promise.

But Jimmy sees through my hollow words and dangles a carrot. "There's going to be an agape meal after the service, followed by plans for an NAACP rally."

Two days later, on Sunday afternoon, I walk over to Canterbury House.[158] There I join the worship, eat, and stay for the meeting that follows. The discussion centering on plans for a demonstration and rally is led by James Forman, Julian Bond, and Ruby Doris Smith.[159] I sit quietly listening, eager to learn as much as I can from this group. I'm impressed by the fact that Father Warren Scott, the Episcopal priest at Canterbury House, doesn't attempt to control the meeting but makes room for the activists to lead it. That evening when the discussion ends, I leave vowing to return, hoping I can somehow become part of this group.

The next day is Monday and time for a new week of classes to begin. I make my way across the campus from biology class toward Morgan Hall. Along the way, I spy a large tree beside the path and decide to lie down under it, hoping the familiar feel of the earth will lift the funk I'm still in at not having made any real friends in spite of the fact that some girls in my dorm want to know how I happen to know Tex and Sippy. *Maybe lying here will carry me back to the days at Tougaloo,* I think, *when I lay beneath the Tougaloo oak feeling so much a part of nature and everything that lives.* I kneel down, take a deep breath, lie back, and lose myself in the blue sky and drifting clouds, as I did so many times as a child. I am here only a few minutes when I hear a warm, almost loving voice. "Hello."

I didn't even hear anyone approaching. Cupping my hand over my eyes to block the sun, I look up into the eyes of Jenelsie Walton, one

---

158 Canterbury is part of the Episcopal Church's college ministry, and Canterbury House is open to all students for worship and fellowship.

159 Ruby Doris Smith is a student at Spelman like me and has not yet grown into the position she will later earn as "most powerful woman in the Student Nonviolent Coordinating Committee" (SNCC). Julian Bond has been attending Morehouse and is becoming well known as a student activist, but the status to which he will rise still lies years into the future. Of the three, James Forman is the only one who has already made a name for himself in the SNCC.

of Mother's girlhood friends. Jenelsie used to be a frequent visitor at Madre and Papa's when Rosemary and I were little girls. Smaller in stature than Mother's five foot four inches, Jenelsie was always bubbly and full of life, one of Mother's friends who brought happiness whenever she came. Since those long-ago days, she has married and become an art instructor at Spelman—Professor Jenelsie Walton Holloway. *Has she come to rescue me?* I wonder. *Has Mother gotten word about my failure to blend in and make friends and asked Jenelsie to help me?*

"I came to ask if you would like to pose for one of my art classes," Jenelsie asks.

"Me?"

"Yes, you'd make a good subject. You don't have to wear anything special. Just come as you are."

The thought of posing for anything leaves me anxious and self-conscious, especially an art class where people will be dissecting every part of me for over an hour. Just thinking about it feels like the ultimate torture, so I am shocked to hear my own voice utter, "All right." *Where did that come from?*

Two days, later I'm sitting on a stool in front of a combined class of male students from Morehouse and female students from Spelman, trying not to appear as nervous as I really am and trying not to move. The most excruciating part of posing is holding still for long periods of time. So to steady myself, I indulge in my favorite pastime—daydreaming. It makes the hour go more swiftly. At the end of the session, I say good-bye to Jenelsie, who responds, "We'll see you Friday."

*What?* I think. *Did I sign up for a series of sessions?* But I agree. I collect my books and begin the walk back across the campus to Morgan Hall, unaware of anything except getting to my room.

A voice calls from behind. I look over my shoulder to see a girl walking fast to catch up with me. She is one of the artists from the class I've just left—the only white student who was there.

"Hi," I respond. I've seen her before. She's one of about twelve white exchange students on this campus of five hundred girls, and the only one who has a job on campus. I've noticed her in a hairnet, standing behind the counter in the dining room, serving plates of food to those of us lined up on the other side with trays. And I've seen her in the snack shop taking orders for ice cream, cherry Cokes, and hamburgers. I like her immediately, because the one thing I've noticed is that she doesn't act like she's better than the rest of us, and she doesn't act like she's afraid to be alone with Negroes. All the other white students travel in pairs, as if they are afraid we're going to do something to them if they move around campus alone. But she's not like that; plus, she's working her way through school like a lot of the Negro girls who are here. I've also seen her in my French class, because not only is she the only white girl in that class, but she is as tall as I am.

"You're a good subject," she says, referring to the art class we've just left, "but I don't think I did you justice with my sketch."

I'm not sure how to respond, but I don't have to because she keeps talking. "I'm Anna Jo Weaver."

"Nell Braxton. Where are you from?" I ask as we continue to walk toward the dorm.

"I'm here for an exchange year from Bethel College."

"Where's that?"

"North Newton, Kansas."

"What made you come to Spelman for a year instead of a semester like the other girls?"

"I wanted to get into the life of the college and do some civil rights work."

"Is your family in Kansas?" is what I say, but I'm thinking, *What? She came down here to get into civil rights work?*

"No, I'm from a little island off the coast of Washington State called Waldron."

"What do you mean—little?"

"Well, the island is so small that if you wrote me a letter, all you'd have to put on it is Weaver, Waldron, Washington, and I'd get it."

We both laugh. "That's smaller than Tougaloo."

"Tougaloo?"

"That's where I'm from. Tougaloo, Mississippi."

I learn during our short exchange as we make our way across campus that Anna Jo is a Mennonite. Arriving at the dorm, we climb the stairs to the second floor where her room is.

"Want to come to my room?" she asks as we reach the landing.

"Okay."

We continue sharing stories about our families and hometowns. We each have younger sisters, but she also has a younger brother. She tells me she has a boyfriend in Waldron named Tony, and I tell her about Bert. She says she sometimes goes to the student movement office at Rush Memorial Baptist Church to help out and asks if I want to walk over with her sometime.

*At last,* I think. *The chance I've been longing for to get involved in the movement.* "Yes," I tell her.

She's having a hard time adjusting to the rules of the school, just as I am, but she has the kind of parents she can write home and complain to.

*September 26, 1961*

*We have to go to chapel at 8:00 on Monday, Wednesday, and Friday mornings. It was five days a week last year. We're also required to go to Vespers every Sunday afternoon at 3:00. They also have what they call midweek services every Thursday evening for everyone who wants to go. Miss Taylor does not look with favor upon those who don't heed her reminder to attend midweek. She sits at the sign-out desk, which almost everyone has to pass in the course of a Thursday afternoon, and to each and every passerby she says, in her small ominous voice, "Sadye, midweek tonight, darlin'...Don't forget midweek, Clara...Girls, midweek tonight."*[160]

We both break into laughter as she mimics Miss Taylor. Anna Jo promises to let me know the next time she heads to the student movement office, so I can accompany her. Then she begins getting ready for her shift behind the counter in the dining room downstairs, and I leave to climb one more flight of stairs to my room.

On the third floor, I get into comfortable clothes and begin my homework. In English literature we have begun reading Erich Fromm's *Escape from Freedom*. "[T]he right to express our thoughts...means something only if we are able to have thoughts of our own; freedom from external authority is a lasting gain only if the inner psychological conditions are such that we are able to establish our own individuality...powerlessness leads to the kind of escape found in the authoritarian character, or to conforming in the process in which the isolated individual becomes an automaton, loses his self while at the same time conceives of himself as free."[161]

---

160  From the Weaver collection of letters, 1961–62.

161  Robert Hoopes, *Form and Thought in Prose*, ed. Wilfred H. Stone (New York: The Ronald Press Company, 1960), 199. Taken from an original reprint from *Escape from Freedom*, by Erich Fromm, 1941.

*This is revolutionary,* I think. It explains exactly what is happening to Negro people. White segregationists try to convince us that we exist only to do their bidding; try to keep us from thinking freely; definitely work to keep us under external authority (theirs), so that we do not establish an independent identity. They do everything to make us conform, to stay under their power. Why haven't I seen the condition of segregation this way before? I read until the dinner bell sounds, and then I go down to the first floor, where I eat with the rest of the girls. Afterward there's more study followed by bedtime.

Bert Gibson calls me every Tuesday on the public phone in the snack shop. Each week I sit there waiting to hear from him, hoping no one will come in and place a call from that phone before he can get through. Today the phone rings at exactly 2:00 p.m. as planned, and after we tell each other how much we miss each other, we talk about the movement and the Freedom Rides taking place across the South. I tell him I've received a *New York Times* article he sent from the September 10, 1961, edition. It is written by Martin Luther King Jr. and is called "The Time for Freedom Has Come." The words of King have always inspired me, stirred my longing to become part of something bigger than myself. Now that longing is becoming a determination to be among the students who make up the moral consciousness of the movement. I share these thoughts with him. Then we tell each other how much we love each other and say good-bye, but not before I promise to wait at this same phone booth next Tuesday, same time. I go over to the counter and order a cherry Coke from Anna Jo, who is there working. Then I head for my English class.

We have moved from Erich Fromm to Ortega y Gasset's *Revolt of the Masses.* The excerpt we are reading is titled, "The Illusion of Individuality."

While others in the class discuss it, I look out of the second-floor window and think, *I am part of the masses.* Gazing outside, I see for the first time "colored projects" across the street. I stare in disbelief at the street below. How could I have missed seeing them all these years? In all the time we've traveled back and forth to Atlanta I never knew the projects were so close to Spelman. Today, for the first time, I see poor Negro children playing in the colored world to which they've been consigned, and I realize it is a microcosm of the world of every southern Negro. The spontaneous feelings and genuine individuality to which the book refers have been suppressed in southern Negroes in order to maintain the status quo, and that suppression governed our lives until the Montgomery bus boycott began and changed everything. After the boycott came the Freedom Rides, and now through the student movement we've begun to let our suppressed feelings and individuality emerge. The demand for justice is spreading across the South, and as it does, I wonder if the children outside my classroom window will ever know what it means to embrace spontaneous feelings. I wonder what role I have in their freedom, what role I have in my own. Then it hits me. Like a bolt out of the blue, it hits me that if I let my chance to make a difference go by, I'll never be able to live with myself or face my children in years to come. What will I answer when they ask, "Mommy, where were you when Martin Luther King was marching?" I missed the opportunity to get involved at Tougaloo, but that won't happen again. Sitting in this classroom today, I know it won't be long before I join the foot soldiers of the movement here in Atlanta. I want to be more than just a student passing through. I want to make a difference. School can wait; the movement cannot. The sound of a bell brings me back to my classroom; I jot down the next class assignment.

I move on to French class, where I want to do well. Madame Thomas was Mother's French teacher back in the days when she was Mademoiselle Geter. I have grown up hearing about how Mademoiselle Geter was one of the very few Negroes who, during the Depression, had enough money to travel back and forth to France and return with stories of French markets and museums that whetted her students' appetites with a desire for travel.

As fall progresses, Anna Jo and I start to spend time at the student movement office on the second floor of Rush Memorial Baptist Church. Incredibly, the Reverend Joe Boone, a former football player for Dad, is pastor at Rush. I never cease to be amazed at the number of former track men and football and basketball players of my father's whose paths I cross.

The small two-story brick church building has a second-floor back-door entrance that leads to the movement offices that overlook the interior of the church below. The movement office comprises two rooms. We enter the larger one where meetings are held. Off to the left is a small room with files, a desk with a telephone, a radio, and a typewriter. The larger room also has a desk, with wire in and out baskets, and a telephone. A bulletin board on the wall opposite the door has newspaper articles about students involved in the movement. Couches and chairs rim the room. Photographs are on all the walls. In them, some people carry picket signs, some are behind bars, others are giving speeches at rallies. One photograph is from a *Time* magazine article that tells the story of a white boy who was beaten mercilessly during his participation in the Alabama Freedom Rides.[162] The photo has appeared

---

162 Quite possibly the photo is of James Peck, who received fifty stitches from a beating he took in Birmingham during the Freedom Rides in the summer of 1961.

in thousands of newspapers and shows blood flowing from the boy's head, a look of agony on his face.

On the bulletin board next to the door we have just entered is a corkboard with a copy of the US Constitution attached and a flyer titled, "Rules for Conduct While on Picket Lines." Between these two documents hangs a black-and-white picture of Georgia's two highest-ranking state officials and below them a photo from *Life* magazine of a circle of children from every land standing hand in hand against desert sands and a setting sun—an image of what the world *could* be. Several coeds are crowded together on a couch under the children's picture. On another sofa to their right beneath four curtain-covered windows sit three fellows. The rest of us are seated on chairs circled around the room—except for Charles Black, chairman of the Committee on Appeal for Human Rights (COAHR). He sits on a corner of the desk, wearing dark slacks, dress socks, dark shoes, and a white shirt with the sleeves rolled up. He is speaking to the assembled group I am taking in so much of my surroundings and the faces of fellow students that I hardly hear a word Charles says. The next thing I know we are standing, crossing our right hands over our left and holding onto the hands of students on either side, praying. Afterward we sing "We Shall Overcome." Every meeting will end this way.

Turning to leave, I bump into a young man who has been up and down answering the phone in the smaller office during the entire meeting. I say hi. He greets me too and says his name is Frank. I tell him my name and ask, "What's in the steel cabinets?" gesturing behind him.

"Those hold research materials and copies of all COAHR's documents—letters, notes, speeches—so each succeeding chairman will have as much information as possible when he takes over." This is one of two

Franks involved in COAHR. Frank Smith, whom I've just met, is often called "Smitty." The other Frank is Frank Holloway, often referred to as "Big Frank." I will learn that Smitty is an introspective person. His patient determination makes him seem more mature than the rest of us, in spite of his quiet sense of humor. Smitty is a junior at Morehouse and has such an infectious intensity about the work of the movement that it hooks others, getting them to participate, too. After that meeting, Anna Jo and I begin working afternoon shifts at the COAHR office, answering phones, typing, helping to plan demonstrations, and absorbing lessons in nonviolence and instructions for picketing.

**A GUIDE FOR PICKETS**

1. Remember that each individual participant in the picketing is required to remain disciplined, peaceful, and nonviolent at all times.

2. Picketers are to keep walking while on duty and are not to engage in discussion or debates with customers, store personnel, or passersby. They are not to block entrances or exits.

3. Everyone who participates in picketing pledges himself (sic) to abide by the decisions arrived at by the group. If he does not think he can abide by those decisions, he should withdraw from participation.

4. During the picketing project, every participant must take orders from the project leader or picket captain. All press inquiries and other questions should be directed to him, and he should be allowed to speak for the group. Should it be felt that he is not

performing his duty properly, objections should be raised at a review meeting and not at the scene of picketing.

5. Direct orders from police personnel are to be obeyed. Write down all particulars of this or any other incident as soon as possible, complete with such details of time and place, persons involved, etc. as are available. Submit your account as soon as you can to the office of the student movement.

6. If you should feel at any time that you are losing control of yourself during picket duty and cannot abide by the agreed-upon discipline, please notify the picket captain quietly and leave the picket line.

7. Every participant should understand that while things have generally gone smoothly, this may not always be the case. Picket(er)s may be abused verbally or physically and may be arrested. They should be prepared to accept arrest. The best way to be able to withstand verbal and physical abuse is to discipline oneself in advance for it and to keep in mind that the picketing project represents a cause greater than any individual.

8. All persons participating in the picketing must remain orderly and peaceful in acts and language. They should be as calm and relaxed as possible, knowing that they are fighting for their rights and are within their rights. It is also important that persons participating not be inappropriately dressed. All should be

clean and well-dressed and should speak and behave courteously even when exposed to great stress and strain.[163]

After an afternoon of work at the office, I walk back to the dorm with Anna Jo. I am impressed by the discipline and seriousness with which these students conduct themselves. Everyone in the meetings is quiet and respectful of Charles when he speaks, raising their hands to ask questions, politely listening to answers. No one interrupts, and few people carry on side conversations.

Back at the dorm, Spelman life is the focus again as Miss Taylor prepares officers of the dorm council for tomorrow's installation. All the officers, of which Anna Jo is one, are expected to wear black dresses, no jewelry, and little white caps, she informs them, and Miss Taylor will provide the caps. Tomorrow a white pillowcase will be placed on the back of each officer's chair to signify that she's being installed.

I wearily climb the stairs to my room and begin my homework, but before I do, I read the Oath to Nonviolence that was distributed at the meeting.

I, _____, willingly participate in the programs and activities of the Atlanta Committee on Appeal for Human Rights as a volunteer, of my own free will without coercion. I will adhere to the following six basic principles of nonviolence:

1. Nonviolence is not a method for cowards. The method is passive physically but strongly active spiritually. It is not passive resistance to evil, it is active nonviolent resistance to evil.

---

163 From the office of the Atlanta student movement, the Committee on Appeal for Human Rights, 236 Auburn Avenue NE. From the Russell C. Campbell Sr. collection of COAHR documents.

2. Nonviolence does not seek to defeat or humiliate the opponent, but to win his (sic) friendship. The aftermath of nonviolence is the creation of the beloved community, where(as) the aftermath of violence is tragic bitterness.

3. In nonviolence the attack is directed against the forces of evil rather than against the persons who happen to be doing the evil.

4. Nonviolent resistance is a willingness to accept suffering without retaliation, to accept blows from the opponent without striking back. If going to jail is necessary, the nonviolent resister enters it "as a bridegroom enters the bride's chambers."

5. Nonviolent resistance avoids not only external physical violence but also internal violence of spirit. At the center of nonviolence stands the principle of love. The nonviolent resister not only refuses to shoot his opponent but also refuses to hate him.

6. Nonviolent resistance is based on the conviction that the universe is on the side of justice. Consequently, the believer in nonviolence has deep faith in the future. This faith is another reason why the nonviolent resister can accept suffering without retaliation.[164]

As I put down the oath, I become aware of noise at the other end of the hall. Following the sounds, I find myself outside the

---

164  From the Russell C. Campbell, Sr. collection of COAHR documents.

door of Joann Merry where squeals of delight float out into the hall along with the strains of an Ahmad Jamal album. Joann almost always has a Jamal album playing. My roommate, Delores, looks up and invites me in to where she is sitting with three other girls playing bid whist. I join the game, which Mother and Dad taught Rosemary and me when we were very young, as soon as the losers get up. Bid whist will become one of my several outlets this semester as I get to know these girls who play cards, smoke cigarettes, and manage to sneak in a bottle of vodka once in a while to mix with orange juice. Tonight I relax from the work at the movement office by playing cards and smoking, and I establish my reputation as one who can hang with the best of them. Maybe what it took all along was for me to take the first step.

# CHAPTER 23

# WE SHALL OVERCOME[165]

A NNA JO AND I are spending more and more time between Canterbury House and Rush Memorial Church at the office of the Committee on Appeal for Human Rights. In the fall of 1961, the COAHR (pronounced koar) organization is barely a year old. It was formed the previous spring when students from the Atlanta University Center came together to protest segregated facilities in the city. Lonnie King, Julian Bond, and Joseph Pierce had called the group together for the protest, but presidents of the AU (Atlanta University) Center colleges were not pleased with the planned demonstration and urged the students to concentrate on their studies instead. Dr. Harry Richardson of the Interdenominational Theological Center felt the students were right, as did Dr. Cunningham of Morris Brown. That is when Dr. Rufus Clement, president of Atlanta University, suggested that the students lay out their grievances to help others to understand why they needed to move their plans forward. He promised to raise money to pay for an ad that listed their grievances in major Atlanta newspapers. Following

---

165 Original words and lyrics by the Reverend Charles Tindley, 1903.

his advice, students put a document together called, "An Appeal for Human Rights." According to Lonnie King, Rosalyn Polk authored much of the appeal, and after it was published Lonnie suggested three students from each AU school comprise the council of COAHR.

The students from Spelman were Marian Wright, Rosalyn Pope, and Josephine Jackson. From Morehouse they were Julian Bond, Albert Brinson, and Don Clark. James Felder, Benjamin Brown, and Lydia Tucker represented Clark College. Mary Ann Smith, Robert Schley, and William Hickmon were the representatives from Morris Brown College. Johnny Parham, Willie Mays, and John Mack were from Atlanta University. The Reverend Marion D. Bennett, Otis Moss, and James Wilbon came from the Interdenominational Theological Center. After presenting their platform, two hundred students sat in at ten downtown restaurants to protest racial segregation. Seventy-six of them were arrested and then released on bail.[166]

Anna Jo and I become active in COAHR in the fall of 1961. By that time, Morehouse founders Julian Bond and Lonnie King are coordinating COAHR's work with that of other student organizations; student activities are being supported by some professors who consider participation in demonstrations a "living civics lesson." Other professors want to make sure we finish college while participating in historic change and will support us only if we keep our grades up; otherwise, they say, they cannot back what we are doing. Of course we all think we can participate in the movement and keep our grades up, too, and some like Ruby Doris Smith (a senior) do exactly that. Most of us, however, discover that we cannot do both, and many opt for the movement

---

166 From an interview with Lonnie King, founding member of the Committee on Appeal for Human Rights, February 3, 2012, Atlanta, GA.

over school. This eventually forces many of us who made that choice to make up our courses in summer school or take additional years to finish college.

One day a special meeting is called at the COAHR office to discuss possible steps to be taken against the local public hospital, Grady Memorial. Chairman Charles Black, a senior at Morehouse, sits on the edge of the desk (his usual perch) in the larger outer office and tells us that a little Negro boy was rushed to Grady Memorial hospital for treatment but was denied care because his mother had taken him into the "white" emergency room when she saw that the "colored" emergency room was filled. Doctors in the white section refused to treat the child, and he died.

Suddenly I'm transported back to Mississippi in 1955, when hospital authorities refused to send the ambulance they used for white people to get Howard, my first love, as he lay dying. Sitting here now, I'm hit with the fact that this is a symptom of an evil that will continue to occur unless someone does something soon. That's when I know I'll do anything in my power to bring about change at Grady Memorial. Enough Howards, enough little Negro boys have died at the hands of racist hospitals.

Charles is drawing his talk to a close. "COAHR asked Ruby Doris to go to the hospital to see what kind of action we should take to protest the death," Charles says.

Ruby Doris Smith (no relation to Frank) offers her assessment. "The hospital is overcrowded, especially the area for Negroes, and the doctors are overworked. They're harassed and prejudiced against the Negro patients they're taking care of. In addition to the two emergency rooms, there are two clinics—one for whites and one for Negroes. I suggest we start by picketing outside the hospital."

"Thank you, Ruby D." This is what Ruby Doris is often called. "The floor is open for questions and discussion."

We agree that we can't boycott a hospital, especially one that treats poor people; we can't sit in, either, because sick people have to be able to receive treatment. But we can take Ruby Doris's suggestion and picket outside, drawing attention to what is happening inside. Hands pop up all over the room as students vie for the opportunity to share ideas. Someone says we have to make sure demonstrators understand the difference between picketing and boycotting. Picketing should make a statement that alerts people to the injustices taking place inside the hospital. Maybe it will get the attention of lawyers, who can go through legal channels to ensure every patient has the right to fair treatment. The meeting ends with a decision to picket Grady Memorial the following day, and then everyone stands for prayer and the singing of "We Shall Overcome."

The next day, Anna Jo and I are among the students who go to the hospital to picket. It is my first experience on a picket line, and in the beginning, it seems easy. All I have to do is walk and keep quiet. The pace is moderate, so we won't get tired and so our signs can be read. The boys march at both ends of the line, alternating boy, girl, boy, girl to protect the girls if we are attacked. Slowly we are becoming a cohesive group that feels the need to take care of one another.

A couple of hours into the picketing, my legs start to get heavy. I feel as if I'm climbing a sand dune and going nowhere, but the thought of another mother with a dead son keeps me going. After four hours, the leader takes off his sign and says it's quitting time. I fall into a car with Smitty at the wheel and am driven with other students to within a few blocks of the Spelman campus. We get out here, because we're not allowed to ride in cars without permission, so we walk the rest of the way to school. Back on campus, I drag myself up two flights of stairs to my room before falling across my bed fully clothed and falling asleep. I awake in the middle of the night and change out of my clothes into pajamas.

Other demonstrations have taken place in the city that week in November, too. One was at Dinkler Plaza, where Secretary of Defense Robert McNamara was scheduled to speak. Many white Democratic Party leaders were gathering, but Negro Democratic leaders were left out, and the NAACP objected. In another part of the city, a small mixed group of students attended a movie together. A white person bought the tickets, then Negroes walked up, and everyone went inside.[167]

Anna Jo and I continue to put in long hours at the COAHR office, returning to campus just in time for her to race to her job serving food in the dining room and me to try to get some homework done before dinner and sleep. She and I travel to and from the church together so much that Smitty dubs us soul mates.

Diving deeper into the fervor of the movement, I lose track of time, my studies, and my homework assignments, but I still manage to make decent grades. Bert's special-delivery letters and weekly phone calls arrive with such regularity that I feel guilty when participation in the movement keeps me from writing him back immediately.

Another Tuesday arrives, and he calls me on the public phone in the snack shop.

"Hi, honey, I really miss you. I can't wait to see you next month and hold you in my arms again," he says.

"I miss you, too," I confess. "I can't wait to see you, either." Of all the boys I've ever dated, Bert makes me feel as if I'm the most special person

---

167 From Anna Jo Weaver Scruton, Weaver/Scruton collection of letters from Spelman, 1961–62.

in the world. He and Mike Peters are planning to come to Tougaloo for the Christmas holidays, and now he's telling me of those plans.

"Mike Peters's mother called me last night to ask when I'm planning to go down. I told her I'm not sure but will let her know as soon as possible. She told me it will be difficult making reservations if we wait too long, so I'll have to look into it soon. I don't know when Mike wants to come down, but the best time for me would be around the twenty-second."

"The twenty-second will be great. I can't wait to be in your arms again."

He says he's read a *New York Times* article that he is sending me. It has photographs of the first white students to integrate Tougaloo College. I tell him about the picketing we are doing at Grady Memorial. Then we say good-bye.

Mother and Dad arrive in Atlanta just before Thanksgiving, bringing with them the Tougaloo basketball team, which has come to play Morehouse. Tougaloo loses the game, but girls from Spelman gather around Rosemary and me behind the Tougaloo bench to find out the names of the cute Tougaloo players.

Thanksgiving with Madre and Papa is gone in a flash, and we are back at school plugging away at our studies. Seeing Mother and Dad for such a short time makes me realize how much I've missed them. Just as I start to feel homesick, Mother writes.

*Dear Nell,*

*So good to see you! Sorry we didn't bring you a victory, but I think we did give you some cause for pride. No doubt the fellows were tired from their long trip and game the night before. Perhaps we ask too much of our bodies sometimes...*

*Have you decided on your (Christmas) gift for Bert? What would you like to do in the way of entertainment when he is visiting with us? We want to make plans so that we ensure his good time as well as yours. Will check on dates that other schools close so that we can figure on the presence of other friends during the holidays...*

*Hope you continue to be happy in the work and your location as this is of deep and genuine concern to me, always. (Also) hope I may get to Canterbury House on some of our visits to the city. It is one of the "new" additions to the system. Know you are grateful to find an opportunity for worship so near and convenient. This is always an important factor in one's spiritual life. Hope you enjoy reading,* The Life of Jesus, *(by) Renan. At some time you may want to discuss it with Fr. Scott during your "Radical Hour" sessions.*

*We are looking forward to your homecoming Christmas. Glad you have as long as you do, so that you may rest and accomplish some of the things you may wish to do on your own. There are always some personal things that we need to do for ourselves but which we might neglect when we are busy with a full schedule...*

*Have always enjoyed your letters and the talks we get a chance to have from time to time. I consider myself very fortunate to have you lovely girls and to have the privilege to share your thoughts, plans, and experiences. Life has richer meaning when our memories are full, meaningful, and frequently happy...I am pulling for you and know that you will continue to do well.*

*Love you always,*
*Mother*

It is early December. The evenings are clear and cold. Early darkness has already settled in by four o'clock. I breathe deeply and see my breath like a mist in front of me. The trees have changed, and girls have pulled winter coats out of their closets and are wearing them again. The East African country of Tanganyika[168] has gained its independence. I take notice and (in my mind) add it to the growing list of freedom struggles being won on the African continent. For a brief moment, I think back to the conversations Judy, Gus, Joel, Manny, Peggy, and I had about African independence during the summer we sat in Al's Seafood Bar in the Catskills, and I vow to use the successes taking place in Africa to fuel my efforts here in the States.

A couple of weeks pass before Rosemary and I are at home welcoming Bert and Mike to Mississippi. On the way down from New York, they stopped and spent a night in Atlanta with Madre and Papa, where they were taken on a tour of the Spelman campus even though it is closed for the holidays.

During their stay in Mississippi, we barnstorm the state with Daddy and the basketball team. When we return home, we host a Christmas party, so friends at Tougaloo and in Jackson can meet our visitors. It is so good to be with Bert again—to feel excitement at the touch of his hand, my heart racing each time we kiss.

On Christmas morning, I awaken to the sounds of Nat King Cole. Getting out of bed, I clean up, get into slacks and a sweater, and then join the family, Bert, and Mike around the tree to open presents. Breakfast soon follows with orange juice, eggs, bacon, grits, and Mother's homemade cinnamon rolls. When the dishes are done, Rosemary, Mother, and I begin preparing dinner in the kitchen. Bert and Dad watch football games on

---

168  Known today as Tanzania.

TV, and Mike keeps up constant chatter as he moves between the kitchen and the living room. In the late afternoon we get dressed for dinner and sit down to a scrumptious turkey. Stuffed to the gills, we clear the table and gather in front of the television to watch Dickens's *A Christmas Carol.*

When New Year's Eve arrives, Rosemary, Mike, Bert, and I attend a reception at the home of friends and then return to our home in time to turn on the television. We join Mother and Dad for eggnog and watch the ball drop in Times Square. A couple of days later we are at the Masonic Temple in Jackson at the first public dance Mother and Dad have ever allowed us to attend. Back at Tougaloo, we take Bert and Mike around the Tougaloo campus pointing out areas of interest. Bert and I never seem to have enough time when we're together, and this trip is no different. The two weeks he and Mike are in Mississippi fly by, and before long it is time for them to return home. At the airport we share a kiss before I watch his and Mike's plane ascend into the sky. As tears fill my eyes, Daddy looks into my face, puts his arm around my shoulder, and says, "If it's real, it will last." I nod.

Returning to Spelman, Rosemary and I discover that new girls have been added to the glee club we sing in. They have all come from Albany State College, and because of their participation in the NAACP/SNCC student sit-in at the Albany bus terminal, they have been expelled from school. Albany receives government funding, so the administration has buckled to Georgia state officials who are determined to punish the students for the stand they have taken against segregation. Spelman, being a private school, welcomes the expelled students. The student everyone gets to know immediately is Bernice Johnson, whose beautiful contralto voice adds incredible texture and richness to our glee club and eventually to the work that we are involved in at COAHR.

On Sunday, Anna Jo and I go to Canterbury House for worship and to participate in the theological debates that take place there. Anna Jo writes home describing one of those debates. "At Canterbury House this morning, they served breakfast...and two men from the Black Muslim movement spoke to us. They were interesting and very adept at side-stepping questions. In the evening some of us went back, and they were still there going strong. Everyone was arguing against them, but that didn't make any difference."[169]

I am amazed at how much Father Scott exposes us to different points of view during Canterbury House's "Radical Hour." So many of these debates help shape our thoughts on civil disobedience and clarify our commitment to nonviolence. He's not like any priest I've ever known, and because of his tolerance and openness, he is respected by a lot of students in the Atlanta University system, not just the Episcopalians.

On Sunday night I go down to the basement of my dorm and discover my bid whist buddies washing clothes and using an illegal hot plate to straighten their hair. Anna Jo is down here, too, asking to have her already straight hair curled with the hot curlers. One of the girls obliges her, and the rest of us take this well-scrubbed Mennonite girl and apply her first mascara, eye shadow, lipstick, and nail polish. Over the next few months we will gather in the basement on a regular basis to laugh, talk, "fry" our hair, and experiment with makeup. And since all of us are over five feet seven inches tall, we call ourselves the "Sisters of the Sky."

Back at the movement office, a number of COAHR members decide it is time to enter the white clinic at Grady Hospital and apply for hospital cards. Since Grady is a charity hospital, everyone who applies for a

---

169 From Anna Jo Weaver Scruton, Weaver/Scruton collection of letters from Spelman, January 6, 1962.

card must be investigated to discover whether or not they can afford to pay for services. When we arrive to apply for cards, we are all refused service. But for reasons we never figure out, two Negro boys are given appointments for the following week.

The following day, January 9, we return to Grady and surround the counter for five hours. No progress is made with hospital personnel regarding the cards we want, and hospital personnel do everything in their power to ignore us while making conversation with one another.

That night between the hours of seven and ten, Anna Jo and I go to three different dormitories on campus to give a brief rundown of the incident at Grady and ask anyone who is willing to picket or stand in at the clinic the following week to sign up. Many of the kids we talk to don't want to risk being arrested.[170] That's when we decide to go to the freshman dorm to try to get volunteers. In doing so, we know full well that we're in violation of the rule prohibiting first-year students from participating in movement activities, but we need bodies. Some of the freshman girls are afraid to sign up, but others really want to be part of the movement. The more I talk with those willing to sign up, the guiltier I feel. I sign them up anyway and hope this will be more of a one-time demonstration for them than a longer commitment. By ten o'clock (the time we have to be back in our dorm), Anna Jo and I have two lists—one for picketers, and one for people willing to enter the clinic. At the other AU colleges, students are signing up volunteers, too, with the hope that together we'll have the fifty or more students we feel we need for the demonstration. We leave the "Guide for Pickets" with small groups of students and return to our dorm to make a graph of the names we have collected, the time of participation, and the dorm

---

170 Ibid.

of each volunteer. That way we can be sure we have enough people for the hours that we need to cover at Grady Memorial Hospital. After we enter the dorm and sign in, I go up to my room and get a yellow notepad as well as the stuffed tiger Bert has sent me. Then I return to Anna Jo's room so we can make a schedule of participants for the next day, but we are so exhausted from the demonstration at Grady and from going from dorm to dorm all evening that the two of us fall asleep on her bed—I holding my stuffed tiger, and Anna Jo holding a teddy bear. Later that night, Anna Jo's roommate, Joyce White, comes in and can't resist taking a photograph of the two of us. Many years later when I see the photo, I remember how strong and in charge we felt back then. Yet for all our bravado, as the photograph attests we were still kids sleeping with stuffed animals in our arms.

ANNA JO AND NELL 1962 (COURTESY OF ANNA JO SCRUTON)

We go through another day of demonstrations at Grady Memorial Hospital before the temperature in Atlanta drops to eighteen degrees, and snow covers everything. The archaic rules governing Spelman have once again gotten to be too much for Anna Jo, and she bundles up and walks off campus. For the same reason, I have called Madre and am spending a few days with Papa and her. Sometimes on days like this I take Anna Jo to my grandparents' home for dinner, but Spelman won't let her spend the night. When Anna Jo returns to the campus, the fun of being out in the snow has already begun for the girls. She later writes home to her parents about it.

*I was in one of my spells of being sick of this place with its rules and regulations, so I bundled up and walked off campus. When I got back people were running around screaming and shouting and laughing...We had to come in by 10:00 (p.m.) of course, and then people were running up and down the halls...They were so excited. Then Miss Taylor put this little notice on the bulletin.* "Girls, please do not go out and play in the snow in the morning. You are inviting a spell of illness if you do. Please be sensible and obey this request. Stay in and study if there is no school tomorrow. It will profit you more." *And then at the bottom of the page in smaller print,* "...demerits for playing in snow."

*As it turned out, they did close school for today, and the dean sent a notice saying we could play in the snow and that there would be no classes and that we could wear slacks on campus... When we went outside, (Miss Taylor) said,* "Now girls, just stay out about fifteen minutes. Come back in soon, and don't fight with the Morehouse young men." *Very easy for her to say, very difficult for her to enforce; we tore into each other first of all and then into the Morehouse guys when they came over and had a frenzy of a battle between Morehouse and Spelman on Spelman's campus, while keeping Clark College on their side of the street at the same time. We were at it for several hours—fifteen minutes, don't fight with the Morehouse men. My face got washed so many times— scoured, I should say—that I think they took the epidermis off; such a riot of fun. My cheeks look like beets. Everyone who sees me laughs. I scrubbed a good many faces myself. Some girls really got it. The boys scrubbed snow into their hair until it was absolutely white, and once in their hair, the snow didn't shake out. Their hair got all nappy but everyone was uproariously happy...Every time a Morgan Hall girl would see another we'd chant, "Demerits for playing in the snow" and then throw a snowball."*[171]

The cold spell continues for the remainder of the week, slowing down our demonstrations at Grady Memorial and ensuring that some of us (like me) return to our classes and try to catch up with the work we've fallen behind on. A week or so later the weather has gotten warmer, the snow has mostly melted, and a small group of COAHR members are back at the office answering telephones and planning nonviolent training meetings. Picketers outside Grady Memorial are keeping a steady pace, while those inside are challenging the segregation policies. Entering the white side of the clinic with Anna Jo, I pass a picket sign that catches my eye. It says, "Health is too precious to be Jim Crowed." A small group of us enters the white clinic and approaches the desk to ask for clinic cards. The receptionist ignores us. We sit and read our

---

171 From Anna Jo Weaver Scruton, Weaver/Scruton collection of letters from Spelman, January 10, 1962.

school books, taking note of the occasional white person who enters the reception area to get a hospital card and is given one. Meanwhile, in the crowded colored clinic—which is on the other side of the receptionist's area and which we can see—Negroes are straining to see what we are doing in the white area.

While we sit reading, a chubby white security guard strolls in from another area inside the hospital. He is holding a billy stick in his hand. "All right, you niggers, I'll give you to the count of ten to get outta here!"

Anna Jo and I hold each other's hands in a viselike grip as he begins his count.

"One...two...three..."

*Be cool,* I say to myself.

"Four...five...six...seven..."

"Don't move," Anna Jo whispers through clenched teeth.

"Eight...nine...ten!"

As if on cue, every student rises to face him.

"You miserable..." He turns and walks back down the hall. I don't know if someone called him to put us out or not, but I am relieved that he doesn't have any backup with him and therefore returns to the place he has come from. Danny Mitchell (vice chairman of COAHR) says we've made our point, and the picketers outside are knocking off. It is four thirty by the clinic clock, so we leave, too, and are driven back to the COAHR office for a short meeting before returning to our respective schools.

The following morning I rise, get dressed, skip breakfast, and race off to my advanced English composition class. I breeze through it and two other classes before grabbing a hamburger and cherry Coke and heading off to the movement office. Anna Jo and I arrive about the same time and find the place nearly empty. Several carloads of students have already been taken to the hospital, and we are directed to the last car bound for Grady. At the meeting in the COAHR office the previous night, we decided to change our tactics inside the clinic. Anna Jo has volunteered to be our "guinea pig" and apply for a clinic card first. If she's successful in getting one, the rest of us will try to get one, too. If they ignore those of us who are Negro or turn us away, we'll have a case of discrimination, because they will have given a card to the white member of our group.

Jumping into the waiting car, Anna Jo says, "It doesn't matter if we can use the cards or not. What matters is whether we get service. If everybody gets cards, we'll know other Negroes can get them from that side, too."

Danny Mitchell interrupts. "Listen, if you go in there today, you may be arrested."

Neither Anna Jo nor I respond. The car we're in pulls to the curb in front of Grady, and we get out. Charles Black is back at the office waiting by the phone to receive updates from Danny, ready to call other civil rights organizations that will get us lawyers if we are arrested.

Smitty leads a dozen of us into the white clinic room. Everyone takes a seat as Anna Jo approaches the receptionist's desk. The receptionist today seems more prepared for us than some of the previous ones, because she allows Anna Jo to fill out forms and gives her a number before telling her to take a seat until her number is called. While Anna Jo waits, a Negro boy in our group goes to the desk to ask for a card. He is ignored. The rest of us approach the desk to ask for cards, too, but we are all ignored.

Anna Jo approaches the receptionist and asks, "Have you run out of numbers?"

"No, ma'am," the receptionist responds.

"Then why have you refused to give numbers to my friends?"

The woman behind the desk gives Anna Jo a cold, hard stare just as a television crew arrives and starts filming. Smitty, who has been appointed spokesman, answers questions from reporters, explaining that we are here at Grady to protest the segregated clinic rooms. He responds to a battery of additional questions before we all leave.

That evening after dinner, Anna Jo and I enter the small TV room in our dorm to watch news coverage of the picketing outside Grady and the demonstration inside. As we watch cameras zoom in on the two of us inside the clinic, the pay phone down the hall rings.

"Phone call for Nell Braxton!" a dorm mate yells.

I leave the TV room and go to pick up the dangling phone. Madre's worried voice is on the other end. She has just seen the news, too, and she is distraught. She begs me not to go to the hospital again, telling me it's too dangerous. She says she doesn't know what she'll do if she turns on the television and sees my brains splattered across the sidewalk.

I've always done what my grandmother wanted me to do. She is one of the best friends I've ever had, a kindred spirit, the person who, as a nine-year-old, I didn't want to live without. She's always been present for me in every way. Now she's asking me to make a promise I can't keep—to leave the demonstrations. It is the only time in my life that I've disobeyed her. I tell her how sorry I am to be causing her worry, but I can't promise to stop working for the movement. We tell each other good-bye and hang up. I go back to the TV room to let Anna Jo know I'm going upstairs. In my room I fall across the bed. I've finally stood up for the things I believe in, but in doing so I've caused Madre heartache and worry.

On January 15, there is a nationwide student protest against nuclear testing in Washington, DC. That same day, students are arrested at Grady Hospital for disturbing the peace. At the time of the arrests at Grady, Anna Jo and I are in class, and by the time we get to the COAHR office, the arrested students have been released. Our picketing there continues.

The weeks grind on, and the demonstrations at Grady continue. By Sunday I am exhausted, and I decide to cut chapel and sleep until the afternoon. When my alarm clock sounds, I struggle to move my aching body to an upright position and head to the communal show- ers next door where the blast of water shocks me awake. Pellets beat into my tired muscles like prickly massage pins as I lather my body with soap. I return to my room, get dressed, and go outside to sit in the tranquility of the afternoon solitude. I'm still there when students pour out of chapel, and a large bell starts to ring. Everybody seems to be walking toward the center of the campus so I follow, curious to see what is happening. There, near the Spelman arches, a large group has gathered.

A Morehouse man is climbing onto a wooden crate and shouting through a megaphone, "Jim Crow is dead!"

A crush of students crowd around him as he takes on the air of an old-time evangelistic preacher. "Dearly beloved," he begins. "We have gathered here today to bury a sinner by the name of Jim Crow. Jim was born almost ninety years ago and grew up in the Southland, where he thrived. As the years passed he moved north, east, and west, despite feeble attempts to keep him down. He took over schools and parks, libraries, lunch counters, restrooms, buses, trains, jobs, hospitals, and even drinking fountains."

Shouts of "Lord have *mercy!*" and "Umph, umph, umph," arise from the crowd. One student (impersonating a deacon) helps a "sister of the congregation" so "overcome with grief" that she "nearly faints." Another female student pretends to sob hysterically as "church elders" work to revive her, fanning white handkerchiefs near her face.

The "preacher" continues: "In 1954, Jim was arrested and sentenced to life imprisonment by the Supreme Court, but he escaped and changed his name. Alias Jim Crow took on the identity of relatives like the Ku Klux Klan and continued to inflict injustice with numerous hangings and lynchings in the South. Mack Parker and Emmett Till were two of the lives he mercilessly snuffed out."

The response from the gathered students is growing louder now. "Preach, brother, preach! Tell the story!" Everyone seems caught up in the drama, seeking to make it an old-fashioned revival-like experience.

"Today," the preacher continues, "at nine o'clock, Jim Crow passed away."

"Oh Lord!" a mocking member of the crowd cries out as a giant black-and-white cardboard crow is raised and set ablaze.

"Ashes to ashes. Dust to dust. In human minds he was born, and in human minds he dies."

Shouts and applause follow and then singing. "Oh, Mary, Don't You Weep, Don't You Mourn."

Once the crow is burned, the crowd disperses as quickly as it gathered.

Sometime near January 20, a group of Negro teachers and students go downtown to the Georgia State Capitol Building where the state legislature is meeting. The galleries have been integrated for a year, but the group is put out for sitting in the "wrong place." A few days later, a large group of students marches downtown. That leads to "a law being passed making it unlawful to picket on or adjacent to state property."[172] There's no way we're going to sit quietly with an injunction like that hanging over our heads, so we return to the COAHR office to plan a mass protest.

---

172 Ibid.

# CHAPTER 24

# MY MIND ON FREEDOM[173]

O N MONDAY, FEBRUARY 12, over a hundred Negro students from the five universities that make up the Atlanta
University Center complex get into formation to begin a march to
the state capitol building, many are still revved up from the mock
burial of Jim Crow at Spelman on the previous Sunday. I move down
the middle of the street between Anna Jo and Joycelyn McKissick
in a group of eight abreast singing songs of freedom. We are the
group from COAHR. On this relatively warm February day, I'm
wearing a white blouse and cardigan sweater with a straight navy-
blue skirt and comfortable flat walking shoes. If I strain my neck I
can see my childhood playmate, Jimmy "Tex" Murray, leading the
marchers as we sing:

> Walkin' and talkin' with my mind stayed on freedom
> Walkin' and talkin' with my mind stayed on freedom

---

173 "My Mind on Freedom" was taken from a Gospel call-and-response hymn, "Woke
Up This Morning with My Mind on Jesus," written by Mississippi Fred McDowell.
The original words were adapted to meet the hopes of the civil rights movement.

# My Mind on Freedom

*Walkin' and talkin' with my mind stayed on freedom*
*Hallelu, hallelu, hallelujah*[174]

Every group of six lines of students has two captains on either side to keep us moving in orderly formation. They relay information—like which songs to sing—that comes back via individual runners from the front lines. News trucks crawl along beside us, carrying photographers on flatbeds clicking their cameras continuously. The captains leading our section move with a sense of purpose, answering questions and sharing information as to how close to the capitol we are. The two young men to our right are too self-assured to be freshmen, I say to myself, and as unsure as I am of my sophomore self, I don't think they are second-year students, either. From their composure I suspect they are juniors. One is a cute Johnny Mathis lookalike, the other a handsome broad-shouldered fellow with a wholesome look. Both are wearing dark slacks, sports jackets, and oxford shirts with the collars open—the Morehouse "uniform." Someone in front begins a new song, "Keep Your Hand on the Plow, Hold On," followed by "Oh Freedom!" We've changed the last line of "Oh Freedom" from "And before I'd be a slave, I'll be buried in my grave and go home to my lord and be free" to "...and before I'll be a slave, I'll be buried in my grave, and I'll *fight* for my *right* to be free." Our voices grow stronger with every verse, and so do we. We feel unstoppable. Arriving at the state capitol, students at the head of the march turn left at the corner (across the street from the capitol building) and lead us away from the capitol around that block and back again. When we come back to the corner facing the capitol, Julian, Smitty, and Danny are passing out signs for us to carry and whispering

---

174  Ibid.

encouraging words. I can hardly hear them. I'm looking beyond where they are to the other side of the street—the side in front of the state capitol where thirty or forty policemen stand in full regalia. Some have their hands on their pistols; others hold billy sticks. Vicious dogs are barking and straining at the leash, and a mob of angry whites is hurling insults and racial epithets.

Smitty brings my attention back when he shoves a sign in my hand and says, "Take the sign and march on *this* side of the street unless some other decision is made." I take the sign and keep marching, wondering what *other* decision might be made. I have come to march to the capitol. That's all. Up front, Bernice Johnson begins a new song, and I join in as much to build up my courage as to be part of the group. We march around the block across from the capitol again. As my section of demonstrators nears the corner once more, I see a small group of students standing off to the side with Smitty. Coming near to them I hear Smitty say, "Some of us are going to cross the street and try to gain access to the capitol. If you are willing to go with us, step out of line."

Anna Jo and I keep walking and singing. I'm not prepared to face the angry mob across the street, and I don't think she is, either. I've witnessed worse mobs than this one on television, but I've never seen one face-to-face. Besides, today all I've come to do is sing and demonstrate the way we've been doing at Grady Hospital, not to gain access to the capitol. Our section of demonstrators rounds the block again. I feel shaky as we approach Smitty and his small group for the second time.

Suddenly a white woman in the mob spots Anna Jo and yells, "Look at that nigger-lover!"

People behind her take the cue and begin to chant, "Nigger-lover! Nigger-lover! Nigger-lover!"

Immediately a host of accusations fly at us from every direction. "We don't need no northun' agitators down here!"

"Goddamn niggers! Why don't you go back to Africa?"

What in the world am I doing here? The air is charged with hatred, the mob is yelling obscenities, cops seem ready to let the dogs go, debris is starting to fly, students are marching and singing freedom songs, and in the midst of the confusion my mind takes me a thousand miles away to New York City. Will I ever see Bert again? Ever feel his kiss and gentle touch, ever hear his voice again? I want to marry him and have his children, but will that ever happen either? I'm nineteen years old. Is this the way my life is going to end? Immediately I feel guilty for thinking about myself at a time like this. Negro children have already died—the little boy at Grady, Emmett Till, and all those names I'll never know. But *I* don't want to die. There's so much I want to do with my life. But if I don't go across the street today, what'll I tell my children when they ask me where I was when Martin Luther King was marching?

So it's come down to this—come down to putting my life on the line if that's what this turns out to be. I think about the freedom I've experienced in New York and the oppression I've felt each year returning to Mississippi. I think of all the children—some right outside my English class at Spelman—who will never know that kind of freedom if someone doesn't take a stand. Negro children in the South *have* to experience what I've felt at Camp Woodland, and I know the only way for them to do that is for me to cross the street. One day my children have to have that freedom, too, if I live long enough to have children; if I don't, somebody's children have to experience it. My grandparents have done their part to advance the cause for freedom. My parents are doing theirs. Now it's my turn. I think of the promise Rosemary and

I made to Mrs. Bethune a decade ago—a promise to make the world a better place for the children who come after us.

Anna Jo squeezes my hand and answers the question I've almost forgotten. "We're willing," she says. *We?* I think, but I stop myself midthought. If she's willing to face what these white people may do to her, how can I say no? This is what I've been working toward since I joined the movement. I just thought I'd be braver when the time came. I nod my head. I don't hear a word of Danny's instructions as we start to cross the street.

Suddenly we are blocked by a police captain who I later learn from a newspaper account is J. L. Moseley.

"Why can't we cross the street?" Charles Black asks.

"Look right over my shoulder and you'll see why," Moseley replies.

Across the street stand thirty state troopers. "We don't want anything to happen that will reflect on you or on the city," Moseley continues as he walks beside us. When reporters question him later about diverting our march, he says he did it because "we obviously had a condition today that was tense."[175]

At this point Charles Black and James Forman, who have been walking with us, step aside and attempt to speak to Colonel Connor, who is head of the State Department for Public Safety, but they are redirected by an Atlanta policeman and sent to a Georgia Bureau of Investigation man who produces an executive order from the governor. Charles and Jim read the order and bring it back to our small group, which is now across from the capitol building on the steps of a church, where the bells are tolling.

---

175 *The Atlanta Constitution*, February 1962. From the Russell C. Campbell Sr. collection of COAHR material.

After reading the order to us, Charles says, "The adjectives used here do not apply to us. Now, who is ready to cross the street?"

We all raise our hands, but Captain Moseley blocks us again. Looking at the people across the street where the capitol building is, then past them to the capitol itself, he refers to the politicians inside the building. "All they want to do is get elected...It's not good for Atlanta for you to go over there."

"Some of us still want to go across the street," Charles Black responds.

The captain reluctantly escorts us across but warns, "There won't be a lot of conversation over there like there is over here. You'll be arrested pretty quickly."[176]

As we begin to move forward, James Forman asks Captain Moseley, "Is this suggesting that we as people can't walk across the street just because we're of a different complexion?" Forman's question is never answered. We cross the street and are blocked by a phalanx of state troopers when we reach the capitol steps. Charles Black climbs the steps while troopers hold the rest of us at bay. At the top of the stairs, he takes out a prepared statement to read and then responds to a barrage of questions from reporters. Afterward he descends the steps and leads our small group back across the street where the mass of demonstrators disperse. Those of us who crossed the street get into the cars that Julian and Frank have driven, and we head back to the movement office.

At Rush Memorial Church, we climb the back steps and assemble inside the office to decide what to do next.

"The police knew we were going to hold a demonstration today, so they were prepared to keep us from getting into the capitol. The only

---

176 Ibid.

way we're going to get inside is to go when they're not expecting us," Danny offers.

"Okay," Charles responds. Then he lays out the plans we've already made for tomorrow. "Some people are signed up to go back to Grady tomorrow, and the city knows we're going to keep that going. So it seems like a good strategy is for a small group to go back to the capitol and try to get into the legislative chambers while the Grady demonstration is going on."

"I'll go back to Grady," Anna Jo volunteers.

"Me, too," Joycelyn says. Danny says he'll go there, too, because he's been one of the spokesmen at that site.

"I'll drive whoever's willing to go back to the capitol," Smitty offers.

"I'll go," Ralph Moore volunteers.

"Me, too. Me, too. I'll go, too." In addition to Ralph the list grows to include Leo Meadows, Larry Fox, Ruby Doris Smith, Russell Campbell, Billy Mitchell, Frank Holloway, me, and one or two more. Charles, our chairman, says he will stay at the office in case we're arrested, so he can work on getting lawyers for us and deal with the media. When the meeting ends, we form our usual circle, join hands, say a prayer, and sing, "We Shall Overcome."

I walk back to Spelman more fearful than excited about the day ahead, because I can still see the hatred on the faces of the angry whites we left at the state capitol earlier in the day. When we return tomorrow, we'll be a much smaller group—isolated, vulnerable, exposed. I climb the stairs to my room and flop across my bed surrounded by the sounds of dormitory life down the hall.

"Myrtis!" someone yells. "Phone call!"

"I need to borrow a curling iron," another voice calls out. A blast of water from one of the stalls in the showers next to my room hits the shower wall. Squeals erupt from winners of a whist game farther down the hall.

I pull myself up from the bed and close my door. The need to study crosses my mind, but then I ask, *What for? I'm not going to be in class tomorrow anyway. I'll be at the capitol.* I lie across my bed again. Lying here alone, I can finally admit I'm scared, but this is something I can't let anyone else know. Everyone else seems so sure of the decision they've made, so strong in their commitment. I search through my books of Negro poets for a poem or a piece of prose from which to draw the courage I need to face tomorrow. After nearly half an hour I find what I'm looking for: Claude McKay's "If We Must Die."

> *If we must die, let it not be like hogs hunted and penned in an inglorious spot while round us bark and mad and hungry dogs, making their mock at our accursed lot.*
>
> *If we must die, O let us nobly die, so that our precious blood may not be shed in vain; then even the monsters we defy shall be constrained to honor us though dead!*
>
> *O kinsmen! We must meet the common foe! Though far outnumbered let us show us brave, and for their thousand blows deal one deathblow! What though before us lies the open grave? Like men we'll face the murderous, cowardly pack, pressed to the wall, dying but fighting back!*[177]

I won't face the possibility of death tomorrow, and I can't figure out why I've chosen this particular poem. Maybe it's because it is the only release I have from the fear I felt this afternoon at the capitol in the

---

177 Claude McKay, "If We Must Die," *Voices of the Harlem Renaissance*, ed. Nathan Irvin Huggins (New York: Oxford University Press 1976), 353.

midst of that angry mob. Maybe I have to let those feelings go before I can face a new and unknown challenge.

The next day is Tuesday, February 13, 1962. Julian drives his car to the capitol loaded with one group of students, and Smitty borrows Andrew Young's car to take the rest of us. James Forman comes along so he can let Charles Black, who is waiting back at the office, know what happens once we're inside the capitol building. Jim Forman's wife, Mildred, is with him.

There isn't a soul outside the capitol when we arrive. We get out of the cars, enter the building, and head down a hallway that we think will lead us to the legislative session already in progress, but halfway down the hall it becomes apparent that we are walking away from the session. The hallway is too quiet. We don't hear gavels banging or the murmur of voices in session. So we start down a second hall. Not having been here before, we're confused about where the legislature is meeting. Then we see members of the custodial crew and say, "We're looking for the legislative session. Which way is it?"

They look somewhat confused to see us inside but point us in the right direction. We thank them and walk toward the gallery, determined to desegregate it.

Mrs. Forman announces she has to use the restroom. Everybody stops. "I *have* to go," she says. Since we are not about to leave her, we double back to the women's restroom and wait for her to go inside. I don't think much about it at the moment, but later I realize she has integrated a public restroom inside the capitol building. As she emerges, several policemen show up out of nowhere and surround us. One says, "Get the hell outta here, or you'll be arrested."

"We're going to listen to the proceedings," several of us respond.

"If you enter those chambers, you'll be charged with trespassing."

"We're on public property," Ruby Doris says. "We're citizens. We're *not* trespassing."

"You're on *state* property, and that means you are trespassing."

We refuse to move.

"You're all under arrest," they say and begin to lead us toward an exit door.

As I walk toward the exit, I think of the irony of entering the capitol to make a public statement in protesting segregated seating inside the legislative chambers (where there are no Negro legislators) and instead being arrested while taking care of a basic human need to use the toilet.

James Forman moves away from the group as soon as the police show up, so he can contact Charles back at the office and let him know what has happened.

I follow my fellow students into the sunlight and into the back of a waiting paddy wagon. Hard benches line both sides of the vehicle. I'm nervous but struggle not to show it. I want to be as strong as everyone else, but my feelings are all over the place as horror stories I've heard about other Negro students come to mind. I've heard about some girls who got arrested, who were stripped and forced to walk naked in front of white male prisoners; others were raped by white prison guards. I know of Negro male students who had cattle prods placed on their genitals. One boy who was abused that way was left sterile *and* crippled. Other males were beaten. What will our fate be?

The Spelman administration is going to have a heart attack when they find out Ruby Doris and I are in jail. They pride themselves on protecting us. How will they handle our arrest? I hope I'm not thrown into solitary confinement. That's the one thing I know I cannot handle.

Smitty, who had only planned to drive Andy Young's car downtown and drop us off, is seated on the opposite side of the paddy wagon from me. Instinctively he begins to pray aloud. We all bow our heads. As soon as he says, "Amen," we sing, "We Shall Overcome."

The paddy wagon comes to a halt at the Fulton County jailhouse, and cops open the doors. When all of us are assembled outside the vehicle, we're led inside to a booking room. Some of us sit, while others stand. I sit near the place where our names will be given and where fingerprints are to be taken.

"Name?" a burly cop shouts to the boy next to me.

"Billy Mitchell," the young Johnny Mathis lookalike responds.

"Home?"

"New York."

"School?"

"Morehouse College."

"Class?"

"Freshman."

*Freshman?* I say to myself. *I thought this guy was a junior.*

"Over there," the cop says, directing Billy to another cop, who is taking fingerprints.

"Name?" the same cop says to Billy's co-captain from the march the day before.

"Russell Carmichael Campbell."

"Campbell?"

"Yeah, like the soup."

Listening to his response, I begin to pray that he'll keep his cool, because he has just looked at the answers the cop is writing down and is now correcting the spelling of his middle name. "C-A-R-M-I-C-H-A-E-L."

*My God, this guy is going to get us thrown* under *the jail,* I think. *Doesn't he know where he is? This is Atlanta, Georgia.*

"Home?" the cop asks.

"Detroit, Michigan."

"Class?"

"Freshman."

*Not another freshman,* I think.

"Name?" the cop says to the next boy.

"Larry Fox."

Larry, I learn from his answers, is a freshman, too. Good Lord, I can't believe I've followed freshmen into jail, freshmen who don't have any more experience than I do. Thank goodness Smitty, a junior, has had experience with demonstrations.

"Name?" the cop yells to me.

"Nell Braxton."

After getting the information he needs, he directs me to another cop who takes the little finger of my right hand and rolls it over an ink pad. Then he rolls it onto the clear bottom portion of a piece of paper that has writing on the top. He then rolls my ring finger over the ink and continues with all the other fingers on that hand, and my thumb. He does the same thing with my left hand before commanding, "Stand over there," pointing to a spot in front of a white wall lit up with bright lights. I walk over and stand in front of the camera on the spot marked X.

"Face forward!" he commands. "Turn right! Turn left!"

Click, click goes the camera.

"Next!" he yells as I move away.

As other mug shots and fingerprints are being taken, Smitty reminds a cop standing near him that we are each entitled to one phone call. At about the same time, he remembers that he promised Andrew Young he wouldn't get arrested so he could return Young's car in time for Andy's wife to use it that night. Now Smitty tries to explain this to one of the cops. "I've got to get that car back to Andrew Young," he says.

For a moment the cop looks as if he might be softening. Suddenly his face hardens, and he snaps back, "Boy! Do you know where you are? You're in jail!"

Seeing that he can't press his luck any further, Smitty puts a dime into the public phone on the wall and places his call. When he is finished, another student drops a dime and begins to talk. While he talks I try to decide whom I should call. If I call Madre, she and Papa might try to bail me out, and this is no time to be separated from my friends. Dad will understand, but what if I call his office in the gym at Tougaloo and someone else answers? I will have wasted my call. I should call Mother's office at Brinkley High, I finally tell myself. When my collect call is accepted, I try to sound reassuring in breaking the news.

"Mother, I've been arrested for demonstrating downtown in Atlanta, and I'm in jail being fingerprinted."

"You are?" She hesitates for a minute and then says, "Thank you for calling to let me know. Are you all right?" I can tell she's struggling to mask her anxiety. I tell her I'm fine. "I know you'll be strong. Daddy and I will be praying for you," she assures me. "Is there anything I can do?"

"No," I tell her. "Thank you. I just wanted to be the one to tell you and Daddy. Everything is being taken care of from this end." Then, not wanting to cost Brinkley too much money for this collect call and not knowing what else to say, I say good-bye.

Pulling down the lever to disconnect the call, I feel I've earned a new kind of respect from my mother—one that says that, whatever happens, I'm going to be all right. It helps me feel stronger because in attempting to convince her of my well-being, I've gathered the courage I need to face whatever lies ahead. Since my call to her was a collect call, my dime falls into the cup at the bottom of the pay phone. I take it and look over my shoulder to see if any of the cops have noticed, but they're all too busy taking names, mug shots, and fingerprints of the other students to notice me, so I ease the coin into the slot again and call Madre. I've decided that I don't want her to learn of my arrest from the television news.

When I hear her voice I blurt out, "Madre, I've been arrested."

"Oh, baby, I'm so sorry," she says through tears she cannot hold back.

"I'm all right. Please don't worry about me," I say, knowing she will regardless of what I tell her. "James Forman and Charles Black are taking care of everything. Please don't bail me out," I beg, realizing that her worse nightmare of turning on her TV and seeing me have come as close to being true as anything she has ever imagined.

"I love you," she tells me. "You know I'm in your corner no matter what."

"I love you, too, Madre. Good-bye," I say, my eyes filling with water as I turn to hand the phone to Ruby Doris. For the first time in my life I have broken my grandmother's heart.

Walking back toward the other students, I overhear Ruby Doris talking on the phone to Charles about getting us a lawyer. The boys are lined up and led off in one direction down a long hall. Ruby Doris, Mrs. Forman, and I are led down another hall where we're searched by a female trusty. It's the first time I've been searched, and I feel awkward letting someone run her hands over my body. She acts as if it's all in a day's work. When the three of us have been searched, we follow the trusty through a series of bars that slide open as we approach and shut when we've passed through. After a long walk we reach our destination—a cell with Negro females—seasoned criminals, hard-timers. The bars to their large cell open and then slam shut behind the three of us. Standing in the middle of the room, I look into an adjoining one that is larger than this one. It is shut off by bars and filled with single beds. Next to it is another partially barred area where toilets and washbasins stand. The toilets are far enough inside the room so that guards cannot look into them from their station outside the room we are in, but there are no doors to make that area completely private. The washbasins are in full view of the prison guards, all of whom are white males.

A television is playing inside the room where we stand, and a majority of the inmates are watching a soap opera. Smaller groups of three or four inmates are seated in straight-back chairs and rocking chairs, holding conversations. There are twenty to twenty-five of us in this cell.

"This place is like a resort," Ruby Doris says. "I've been in a lot worse jails than this."

*Thank God I'm with a veteran,* I think. Looking around, I have to admit this is not what I expected, either. The room is spacious and filled with light, but the windows are so high that I can only see sky and the tops of trees. Benches are on either side of metal tables where we can play cards or read newspapers, but this is still jail. There are bars everywhere—in front of the toilets, around the area where we'll sleep, and over the windows. Already I feel trapped. I look for a spot to sit on one of the benches in front of the television. I've taken so much for granted—the wind and sun, the earth under my feet, even a refreshing rain and the cool chill of winter. Now what do I do, locked away with all this time on my hands? I don't have a book, a piece of paper, a pen, or a magazine. The newspapers on the table have been censored, and all the articles I'd be interested in reading have been cut out. If I were back at school, I'd be preparing for my English class—the one in which we're reading *Walden*. Thinking of that reading now, I imagine my own body stretched out against a cool patch of earth at Walden Pond. Thoreau watched ants wage war and thought about their universal urge to destroy, but I used to watch ants move back and forth carrying lumps of dirt to add to the other lumps that made up the anthill nearby. They carried pieces of earth twice their size, working together to build something bigger than any one of them could build alone. I hope we're like *those* ants. I hope that by sitting in the Fulton County jail today, each one of us is building something greater than any one of us can build alone.

# Chapter 25

# Ain't Gonna Let Nobody Turn Me 'Round[178]

SITTING DOWN ON A bench beside a metal table, Mrs. Forman, Ruby D., and I say hello to the women with whom we've been placed. Some look up from their soap operas and mumble a hello, and others ignore us.

We sit in silence until the programs are over. Then one of the inmates asks, "What y'all in for?"

Ruby Doris begins to explain what happened at the capitol, but she is interrupted by an inmate. "You mean they's arrestin' peoples for goin' inta buildings now'days?"

They all laugh. They don't have a clue about the civil rights work taking place in Atlanta or about much of anything else that's going on outside. Their world is here in this cell, in the newspaper articles that

---

178  This song is believed to be based on an old Negro spiritual, "Don't You Let Nobody Turn You 'Round," and adapted by the civil rights movement.

haven't been censored, and in the soap operas they watch on TV. The very thought of our being arrested for entering the capitol building is ludicrous to them.

"I'm Blood," a big dark-skinned woman on the other side of the room declares.

The inmate sitting next to me whispers in my ear, "That's Blood. She called Blood 'cause she kilt a man in cold blood."

"This here's Tough Titty," Blood says, pointing to the medium-size, brown-skinned woman with short hair who is seated beside her. Tough Titty, the woman seated beside me whispers, got her name by surviving a hideous slashing from a man she was in a fight with who left a deep gash across one of her breasts from his knife. A few more women introduce themselves, but none of them have names as unforgettable as the first two.

Some prisoners look as if they should be sitting on a front porch rocking grandchildren; others look tough, like street fighters. As I scan the room, it occurs to me that it isn't just my freedom and the freedom of the children I've seen in the projects that we're working toward. It's the freedom of all of us—these women, too. That white world outside doesn't see any difference between me and the women in here. To them we are all just niggers.

Dinner arrives on a sectioned metal tray with plastic utensils. The meat looks like a dark-brown piece of dried leather. The rice is mushy, and the green beans are soft and overcooked. There is a slice of white bread on the tray—something totally alien to my upbringing. We always had whole-wheat or corn bread when we were growing up. I take a taste of the rice, which is very mildly seasoned. It all tastes like water that has been thickened and colored to look like rice and vegetables, and I unconsciously turn my nose up at the first bite, but Ruby D. tells me, "Jail is one place you don't want to be sick. Eat it." And so I do.

That night I "brush" my teeth by putting salt on my fingertip and running it around in my mouth. Then I wash out my underwear, hang it on the rail at the foot of my bed, take off my skirt and blouse, and get under the sheets in my slip and bra.

The next day after washing my face, underarms, and private parts with a dampened paper towel and soap, I put on my clean underwear, skirt, and blouse, and I go sit on one of the benches. I'm feeling pretty low. Ruby Doris comes over and tells me to get up and do calisthenics with her. "You need to keep strong," she says. We spend a good part of the morning exercising before we attempt to read what is left of the censored newspaper that has had whole articles or portions of articles cut out. During breakfast, news of our arrest appears on the prison television screen, and fellow inmates take notice. They begin asking us questions about what the movement is and what we are trying to do. We talk to them about civil rights. They listen attentively, then ask if we can help them see a chaplain. When Ruby D. says yes, they say, "Anythang y'all kin do so we kin go outside an' exercise?" Ruby says she'll see about that, too. Later that day, I see her talking to one of the prison guards, and the following day we are all taken outside for a game of volleyball. Breathing in the fresh air for the first time in three days, I ask Ruby Doris what she said to the guard.

"I just reminded him that exercise is a right these women are being denied."

Hearing her response, I figure the guard must have decided he didn't want any civil rights uprisings inside the jail, so he let us go outside. That same afternoon we are led to the chapel in small groups so we can pray. The chapel space feels tight and close. It has linen and bro-cade trappings on the altar and paintings of Jesus, the Virgin Mary, and the disciples on the walls. There are limited rows of pews, and there are kneelers at the rail in front of the altar. Even though the space is small, it feels good to get down on my knees and pray. Some of the women say this is the first time they have been outside or to a chapel since they've been in jail.

At the end of the day, I wash out my underwear and hang it up again before I climb between the sheets. In the middle of the night, a loud bang causes me to shoot straight up in bed.

"Sorry," Mrs. Forman says, pointing to a large book. "I hit it on the way to the toilet."

Two inmates are standing near her as she makes her way from the sleeping area through the bars and around the corner to the left to go to the toilet. The two inmates who had been standing near her saunter back to their beds.

Ruby Doris beckons for me to come over to her bed. I sit on her cov-ers as she explains, "They"—referring to the inmates—"were bending over you while you were sleeping. They've been locked up a long time." No other explanation is needed.

After that night, the three of us decide we will take turns, with one of us staying awake all night keeping watch while the other two sleep; but my natural proclivity toward insomnia doesn't allow me to get much sleep after that, regardless of who is scheduled to stay awake.

The next morning I make my way to the sink to brush my teeth with salt and water on my index finger. Then I sponge myself off and complete my exercise routine with Ruby Doris before we all eat breakfast. The rest of the morning moves along slowly. At lunchtime the Negro trusty who usually brings our food calls Ruby Doris aside and gives her a pack of cigarettes, which she puts in her pocket. I've never seen Ruby with a cigarette in my life, and so I say, "I've never seen you smoke before."

I'm wondering why the guard didn't give me the cigarettes, since I'm the smoker, but Ruby says, "Jail can make you do some strange things," and she offers me a couple of cigarettes.

The afternoon drags by with soap operas droning in the background as some inmates play poker with matchsticks and others talk with Mrs. Forman. Ruby Doris makes notes in a makeshift diary of paper towels, and I sit daydreaming.

"Mail call!" a trusty yells and motions for me to come to the bars. He hands me an envelope that I can see has already been opened and read by prison officials. Inside is a Valentine's card from Bert with a heart and roses on the front. The card reads,

> *Darling, you alone can bring*
> *True happiness to me,*
> *You and you alone can make*
> *My dreams reality—*
> *That's why on special days like this*
> *What I want most to do*
> *Is just to tell you once again*
> *How dearly I love you!*
> > *Yours always,*
> > *Bert*

I sit staring at the card, aware for the first time that, in the middle of preparing for the first demonstration and our return to the state capitol building, I've forgotten to buy a Valentine's card for him. He probably called the snack shop to talk with me the day we were arrested and is worried now because I wasn't there. It makes me sad just to think of him, because there's nothing I can do to reach out to him now.

The monotony of the institutional routine sets in again after dinner, and as evening approaches we ready ourselves for bed. After a long silence with inmates shifting around in bed, everyone starts to settle down and drift off to sleep. The next thing I know Ruby Doris is shaking me awake and motioning for me to follow her and Mrs. Forman. Groggily I swing my legs over the side of the bed and trail them into the toilet area where we huddle under a dim light. Ruby reaches into her pocket and pulls out the cigarette pack the trusty gave her earlier in the day. Feeling around inside, she carefully extracts a long piece of toilet paper.

"The trusty said he'll take notes back and forth between us and the boys if we want him to," she whispers as she prepares to read the note the boys have written to us on toilet paper.

*Dear girls, we are writing to see how you like your "hotel accommodations." Atty Donald Hollowell has been secured for us and has been here to talk with us about bail. All of us refused, so don't let him talk you into accepting it when he visits you. He'll probably come to you tomorrow. Billy was separated from the rest of us and put in a cell with other inmates.... Frank Smith is keeping a diary. Leo's writing poetry. Some of the others have made friends with the men in the cells. I made a chess board out of matchbook covers. I use burned matches for the black pieces and unburned ones for the white. One of the inmates and I have a good game going. We shall overcome because what we are doing is "all for the cause." Russell*

I'm surprised that the guy from Detroit, who I thought would get us all thrown under the jail with his smart-aleck answers, is the one writing notes to keep our spirits up. But the thought of his buddy, Billy, being alone in a cell with hardened criminals worries me.

"We should write them back and let them know we got the letter," Ruby says. And so we carefully unroll some toilet paper, get a pencil, and compose a response to give to the trusty the next day. He'll continue to take letters back and forth between us for a few loose cigarettes.

*Dear fellows, we are glad to see you found a good use for this "Bronco Buster" toilet paper. Using it we have discovered the true meaning of "raw hide" (smile). We are glad to know about Atty Hollowell. Have you heard anything from the outside? Do you know what's happening at Grady? We saw something about it in the paper but most of the article was cut out. We miss all of you. "All for the cause."*

Each of us signs her name before Ruby D. folds the note to stuff into the cigarette pack.

The following morning, Attorney Hollowell comes to us, and Mrs. Forman, Ruby Doris, and I gather at the bars to talk with him.

He says, "Bail money is ready if you want to get out. But if you decide to stay, I can't predict how long you'll be here, so you should consider your options carefully."

"We've already decided," Ruby tells him. "We're going to stay."

"Are you sure?" he asks. We all nod.

"Then I'll see you in court." He heads for the door.

The next day, after we've eaten and cleaned ourselves up, a couple of guards arrive to lead us through narrow corridors, down a flight of stairs, through another short hall, and into a courtroom. Upon entering I spot the fellows who were arrested with us standing on the opposite side of the room. All of us are between a highly shined low wooden gate to the right and a white judge who sits to our left behind a desk on a raised platform. Our attorney stands near the gate to our right. Taking in the scene, I become aware of a sight on the other side of the low gate that causes a lump to rise in my throat. The entire courtroom is filled with faculty and students from the Atlanta University Center campuses. That means the whole administration is behind us. If they are behind us, I can endure almost anything.

The bailiff calls our names one by one. We stand side by side facing the judge, with our backs to the rest of the courtroom. He asks us one at a time how we plead. "Not guilty," we answer down the line one after another. Attorney Hollowell informs the judge that we have refused bail because we do not feel we have broken any law. "They've chosen to remain incarcerated until their trial date," he announces.

Students from the Atlanta University schools cheer when our decision is announced, causing the judge to rap his gavel and yell, "Order!"

Our lawyer and the judge speak to each other in legal terms, and then it is over. Not until I turn to leave the courtroom do I see Rosemary, who has made her way up to the wooden gate that separates us from those who've come to our hearing. She has been clear from the beginning that she could never take the oath to nonviolence, because she can't imagine herself being hit and not retaliating, but her decision has never stopped her from supporting me. Rushing forward, she throws her arms around me, and I hug her tightly, struggling to keep my emotions under control. She shoves a brown paper bag in my hands and tells me, "Madre was here waiting to take you home. She left when you refused bail."

"At least she saw me and knows I'm all right," I say.

We say good-bye as a policeman tugs at my elbow and leads me back toward the hall, where I ascend the stairs and follow the narrow hallways back to my cell. The guard takes the bag Rosemary gave me, so it can be inspected.

Inside the cell I wait at the bars until I get the bag Rosemary brought. Inside is a letter from Bert that has been opened and read. There is also clean underwear, chewing gum, several packs of Winston cigarettes, a toothbrush, toothpaste, deodorant, a clean blouse, and a comb and brush. I tear into Bert's letter.

*February 15, 1962*

*Hi Darling,*

*I called you today and talked to a girl named Yvonne. She told me that you had been arrested on Tuesday and were probably out by now. However, you weren't in the snack shop when I called. The young lady said she would be sure to tell you that I called.*

*I miss you so-o-o-o much I don't know what to do. You are my one and only. I hope I never lose you.*

*Yours always,*
*Bert*

*P.S. I was thinking about "Until Eternity" all week. I love you.*

Just before my arrest, I had composed a poem that I sent to him.

*Until Eternity—Nell Anne Braxton*

*How long will I love you, dear?*
*How long will you love me?*
*Will our love last forever?*
*Let us stop to see.*

*We'll love till birds stop singing and sound has ceased to be*
*until the fish stop swimming and nothing fills the sea*

*Until the black of death has come and taken you from me until*
*the earth shall be no more Until Eternity.*

I light the first Winston cigarette I've had in four days, clutching Bert's letter in my hand. I take a deep breath and turn to watch soap operas until dinner comes. We eat, and I brush my teeth with real toothpaste and a real toothbrush before settling down for the night and going over the events of the day in my mind. After days of the dull routine of prison life this day has felt eventful, even though all we've done is go to court and turn down bail.

It will be thirty years before I learn how hard prison was on the boys. For all his newsy reporting on things taking place in their cells, and for all the encouragement he gives us in his smuggled note, Russell Campbell sends a very different kind of letter home to Detroit.

February 1962

Dear Parents,

150 students marched on the State Capitol in downtown Atlanta protesting a bill making it illegal to picket the Capitol building. Looking across the street we could see state and local police guarding the Capitol against picketers.

Captain William Holt of the Atlanta police tried to reason with the students and threatened them with arrest for simulating riot conditions. (Later) We had a meeting at the office of the Committee on Appeal for Human Rights (COAHR). The problem of going to jail was discussed. Those who agreed to picket understood that they would probably be arrested...

We were fingerprinted and confined to cells which normally hold two prisoners. There were four to a cell, the beds were infested with vermin and the food was served in dog cans.

When our hearing came up the arrested students walked into the court room with dignity. In a matter of minutes the room was filled with students from Spelman and Morehouse. My heart was overjoyed when I saw them.

The Attorney General's remarks alleged that our actions tended to (disrupt) the peaceful relations existing in Atlanta. After the hearing we were taken back to our cells. This is our fourth day in jail. It has been very trying. If we are subsequently found guilty, we will be sentenced for six months. I shall keep you informed. Say hello to everybody.[179]

---

179 From the Russell C. Campbell Sr. collection of letters home from Morehouse, February 1962.

Today is the fifth morning of our incarceration. I have already cleaned myself up, exercised with Ruby D., and had breakfast.

"Quiet!" one of the inmates yells. "Ain't that y'all on TV?"

Turning to the television, we see that the students demonstrating outside Grady Memorial Hospital are being arrested. Suddenly the story is interrupted and replaced by other local news. Anxious to know more, we call a trusty over to the bars, but he can't tell us anything. That evening another pack of cigarettes arrives and is handed to me by the trusty. Unable to contain myself and hoping it is news of the arrests we saw on TV, I take it and go straight to the toilet. Sitting on the toilet seat farthest from the doorway, I light a cigarette and slide the note out of the pack. It's from Anna Jo. *How in the world has her note made it through the system from the white section of another jail to me?* I wonder. The underground system among trusties must be incredible. Anna Jo is among the students who were arrested outside Grady earlier in the day, and her experience sounds more like what I expected mine to be. The cell she describes is sparser than ours, and the Negroes and whites in her area are in closer proximity to one another than those of us in the Fulton County jail seem to be, although I have no idea where white prisoners are located in this jailhouse. From the white section where she is confined, Anna Jo can hear the Negro male and female students singing back and forth to one another.

> *My dear Soul-mate,*
>
> *I guess you know by now that we were arrested for causing a disturbance outside Grady. The hospital administration got tired of hearing us demonstrate everyday so they had all of us arrested. There were about twenty of us and as we were being carried off other students said they were going to Grady to get arrested too so they could fill up the jail. Joycelyn was taken into custody with us*

*and when they led her into the paddy wagon, she started singing,*
*"Ain't gonna let nobody turn me 'round." All of us joined in. When*
*the cops saw me they separated me from the others and put me in*
*a patrol car by myself. I'm in a cell by myself, too. I can hear every-*
*body else singing songs in their cells. They have such spirit and I*
*want so much to be with them that it makes me cry to hear them.*
*I feel completely alone. This is the worst part of it for me. I'm in a*
*cell with one bare light bulb and a window so high I can't see out.*

*The guards are really mean. Some of them have been coming on*
*to me and I'm afraid of what they might do when I fall asleep. There's*
*a lot to be said for (safety in) numbers but I know I can't give in to my*
*fears because that's what these red necks want me to do. I know you*
*are all with me in spirit and that keeps me strong. "All for the cause."*

*With love from your Soul-mate,*

*Anna Jo*

I flush the toilet, slip the note back inside the cigarette pack, come out, and give the pack to Ruby D. Anna Jo has become so much a part of us that I sometimes forget she is not one of us. Nothing brings this home more clearly than our separate and unequal experiences in jail.

When Ruby Doris and Mrs. Forman have read Anna Jo's letter, they come out of the toilet area. Ruby takes our hands in hers and prays. Later that day, a trusty calls Ruby to the bars and says he's heard we're getting out of jail soon. Ruby tells him he's wrong, because we've chosen to stay in jail.

A fast trial takes place following the arrest of Anna Jo and the twenty-two others from Grady Hospital—a trial she writes home about.

*All 23 of us had to stand through the whole thing (the trial)*
*about an hour. That got pretty old, what with our stomachs*

*scraping up and down against our backbones. We were found guilty of disturbing the peace at Grady Hospital and sentenced to 15 days or $17.00. We'd hoped to be arrested on a state offense so there'd be a chance of a retrial just as with those who picketed the Capitol, but on this city offense they just settled it then and there and we could do nothing more...We drove to the COAHR office and ordered food in a hurry. We were all very happy and had a good time. When the food came we couldn't eat it quick enough. Then we girls walked back to campus (the Dean said we had to be in at 11:00) and had a big reunion in Morgan Hall. Everyone came tearing down the halls to greet us. I've never seen Miss Taylor look so happy; she looked ten years younger.*[180]

On this fifth day of our incarceration at the Fulton County jail, Attorney Hollowell comes to the bars, calls Ruby Doris, Mrs. Forman, and me over and says our bail has been paid. Confused and angry, we refuse to leave.

"Who posted bail?" we demand.

"Reverend King," Hollowell says.

"What are you talking about? He's not even here." As far as we know, Martin Luther King Jr. is in Albany working to desegregate that city.

"No," Hollowell says, "Daddy King," meaning Martin Luther King Sr.

"But why?"

"I don't know. I was just told your bail has been paid, and I'm to take you to Rush Memorial Church, where the boys are waiting."

---

180  From the Weaver/Scruton collection of letters home from Spelman, February 1962.

"If the boys aren't at Rush when we get there, we're going to get ourselves rearrested," we threaten, wary now of whom we can trust.

We collect our personal belongings, say good-bye to the other women prisoners, and move through the bars. The sun has set by the time we are driven to Rush Memorial. Getting out of the car, we enter the back door the way we've done so many times going to the COAHR office, but this time Attorney Hollowell avoids the back stairs to our office and ushers us into the church through a door that opens in back of the pulpit. As soon as we appear, a roar goes up from the crowd inside that sounds as if it will blow the roof off the building. Students have filled the church to overflowing and are cheering and clapping as we enter. That's when I spot the boys we got arrested with and the twenty-three students who were arrested at Grady Memorial. I walk across the platform area toward them and throw my arms around Anna Jo.

Charles Black, Julian Bond, Attorney Hollowell, and "Daddy King" make speeches. Frank Smith speaks for our group, and Danny Mitchell (no relation to Billy Mitchell, the young Johnny Mathis lookalike) speaks for the group that was arrested at Grady Hospital. Applause follows each speech.

*If anything was worth going to jail for,* I think, *this is it! What a welcome.* Following the speeches, Bernice Johnson begins singing, and we join her in a series of movement songs. When she leads us in singing "Amen," everyone starts to file out of church. Still singing, we head back to our several campuses.

At Morgan Hall I climb the stairs, go to my room, take off my clothes, and head straight for the stalls to take the first shower I've had in a week. As warm water runs over my body, I luxuriate in its massage and then lather myself with soap and let the beads from the shower rinse me off. I lather up a second time, washing away the dirt *and* the experience of having been locked up. Stepping out of the stall, I dry off and head next door to my room where a stack of letters sits on my desk. I rip Bert's open first. In it he says he has accepted an offer to be a senior camp counselor at Woodland for the coming summer so he and I can be together. He asks if I've sent my letter of acceptance back yet. That's when I find a letter from Norman Studer, the director of the camp, and open it. Norman's letter says that since I didn't complete the forms indicating my desire to return to camp as the head counselor of junior camp, the position has gone to someone else. I'm brokenhearted. I look and look for the letter he says he sent with the forms, but it's not among the ones on my desk. I do find a letter from Katy, though, that says she has decided to work as a waitress at a place called Green Mansions during the summer because she can make twice the money there as she can at camp.

After a fitful night of sleep and a morning of classes, where I try to catch up on the schoolwork I've missed during my time in jail, I race over to the snack shop and call Bert to tell him what has happened with my summer job. He is as upset as I am. We were both counting on being together for the summer. I was also looking forward to making some money and being with the kids I've grown to love. We profess love for each other before hanging up the phone; then I go to the school post office. There I discover a batch of letters that have been held until my release, and that's where the forms for camp are. Back in my room, I write Norman Studer explaining what happened and why I didn't get the forms until I was released from jail. I know the camp can't take back a job it has already given to someone else, but I write hoping that if someone drops out at the last minute Norman will keep me in mind.

Those of us who were arrested and are awaiting trial, and those who were arrested at Grady Hospital, aware that if they go back they'll only be charged with some other city offense, decide to regroup. With heightened awareness in the community of the injustices taking place at Grady, legal methods will be pursued through other civil rights organizations. We know through our student coordinators like Julian and Lonnie that some student organizations are sitting in at locations throughout the city, so we put our efforts into voter registration—beginning with the public housing projects near Spelman.

Meanwhile, word reaches us that a party is going to be held at a home off campus and that everyone who was arrested is invited because the party is to honor all those who spent time in jail. The party is off-limits to the girls at Spelman, so we will have to pull a "creep" (slip off campus) if we intend to go.

On the night of the party, the movement girls who live in Morgan Hall make up our beds to look as if we are in them. Then we get dressed in black clothing to keep from being easily detected as we slip off campus. We follow a series of hallways that lead us out of the rear of the dorm. We stick paper in the door so it will stay unlocked, and then we ease it shut. One of our members has made friends with Mr. Little, the security guard whom the Morehouse men call "Will Shoot." He'll leave the campus gate at the side entrance unlocked so we can sneak out and then back in again. If we make it to the side gate, a car will be waiting to drive us to the party.

We tiptoe down to the basement of Morgan Hall through a series of corridors and slip out the side door. Crawling across campus on our bellies like reconnaissance soldiers, we make our way to the midpoint of the campus, which is where President Manley's home is located. Just as Mercedes, the lead girl, begins to stand up, the front door of the president's home swings opens, and a group of laughing adults emerge, saying their good-byes. In the stillness of the moment, pleasantries can be heard over the ice in cocktail glasses inside as the evening winds down. Unknown to us until very this moment, President and Mrs. Manley have been entertaining members of the board of trustees, and the festivities are beginning to break up. The five of us duck down and struggle to get far under the bushes at the side of the house so as not to be seen. It's only now that I think my parents would kill me if they found out that this was what I was doing in the middle of the night.

A group of trustees lingers talking and glad-handing for what seems like forever before they descend the front steps and walk away. The front door closes, and everything starts to quiet down again as the remaining guests continue their conversations inside. Holding our breaths and making sure the trustees are out of sight, we slither across the campus toward the unlocked gate.

"Oh-ma-God! What the hell is that?" Joycelyn says just above a whisper.

We all look back. Brenda has grabbed Joycelyn's foot just as Joycelyn was moving to join us because Brenda's caught on the thorns of a rosebush at the president's house. As we catch sight of her Brenda lets out a low "Shit!"

Mercedes, Anna Jo, and I crawl on toward the gate, and Joycelyn whispers to Brenda, "We'll wait for you at the car." But we've been delayed so long by the president and trustees that I wonder if the car is still there.

Reaching the unlocked campus gate, four of us slip through, squat down, and look for a car. A shadowy figure makes its way up the sidewalk to where we are.

Frank Smith motions for us to follow him. We tiptoe down the street toward an idling car with its headlights turned off. Frank opens the back door and tells us to get on the floor. We do, and tell him Brenda is stuck on a bush, so he goes back to wait at the gate for her. Inside the car, Russell Campbell, Billy Mitchell, Danny Mitchell, and Leo Meadows are scrunched together on the backseat. Up in front are Julian Bond at the wheel and his wife, Alice, holding the passenger seat for Frank, who soon returns with Brenda. Hardly able to breathe squeezed together on the floor in back, we girls slap one another five, because we've made it off campus without getting caught.

Arriving at the home where the party is being held, we enter a living room where records are spinning and fried chicken, potato chips, deviled eggs, nuts, and sandwiches are being served. We get ourselves drinks—mostly screwdrivers—and look for seats. After the huge reception we received at Rush Memorial Church when we got out of jail, this party is a letdown for me. There's very little furniture in the house, as if the host has recently moved in. A few folding chairs are scattered around the living room. In the kitchen, a Formica table is loaded with food. A couple of folding chairs are near the table, but most of the people are standing around talking. Billy Mitchell takes my hand and leads me into a bedroom where couples are seated around on the carpeted floor because there is absolutely no furniture. He and I slide down on the carpet, too, talking and nursing our drinks. I light a cigarette and we talk about our time in jail. By this time my glass is empty, so he heads back to the kitchen to get me another. I light a second cigarette and look around the room, which is lit only by the street lamp outside. Couples are kissing, drinking, and smoking. Billy returns with another screwdriver for me. I take a gulp and another drag from my cigarette. My mind gets hazy from the two drinks and very little food. I lean back against the wall as Billy starts kissing me. I don't resist.

After more kissing and the consumption of the remainder of our drinks, the two of us get up from the floor and go back into the living room. Forty-fives continue to spin but nobody's dancing. Billy goes out the front door, and Russell Campbell starts talking to me. I sit in the living room with him for a while, lighting one cigarette after another. The evening drags on until someone says we should get back to campus. The same crowd of girls and boys piles back into Julian's car, and he drives to Spelman where the gate is closed but still unlocked. From here Julian will drive the boys to Morehouse. Outside of the car, we girls sneak through the gate. Crawling on our stomachs, we cross a very still and quiet campus. The president's party has long since ended, and the whole campus seems to be sleeping. We enter the side door of our dorm where paper has been stuffed to keep it unlocked. All of us reek of liquor. A couple of the girls are so giddy that we have to make sure they don't bang the door as we sneak back in. The five of us move through several passages in the basement under the dining hall; on we go through a hallway and another room before we reach the kitchen and head upstairs. Since no one's been moving around for a while, everything we touch and everywhere we step creaks and squeaks like in a haunted house. Suddenly someone starts turning on lights right behind us, and we find ourselves in a panic to get out of each area and escape before we are detected. We race to our rooms and hurriedly hang everything up before jumping into bed.[181]

In the ensuing days I find myself pouring more time into the movement than into my schoolwork, and my teachers notice it, too. Madame Thomas asks me to remain after French class to tell me she's concerned about the plunge in my grades. She warns me that I'm in danger of having my grade slip below a C in her class, and she lets me know I have used up the maximum number of cuts allowed for her class. I thank her and head to my next class, thinking of how much I loved French in high school and how I won the biology award at Lanier High, but now my biology grades are bordering on a C-minus. I'm paying a heavy price for my student movement involvement. Vowing to do better, I start taking my school books to the movement office when I'm on duty there answering the phones.

Since we've pulled back from demonstrations at Grady Memorial and are awaiting trial for "trespassing" at the state capitol, we've decided to concentrate our efforts on voter registration these days. We take turns manning the office telephone, which allows us to stay abreast of what other student groups are doing throughout the city. We've agreed not to go back to Grady Hospital, because we'll only be arrested, charged with a city offense, and released. Forming male and female teams, we augment our office vigil with a voter registration drive in "the bottom," one of Atlanta's most depressed areas of the housing projects. From now on, pairs of students will go into the projects to try to talk people into registering to vote while other pairs will stay at the office to answer the phones and coordinate the work of COAHR with other student movement groups.

---

181 Ibid.

CIVIL RIGHTS DEMONSTRATION AT ATLANTA UNIVERSITY
(COURTESY OF RUSSELL C. CAMPBELL SR.)

Students who go to the bottom enter homes in male/female pairs, taking with us pencils, writing pads, and a map of the projects obtained from the COAHR office. The bottom is close enough to the five university campuses for us to get there on foot, so Russell Campbell and I form one team and walk over to the area.

We begin knocking on doors. "Hi, I'm Russell Campbell, and this is Nell Braxton. We are students at Spelman and Morehouse College, and we want to talk to you about voter registration. Do you have a few moments?"

Sometimes people slam the door in our faces before we can finish introducing ourselves. Sometimes they say they don't want to talk to us. Some people let us in, and we take that opportunity to explain to them why it's important for them to vote. Regardless of how people treat us when they answer the door, we are polite. Often when we are invited inside, there are small children running around. I sometimes pick up one of the children while Russell talks with a parent about the importance of voting. I hold the child on my lap while at the same time adding to the conversation Russell is having with the little one's parent. Sometimes holding a child is a good way to break the ice with a parent. Russell and I make a point of telling the adults they can change the face of city politics if they register, because they have power in their numbers. We promise that a group of students will take them downtown on a school bus so they can register, and that there will be other students to meet them downtown who will stay with them through the registration process and bring them back home again.

When we enter the homes of elderly people, we can tell that some of them feel intimidated. After we spend time talking with them, we learn the source of their fear. A few have already attempted to register and have been mistreated. One elderly woman says, "First time I tried to register, peoples say I had ta recite parts the Constitution and explain it. I knowed most of it by heart," she says, "but I couldn't answer their questions the way they wanted me to."

Interpreting the Constitution is not a requirement for voter registration, we tell her. "You won't have to go through that kind of thing when we take you downtown," we promise. So she agrees to go.

Another elderly woman, who is initially hesitant about letting us in, spends a few minutes in her doorway. She talks with us from behind her screen door, and then she says, "If y'all young people care enough to come 'round here, I'll go. 'Cause nobody ever cared that much b'fo."

As I leave her home, I think back to my English class and the days when we studied Erich Fromm and Ortega y Gasset. *Finally,* I say to myself, *I've stepped into the world of the people I saw from my classroom window, the people whose world I wanted so much to change.*

Following an afternoon in the bottom, I return to my dorm often tired and smelling of urine from the babies I've held on my lap. I have only minutes to put down my papers, collect my bathing suit, goggles, and bathing cap, and make my way across campus and into the showers that lead to my swim class. Last semester I took a dance class to relieve the stress I felt from picketing and demonstrating. This semester I've decided to learn to swim. It has been a good decision. Not only have I mastered swimming, I have reveled in the therapeutic effect of the water and emerged from each class feeling refreshed.

On the way back to Morgan Hall, I see girls in the distance coming from the other dormitories queuing up outside the dining hall where dinner is being served. I'm lucky to live in the dorm where the dining hall is located, because after I go upstairs and hang up my wet swimsuit, I can look out one of the front windows and wait until the line is short before I go down to join it for dinner.

After I've eaten, I go back to my room to gather my schoolbooks and walk over to the COAHR office. There I will study and answer phones, which isn't nearly as satisfying as picketing and getting arrested, but it allows me to catch up on some schoolwork. Russell Campbell is my partner tonight, and after we've spent an hour or more studying, we take a coffee break. Lighting a cigarette and taking a sip of coffee, I ask him how he got involved in the movement.

"It's something I wanted to do ever since I left home," he tells me. "It's one of the reasons I came to Morehouse, that and the fact that my brother, Finley, taught at Morehouse."

"Really?"

"Yeah, up until about a year ago."

During the course of our conversation, he tells me he grew up hearing his mother talk about a race riot that took place in Detroit the year he was born. "She told me she laid me on the floor under the dining-room table and covered me with her body when the rioters came onto our street looting shops and breaking streetlights."

The year was 1943, the same year my parents and I escaped the race riot in Beaumont, Texas, the year rioting took place in Harlem and Los Angeles, too. The most serious riot it turns out was the one Russell's mother remembered in Detroit. It occurred on June 20, one month after Russell was born.[182]

I reach for my half-empty pack of cigarettes and tap one out, but before I can strike a match, a flame appears in Russell's cupped hand. I thank him and offer him a drag. I've learned that even though he's not a smoker, he'll occasionally take drags off other people's cigarettes as a way of being part of the crowd. Continuing our conversation, I learn that he is the youngest child of a Baptist minister. He tries to adhere to the tenets of the church, including its rules on no smoking or drinking. His father, the Reverend Stephen C. Campbell, is pastor of the Russell

---

182 Detroit's three-year increase in the Negro population to 50,000 and in the white population to 450,000, mostly from the South, all competing for work, led to a combustible situation. The Detroit riot killed twenty-five Negroes and nine whites and exceeded $2 million in property losses. It had a profound effect on the country (and) "shocked people into realizing the status of the Negro had undergone a significant change that could not be ignored." Benjamin Quarles, *The Negro in the Making of America* (New York: Collier Books, Macmillan Publishing Company, 1964, 1969), 227.

Street Baptist Church in Detroit and has five other children—a son and daughter from his first marriage and four sons from his present marriage to Russell's mother, Pauline, whom he wed after the death of his first wife. Finley, Major, Anthony, and Russell are the children from his second marriage.

Russell asks me how I got involved in the movement, and I tell him about the night I ran into Jimmy Murray after more than ten years of separation as friends and of how Jim extended to me an invitation to a meeting at Canterbury House. I also tell him that first day when we were part of the mass march to the state capitol, I thought he and Billy Mitchell were juniors, and that was the reason I followed their directions and was willing to go to jail.

"I thought I was with movement veterans," I confess. "I might not have been so dutiful if I'd known you were freshmen." We both laugh.

"Are you dating Jim Murray?" Russell asks.

"No, my boyfriend lives in New York."

"What's his name?"

"Bert Gibson." I relate how Bert and I fell in love at camp down by the Esopus Creek. I don't ask who he's dating, because I've seen him with a lot of girls at Spelman, but he volunteers that he has a girl in Detroit whose name is Gail. He says she is sweet, delicate, and different from his other girlfriends. She's in love with him, and he with her. She's someone he wants to go back to when the school year ends. We quiet down and turn back to our books, but I feel we've somehow crossed a line. I'm not sure when it happened, but I know I feel differently about him now—attracted to him, and comfortable and at ease in his presence. We've walked on picket lines together, gone into strange homes to register voters, shared small talk during those walks between homes.

I've trusted him with my life as we stood facing an angry crowd in front of the state capitol. I glance over at him. He is quiet and reflective, too. Suddenly he leans over and kisses me. I melt into his arms with emotions that bubble up in a mixture of excitement and confusion. What are we doing? We've just talked about other people we love, yet here we are entangling ourselves in ways neither of us seems to have foreseen. Are these the pent-up emotions of the movement spilling over or something deeper? It's a question I cannot answer. We pull away from each other; mercifully the office door swings open, and students start to file in. They all check in before we head back to our respective campuses.

# CHAPTER 26

# RAINY NIGHT IN GEORGIA[183]

S ITTING IN SPEECH CLASS the following day, I think of the small cadre of students that has continued to show up at the movement office and in the bottom to register voters. Somehow I know I am living at a time that will never come again; if I miss this opportunity to be part of it, I may never have another chance to make a difference. So even though I have pangs of guilt about falling behind in my schoolwork, I convince myself that what I'm doing is important, because the movement won't last forever.

As soon as class ends, I meet Russell and return to the bottom to convince more people to register to vote. When Russell and I arrive, we find that a school bus is already waiting for folks who signed up to register earlier in the week, and the melodious sound of a movement song is wafting through the air. It is the voice of Bernice Johnson weaving her way along the maze of sidewalks like a Pied Piper, singing "We Shall Not Be Moved." People flow out of their houses all along

183 *Written by Tony Joe White, 1962, recorded by Brook Benton.*

the walkways to follow her. I've never seen anything like this before, but I understand why everyone wants to be within hearing range of her beautiful contralto voice. Today she's doing the work of gathering people for us, leading the ones we've been talking to onto the bus that will soon be headed downtown to help them register to vote. She walks onto the bus with hordes of people following her and is still singing when the driver pulls away from the curb. As the bus moves from the bottom toward downtown, Charles Black will remind folks that they cannot legally be quizzed about the Constitution or asked to interpret documents. He will tell them the bus will wait and bring them home after they've registered. There isn't much for us to do after they've left, so Russell and I return to school.

In the evening after dinner, Anna Jo and I man the phones at the COAHR office. We study for a couple of hours and then pack up our books and begin the walk back to Morgan Hall, as soon as two other students arrive at the office to relieve us.

Back on campus, we climb the stairs inside Morgan Hall. I say good night at the second-floor landing and continue to my room on the third floor. Then I open a letter from Mother that awaits me. In it she says she and Daddy have decided to leave Mississippi and move to California when summer comes. She says she realizes that because of the experiences Rosemary and I have had at Camp Woodland, we won't want to return to Mississippi once we've finished college, and they don't want to live in a place that has held unhappy memories for us. Even as I read her letter I know there's more to their decision than she's telling me, but I also know better than to ask for more information than she's willing to share. Besides, the thought of moving to California is more exciting than any reason she can give for leaving Mississippi.

Toward the end of her letter, Mom says Katy Wechsler and five friends from Oberlin have driven to Tougaloo from Ohio and are spending spring break in our home. I shudder to think of the Oberlin kids traveling to Tougaloo by car. According to Mom there is one Negro boy among them, and in Mississippi Negro and white people can be arrested for riding on the same car seat. White people are expected to sit in the front seat, and Negros sit in the back, or vice versa. It seems that three of the Oberlin kids have specific purposes for making the trip. Gilbert Moses, an actor and the lone Negro student, has gone to learn about the Mississippi Freedom Theatre, Charles Butts to explore the possibility of starting the *Mississippi Free Press*, and Katy to see if she can start an exchange program between Tougaloo and Oberlin, which she manages to do.

Meanwhile, back at Spelman, Rosemary has just returned from Washington, DC, with a busload of students who went to represent the Atlanta University Center and Emory University. Several chaperones were with them, including Dr. Howard Zinn from Spelman. Their purpose was to protest nuclear testing in a Quaker-led march known as the "Friends Witness for World Order." Rosemary's participation was her way of honoring the promise Mrs. Bethune asked us to make toward bettering the world for children of a future generation

Through continued work in the projects and at the COAHR office, my relationship with Russell heats up, and on April 9, after returning from the office to Spelman and signing in at the front desk in the dorm, I manage to sneak off campus to meet him at the Paschal Brothers' Restaurant where we celebrate my twentieth birthday. Sitting in the glow of a candle radiating inside a cone-shaped red glass covered with white plastic netting, we drink milkshakes and eat hamburgers while listening to Ray Charles's recording of "What'd I Say."

"Happy birthday," Russ says, picking up the bill a waiter has placed on the table. I reach across and put my hand on his.

"I love you," I say, suddenly embarrassed by a confession I hadn't planned to make and wishing I could take it back.

He responds, "I like you a lot, Nell, more than I ever thought I would, but love is something I'll only say to the woman I marry."

"I understand," I tell him, "because even though I love you, I am *in love* with Bert." The declaration sounds hollow as soon as the words leave my lips, and I have to admit that what I really want to hear him say is that he loves me, too.

We've snuck into Paschal's and managed to avoid getting caught at a place that is off-limits to college students. Not wanting to put ourselves at any greater peril of being seen, we tiptoe down the dark staircase, ease out a side door, and make our way across the parking lot and back to Spelman. Once on campus again, we walk up the sidewalk to Morgan Hall where Russell takes my hand and squeezes it as he pulls me toward him.

"You need a nickname," he says, "and I'm gonna give you one. It's got to be something no one else has ever called you. Something like 'Nellie.' Has anyone ever called you that?"

"No, and you'd better not, either. I *hate* Nellie."

"Okay, what's your middle name?"

"Anne, but that's my mother's first name. Friends I grew up with in Atlanta call me Nell Anne," I offer, hoping he'll take the hint.

"No, I want to call you something you've never been called before. Has anyone ever called you Nellie Bee?"

"Nellie *what*?"

"Nellie Bee?"

— 516 —

"No, and they'd better *not!*"

"Then that's what I'm gonna call you—Nellie Bee."

"Russell, if you call me Nellie Bee, I swear I'll call you Rusty C."

But the name sticks, and before long Anna Jo is calling me Nellie Bee, too. I quietly enter the dorm and stop in to see Anna Jo on the second floor. That way it will look like I'm coming from her room when I go up the stairs past the sign-in desk to my own room.

A week later Russell and I are headed back to campus from the movement office with a group of students; we've all just left a movement meeting. Joycelyn calls back to me over her shoulder, "Take your time. I'll sign you in at the dorm."

Russell and I slow down and enter the gate to Spelman a fair distance behind the others. Halfway up the walk to Morgan Hall, he moves between me and the dorm. He looks into my eyes as light inside the front door streams across his shoulder and onto my face. Smiling, he rubs the back of his index finger against my cheek.

"You've cut your hair," he says.

I nod.

"You've never looked more beautiful. I wish I could bottle this night and keep it forever." Leaning forward he squeezes my hands in his and kisses me. "Good night," he says and walks off into the darkness.

I climb the steps of my dorm, not trusting myself to look back, fearing it will destroy the magic of the moment. I ascend the two flights of stairs to my room and fall across the bed, thrilled. The next night he calls and invites me to an end-of-the-year dance at Spelman. It's the first date I've had all year.

On the night of the dance, I descend the third-floor stairs with Joycelyn, Brenda, and Liz, whose dates Danny Mitchell, Big Frank

Holloway, and Franklin Gordon are waiting in the lounge with Russell. Taking my hand in his, Russell leads me down to the first floor and out into the warmth of the spring air. We stroll to the gym and enter. Inside a forty-five record drops onto the turntable, and words from the velvet voices of the Duprees float above students on the dance floor. "See the pyramids along the Nile..." Russell leads me into the midst of couples already dancing and hugs me to him as we slow drag across the floor. When that song ends another platter drops, and Marvin Gaye belts out "Hitchhiker." Russell teaches me the hitchhiker dance and another dance, called the swim.

"Dive in!" he calls out. "Now do the backstroke! Side stroke, breast-stroke!" Following the swim a third record drops, and the floor fills with students as the Contours sing, "Do you love me, now that I can dance?" I haven't had so much fun since the beatnik social at Tougaloo.

When the night is over, Russell and I head back to Morgan Hall. On the way he tells me that Miriam Makeba and Harry Delafonte are coming to Atlanta to do a benefit for the civil rights movement. He says if we sell enough tickets, we can get into the concert for free. We spend the next two weeks between the voter registration drive and schoolwork pounding the pavement selling tickets, and by the night of the performance we've sold enough tickets to get free passes for ourselves and for Rosemary and her date, Leo Meadows, one of the guys from Morehouse who was incarcerated with Russell and me.

On the night of the benefit, civil rights volunteers are seated in a balcony that juts out over the orchestra seats. Russell, Leo, Rosemary, and I find seats together and settle back. Harry Belafonte comes out first and greets people in the orchestra section, and then he salutes those seated in the mezzanine. After sustained applause he leans back, looks up into the balcony, waves to us, and calls out, "And hello to all you up there on scholarship!"

Everyone laughs and breaks into applause again. He motions for Miriam Makeba to join him on stage. He introduces her and exits. Her electrifying performance explodes across the stage as she undulates, gyrates, wiggles, teases, and seduces the audience. Negro and white men rise to their feet, calling out to her. One white man even reaches out to touch her from the front of his orchestra seat. Watching her move and listening to her sultry voice, I wonder if those of us who've been snatched from the African shore have lost the ability to enjoy the kind of sensuality she so fully embraces. Glistening under strobe lights, she beckons us all to join her in song and dance, and we instinctively and ritualistically stomp out the rhythms of the drumbeat. The gift she gives us this night is deeply felt, for it is offered at a time when she is banned from returning to her own country to help her people, who are breaking under the whip of an evil apartheid regime.

When she has whipped us into a frenzy, Harry Belafonte reappears. Wearing tight black hip-hugging pants and a red bolero shirt open to the navel, he calls out, "Sing out the chorus! Matilda, she take-a me money and run Venezuela." Then he quiets us with the hushed sounds of "Bring Me Little Water, Sylvie." Mesmerized, I become a part of his song, taking on the role of Sylvie, straining to balance pails of cool water on my head for him as he sits parched beneath the hot island sun. There I stand leaning over him, mopping sweat from his brow, fanning him with palm leaves as he rests from his work. Cheering and applause snap me back from my island paradise. Harry Belafonte appears for encore after encore, finally exiting the stage for good as Russell and I turn to face each other, nodding our approval.

The music of Miriam Makeba and Harry Belafonte has set us free this night, and our feet barely touch the ground as we exit the concert hall. Leo and Rosemary say good night to us and head back to Madre and Papa's, where Rosemary and I are spending the weekend so we can stay out later than our Spelman curfew allows. Russell and I leave for the home of T. J. Alexander, a wealthy Atlanta Negro who frequently posts bail for student activists. When we arrive, his yard is aglow with lanterns. A giant sterling silver flagon stands on one table, sending champagne cascading down like a waterfall. Underwater pool lights shimmer in the night as tuxedoed young men stop near us carrying silver trays loaded with finger food. Waiting for the food to reach us, we sip champagne. Lost in the magic of this night, I have the sensation of watching a movie of my life. It all seems too good to be real. All of a sudden, I let out a gasp. Harry Belafonte has just walked by me and is even more beautiful close-up than he was on stage. He and Miriam Makeba stand at the head of a long receiving line reserved for dignitaries, and then disappear inside the house as students begin to join the tail end of the queue. I feel cheated as they are whisked away. We're the ones who worked hard to sell tickets for the concert, yet it feels like we've been pushed aside and ignored on this night set aside to make money for our struggle.

Seeing my disappointment, Russell suggests we go home, so he and I head for Mr. MacDowell's car (the man Madre hired to escort us and her everywhere). Just at that moment Belafonte reemerges and passes us again. Still enthralled by the concert and surprised at suddenly coming face-to-face with this icon again, I ask him for his autograph.

"No," he says. Then he turns and walks away.

Crushed, I climb into the backseat of Mr. MacDowell's waiting car, contrasting this recent exchange with a day long ago during a summer in New York City when Katy, Rosemary, Nick, and I stood at a stage door waiting for Sidney Poitier to come out, talk with us, and sign our Playbills. I take a cigarette from my purse and light it, consoling myself with thoughts of the importance of being part of a movement when it is still in its infancy. I think of all the young children who have faced dogs and fire hoses, of those who have been maimed or killed, of elderly people who've registered to vote for the first time, of leaders less famous than the big names everyone is hearing now, and I know they are the real heroes. Yet on this night I can foresee a time when the work of the foot soldiers will be eclipsed by celebrities on the front lines bathed in the spotlight. And even though I know we need their name recognition to get the newspaper and television coverage that will eventually let the world see the real conditions in the South, tonight I am glad to be part of a small group of students and dedicated leaders walking the sidewalks and going to jail at a time when few are watching. I'm proud to be part of a group that has taken on a sick society in the belief that our children and our children's children will live lives free of the kind of racism we have known. I think of Miriam Makeba, who has come to Georgia to sing for our freedom at a time when she can't go home to South Africa and sing for her own. My reverie is suddenly interrupted by Russell, who wrests the concert program from my hand and begins writing on it.

"What are you doing?" I bark at him.

He doesn't answer but begins writing on the program. Seeing him write all over my program makes me furious, but I know arguing with him is a waste of time, so I light another cigarette and inhale deeply as Mr. MacDowell's car rolls through the night.

Russell shoves the program back into my hand and I look down, curious to see what he has written.

*"To a dedicated soldier,"* it says, *"with respect and admiration. Yours, Harry Belafonte."*

"What the hell," he says. "It's just a name. Nobody'll know he didn't sign it."

We both laugh.[184]

Mr. MacDowell pulls the car up at Madre and Papa's. Russell gets out, opens my door, and walks me to the front door of the house. Kissing me good night, he asks if I will go to the Kappa dawn dance with him. It is an annual breakfast dance hosted by the Kappa Alpha Psi fraternity and one of the most anticipated events of the year. I accept and invite him to dinner at Madre and Papa's later that week.

On the evening of the dance, Russell appears at my grandparents' home in a black tuxedo, a corsage in hand for me. I am wearing the pink gown and gold slippers I wore to Rosemary's debutante ball, and I feel like a princess. Mr. Mac drives us to the hotel, where a band already has everyone dancing to "Twist and Shout!" We join the frenzy and then melt into each other's arms when "Smoke Gets in Your Eyes" is played. We dance the watusi to "I Can't Sit Down" and get so giddy on spiked punch that the floorboards seem to be moving.

At intermission I look for my childhood friend, Jimmy Murray, so I can say good-bye. We talk about our paths crossing again after so many years, and we dance together when the band returns. We send love to each other's families before parting company. I look around for Russell and spy him standing in front of a row of windows that look out over a small park across the street. I go to stand beside him, slipping my arm

---

184  Forty years later, Russell attended a special ceremony at which Harry Belafonte was presented with the Paul Robeson Award. After the affair, he approached Mr. Belafonte and confessed to having once forged his name. When Russell explained the circumstances under which the forgery occurred, Belafonte laughed and gave Russell a program to send to me, signed, "Peace, Harry Belafonte."

around his waist. He places his arm over my shoulder and nods toward the park below. "I've been standing here watching it change colors," he says, referring to a fountain inside the park.

I look down at the water gushing up and tell him about a time when I was a little girl, and Madre brought me to the same fountain. "At the time, I was so mesmerized by it that I didn't want to leave. But a wrinkle-faced white man was standing near us with callused worker's hands, smoking a cigarette, and Madre is allergic to cigarette smoke, so she said we had to leave. I wasn't ready to leave, so I reached up and held her nose to keep her from inhaling the smoke. I was too young to realize that I'd also stopped her from breathing. When the smoker asked why I was holding my grandmother's nose, Madre explained that I wanted to stay and watch the water change colors, but she was allergic to cigarette smoke, and so we had to leave. The man immediately crushed his cigarette under his foot so we could stay."

Russell takes me by the hand and says, "Let's leave this place."

We race for the elevator doors. "First floor!" we shout to the startled attendant. When the doors open again we run through the hotel lobby, out the front door, and into the street. A light rain begins to fall, but we dodge traffic and race toward the fountain. Reaching it we embrace and kiss with the urgency of lovers who feel the moment slipping away. As we cling to each other in the rain, struggling to keep time at bay, I whisper, "Detroit isn't on the way to anywhere but Canada, and I'll probably never get there."

"Maybe for the Montreal Olympics," he offers. "California isn't on the way to anywhere either but Hawaii, and who knows when I'll get there."

Russell has given me a zest for life, taught me to seize and embrace life exuberantly. As we stand at the edge of the fountain, facing the fact that we may never see each other again, I spy coins at the bottom of the shallow pool surrounding it.

"I wish I had a penny to throw in," I lament offhandedly. He reaches down and scoops up a handful of coins. "Just because they've been wished on before doesn't mean we can't use them."

I take a penny from his dripping palm, and each of us throws a coin in, spontaneously singing the first line to, "Three Coins in the Fountain," changing the "three coins" to "two."

"What did you wish for?" he asks.

"If I tell you, it won't come true."

The rain falls harder.

"We'd better get back inside," he says, "before your hair goes straight."

We laugh at the absurdity of the statement and turn to go back. As we cross the street, I look up at the windows of the room we've left. It is filled with partygoers whose silhouettes are still twisting to the music. A small group has gathered near the window where we stood earlier. Now they are watching us. We wave, and they wave back. Then we enter the building and head back to the dance hall to gather our wraps.

Outside, Mr. MacDowell waits to take us to the Kappa breakfast, where we enjoy more music and laughter. Russell confesses to having been one of the fellows who found the main switch to Spelman's electrical system in an underground tunnel and plunged Morgan Hall into darkness on the night of the school's infamous panty raid. When we have finished eating, he suggests we go out and watch the sunrise. A mild drizzle has begun again as we walk toward the dawn. Suddenly he sweeps me up in his arms and begins running up the middle of the street. He races uphill along the white line that divides traffic just as Mr. Mac's car comes over the hill and to an abrupt stop. We shriek with laughter while the sunrays creep over the horizon. Then we fall into the backseat as our driver heads for home. Russell asks if I will come see him off at the railroad station when he leaves for Detroit. I promise I will, and we kiss good night.

The next day I go to Spelman to pick up the last of my personal belongings and to say good-bye to Anna Jo. We hug as our eyes fill with tears. I realize I'll probably never see her again either and ask her to sign my yearbook. She gives me an autographed school photo instead. On the back she has written:

> *To Nellie Bee,*
>
> *You are a strong and beautiful human being. A* true *piece of humanity.*
>
> *Don't Let Nobody Turn You 'Round, and one day We Shall Overcome.*
>
> 

*With love from your Soul-mate,*

*Anna Jo*

I walk over to Graves Hall where Russell lives and wait in the lounge while a classmate goes to get him. Russ comes bounding down the stairs, a big smile on his face. "I knew it was you when the kid who came to get me said, 'The most beautiful girl I've ever seen is waiting downstairs for you.'"

I blush, embarrassed by the compliment, and ask him to sign my yearbook; then I sign his.

The next day, Rosemary and I go to the railroad station to see him off. I've asked her to come with me, so I won't have to ride home alone after he and I say good-bye. Rosemary and I ride in silence, and I wonder how spring has passed me by. A feeling of déjà vu engulfs me as I gaze out the car window, feeling as if I am back in the middle of the spring following Howard's death. I notice for the first time the delicate pinks of mimosa trees, the beautiful blossoms of the dogwood, the sweeping limbs of the weeping willows.

We pull up at the railroad station, and as I leave the car, I am snapped back to reality by the mustiness of the old train depot. I remember the days when Rosemary, Madre, and I traveled to New York—meeting the Harrises in Gaffney, eating in the dining car after leaving Washington, speaking Spanish so no one would understand us. I see myself lying in the top berth of the train again counting telephone poles, waving to barefoot children who run alongside our Pullman car. What happened to the girl I used to be?

Rosemary and I enter the station house. We walk across the waiting room floor crossing under the sign over the door that screams WHITE ONLY. The struggle for freedom has been too hard fought, too costly for us to be governed by that sign anymore, and I know Russell will look for me here in this room, not the "colored" waiting room. I light a cigarette as Rose and I sit and carry on mindless conversation. So little has changed since the days when we boarded the train with Madre. I look around the station house more aware than ever of how much has *not* changed. There are still two waiting rooms—white and colored. Civil rights groups have been struggling for two years to end segregation in public places, but Rosemary and I are the only Negroes in this white section. Peering into the colored section at the apprehensive faces of Negro women and men looking back at us, it slowly begins to dawn on me that true integration is going to take more than legislation. Segregation is so much a state of mind—a state of enslavement—that freeing people from it will be more difficult than the passage of a few laws.

I look toward the door Russell has just entered. He takes long strides into the waiting area, his eyes searching it for me. I stand to make finding me easier. We meet and walk outside to the platform, and Rosemary walks away to give us time alone. There isn't much to say. It is ending. We both know it has to. The whistle blows as the porter takes Russell's luggage from the platform and places it on the train.

"All abo-o-oard!" the trainman yells.

We embrace and kiss a long last good-bye as smoke shoots out from beneath the wheels. The train lunges forward, and Russell hops aboard. Then his face appears in a window of a car. I wave good-bye and turn to join Rosemary as we head toward Mr. MacDowell's waiting car.

"He's saying something," Rosemary tells me, looking back at the train.

I turn and look back, too, searching the windows for his face, but when I find it I can't make out what he is saying. I begin running alongside the train, mouthing, "What? I can't hear you." Pointing to my ear, I try to keep up with his car.

The train picks up speed as he repeats what he has said, but I still don't understand him. He takes out a pocket handkerchief and rubs a clear small circle on the windowpane. Then slowly and deliberately he mouths the words, "I love you!"

I stop dead in my tracks. Covering my face with my hands, I begin to sob as his train speeds off down the track. Rosemary puts her arms around me and leads me back to the car. As we wend our way toward home, I remember the words he wrote in my yearbook the day before when I stopped by his dorm.

> *Nellie Bee,*
>
> *You have chosen a road to take and you have taken it. This road is leading you down a strange and wondrous path—to reach*

*a subsequent peace of mind. Our two roads have junctioned,*
*and for a while we are both on the same highway. COAHR, jail,*
*gigs, creeps, crazy puns on birthdays, and a complete (sic) ber-*
*serk environmental condition, but still we are on the same road.*
*The day is coming when my road will no longer be with yours.*
*In time and space it will only be a mi-nute (sic) fraction of a*
*second, but in my mind it was an eternity.*

In the fifties and sixties, it was the youth of the nation who shaped the tenor of the times. We were kids, just kids who'd grown up in an era of lynchings, beatings, cattle prods, and rapes. Kids who'd lived through a Cold War, race riots, cross burnings, and threats from the Klan. Kids who'd been forced to urinate at the side of dusty roads along hostile southern byways, who'd lived segregated lives in segregated towns and who'd seen adults we respected called "boy" and "girl." We'd been stunned by the murder of Emmett Till, seen the photos of Mack Parker's body dragged up from a muddy Mississippi riverbed, lost loved ones to the hatred, rage, and frustration of the times. Most of us hadn't known the pleasures of trying on clothes in department stores or the luxury of checking into hotels, but we'd been stirred by the speeches of Martin Luther King Jr. and challenged by a young President Kennedy who inspired us to ask what we could do for our country. Our decision to respond to the president's challenge and Dr. King's example of non-violent protest wasn't always well thought out. Sometimes it was simply our reaction to the violence permeating the Jim Crow South and the failure of our government to take action. But we were young enough and idealistic enough to really believe we could change the plight of our people and create a different reality for the children yet to come.

Nonviolent protest was the method we chose, believing that through prayer, commitment, and discipline, we could create a brighter future for ourselves and for our people. I don't think any of us truly realized, as we marched that long road to freedom, how profoundly we were changing the course of history and the future of the world.

# EPILOGUE

# JOSHUA FIT THE BATTLE[i]

*Joshua fit the battle of Jericho, and*
*the walls came tumblin' down.*

IT IS THE EVENING of January 18, 2009, when our daughter Erika Anne, my husband Bert, and I find ourselves seated at the table with our friend Archbishop Desmond Tutu ("the Arch") and his son-in-law, Mthunzi Gxashe. We are here to attend one of the many preinaugural balls for President-elect Barack Obama. This one is being hosted by an HIV/AIDS prevention group called The Balm in Gilead, Inc., and it is being held to honor twenty-five Black "Keepers of the Flame," among them, Julian Bond, Myrlie Evers, Dorothy Height, and the archbishop.

While waiting for the festivities to begin, I lean over and say to the Arch, "The last time I was in Washington for a presidential inauguration was 1953. I was ten years old and a member of the school safety patrol that was scheduled to lead President Eisenhower's inaugural

---

This traditional Negro spiritual is thought to be a product of pre–Civil War slaves dating back to the first half of the nineteenth century. Copyrighted by Jay Roberts. Obtained at Wikipedia: allmusic.com.

parade. I remember being humiliated when we Black kids were forced to march behind the white safety patrol kids in Jim Crow formation. Now here we are over fifty years later, celebrating the election of the first African American president."

The Arch responds, "God really does have a sense of humor."

*A sense of humor indeed,* I think. Who would have believed that a little Black girl born in the red clay hills of Georgia, barely discovering who she was in a 1953 segregated society would one day end up seated beside a Nobel Peace Prize laureate celebrating the inauguration of America's first Black president? Yet here I was, seated with a Nobel Peace Prize laureate, who himself had grown up in a harsh apartheid society. But maybe that's the thing that had brought us together so many years ago—the fact that we both knew what it was to be hated by a larger society but were encouraged to persevere by our loving, small Black communities. And we both have had Black and white role models who encouraged us to rise above our beginnings.

The two of us continue to reminisce, comparing the election of Nelson Mandela to that of Barack Obama until we are interrupted by a group of people wanting to take the Arch's photograph. While he accommodates them, my mind wanders back over the road he and I have traveled together.

We became friends through antiapartheid work in the eighties in the days when he was the Archbishop of Southern Africa, and I was a social justice advocate here in the United States serving as executive assistant to Paul Moore Jr., the Episcopal Bishop of New York. At that time I was close to a community of South African exiles living in New York City and a member of the Episcopal Church's Executive Council, a forty-member body that serves as the Church's board of directors between its triennial conventions. It was in that capacity that I was appointed one of three US representatives to a Partners-in-Mission gathering in South Africa, where we joined clergy and laity of southern Africa, as well as other international church leaders, to spend time living among the people of southern Africa before coming together under the leadership of Archbishop Tutu to design a five-year plan to dismantle apartheid. During those heady days of the antiapartheid struggle, the archbishop and I had become personal friends as well as working colleagues, and over the next twenty-five years, we had exchanged numerous letters, phone calls, e-mails, and visits to one another's countries. Over that period of time, I had grown close to his wife, Leah, and their children, just as he had to my husband and children.

Eventually the photo taking with the Arch is interrupted, coinciding with the interruption of my thoughts as the opening strains of the Negro National Anthem, "Lift Every Voice and Sing," resounds throughout the ballroom. Everyone in the Grand Hyatt Hotel stands to sing and view a montage of photographs chronicling the struggle of African Americans from the time we arrived on these shores in chains to the election of Barack Obama as president. As I stand there singing and viewing the video, my mind again wanders. This time it focuses on the November 4, 2008, election that has brought us here.

On that night, Bert and I were seated in the room in our apartment that I use as my New York home office, watching television election returns. A few minutes past 11:00 p.m. EST, Senator Barack Obama was declared president-elect of the United States. Tears slid down my cheeks as Bert popped the bottle of champagne we'd had on ice for such an occasion. Instinctively I reached for the phone to call my mother in California, who was watching the results with my sister, Rosemary.

"I'm so glad you lived to see this day," I said as soon as Mother picked up the phone. She, Rosemary, Bert, and I spoke on extension phones, reveling in the moment all talking together, wishing Dad were still alive to revel in it, too. Suddenly my Skype phone began to ring. It was our daughter, Erika, calling from an election party in Cambridge, England, where she was working as a veterinarian. Bert and I said good-bye to Mother and Rosemary and screamed into the Skype microphone, blending our voices with Erika's squeals and those of people in the background at the election party she was attending.

"It's incredible here!" she yelled. "The Cambridge Union Center is jam-packed...[with people] screaming, jumping up and down on chairs, and chanting, 'Obama! Obama!'"

"People are going crazy here, too," Bert and I reported. We spoke for a few minutes more before promising to talk again the next day; then we said good-bye and hung up. Bert and I went back to watching the results of President Obama's election; then, from what seemed like very far away, we detected faint rumbling.

"Listen," Bert said. We turned the volume on our TV down and became conscious of muffled sounds outside on the street below. We live on the twenty-first floor of an apartment building in Manhattan. Every unit has an outdoor balcony, and it was the crowds outside we were hearing through the half-closed windows of our unit. We left my office and went down the hall, through the living room, and outside onto our balcony, where we joined people on other balconies in our building and on the balconies of neighboring buildings all chanting, "Obama! Obama!" Young people spilled onto the sidewalks below from neighborhood buildings, cheering. Taxis and trucks along Columbus

Avenue honked their horns. Bert placed his arm around my waist, and I put mine around his.

"I didn't think I'd live to see this day," I said.

"I wish Bert III were here," he responded.

A feeling of sadness overtook us in that moment as we remembered our son, who died sixteen years earlier in an accident. The chill of the November night sent us back inside our apartment and back to my office, where the television was still going. The scene had switched from "talking heads" to people dancing along 125th Street. Suddenly cameras went to Times Square, which looked like New Year's Eve. New York City, after a horrendous stock market crash, was erupting in jubilation!

I was awestruck as Bert and I sat on the couch watching celebrations of the momentous election take place around the world. As I tried to take all of it in, I remembered the two communications I received a day earlier—one a letter from Anna Jo, the other an e-mail from Russell. I had been thinking about them a lot during the election process and about the other foot soldiers from our days in Atlanta. I hadn't been in touch with most of them since our student movement days and hadn't heard from Russell or Anna Jo for a long time. It seemed we were all reminiscing about the past as we watched the election unfold.

In her letter Anna Jo said, "This is my first time ever to vote for a president that I feel wholehearted about and really care for. His story and the timing of this race occupy my mind a lot. Such hope and tension."

She went on to tell me that she'd recently removed boxes she'd placed in her parents' storage shed years earlier, including those from her time in Atlanta—"a few old newspapers, issues of the SNCC

*Student Voice*, schoolwork, flyers, letters. Things *have* changed," she wrote. Then remembering the long-ago first night some forty years earlier when she arrived at Spelman, she continued, "I left the coast of Washington State beginning with a full day of boat and bus travel from where my family lived in the island boonies just to reach Seattle. I arrived on the Spelman campus in early September 1961, a day or two before most other students...I'd never been anywhere near the fabled Deep South. Like others headed to Spelman, I was unacquainted with big cities, the hiring of taxis, the negotiation of international airports. I had only a vague idea of all the things to beware of, yet arrive I did. Since I was a sophomore, Morgan Hall would be my residence. I stood rumpled and unladylike under the light at the door, and Miss Taylor and Venecia Gardner (a student resident assistant) graciously and warmly welcomed me...but I was too late for supper.

"Alone and settled in my room in the quiet building, ready to lie down at long last, I lingered at the tall windows, examining their wooden louvers. Louvers were new to me, wonderfully southern. The windows were open (due to the unaccustomed, overbearing heat!), and so I became aware of people singing somewhere in the distance across the darkness. The tune was sort of familiar—'Amen.' We didn't sing it where I'd gone to church. But with the greater clarity of the higher notes of the song, it wasn't 'amen' that I made out, but 'freedom, freedom....' They sang it over and over and then some more.

"I heard some pretty remarkable words at Spelman, but that word, *freedom*—the word that caught and grew in my imagination as I learned about slavery in this country; then upon my arrival in the context of Spelman and the South, the word that reached me in disembodied song through the quiet of the night and subsequently in the particular nuances of all the different voices raised in all the different settings at that time—it was everywhere, and it riveted me over the next couple of years in Atlanta. And it is the enduring word."

Russell's e-mail arrived moments before Anna Jo's letter, and it said, "On October 1, 2008, I voted for a Black man, and I cried.[ii] A few weeks later I was asked to speak at an Obama rally as a representative from the student movement. Just before I got up to speak, they showed a movie about Obama, followed by a movie about the movement. They showed the people who gave their last full measure of devotion...Then I spoke. Nell, I broke and started crying before I regained my composure. It was emotionally draining (as) I remembered what we did and who did it. People like Frank Smith, Big Frank Holloway, Anna Jo Weaver, Elizabeth Heath, Ralph Moore, Larry Fox, Gwen Iles, Ruby (Doris) Smith, Leo Meadows, you, me, and thousands of others. We changed history. Many who started with us did not (live to) see this day..."

How heartbreakingly true. I especially remembered Ruby Doris Smith, my salvation in the Fulton County jail. After she graduated from Spelman, Ruby Doris became a full-time freedom fighter, the most powerful woman in the Student Nonviolent Coordinating Committee, working as James Forman's right hand. A wife and mother of a young son, she died much too early in October 1967, following a battle with a rare form of cancer known as lymphosarcoma.[iii]

But there were others who marched with us who did live to witness President Obama's election. And a number of them had gone on to have outstanding careers. Julian Bond, a cofounder of both the Committee on Appeal for Human Rights and the Student Nonviolent Coordinating

---

ii He said he couldn't wait for Election Day, so he had voted early.

iii Cynthia Griggs Fleming, *Soon We Will Not Cry: The Liberation of Ruby Doris Smith Robinson* (New York: Roman and Littlefield Publishers, 2006).

Committee, had served as a Georgia state senator before becoming the first African American nominated for vice president of the United States in 1968. He later served as chairman of the National Association for the Advancement of Colored People. Bernice Johnson Reagon (our singing Pied Piper who brought people out of the Atlanta projects so we could register them to vote) was an original member of Sweet Honey in the Rock. She became a curator at the Smithsonian's National Museum of American History, and she was the subject of several of Bill Moyers's PBS programs on music and the movement. She continues to be a self-described "song talker" engaged in the struggle for liberation. Frank Smith (Smitty) followed Charles Black as chairman of the Committee on Appeal for Human Rights (COAHR) and then became a respected city councilman in Washington, DC. He serves today as director of the African American Civil War Memorial Freedom Foundation and Museum.

And there are those of us who continue in our roles as foot soldiers. Russell Campbell served for a time as secretary of COAHR and continued in the student movement for a number of years. Today he lives in Washington, DC, where he is still active in civil rights activities. He married, became the father of four, served as a deacon in the Baptist Church, and now works for the Environmental Protection Agency. After her sophomore year Anna Jo Weaver transferred from Bethel College to Spelman where she continued to be part of the student movement. She later moved back to Waldron Island and married Tony Scruton, the fellow so many of us heard about during her days at Spelman. The two of them are the island's conservationists and have three daughters, the second of whom is named Nell.

Bert Gibson and I were married three and a half years before our children arrived. During the early days of our marriage, we were part of the Black and Brown Caucus at St. Mark's Church-in-the-Bowery in New York City, where we worked with members of the Black Panther Party to set up a breakfast program as well as establish the first prison law library in New York State. As a stay-at-home mom, prior to going back to work full time, I labored on behalf of the homeless, people with AIDS, prisoners, migrant workers, women, and lesbian, gay, bisexual, and trans-gendered persons, and in support of poor people and people of color everywhere. I became heavily involved in the antiapartheid movement, getting arrested outside the South African consulate in New York City and spending time in apartheid South Africa working with Archbishop Tutu and international religious leaders. I served as executive assistant to the Episcopal Bishop of New York, and in the ensuing years I became Associate General Secretary for Inclusiveness and Justice at the National Council of Churches before becoming national coordinator for the Episcopal Urban Caucus, whose mission is to stand in solidarity with poor and oppressed people and hold the feet of the Episcopal Church to the fire of social justice.

We are the members of the Moses generation who lived to see Joshua lead our people (and the nation) into a new reality of hope. But we civil rights leaders of the twentieth century are wise enough to know that challenges for the Israelites did not end with their entry into Canaan, and neither will the challenges of the twentieth century solve the issues that twenty-first-century activists encounter in today's Promised Land. The history of racism in America has a much too checkered past to end with the election of one man or be erased with the rise of a new group of activists, some of whom make up the Occupy movements around the world. But the election of Barack Obama to the highest office in our land has helped straighten the path toward equality, and the Occupy movements have helped ease the load we twentieth-century activists carried for so long. Our goal was never to elect the first African American president but to open the avenues of access across the land to all Americans regardless of color; to give every American an equal opportunity to pursue his or her dream without fear of malice or harm; to ensure that each had the equal rights that are guaranteed under the law.

---

BACK INSIDE THE INAUGURAL ball, twenty-five presenters have handed out twenty-five awards, and performers have displayed their talents; the evening is winding down now. We have all eaten dinner, and the Arch and I have shared a dance. Erika has taken photos with her activist idols. Bert and I have met friends attending the ball, and twenty-five outstanding Keepers of the Flame have accepted awards and given speeches.

We now sit waiting for the young man who is assigned to lead the archbishop and his son-in-law to the car that will take them back to their hotel. When the young man arrives, he, the Arch, Mthunzi, and I make our way through the crowds. People are still asking for one more photo with the Arch. Archbishop Tutu obliges, teasing the children with whom we come in contact along the way. Outside, he and Mthunzi face the searing cold before sliding into their chauffeur-driven car and waving good night. Tomorrow we will watch history being made as Barack Obama becomes the first Black president of the United States.

Archbishop Tutu and Nell dancing, Inaugural Ball 2009

I wish my father could have lived to see President Obama's election. After an illustrious career in education and coaching in the South and the West, he became the first African American coach in the Sacramento City Unified School District, enjoying a full and satisfying career in high-school athletics—coaching winning football and championship track teams. He followed my mother in becoming the second African American vice principal in the district. Up to the time of his death, he kept in touch with the young men he had coached at various colleges throughout the South. He was an active layman and lector at Trinity Cathedral, the Sacramento church that came to our rescue in 1962 when we arrived homeless, friendless, and worn out from our travels to the West Coast. He died on February 2, 1997.

After years of teaching in the Sacramento City Unified School District, our mother became the district's first African American counselor, then preceded my father as its first African American vice principal. She is a founding member of the Oak Park Preschool, which serves children in the inner city, and is an inductee into the Youth on the Move Educators' Hall of Fame. Having reached her nineties, she stays alert playing bridge and attending civic, social, and church events in the Sacramento area. She too is a church lector and is active in the life of Trinity Cathedral.

Following a stint in Brazil, Rosemary spent several years teaching English as a second language in Arequipa, Peru, before returning home and earning two master's degrees. She became dean of students at the University of California at Davis, then moved to Sacramento, where she worked for the state of California in telecommunications until her recent retirement. She is a licensed lay preacher at Trinity Cathedral.

My husband, Bert, has been my supporter throughout our married life, joining me in demonstrations in the early days and taking over as the "at-home" parent during my travels around the world representing The Episcopal Church and later the National Council of Churches. He has enjoyed a fulfilling career in financial management and today is the chief financial officer for a New York City nonprofit organization.

To our regret, our son, Bertram Maxwell Gibson III, did not live to see the election of President Barack Obama. He would have been as excited as Erika was. He was a 1991 graduate of Franklin and Marshall College in Lancaster, Pennsylvania. An aspiring writer, he published his first newspaper article in July 1992. On August 2 of that year, he died in a fall at Barnard College while working on a summer project. He has been my muse throughout the writing of this book.

At age eight, our daughter, Erika Anne, began a stellar career in track and field, winning more gold medals and trophies in the high jump and hurdles than we can count. She is a 1995 graduate of Duke University, having taken a semester off in the wake of her brother's untimely death. In 2001, she graduated with honors from the Tuskegee School of Veterinary Medicine in Alabama, and in 2008, she completed the University of Pennsylvania's veterinary program in neurology/neurosurgery. Today she is a practicing veterinary neurologist/neurosurgeon, the first board-certified African American in the field.

# About the Author

IN 1970 NELL BRAXTON Gibson became the first woman to serve on the Board of Trustees at Berkeley Divinity School at Yale University and in 1985 was awarded an Honorary Doctor of Divinity Degree from the school for her work in bringing more women and people of color onto the Board. She holds a Bachelor of Arts Degree in English and is listed in, Who's Who Among Black Americans. In 2007 she was awarded a Trinity (Wall Street) Transformational Fellowship for her social justice work. The fellowship allowed her to spend a month in South Africa and Namibia gathering information on the bloodless transition of both countries from apartheid to independence. In 2009 the Manhattan Country School honored her with a "Living the Dream" Mentor Award and in 2010 the Episcopal Church Women of the Church of the Intercession in New York honored her Humanitarian Achievements. On March 1, 2012 the Episcopal Church's President of the House of Deputies (PHoD) presented her with the PHoD Medallion for Exemplary Service. During the presentation Bonnie Anderson, President of the House of Deputies said, "The prophet Micah tells us that it isn't enough to love justice. God wants us to do justice and Nell Gibson is one of the greatest doers of justice our generation of Episcopalians has ever seen."

CPSIA information can be obtained
at www.ICGtesting.com
Printed in the USA
FSOW03n2222230217
31212FS